Holy Wisdor
Logos o

The Four Lost Apocryphal Christian Gospels of Truth, Philip, Mary & Thomas, and The Secret Revelation of John

Interpretation and Commentary by James Brantingham PhD

Holy Wisdom and The Logos of God

Interpretation and Commentary by James Brantingham PhD

Copyright © 2021 (Second Edition 5 19 2021; 6 26 2021) by James Brantingham

All rights reserved. No part of this book may be reproduced in any form or by any electronic or mechanical means, including information storage and retrieval systems, without written permission from the author, except for the use of brief quotations in a book review.

A Prayer

' My prayer, Father, is not that you take them out of the world but that you protect them from **Error** and the **Evil one**. *They are not of the world, (even) as I am not of this world!* Sanctify them by the Truth; Father, your Word is Truth! Pilate retorted... '*What is Truth?*' With this, the Procurator took him out ...and said, 'I find no basis for a charge against him' (paraphrase - mine).

Dedication

This Book: Holy Wisdom and The Logos of God is dedicated to my wife, Kathy Brantingham, my Sons Christopher and Jon, and my daughter-law Cindy and our three grandchildren: Miles, Matthew, and Violet.

Table of Contents

Holy Wisdom and The Logos of God

A Prayer 3
Dedication 4
Table of Contents 5
A Note About this Edition 7
A Brief History about the Discovery of these Gnostic-Christian Gospels Gnostics, and Gnosticism 8
The first Gnostics Simon Magus, Menander and Basilides 29
References to "Holy Wisdom and The Logos of God?" 38

The Gospel of Truth

Introduction to The Gospel of Truth Today......................53
The Gospel of Truth 74
References for "The Gospel of Truth" 93

The Gospel of Philip

Introduction To The Gospel of Philip..............................103
The Gospel of Philip (the Gnostic Gospel) 107
References for "The Gospel of Philip" 135
Appendix A, Barbēlō and Consorts..................................151

The Gospel According To Mary

Introduction to The Gospel According To Mary (of Magdala)....154
References for "The Gospel According to Mary of Magdala" 181
The Gospel According to Mary of Magdala (the Coptic Gnostic Gospel) 191
References for "The Gospel According to Mary of Magdala" 199

The Gospel of Thomas

Introduction to the Gospel of Thomas 211
The Gospel of Thomas (the Gnostic Gospel)..................216
References for "The Gospel of Thomas" 242

The Secret Revelation of John

Introduction to the Secret Revelation of John 250
The Secret Revelation of John (the Gnostic Book) 256
Six Questions that John asks the Savior About life (and the Savior Prophetically answers): 290
References for The Secret Revelation of John 4 28 2021 300
Appendix 1 315
Appendix 2 318
Appendix 3 334

A Note About this Edition

This text is a new book. It is called "Holy Wisdom and The Logos of God' (The Four Lost Apocryphal Christian Gospels of Truth, Philip, Mary, and Thomas with the Secret Revelation of John)." Though new, I have extensively redone or rewritten most of the material found in my previous book, Truth. What is Truth? In place of the full title, it will most often be referred to as, ' *Holy Wisdom and The Logos of God.*' In this text, I have decreased (some) over-explanation or interpretations across the board. Especially in *the Gospels of Truth, Mary of Magdala, Thomas* and the *Secret Revelation of John.* The *Gospel of Philip* (except for a few verses) is essentially the 2017 publication. Comments on science are now in Appendices or here or there within Introductions. I endeavored to make all of the books closer to the core Coptic (and "Gnostic") message. It is a text along the *"Judeo-Christological Gnostic"* spectrum. Yet, I have consciously written it for anyone of a "loving and caring" spiritual persuasion or practice.

I might suggest first read the Gospels and Secret John - then go back and read the introductions, appendices, addendums (and so forth).

A Brief History about the Discovery of these Gnostic-Christian Gospels Gnostics, and Gnosticism

In 1945 CE, peasant farmers digging for fertilizer struck a sealed container and uncovered a buried (purposely hidden) jar near Nag Hammadi next to the Nile and Luxor, Egypt. Eventually, it became clear that they had found twelve complete and a thirteenth incomplete Codex (see discussion on a Codex, Codexes, and Codices below). Inside these "books" were fifty-two mostly "Gnostic" texts. But the Truth is that whoever hid these texts one thousand, five-to-six hundred years ago considered them "Christian books." Today, some (but not all) mainstream church leaders label them heretical (Taussig, Hal. Ed. 2013). Of course, today, Gnostic-Christian churches are increasing. And of course, they consider the Gnostic texts (*most* but not *all* of them) part of the "New Covenant" alongside the Old (OT) and New (NT) Testaments (Ecclesia Gnostica, Los Angeles 2002; Johannite Church, The Apostolic. 2018; Ecclesia Pistis Sophia. 2019). Indeed a few mainstream churches, such as the clergy in the Episcopal or the United Methodist churches, may occasionally integrate them into talks, sermons, or homilies (Bourgeault, Cynthia. 2008; Hal Taussig 2012). Many biblical scholars and authors do not automatically label *all* of the Nag Hammadi Library (*NHL*) heterodox, heretical, or apostate in the modern era.

Before 1945, scholars, adventurers, and collectors had found a few other Gnostic codices. In 1769, James Bruce purchased a codex in Upper Egypt that contained the '*Books of Jeu*' (mentioned in another early find, the '*Pistis Sophia*') called the Bruce Codex. First acquired by the British Museum, they have been in the Bodleian Library, Oxford, since 1848. Other Scholars purchased a few other Gnostic books before the eighteenth century; one is the extensive text '*Pistis Sophia*' (technically meaning, "Faith and Wisdom"). It has had various names derived from these two words (like the "*Faithfulness of Wisdom or Sophia*") since "Sophia" is Greek for "Wisdom" and was a divinity (especially) in the Canonical texts of the OT and the NT but mainly in the NT Apocrypha (Hart, David. 2017; See Ecclesiasticus in the OT). She was (and is) an indispensable divinity *yoked with Jesus Christ* in Gnostic theology. Today the title *Pistis Sophia* seems to be its primary designation. The British Library purchased *Pistis Sophia* in 1785 from Anthony Askew (and called it the *Askew Codex*). Also purchased in 1896 through the "Cairo antiquities market" was the *Secret Revelation of John*. This Codex also contained Mary's Gospel and a few other Gnostic texts.

Later in 1945, at Nag Hammadi, scholars found the full text of the *Gospel of Thomas*. And beginning on its last page (and 'attached to it) was the *Gospel of Philip*. Today, Thomas's Gospel is the most popular and most studied Gnostic Gospel in all of history (Smith Andrew P. 2015.)

The *Gospel of Philip* was unknown in the West for the last 1,500 years. A few "late Church Fathers" in the Eastern Byzantine or Orthodox Church briefly mentioned Philip's Gospel. They may have commented on a few phrases written down by earlier Church Fathers (without having the actual text before them). The late Eastern Byzantine Orthodox Church Fathers did note curiously that the *Gospel of Philip* was found just after and next to the *Gospel of Thomas*. Found physically attached in 1945 (Philip followed immediately after and *on* the last page of, the *Gospel of Thomas*). The Byzantine comments followed in the same order! In the modern era, these **same** *Gospels of Thomas* and *Philip* are the most "popularly purchased, and read singular Gnostic books" (in popular non-academic readership). Interestingly they are also used in Christian academia and worship (including in churches for occasional sermons or homilies) more than all *other* singular Gnostic Gospels or texts (Smith Andrew P. 2015; Bourgeault, Cynthia. 2008; Smith, Geoffrey S. 2019.)

The Codices

These codices were ancient, handwritten books in the Coptic language and found about found fifty-two, mostly 'Gnostic' treatises (Meyer M., Robinson, J. 2007.)

This book *'Holy Wisdom and The Logos of God'* (*Wisd&Logos*) presents four of these lost Christian Apocryphal Gospels. The *Gospel of Truth* (*Gtr*), the *Gospel of Philip* (*GPhil*), the *Gospel of Thomas* (*GThom*), and the *Gospel of Mary* (*GMary*) - along with arguably the most important text of Gnostic Christian theology, the *Secret Revelation of John* (*SRevJohn*). The *Gospel According to Mary* (*GMary*) was **not** found with the *NHL* books. But they did find a copy inside an earlier codex found before the *NHL* with the *SRevJohn*. The *SRevJohn* (also called the *'Apocryphon of* or the '*Secret Book of John*') ties the *GMary* (with its literary structure and content) about Mary Magdalene to the *NHL* corpus (Stevan Davies 2005; Karen King 2006).

Codex and Codices

"A single ancient book in such an archeological discovery is called a Codex, and many books 'Codexes' (or the plural term 'Codices' is used). Like modern bibles, "which are often seen as a single book," a Codex is similar. One book usually contains a few, or many smaller books, texts, or volumes inside it. A simple and good comparison is to the Christian Bible. This 'Bible' includes multiple books found within, such as the Jewish Tanakh called by Christians the Old Testament (OT) and Christian texts such as the Letters of Paul, Gospels, and Revelation. The OT makes up one part of the book (and is essentially the singular Jewish Bible -with its many books within). The Christian "Bible" includes an additional twenty-seven other texts called the New Testament (NT). So both the OT and NT completes the "One book," or the "Bible" (for Christians). Inside the NHL canister was a very large cache of many such "Books" or Codices of ancient "Gnostic-Christian" manuscripts."

There was (in fact) no such thing as ancient "Gnostic" text, nor a "Gnostic book." There was, for example "the Christian" *Gospel of Thomas* ("later labeled Gnostic") and "the Christian" *Epistle of Barnabas* (labeled later a "non-Gnostic, ideologically Canonical" but finally, an excluded *Apocryphal* Christian book"). Ultimately, both of these texts (after hundreds of years) were completely excluded from the Christian Canon.

Yet, there is substantial agreement that most people (in Christianity's first few hundred years) called themselves "*Christians*" (with few exceptions) and did not call themselves "Gnostics," or Gnostic-Christians or other labels." They did **not** (*though their enemies, the heresiologists did*) call them 'Gnostics.' But more often they were 'named' based on the Gnostic books they read ("Valentinians if they read Valentinian books, Sethians if Sethian books"). An example of a Valentinian book is the *Gospel of Truth* or the *Gospel of Philip*," read by "Valentinians." Readers of the *Secret Revelation of John* and *On the Origin of the World* were labeled "Sethians." In fact, after the *Gospel of John* was completed, the Johannine community split (Turner, John. 2019; Brown, Raymond. 1979). So it is believed that all the "Johannine Community"

(followers of the Apostle John) helped write the *Gospel of John*. But the community split after that, and *1, 2* and *3 John* is believed to have been written by the "proto-orthodox." However, another group of the 'Johannine community' (who may have been '*early or proto-Gnostic*') may have named themselves similarly to the 'Johannines.' Anthony Silva (2013) suggests they may have used a term like (his modern '*Gnostic-Christian*' congregation, or) the "Johannites." Both claimed to be '*the true*' followers of the Apostle John. And so the rightful heirs to the *Gospel of John*! And non-Sethian, non-Valentinian Thomasine books were "possibly written by the Syrian 'Thomasine Community'" possibly including *the Gospel of Thomas* (Smith, AP. 2015; Turner, John. 2019; Silva, Anthony. 2003.)

But this could get complicated because both "Valentinians" *and* "Sethians" *and* proto-Canonical Syrians all read and used the *Gospel of Thomas!* In fact, Syrians probably wrote most of the *Thomasine* books (addressed below) and thought the "*Gospel of Thomas*" canonical. Yet the whole of the *Thomasine* literature did not end up being labeled (in the first few hundred years) "*Thomasine.*" Yet modern scholars call these (Apocryphal, ideologically canonical Christian) books that center around the Apostle Thomas, "Thomasine." But, they **still** do not mean that most of these texts are Gnostic (except for the *GThom*)! In fact, like modern Protestantism, Gnostics quickly split off into a mind-boggling variety of different "denominations" with many minor theological variations leading to this or that different title or designation." To get an idea of how many Gnostic groups eventually developed, I suggest googling a 'list of Gnostic sects or groups!' And everyone used the *Secret Revelation of John* to explicate "Gnostic Theology" (Keble, John 1872; Smith Andrew P. 2015). One thing is sure, the Egyptian farmers who found these thirteen leather-bound "books" had no idea what they were, nor what they were worth!

To grasp the point I am trying to make, a recent scholarly book by Geoffrey S. Smith on "Valentinian Christianity" (2019) is wonderfully illuminating. Valentinus, educated in Platonism and Christianity in Alexandria, claimed Apostolic descent through (the 'Gnostic,') Theudas (a disciple of Paul). Smith writes,

> "Now that we have a wealth of texts written by Valentinians, we are confronted by a curious reality: though scholars often regard the Valentinians as a distinct Christian sect that thought of themselves as disciples of Valentinus, no surviving text composed by a so-called Valentinian actually uses the term Valentinian. This designation appears only in the patristic sources—that is, in those writers who were largely interested in refuting the Valentinians. Even more striking is the fact that no text thought to have been composed by a Valentinian mentions Valentinus. In fact, in the Nag Hammadi texts, Valentinus's name appears only two times; he is twice named in a list of "heretics" in the Testimony of Truth. Only one alleged Valentinian mentions Valentinus: Alexander, whose appeal to Valentinus and his writings is reported secondhand by an unsympathetic Tertullian (Smith, Geoffrey S. 2019)"

So, the title of Smith's book (ends up being) an exquisite play on words. For, Valentinus is seen (today) as one of the "great leaders of early Gnostic-Christianity." But I doubt he even thought of himself as a "Gnostic." Did he think of himself as a "teacher? yes," and, as an exegete and philosopher of Christianity?' 'yes" (Smith, Geoffrey S. 2019). Already popular, liked, and sufficiently trusted, Valentinus ran (Tertullian said) for the highest Roman office (Bishop or "Pope")! "He expected to become Bishop because he was an able man both in genius and eloquence," said Tertullian, and other historians agree! (Schaff, Philip., Ed. 2016; Encyclopædia Britannica, Inc. Valentinus. 2021). Yet the most terrible crime Valentinus, Sethians, and all the other Gnostics made before and *after* Valentinus, the Sethians and the Basilidians had disappeared (and which was familiar to all the other Gnostics) was, (the heresiologists said), was their claim "there are two equal and competing 'God's!" One in the OT and one in the NT!

Did Gnosticism teach there were "Two Gods?"

Jews and Christians (in the time of Jesus and into late antiquity) taught that a "god" or *'gods'* of other religions were *"real gods"* but, *not-in-any-way-equal* to the *'God'*^ of Israel! (see ^Tillich, Paul. 1951; 1952; 1957). **"The same God of Israel was and is the *'One God'* of Christianity (and effectively) the 'true - One Most High, - the 'God' of Love'** *in Gnosticism* ('or Gnostic-Christianity')!" Two thousand years ago, Jews and Christians did not deny other nations, cultures, and religions their "own gods." But both faiths taught that (*if*) these other 'gods' were actual - (for not all could be as there were just too many to count or even name - maybe these were fallen angels or demons)! Yet "Baal," the supreme "god" (from Canaan) with an ancient "pedigree" and who had been worshipped by varying groups of Jews in Israel at different times was surely believed to be real (Johnson, Paul. 1976) So, "the Jews and, later the Christians accepted some type of existence for these minor and lesser 'gods.'" But to them they were less important beings, inferior and second-class divinities (or even demons). But (though more powerful than humans) they were powerless "and shabby and deficient gods" next to the "One (true) Mighty and Most High God of Love (*'God' of the World and of the Cosmos*)!"

The answer then is that until or before Manichaeism Gnosticism did ***not*** worship or teach there were "Two (equally powerful) Gods." This is why it is monistic (derived from the Monad) *but* with a mitigated dualism (for there was no Good God and an equally powerful Devil or Evil God duking it out.) Not in Valentinianism. Not in Sethianism nor the Basilideans. Even in the first emanation from *'God'* of His 'First Thought' (*Barbēlō*) it is clear in the *SRevJohn* She is not the Equal to the One God. Clearly Barbēlō (or Sophia) are dependent. A higher God (in conjunction with a lesser divinity, 'god or goddess,' yes.)

Classical Gnosticism

Classical Gnosticism is heavily concerned with the dueling natures of spirit and matter (roughly speaking Good and Evil, and Light and Darkness). But unlike other dualist faiths, it was a form of a mitigated dualism or a 'Monism' (Brons, David. 2015). In this case 'Monism" means both the One true and Good God (historically the Monad) who is Good and much stronger and greater than Evil (Yaldabaoth). 'Classical Gnosticism' sees the world of matter as being in a fallen, lesser state to the world of spirit. In classical Gnosticism, the universe begins with an unknown 'Good' God (the Monad). He (the One Good God) creates a series of divine beings. One of the first 'created or emanated' is divine Sofia or Sophia (or Wisdom; also and discussed later as Barbēlō) that at times appears to be designated the Higher (more Spiritual or Pneumatic) Greater Sofia. This is the 'Sophia' or 'Wisdom' found in the OT Sapiential literature (such as in Proverbs 8), where She is personified as 'Wisdom' and the 'Holy

Spirit' (who is identical to the 'Holy Mother'). Sophia though seeks to prove her worth, and in a lower aeon becomes 'Sophia the (fallen) the Lesser, the more material and less spiritual, divinity.' When She attempts to create a divine being by herself, Her efforts, undertaken alone (without the Good, Holy Father Above) produce a flawed divine being, a *'lower, inferior or lesser god'*. This divinity is described in the Apocryphon of John as 'Yaldabaoth'. But he is often described or referred to in classical Gnosticism as the *'Demiurge.'* The term: 'Demiurge' (though a specific word and definition) does not arise in this literature but is the concept taken from the classical Greek to describe what Yaldabaoth (and other demiurges) do who are divine craftsmen or women.

The True Fall

The Demiurge Yaldabaoth believes he is the only god. And sets about creating our flawed and fallen material world

Later both he and Sophia will interact with it. But he declares that *'he is the only true god'* and that there are no others. Hence he is seen as the *"'god'* of the Old Testament." And Yaldabaoth creates a host of petty rulers (known as Archons) to rule over humanity. Gnostic-Christians believed the failed creation of 'Yaldabaoth' by Sofia was a catastrophe, and that his later molding of the world and of 'matter' was and is the 'true Fall'. These 'Gnostic' Christians asserted that 'matter' is a dense, darker material... that it is less ethereal, and thus less 'spiritual and against what would be the true wisdom of the Spirit...' and that the 'spirit and spiritual... would not become entangled with matter and 'its' materialism and fleshly outcomes.' (DeConick, April D. 2017; Davies, Stevan. 2005; Hoeller, Stephan A. 2010; Gnostic Society Library, The. 2015).

> Classical Gnosticism from around the beginning of the second century viewed the Demiurge as the God (or *'god'*) of the Old Testament (Pétrement, Simone.1984). This 'god' created a world of matter, and out of that a world, all and every form of materialism and fleshly want and need. Yet unknowingly he (Yaldabaoth) passed along a spark of the 'divine spirit' (of the One Most High and Good God) when breathing upon humanity. When he breathed into Adam and Eve, the 'breath or spirit' of the Good God entered them and they lived. Why? Because Yaldabaoth had inherited that spirit from his mother Sophia (as She had when emanated from *'God above God,'* ^ *the Father. And 'He' is 'God' (above every human conception of any God or 'gods' and is beyond human understanding and expression)* ^(See: Tillich, Paul. 1951; 1952; 1957) So if a human attains wisdom and enlightenment through Knowledge they grow closer and closer to the spiritual world and Gnosticism. Instead of trying to believe they 'will experien-

tially know' and become 'one' with the true God. This final 'becoming One with, and attaining experientially knowing of the true One God' is the attainment of 'Gnosis'. With 'Gnosis' they have attained salvation. This type of Knowing is akin to a person having a Near-Death Experience (an 'NDE') or communicating beyond all doubt with someone they know who has already "died." They don't need to 'believe' they Know! This "knowing will be addressed in the pages to come. However, the Demiurge does not wish to see humans ascend above him (for he seeks to be worshipped and to not be alone). So he seeks to keep humanity away from divine wisdom and knowledge (and succeeds in doing this by inducing in them "Ignorance.") Thus, the events of the Garden of Eden in Genesis have an inverse significance in the Gnostic point of view. To Gnostics, eating the fruit of the tree of Knowledge by Adam and Eve (in defiance of the '*god*' of this world) was good. Instead of being seen as a fall from Grace it was rather the first step towards wisdom. And, towards a piece of greater spiritual knowledge and existence leading to heaven.

Events in the New Testament and '*the* Son of Man'

How then do the events of the New Testament figure into Gnosticism? The classic Gnostic view was that the Monad (the true God of heaven) took pity on humanity and sent Sophia. Wishing to save them He sends Jesus (as the Word or Logos made flesh) to help humanity find Knowledge. He imparts the Holy Spirit into Jesus (when he is baptized by John). Then, the human Jesus, already the pious and devout 'son of God' (who had in someway also been prepared for the incarnation of the Holy Spirit 'or Mother;' that is his yoking with Sophia) begins his role as 'Son of Man and the Messiah'.

> Clearly one title held by Gnostic-Christians mutually with the Proto-Canonical Christians was His (Jesus) preferred title the "Son of Man." This is true even if it was slightly broader meaning He (the Christ) and those that followed Him (in the Canonical and Gnostic Gospels) it is his Disciples ("the remnant") and in a few places in Danielic (or Enochic Jews) the Son of Man is Jesus and "a -that- remnant of Israel." In fact in both groups meant: The "*Son of Man*" is the Christ (the Anointed), and the Son of God (Saunders, Craig David. 2021; Pétrement, Simone. 1984).

> It is true that this term can mean the 'Son of Humanity' or a human being, however as Saunders notes (Jesus as) the **Son of Man** is associated with (pertaining to Jewish Scriptures including the Tanakh and Second Temple Jewish writings or texts) His being the mediator of God's will; and here is a major Christological title (i.e., the Son of Man). The perfect God-human, the Son of Man represents God the

Father before his disciples and... represents the disciples/humanity before God; and emphasizes God the Father's will as being a central concern in Jesus the Son of Man's (and, consequently, the disciples') earthly ministry; He is the Son of Humanity... who represents humanity to God; The culmination of Jesus the Son of Man's earthly ministry will be emphasized through His predictions of the Son of Man's sacrificial suffering, death, and resurrection. The Son of Man explains what following God the Father's will entail... like the Son of Man, itinerant ministry requires renunciation of family, home, possessions, and life. And... quoting the Scholar John Meier, Saunders notes, "the ...concept of 'Son of Man' is vital to Matthew's Christology and total message. It is just as important as the title Son of God." I agree with this (*After* Saunders, Craig David. 2021.)

The Son of Man (More about this title)

In fact the expression "Son of Man" is an Indication of Jesus' Incarnation and the realized ideal of humanity. His (the Son of Man's) divinity is assumed, while the humanization of that divinity is asserted. The title "Son of Man" equals God manifest in the flesh, or the Word who was God become flesh; or God with us. I agree with this (*After* Saunders, Craig David. 2021.)

The Son of Man, Jesus ...associated with people, especially the marginalized (e.g., tax collectors and sinners - and His disciples) calling them to repent of their sins and receive his forgiveness; and ...to forgive others when they sinned against them by extending mercy in accordance to God the Father's will. the Son of Man's ...disciples were called to faithful obedience to God's will even when their itinerant ministry would lead to inevitable persecution and possible death. And the Son of Man was the ...Lord of the Sabbath, and had the authority to redefine the Sabbath regulations. And thus defined it as ... acts of mercy (and love) towards human beings in need, fulfills the Sabbath law. Only the Son of Man specifically mediates God's will regarding demonstrating mercy and grace towards humanity. And the Holy Spirit was the agent through whom Jesus the Son of Man accomplished his ministry. Finally it is possible to go on particulars of the this "Specific Son of Man," as opposed to this a 'son of humanity.' He *is* the son of humanity noted above but, (also) so much more related to the Jewish Scriptures and Second Temple texts - and of course the NT which is (and was) part of Gnosticism. I agree with this. Cleary some Scholars do not accept that the Son of Man is an Important Christological title. If not important why would Jesus have said these words? Because the words, "Son of Man" from Jesus' lips certainly were heard by the Romans as someone claiming to be the Messianic, "King of Israel." The Romans were not interested in the "spiritual or messianic title" only the earthly title (*After* Saunders, Craig David. 2021)

Now this (the emanation of the Son through the Holy Mother and Father at His baptism by John is, the 'true' but esoteric and hidden 'Virgin Birth') too Gnostics. Yet I do not believe this was just bluntly shared in church house meetings two thousand years ago. But shared later, carefully and privately as esoteric and hidden special exegetical knowledge given to a select group. Yet, however it was transmitted this 'theology' is that Jesus Christ began to teach divine soteriological knowledge and wisdom leading to '*Gnosis*' and Salvation!

Together, Jesus (with Sophia) brings and teaches this 'sacred salvational knowledge' or '*Gnosis*' to all (who seek it). This teaching *must* have then included the OT, NT and Gnostic scriptures. These scriptures remove from humanity their ignorance. And those who study them learn that the, 'Spirit of the true God is within.' And from the Gnostic scriptures they are helped (and can ask for help by those who already regained this 'experiential knowledge and Truth' from the Father. So, those who attain this '*Gnosis*' will ascend (at death) too, at a minimum, the Aeon of 'Heaven' (this first Aeon is overseen by the Great Angel 'Eleleth'). There it is also ruled over by the 'Lower Sofia' and, by the 'Nous or Logos' (Christ) both leading all who seek it, Heaven above. After that some will ascend higher and even all the way up to where Christ Soter (Jesus) sits at the right and, Sofia at the left hand of the Power ('*God*'); in the Highest Aeon and with the true Good and One God Above (Smith Andrew P. 2009; 2015; Hoeller, Stephan A. 2002).

This mythotheology is minimally touched upon here and in the included 'Gnostic Gospels and 'the *SRevJohn*. But, it is covered to a much greater degree in the included 'Secret Revelation of John'. Yet even before reading the SRevJohn, understanding this small core of the Gnostic Theology at the beginning is helpful. It gives some apprehension and comprehension of 'Gnosticism' found in the Gospels of Truth, Philip, Mary and Thomas. It is not clearly stated as above except in the SRevJohn (and a few other Gnostic text). That said, this minimal outline is useful for what seems to be an assumed back- ground for many of the verses in these texts.

A HISTORICAL EXPLANATION OF MY APPROACH TO THESE TEXTS

Anciently (two millennia ago), '*Gnostics*' first noted that their scripture was derived from Jesus Christ and or, had come from one of His First Apostles (or a Disciple of these Apostles) and was authoritative. Authority in scripture *then* (Gnostically too) came from Jesus Christ. So the authors of these 'scriptures' claimed to be Apostles such as: Thomas, Philip, Mary, and John (John the 'Seer' from Revelation and author of the Secret Revelation).

Or the authors would claim to be a strong disciple in a line extending back to the first Apostles. Valentinus, in about c.100 – 160 CE, is believed possibly to have written the *Gospel of Truth* and claimed to have been a disciple of Theudas. Theudas, Valentinus said, had been a disciple of the Apostle Paul (Smith, Andrew P. 2015.) This is why I note that the first Gnostics were told they should (along with learning the OT and NT) 'learn or read these (Gnostic) Gospels' because, these books (to) could be trusted. For, they were books written based upon Apostolic knowledge and would ultimately be accepted as legitimate 'Christian teaching and knowledge' too.

Sources

I have used many Coptic to English interlinear and Coptic to English translations such as those by Thomas Patterson Brown (2014), Mark M. Mattison (2013), Kendrick Grobel (1962), Michael W. Grondin (1996; 2015), April D. DeConick, (2005), Jean Ives Leloup (2002; 2004; 2005), Karen King (2003), Robert McL. Wilson (1962), Wesley W. Isenberg and Bentley W. Layton. (2000), Harold W. Attridge, George W MacRae. (2000), George W. MacRae, Robert. McL. Wilson (2000), M. Waldstein M, FW Wisse, JM. Robinson. (2000) and have also reflected off of the large body of Academic English translations available to the reader today such as from (Marvin W. Meyer, James M. Robinson. (2007) and William Barnstone. (1984; 2009), William Barnstone and Marvin Meyer (2003.) and Marvin Meyer (2005) Simone Pétrement (1984) and AP Smith (2002; 2005; 2009). I am in complete debt to these Scholars, Authors and Writers and to this large body of (academic but often beautiful) translations available now in English. My "Gnostic texts" are meant to be read, and to "feel-like" (slightly more) of a combined, but mostly "Gnostic" text (with a bit of a Canonical flourish). Yet I also tried to always keep the **core Coptic** suggestive idea and evocative Gnostic translation intact. There is no attempt here to lead anybody into (or out of) "Canonical Christianity" (be it Catholic, Protestant, Orthodox or… Heterodox and *Gnostic!*). Nor am I trying to lead anyone away from certain denominations (or toward a different denomination) nor away from a belief in God. I simply hope my effort brings more joy, peace and happiness for you, the reader.

The *GTr, GPhil, GMary, GThom* and the *SRevJohn* are the most read Gnostic texts in the world. And this is particularly true of the *Gospel of Thomas* (which many hold to be the equal to any NT book). I have tried to achieve an accessible reading by utilizing here and there a small number of interpolations from other texts; from gnostic, canonical or Jewish second temple books. though, in this Second Edition I have actually used less and removed some previous interpolations.

What did the Early Christian Hear?

I asked myself, how would an early Christian 'hear' these Gnostic Gospels and Texts explained to them. And what might they have understood in hearing them (in relation to what they were being taught or reading about in the "Canonical OT and NT books?" I used gnostic, canonical, deuterocanonical or, non- Gnostic non-canonical (but ideologically canonical and apocryphal) texts. And, I used Second Temple Jewish texts (such as 1 Enoch). This was to increase the reading pleasure and grasp of these texts. But this amounts to a very small use of additional words being added to these translations. All extracts and interpolated words were judiciously added and based on words or statements arising from the more or less similar subject matter, akin to or not directly opposed to any interlinear Coptic to English translations, and reflecting off of the many other wonderful extant modern translations (like the work of Marvin Mayer and William Barnstone, Jean-Ives Leloup, Thomas P. Brown, Karen King, Michael W. Grondin, Kendrick Grobel, Stevan Davies, April D. DeConick, David Brons, The Gnostic Society Library @gnosis.org, Miguel Conner, GRS Mead, Elaine Pagels, James M. Robinson, John D. Turner) and I would add today: Geoffrey Smith (2019). I could go on and on. But without these great Scholars (and Artists) I would be nothing!

Several paragraphs and lines in the *SRevJohn* are reflected upon using scientific research. I have a PhD from the University of Surrey in the UK and did Clinical Research for many years. I consider myself a "scientist" and part of my spiritual point of view comes from the transcendent complexity I witnessed (and continue to witness, in science and life.) I am eclectic in my religious and spiritual beliefs (though raised Christian) and I believe in '*God Above God*' (that is, for me, taking into account the current state of science and *per Occam's razor*) I believe the beginning was, "God!" (Brown, T. Patterson. 2014; Grobel, Kendrick. 1960; Turner, Martha L. 1996; Grondin, MW. 2017; Mattison, Mark M. 2013; see also: The Gnostic Society Library at http://gnosis.org/library.html).

The *SRevJohn* brought an additional challenge, in that it has subjects and entities such as 'Barbēlō' (an extremely complex divinity that is first and foremost the Hebrew, feminine 'Holy Spirit' also called, the 'Holy Mother' but is also Wisdom and/or Sofia too; and with masculine and feminine expressions and persona's) that make this a text difficult to follow for someone with minimal reading in Gnosticism and specifically about 'Sethian Gnostic-Christians and Sethianism'. They too like the Valentinians anciently lived and openly worshiped with other canonical Christians. They would have been called to explain their unique beliefs and practice. And explain it in light of the coalescing proto-canonical NT. How did 'they interpret the Way' or being 'followers of Jesus'? It is my hope that my translation can help to delve into this question.

The True Dualism

Applying anachronistic trinitarian views to make *Sophia* (or *Barbēlō*) a "second equally powerful - and coexisting Goddess," is not (and was not then) the solution! Nevertheless there was (in Gnosticism) a dualism not found (or minimally found) in non-Gnostic Christianity and which is the 'true dualism of Gnosticism.' This is the dualism between Spirit *and* Matter; or that which is derived from matter, materialism and the flesh; and that which is spiritual (with the spiritual above such unimportant 'stuff, substance, and dull non-spiritual physicality, things and personnel)!

Further, these lesser divinities were more likely demons, fallen angels, powers, principalities, entities or weak, and minor '*gods*'" of little or no concern! It is complicated, but one example is that of the god, "Baal" (once worshipped by some in Northern Israel, these Israelites later abandoned Baal.) But Baal was still the Supreme God of some northern nations. In these sources, "Baal" came to refer to the Lebanon-Phoenician storm deity (or possibly "Yahweh of Samaria") but earlier Baal or Yahweh of Samaria had been ejected by the Omrides (of Omri) who then reintroduced them. The ruling dynasty of Omri located itself in Samaria and Omri's son and heir Ahab allowed his consort Jezebel to bring back into Samaria (their capital rather than Jerusalem) the worship of Baal and Asherah (and their priests). They likely understood Baal as a form of Yahweh. But (that said) Baal was ultimately wholly rejected by the Prophets of Yahweh and especially by Elijah of Israel as a foreign diety (and not the God of Israel.) Baal in "Northern Israel" is an example of accommodation (for a while), of "Two Supreme Gods" or so it appears. The OT says, Omri "did not do what was right in the sight of the Lord nor walk in the ways of his ancestor David." The Bible stresses this apostasy (in favor of Baal) away from the religion of Yahweh.

Examples from Omri and his Dynasty

Some archaeologists consider the Omri dynasty the first significant regional Kingdom with power (not David's or Solomon's). The first non-biblical source to ever mention a Hebrew king is the Mesha stele. And it says, "Omri, (is the) king of Israel. The book of Kings in the Bible barely mentions Omri's accomplishments, considering him evil. He is the king who repeats the northern king Jeroboam's sin by refusing to acknowledge Jerusalem's Temple as the only legitimate Israelite religious shrine. Some archeologists assert that Omri's rule was the first true "Kingdom of Israel." And note the earlier reigns of David and Solomon had weak "political organization" without the extensive bureaucracy needed to run the Kingdom of the Bible. They believe that Omri was the first major Israelite king. Still, Omri faced internal opposition. While increasing trade and stability, peace with Phoenicia also resulted in the penetration of Phoenician religious traditions (including Baal) back into the kingdom. A violent struggle developed between the Yahweh-only party (personified by the prophets Elijah and

Elisha) and the aristocracy (personified by Omri, Ahab, *Jezebel* and their descendants). Finally, all the prophets of Baal met the prophet Elijah of Yahweh. Yahweh "conquered" on Mount Carmel, after which Elijah slaughtered 450 of Baal's prophets (virtually all his opponents)!

Omri's son Ahab and the Baal and Asherah-worshiping princess Jezebel, the Bible says, became apostates from the religion of Yahweh in favor of Baal. Omri allowed "worship of Baal," creating a religious tradition unacceptable to the Yahwists. They worshiped Baal (and other gods 'at high places') or localized or regional worshipping centers dedicated to 'a god,' which were shrines that included a place to make sacrifices, burn incense, and hold feasts and festivals. They contained altars, graven images, and shrines, where they worshiped Baal as their chief deity. A "High place" did not mean only a place to worship on a Hill. It could be in a valley or a plain. But Yahweh was to be worshiped ultimately in a temple. "He, Yahweh" would build a house that would stand for the name of the Lord, and "'*God*' Most-High." Solomon did this, but before that, local centers, including High Places, were allowed as centers of worship. So, in fact, "Omri and Jezebel had '*backslide.*' Worshipping a forbidden god and, in a forbidden place. (Couturier, Adam. 2021; Omri 2021).

One Supreme God or Absolute Polytheism by Gnostics (or Gnostic-Christians)?

Gnostics (like all Christians) were infused in-depth with 'OT' and 'NT' prophecy by '*God*' about the Messiah and taught that this same '*God*' intervened in history to set the stage for sending the Savior. "He" sent "Him, the Christ" to the aeon of the earth. This history is accurate. So they could *not* have been saying there is an equal but different 'god' of the OT. A 'god' equal to the God of Israel, '*the Father*' of Jesus and 'the Way!' Jews or God-Fearing Gentiles would have heard them speaking outright nonsense "that the God of the OT was 'a pagan or gentile *lesser god!*' So Gnosticism did not teach absolute polytheism (any more than Christianity taught tritheism).

(1 Cor 8:5-6) Paul noted, "...indeed there are many "gods" and many "lords"— yet for us, there is **one God** (*of the OT and 'the Way'*- Italics mine), the Father, from whom are all things, and for whom we exist, and one Lord, Jesus Christ, through whom are all things and through whom we exist. This is 'trinitarian' language. But there was much "trinitarian-*like*" (and it must be stressed - *trinitarian-like* not **actual** (and true) trinitarian theology before the Councils of Nicaea c. 325 and Constantinople in 381 CE. Only those councils solidified the Apostles creed (which became the benchmark of Orthodoxy and its '*first official definition and explanation of the doctrine of the trinity.* So prior to (especially to Constantinople in 381 CE) there were many formulations regarding the 'Father, the Son and

the Holy Spirit (or God the Father the Holy Spirit or Mother and the Son or Logos, etc.').

Examples that Christian-Gnosticism (accepted but adapted the OT and NT) and did not teach Absolute Polytheism:

> Psalms 82 1-2; 5-6 (in the OT): God has taken his place in the divine council; in the midst of the gods he holds judgment: "How long will you judge unjustly and show partiality to the wicked? I said, "You are gods, sons of the Most High, all of you; nevertheless, like men, you shall die, and fall like any prince."

Some hold this scripture is talking about human beings, Kings, or the Aristocracy. Still, Michael S. Heiser (2015) documents clearly that these were "gods" not people (in Jewish scripture). And though seen as weak, nevertheless were still real! (Heiser, Michael S. 2015)

Charles Pope gives what came to be the most frequent and common biblical answer. And was the answer about 'gods' anciently and for today. It is that devils pose as gods, deceiving the nations (Pope, Charles. 2021) Some supporting scriptures:

> Psalm 106:34-38: They did not destroy the peoples, as the Lord commanded them, but they mixed with the nations and learned to do as they did. They served their idols ('*gods*' - Italics mine) which became a snare to them. They sacrificed their sons and their daughters to the demons; they poured out innocent blood.

> Deut 32:16-17: They stirred him to jealousy with strange gods; with abominations they provoked him to anger. They sacrificed to demons that were no gods, to gods they had never known.

And the most enlightening verses (about lesser 'gods or idols' from the Apostle Paul:

> 1 Cor 10:20-22: What do I imply then? That food offered to idols (pagan or gentile 'gods'- Italics mine) is anything, or that an idol is anything? **No, I imply that what pagans sacrifice they offer to demons and not to God. I do not want you to be participants with demons. You cannot drink the cup of the Lord and the cup of demons.** You cannot partake of the table of the Lord and the table of demons. Shall we provoke the Lord to jealousy? Are we stronger than he?

As Gnosticism entered into Judaism and 'the Way,' or Christianity, both had only One Supreme God. The Gnostics knew this too and knew it well. So in their naming the OT "God" *a different "God"* these people were saying (in effect) this is *not* the God of Abraham, Isaac, and Jacob (the God of Israel.) Understood correctly, they were saying "that the OT God or '*god*' is a "pagan or gentile 'god' - a devil or lesser divinity." Just because (in the Gnostic Greek or Coptic) used the equivalent to English 'Capital' letters (in English or in another language and translation) did not signify equality with the 'One God.' Jews and Christians understood this allegation as an insult to Judaism (as did non-Gnostic and Gnostic-Christianity)! But this is the Truth about it! The Gnostics were not uncovering (others implied) two 'hidden' but equal Gods! Gods (each with a 'capital G.') And there has been a lot of spilled ink over "Gnostic mitigated dualism" of unequal divinities. But in fact, the Gnostic *NHL* and related scriptures often (but not always) appear like the Dualism of Zoroastrian or the Manichean 'Gods' contending for the Supremacy of Good over Evil. And thus it seems this way over the local aeon of earth and its Cosmos! But the superstructure of Judaism and Christianity does not support such a "two-God" scenario. The Valentinian scriptures do not mention Yaldabaoth (or 'Yahtzevaot'). Nor could Valentinus have run for the office of the "Bishop of Rome" if they had…

Valentinian Christianity

Thus the title of Geoffrey Smith's book, "Valentinian Christianity," is an exquisite play on words. Valentinus was an early "leader" in "Gnostic-Christianity." But I believe he did not think of himself as more spiritual because he was a "Gnostic" or did Gnostic exegesis. Did he believe he was a better "teacher? yes." Did he think he was an important and even a superior exegete and philosopher of Christianity? yes." (Smith, Geoffrey S. 2019) Already popular, liked, and sufficiently trusted, Valentinus ran for the highest Roman office (or "Pope"). "He expected to become Bishop, for he was an able man both in genius and eloquence," said Tertullian, and other historians agree. (Schaff, Philip., Ed. 2016; Encyclopædia Britannica, Inc. Valentinus Gnostic Philosopher 2021).

There is much controversy about what the term 'Gnostic' means. The words 'Gnostic' and 'Gnosticism' stand for (in *this* book) "Gnostic-Christianity or Christian-Gnosticism." And this holds (in *this* book) at all times unless otherwise noted. Gnostic pre-Christian Jewish, Platonic, Egyptian or other religious or spiritual sources that influenced Christianity and the development of "Gnostic-Christians and Gnostic-Christianity" are not denied (King, Karen L 2003; 2006; DeConick, April D. 2017.) But I do not accept that Gnosticism was overlaid upon Judaism and created "Christianity." And I also do not believe "Gnosticism" would have been the force it *was* and *is* today without having been shaped from Christian roots.' (Pétrement, Simone. 1984; Simon, Bernard. 2004.) I can state one final example of the effect of Valentinus on forcing a cohesive and understandable Christian doctrine. Hermeneutics after Valentinus *had* to prove the continuity of the Old and New Testaments! And further, Valentinian teaching documents (possibly the earliest) primitive trinitarian doctrine. In today's trinitarian language, "the Father, Son, and Holy Spirit," but preceded by or used at the same with, 'the Father, Mother, and Son. "Holy Mother,' meant the Holy Spirit. But it also meant Sophia or Wisdom. And Wisdom had been called the 'Holy Spirit to by various Canonical bodies. The Son (often in Gnosticism called the 'Logos') had an incalculable impact on Christianity's development (Moore, Edward. 2021).

As Bernard Simon (2004) writes about Valentinus,

> It appears that he remained a prominent and respected member of the Christian community, and there is no evidence of him ever being accused of heresy… (in his lifetime)

Bernard goes on to note that GRS Mead had this to say about Valentinus,

> Gnosis in his hands tried to embrace everything, even the most dogmatic formulation of the traditions of the Master. Valentinus recognized the tremendous popular movement of Christianity and its incomprehensibility as an integral part of the mighty outpouring; he labored to weave all together, external and internal, into one piece, devoted his life to the task, and doubtless only at his death perceived that for... "the Age" he was attempting the impossible. None but a very few could ever appreciate the ideal of the man, much less understand it (Simon, Bernard. 2004)

Jesus, 'son of God'

Valentinus held that Jesus only became 'the Son of God' after baptism by John. And before this, he was *not fully* divine, though He is revered greatly before His baptism, as do many modern groups today. Assemblies like the Latter-Day Saints or Ecclesia Pistis Sophia (a Gnostic-Christian denomination). They revered Jesus Christ (as a man, prophet, and the 'son of God'). But, to them, Jesus was a highly devout and spiritual man. A '*son of God*' (with a "small' s'). For in Israel, Christ would have been seen as, at minimum, a holy man during this time. And these groups today see Him in some way divine like Moses (and like the prophets and apostles before Him), but not as the *Son of God equal to God (with a large' S')*. However, as a 'son of God' found in the OT biblical phrase, "I said ye shall be as gods" (Jesus quotes this himself as *one explanation* from the OT). However, this could (and did at times) mean a '*god*' (in the Divine Council). But not a '*god*' equal to the Most High (Heiser, Michael S. 2015).

Bernard Simon (2004) writes,

> Valentinus and his followers believed that the human Jesus was born the true son of Mary and Joseph. When he went down into the water as he was baptized, the divine Saviour, ...the Father', descended on him in the form of a dove. So, by a special dispensation, His body is at one with Sophia (the Holy Spirit or 'Mother') and her spiritual seed. In the Valentinians' eyes, this was the actual virgin birth and resurrection from the dead, for He was reborn of the Virgin Spirit!

Simon also writes Valentinus meant,

> ...Jesus is indeed our Saviour, but in the sense of the Greek 'soter,' meaning healer, and that his role was to cure us of ignorance about life's values, to revolutionize our belief in material things (lust, wealth, power, and self-esteem). And to bring knowledge of the 'pneuma' (literally, the Breath of God); that is, to bring on the Spirit to the soul and mind.

And Simon writes Valentinus was (pro-sex for marriage) noting his opinion that he,

> encouraged sex and marriage for spiritual people only, basing their belief on the Gospel of John: Whosoever is in the world and has not loved a woman so as to become one with her, is not out of the Truth, and will attain the Truth...

Jesus Christ in Valentinian Christianity

Valentinianism is a profoundly Christo-centric form of Christian mysticism. The entire mythology can be seen as Christology. In Valentinian thought, the decisive event in the history of the world was the ministry of Jesus (tritrac 2019;) Prior to his coming, the true God was unknown (Against Heresies 1:19:3-1:20:3). This is because "no one knows the Father except the Son and those to whom the Son chooses to reveal him" (Matthew 11:27 cf. Against Heresies 1:20:3). This is the point of the Sophia myth. Throughout the ages, human beings sought to find God, but in the absence of Christ, they succeeded only in producing a defective image of the divine i.e. the Craftsman (demiurge). In their error they worshipped an imperfect image of God as lawgiver and Craftsman of the material world instead of the true God. See Jesus Christ in Valentinianism by David Brons. (Brons, David. 2019; Grobel, Kendrick. 1960; Schoedel, William. 1980 Brantingham 2019.)

In "Sethian Christianity" (in the book's theology, of the *Secret Revelation of John*), Jesus Christ's importance is revealed. And, He shows up in other significant Sethian "Gnostic-Christian" theological works. He is found and discussed in "*On the Origin of the World*" (Smith, AP. 2015) and in the *tripartite tractate* (*tritrac*) and other texts in the *NHL* which make it clear that to them the Advent of Jesus was (to the Sethians) one of most the decisive events in the history of the world. The *NHL* contains many "books and treatises," and the Sethians were a prolific body of writers (Davies, Stevan. 2019; Thomassen, Einar. 2007).

John D. Turner (2001) is considered one of the most outstanding scholars to have written about the 'Sethians,' and he described "Sethianism" in a variety of ways but especially as a form of "heterodox Christian speculation." Or, 'a distinctly inner-Jewish, albeit syncretistic and heterodox, phenomenon fused to Christianity.' 'Christian Sethianism,' as Pétrement held (1984), and Turner (2001) appeared to concur, was never a "separate religious" movement apart from 'Christianity.' Instead, it was a set of mythological themes novelly illuminated and laid out to give an understanding of and how to practice the most spiritual Christianity... And it was this, "Jesus is indeed the 'Savior' and 'Soter,' but like Bernard Simon (2004) wrote, Jesus brought salvation and deliverance". "Jesus cured us, delivering us from *ignorance*. Jesus removed our ignorance about what were life's truly good and godly values. He revolutionized our awareness about matter, materialism, flesh (and especially lust and sex), power, and self-esteem. He brought us into a '*Knowledge*' of the '*pneuma*' (literally inspiring into us Spirit, or "the Breath of God"). By this, Pneuma could join with the soul and mind in a *spiritual resurrection* before death (Turner, John. D. 2001; Pétrement, Simone. 1984; Simon, Bernard. 2004.) Ultimately, the Sethians tried to offer descriptions explaining the inner theology and the best way to practice and worship *like* "Christians." According to Turner, Christianity, Judaism, and Middle Platonism were the roots of Sethianism, and all three influenced the other (Turner, John D. 2001).

Like the Valentinians (but for a shorter time), 'Sethians' called themselves "Christians." And their writing, texts, and books were "Christian (or Judeo-Christian)." There is no one clear "leader" (of Sethianism) though Turner suggests two different 'Sethian-like' groups fused with Christianity. One group was the 'baptizing Barbeloites.' They viewed (the feminine) Barbēlō as the first emanation of the Highest (and Good) 'God.' Later, Barbēlō (who is also the Pneumatic, Highest Sophia) is named *the "Holy Spirit*," and frequently appears in 'Gnostic books' (in Her feminine guise or similarly) as the "*Holy Mother*."

Barbēlō is not to be confused with Jesus' earthly (Holy) Mother or Theotokos, which uses the same terminology (because, for the proto-canonical, the virgin birth and her son being 'the Son of God,' made Mary 'Holy'). Later, Catholics came to call her "Mother of God" (or "God-bearer") the Theotokos. Theotokos was a topic of theological dispute in the 4th and 5th centuries ("the one who gives birth to God") and was countered by those who thought Jesus had two distinct natures. It was the Patriarch of Constantinople Nestorius who insisted that Jesus had both a divine and human nature which were "distinct," so that Mary could be the (bearer of Christ) or the "*Christotokas*" but not 'God.' This was the great argument that would divide the Churches over the Incarnation. Exiled, Nestorius's followers began the "Nestorian Church," but it reconciled with the Catholic and Orthodox Church in 544. Discussed briefly to clarify the term "Holy Mother," it is worth keeping in mind that modern Gnostics (as Ecclesia Gnostica does) use both definitions. But 'Ecclesia Gnostica' always clarifies this. Mary is esteemed by Gnostics too (Hoeller, Stephan A. 2002.). Although some churches in the East still use "Mother of Christ" (Jenkins, Philip. 2008; 2015.)

From this terminology applied to 'God's first thought' and emanation (some have held), Barbēlō is 'the Holy Mother' and the 'Consort' of 'God the Father.' It is reminiscent of the worship of El in Elephantine, Egypt, where Jews worshipped (at their temple) Yahweh and his (Consort) Asherah. But some scholars now see this as possibly having been a "politically correct" position. It is suggested 'Asherah' was in the (unstated) place of a "lesser goddess" (**see below**). Thus it was an *appearance* of 'polytheistic-*like* practice' (living in assimilation side by side) with the Arameans in Elephantine. Or, an earlier form of the "Israelite Religion" more commonly practiced in Northern Israel," for example, even used to describe Samaria north of Judea. In fact there is documentation of a "Yahweh of Samaria" (as there is a "Yahweh of Teman"). Teman is intriguingly supported by the words of Habakkuk, "God came from Teman, and the Holy One from Mount Paran," before the finalized prescriptive formalization of "Judaism, *Jerusalem*, and '*Yahweh* only" (Van der Toorn, K. 1992). There was likely a similar blending of Barbēlō and 'God' as the 'Mother-Father' (described) in the *SRevJohn*. With this, Barbēlō became (for some anciently and moderns) a Consort.

Some modern Gnostics justify calling Barbēlō or Sophia' *God*' (or more precisely) '*the Goddess Most High*' with a capital' *G*. This was and is possible using Gnosticism's earliest forms of "trinitarianism," but as a consort "God and His goddess," *not* "God and His Goddess (or Two equal Gods.") It is still required from a strictly theological perspective (and on the other foot) to be a "god and his Goddess." Yet, I have never seen (such a paring) in Jewish, Christian, or the Gnostic and associated NHL materials. (Though I admit I cannot speak for all Manichean, Mandaean, Cathar, and other obscure gnostic and apocryphal materials).

It might bother people today, but (I believe) it would probably have been (for ancient Christians and Jews in Christianity (or Gnostic-Christians) fundamentally expected that a 'Patriarchal' practice would be the norm - and in reality (anciently) all that they could bear. Some might object, but it is anachronistic to demand a "Goddess" from (this) history and (their then) ancient practice. It was not a misogynistic statement about religious practice but was Jewish and Christian theology two thousand years ago. It understands theology that the most highly trained (Priests and Bishops could intellectually and abstractly understand) but also what the (usually much less educated) could take in or absorb.

Intellectually and in reality, it was the only workable approach by which Priests or Bishops could maintain a monotheist theology for "Christianity or Gnostic-Christianity," and allow the "ancient tradition" to continue. But it was overly dangerous (to push the equality of the One God or the One Goddess existing concurrently). And it stood (and still stands) a significant chance of falling apart by misunderstandings about "two gods" (as ultimately a religion derived from Israel). Even today, almost all definitions of Gnosticism quickly bring up the belief in the "two gods" theory. Misunderstood, in practice, it immediately makes the average Christian (and probably many observant Jews and others) promptly reject "Gnosticism." Ultimately and long, long ago, *only* "ancient traditions and religions" were considered *'true, valid, and real religions if they were of great antiquity.'* Modern scientific methodology played no role in this type of spirituality (Heiser, Michael S. 2015). But it is not so today.

I stand by my contention about "Sophia and Barbēlō." No doubt, at times, they were described as 'the Holy Spirit or Wisdom' as part of *the* earliest representations of a trinitarian "Godhead." Or, (before the Nicene councils) even as '*God*' in the female guise or with feminine attributes. And I suggest (privately and carefully) by some Gnostics (**as the one** '*Goddess*') or the supreme female principle or feminine attributions of 'the One God (or the '*One Goddess.*' Today, "Sophia and Barbēlō" are often described as the 'Divine Feminine.' Only in this manner could the supreme female principle (as "Goddess") have been called 'the Mother.' But clearly this was a rare (maybe even only an oral) presentation of the "One Goddess Most High."

The Valentinian and Sethian "trinities" almost always used, the 'Father' (or Holy Father) and the 'Son or the Logos or maybe 'Christ Soter' but more often the Logos;' and the Holy Spirit as also the Holy Mother or 'Mother.' Yet often in Gnostic-Christian treatises, there is a trinitarian like 'Father, Mother, and Son.' It is true that a "Mother God or Goddess" can be derived from *SRevJohn's* unique "Mother-Father" presentation of Barbēlō. But I think in practice, it was very uncommon. Certainly, it is scarce in the great body of the *NHL* and its Associated literature. This *is* still a type of "mitigated monism" (and maintains the status of monotheism) and thus of Christianity's and Gnosticism's great antiquity (being tied to the OT.) Strictly (and theologically), the 'One Goddess Most High' maintains this mitigation (and monotheism) too. The *Divine Council* and the "*reality of lesser gods*" (Psalms 82 1-2; 5-6) are found in the OT, and are well described by Michael Heiser (2015) and identified as part of the overall religious landscape in Gnosticism by David D. Brons (2015.) But, now there is incredible research that (stranger than fiction) is the first scientific evidence 'from Sophia' Herself (a subject covered later) in which 'She' self identifies as an Archangel (Schwartz, Gary E. 2010; 2011).

Turner (2001) notes that the Barbeloites were a baptizing party fused with Christian baptizing groups in the mid-second century. They viewed the Christ, who descended 'down to' humanity (from "Heaven,"), giving secret, sacred, salvational knowledge unveiling 'the Way' to Redemption as a manifestation (and Incarnation) of Seth... But Jesus was misunderstood as fomenting 'sedition' and considered (a rebel against Rome) murdered and "hung, or crucified on a tree (or the cross). As the pre-existing "self-generated (Autogenes)" or 'Son of Barbēlō,' Christ was "anointed with the Invisible Spirit's 'Christhood.'" According to Turner, this anointing receiving 'Christhood' by the Barbeloites in *their* baptismal rite that assimilated the archetypal "Son of Man." And Seth the Righteous had (also) been a "Son of Man" who Aeons and Aeons before Jesus delivered secret Salvational Knowledge. Thus the earthly Jesus was regarded (by Sethians) as a messenger of Barbēlō. And he became the divine Logos when He received his Christhood after being baptized in the Jordan by John.

But both Judaism and Christianity and their sophisticated theologians (worth their salt despite anthropomorphism) cleaved to the Tanakh or OT, and "Numbers 23:19." 'Numbers 23:19" said (as it does now) *God* is not just a man, that he should lie, or a son of man, that he should change his mind; without needing to add *God* is not just a woman - *for at minimum (even two thousand years ago) theologians understood this.* *God* is not just a woman! So the concept of Barbēlō as 'God,' portrayed as feminine' was 'not' problematic,' for (*we know*) per the OT, "male and female He created them... (*After* ESV). But two Supreme Gods has always 'crossed a line, and gone too far,' for either faith. And for the greatest, nearly absolute majority of Christians, the trinity is not three Gods! In fact, in a favorite Gospel used by the Sethians, the *Gospel of Thomas* verse 30 (from the Greek fragments), Yeshua says: Where there are three gods, they are godless. But where there is only one, I say that I myself am with him. Raise the stone, and there you shall find me, cleave the wood and there am I (*After,* ESV; and Thomas P. Brown. 2014).

"Sethian Christians finally dissociated first from Christianity and then even Platonism." Fragmenting into various smaller and sectarian Gnostic groups, they became the Archontics, Audians, and Borborites. But also, the ("*sexually deviant*") Phibionites according to Epiphanius of Salamis. The Phibionites heresy may have practiced 'antinomian' fornication connected to their *unique* "Gnostic" religious meetings and rites. Epiphanius said they derived these practices from the *Nicolaitans* (mentioned -and condemned-by John in the *Book of Revelation* 2:6;15). But from today's vista, sexual abuse (or even assaults) are now recognized as having always existed. And in *every* religious or spiritual congregation; (from before history). Not correct practice! And finally admitted today, it may, at last, be stopped (or significantly reduced) now and into the future. But such a report (from any religious community) is not a shock (Benko, Stephan. 1967; Schaff, Philip., Ed. 2016).

Finally, some of this Sethian literature includes Seth, Jesus Christ, Peter, Mary (Magdalene), and Mary (Jesus earthly mother), James, Paul, Philip, Matthew, and more. But beyond the use of the Patriarchs' (and other Christian) names, we remain ignorant about who wrote these incredible Sethian texts! There is no doubt that this group strongly *contributed* to Christianity in ways that we still do not (fully) understand to this very day!

New, New Testaments

The primary "theological writings" Valentinians defined themselves by were the "*tripartite tractate,*" and the "*Holy Book of the Great Invisible Spirit*" (this last product was by Sethians!) Yet much that is "theologically complicated" in Valentinianism, Sethianism (and in other Gnostic groups) is explained from or in the "*Secret Revelation of John*" and, to a lesser degree, the two similar texts above. This is not to discount or belittle Gnostic Gospels, texts, and Letters, but they are not the prominent 'go-to' explanatory theological treatises.

That said, there have been recent attempts at producing canonical-*like* publication of '*New,*' "*New Testaments.*" Under (Editor) Hal Taussig, a Professor of New Testament (retired) from Union Theological Seminary, and a pastor at a United Methodist Church, who formed a new "Council."

This "Council" was a group of modern-day Christians *and* a variety of other Biblical Scholars (one in this "*Council*" - being a woman, not Christian, yet a devout, believing and observant Jew) that made part of this "Council." They then studied and added to the Canonical texts some Christian Apocryphal, but mostly "Gnostic" texts such as "*The Gospel of Thomas,*" the "*Secret Revelation of John,* the *Gospel of Mary* and *Thunder* (a text many believe inspired by "*Sophia*"). This Council named their NT Bible the "*New, New Testament*" (Taussig, Hal. Ed. 2013). Another "*New*" *New Testament* was *The Restored New Testament* by William Barnstone. A Biblical and Gnostic Scholar (by his own description he is a non-observant Jew and agnostic). An extraordinary Scholar Barnstone added significant ancient Jewish and Greek contextual material "back into" the *Gospels* "Markos, Mattityahu (Jewish spelling), Loukas (Greek spelling), and Yohannan." Along with additional Jewish and Greek names, ancient viewpoints, and historical ideas from Israel in the time of Jesus. Barnstone added all of this into his scholarly "NT" and called it the "*Restored New Testament.*" William Barnstone also added in the *Gospel of Thomas* (found in this book) and the recently discovered 'Sethian work,' "*The Gospel of Judas*" (Barnstone, William. 2009).

The first Gnostics Simon Magus, Menander and Basilides

Basilides was also a prominent third-century Gnostic-Christian theologian and leader. Those that later followed him were called 'Basilidians,' say the Church Fathers, but otherwise (at first) were identified as "Christians." Basilides led a "School and Church of Christians" who flourished in Alexandria, Egypt.

Upon his death, his son Isidore succeeded him. The last Basilidian "Christian" school and church was reported extant in Egypt in the fourth century. Basilides claimed to have been a pupil of Menander in Antioch. Significantly Menander (of Alexandria) had been a direct disciple of Simon Magus and took over as leader of Simon's Gnostic Community and Religion after Simon Magus died.

And It appears that Simon Magus had been (*at least for a limited period of time*) a real follower and disciple *(of Jesus Christ)* in the post-resurrection movement, or 'the Way.' Whatever the time was that he had been a follower of 'the Way,' this surely increased his stature, gravitas and fame and importance in the eyes of others when the Magus set out on 'his own.' He is reported to have represented himself in his later Gnostic church and party as "the "Standing One, and a Mighty Power" (both Messianic titles). Simon challenged Dositheus, the "original leader" of this "Gnostic Church." He triumphed over Dositheus in battle, winning as his wife "Helena," whom he believed to be "the Holy Spirit" (and the reincarnation of Wisdom) and claimed her 'Sophia' come to help him help; leading others to salvation." Descending from Above and from the Unknown God, Simon Magus came representing the Father Himself (with Sophia), he said!

As April D. DeConick (2017) and Irenaeus himself inform us, Simon Magus became a "figure" (for some) similar to "Jesus Christ" in his self-descriptions. If there is substance to this, he might have indeed been one of the first to bring "Gnostic" ideas if not a movement" into association with Christianity (Armitage, Robinson, 1920; Keble, John 1872; April D. DeConick 2017.) He baptized Samaritans claiming, "I am the Word of God, the Paraclete, I am and the Almighty, (and) I am all that is God's." Such exalted titles and claims by Simon would have been more than the nascent church could abide. His mission was to save the Father's *Ennoia* (or Thought). And to release "It" from its "captivity" stuck in the "flesh of humanity." According to April D. DeConick (2017), the core theological beliefs of Simon Magus were: Father God, YHWH, whose Ennoia (first thought) or His nous (His mind and soul) emanated the Holy Spirit, the Mother God.

Further, Basilides taught the Father had conceived and willed the existence of archangels, angels, and the (He knew, this '*local*') Cosmos. His first Thought, the Holy Spirit or Mother, understood and leaped forth to bring His will into reality in the lower realms. There as the Mother God, she generated the angels and powers the Father deemed should exist. In turn, these angels and powers created the world the Father had envisioned. But things went awry. After YHWH's first Thought, the creator angels became jealous, and as "fallen angels" lusted after the Holy Spirit's (the Holy Mother's) power. But they failed to seize power. Instead, they grabbed Her and incarcerated her in a material human body. Thus the spirit became subject to a cycle of birth and death. And she underwent reincarnation for aeons and aeons, lifetime after lifetime, until Simon released her.

The Holy Spirit (or Mother) suffered exceedingly, unable to realize her liberation and release and unable to return to the Father. Her very own creation had trapped her! The only solution to this horrific predicament was by the Father's intervention. Thus He descends to earth to save her personally. But, Simon declared himself (on earth) to be YHWH manifest, the Great Power, the son of God, and come to free His First Thought (the Holy Mother or "Helena"). Simon released "Helena" from her enslavement to the rebellious angels. On land, Simon appears to humans to be human. So he wandered around looking for the lost Holy Spirit. He finds her and marries her. She is his beloved Helena, reincarnated into the body of a "prostitute." Simon, "the son of 'God,'" recognized her and released her, liberating both Helena (and in some way all humanity). Simon then declared that all humans are like Helena was, in bondage. But by the "grace and power of God" can be released (if they attain Knowledge). He will also free them from the evil principalities and powers and the rulers of darkness and spiritual wickedness over this world. But through him, Simon, not Jesus (April DeConick 2017.)

Basilides

Basilides' (132-135 CE) core "Gnostic teachings" contradict each other in the Church Fathers' different writings by the heresiologists. Basilides taught some "blending or synthesis" similar to Simon Magus' teaching and Gnostic-Christian or Gnostic teachings.

He developed a cosmogony or explanation for creating the Cosmos through the Sophian myth of classical Gnosticism. For example, from the *SRevJohn* or the *Holy Book of the Great Invisible Spirit* (with no mention of Yaldabaoth) by Basilides but, with other associated names, "Saklas - or Nebruel." One of them cries out, "I am a jealous God, and there is no other God besides me!"). So Yaldabaoth also claims in the *SRevJohn,* and he also reinterpreted key Christian concepts using the popular Stoic philosophy of the era. This, Stoic philosophy was one in which the highest virtue, the highest good, is based on Knowledge; the wise live in harmony with Divine Reason (also identified with the ups and downs in life). But sometimes described as that which is "foreordained." The Stoic indifference to it all was also part of Basilides' popular Gnostic philosophy.

Basilides' taught Simon Magus claimed messianic titles that would have immediately caused confrontation (as it did with certain of the Apostles). But the facts are that Gnosticism or some Gnostic ideas intermingled within many early Christian communities surviving as part and parcel of Christianity into the third century. Certainly, Gnosticism had a Platonic base, and philosophical 'Platonism' has guided (canonical) theology's elucidation of Christianity - and still does to this day. Another concept of Gnosticism taken aboard, especially in the (modern age) and in the last two hundred years, was the "importance of Knowledge." No one in contemporary society denies the profound changes that have come about in their communities because of the 'scientific and common sense use' of *Knowl-*

edge! It is the basis of and the requirement of rational science. As the Psalmist (19:1) says: The heavens declare the glory of God, and the sky above proclaims his handiwork (ESV); "But ask the beasts, and they will teach you; the birds of the heavens, and they will tell you, or the bushes of the earth, and they will guide you, and the fish of the sea will declare to you. Who among all these does not know that the hand of the Lord has done this? (ESV). So many scientists (who are "Christian") state such verses embrace the study of the World and the Laws of Nature (and Science and Christianity co-exist peaceably.)

Through the union of Wisdom and Power, a group of angelic rulers came into existence. They generated a total of 365 heavens or aeons (Irenaeus, Against Heresies). Each of these heavens (or Aeons) had a chief ruler (or Archon) and numerous lesser angels. The final heaven, Basilides claimed, was the realm of matter. In this Aeon, humanity is ruled by "the god of the Jews." He implied because of that; there would be strife for the nations and the Jewish people themselves. This, Basilides said, caused all the Archons in the other 364 heavens (or Aeons) to oppose the *'god'* (a daemon and a lesser divinity) of the Jews. But he meant the *'lesser god'* of the OT. So they sent a savior, Jesus Christ, from the highest Aeon (or Heaven) of the Father, to rescue the human beings under the yoke of Saklas or Nebruel identified in SRevJohn as Yaltabaoth (as Irenaeus wrote about in Against Heresies (Keble, John. 1872). Since the realm of matter is the source and aeon of this *'god,' it is the Adversary's realm (Ha Satan), not of the Father!* Basilides found no redeeming value in the earth's eon (made of matter) and filled with materialism, flesh, and unappeasable craving and desires. Basilides stated, "salvation belongs only to the soul (meaning the mind, soul, and spirit)," for "the body is by nature corruptible" (Keble, John 1872). He declared, shockingly and opposite Christian proto-orthodox teachings, that Christ's death on the cross was apparent (but not historical). For, it did not "occur to Him (his soul and spirit) but only to the flesh of Jesus." Indeed, a doctrine that would come to be called Docetism, or to "appear like" (Moore, Edward. 2021).

Yet in the end and taken from the Basilidean Fragments C, D, he does not call upon his hearers to abandon the material realm. Instead, he offers them a new life by appealing to the grand hierarchy of rulers persisting above the material realm (see Fragment D). When one turns to the more significant order of Being, there is a "creation of good things" coming close to the OT. And strikingly, along these lines (as also found in the OT), Basilides states, "Love between people and the begetting of the Good" should be the final result of his (to a certain degree unclear) teaching. Despite his being "Gnostic," this appears to be one of the most important early expressions of a truly Christian, if not "orthodox," philosophy (Moore, Edward. 2021).

The Logos, Simon Magus, Menander, Valentinians and Sethians

Furthermore, the *extreme* Gnostic emphasis on "*the Logos*" or literally "I say," is a term (and concept) in Western philosophy, science, medicine, psychology, rhetoric, and religion derived from the Greek word meaning variously, the "ground," "plea," "opinion," "expectation," "the word of God," or "the Word." And "speech," "account," "reason," "proportion," and "discourse." It also became a technical term meaning the principle of order and technical application of Knowledge (Freke, Tim., Gandy, Peter. 1997). Jerome felt frustrated that he could not develop an equivalent one-word "Latin" term (and the same problem exists; it could be said in English even today). Though "The Word' is not being demeaned here (of the "unbelievably beautiful" English prologue to John's Gospel, it is beautiful and needs no change! But, I like what Professor David Hart (2017) came up with to rival 'the Logos' from Asia: He suggests the: Tao 道 or 'the Way.' And of course, 道 means a myriad of things similar to the Logos. Reader John wrote, "Logos." Though the "Word" is fine, "*Logos*" is so broad that it is ecumenical even beyond all religious' theology. Knowing this is good.

Simon Magus said, "that releasing the Ennoia of the transcendent Spirit" or the "mind, thought and spiritual essence of '*God*'" was his (Simon's) reason for descending into the world. He came down and recognized the "Holy Spirit." The Holy Spirit or Mother, or Wisdom, was Helena, who was therefore Sophia! He married Helena, "releasing the Holy Spirit." Simon passed this arrogance and pomposity to Menander (DeConick, April D. 2017.) Menander taught in Alexandria during the time of the Emperors Hadrian and Antonius Pius. Basilides claimed to be a disciple of Menander (which therefore is a claim to "Apostolic lineage") through Simon Magus and his Gnostic practice. But also as a disciple of the Anointed (Jesus) and 'the Way.'

Peter condemned Simon Magus for trying to "buy" the 'episcopate' gift and laying on of hands to heal through the "Holy Spirit." Simon Magus witnessed Philip perform (and coveted) this gift of healing in Acts 8:9–24. But actually, the NT gives no explicit statement that he, Simon Magus, was thrown out of the church. In fact, after Peter's denouncement, Simon Magus was asked to "repent" (and Simon asks Peter in Acts 8:9–24 too, "pray ye to the Lord for me").

But from the Apocryphal scriptures, Menander taught that although Simon had descended in Samaria, he (Menander) had come to save all nations—and all humans generally—from enslavement. Enslavement to the fallen angels and powers that ruled the world. Menander also said that recognizing, marrying, and "releasing" Helena (the Holy Mother and Sophia) had - accomplished this mission. And that, "Heaven" sent *Menander*. He was the actual Savior, for the deliverance of all men." Entirely rejected by Irenaeus and other proto-Canonical Church Fathers, heresiologists, and overall the church. It would be the Valentinians and the less narcissistic and self-important but somewhat anonymous "Sethians" that would join for up to a few hundred years the "proto-canonical churches" (Irenaeus, Against the Heresies (Armitage, Robinson, 1920; Keble, John 1872; April D. DeConick 2017.)

Marcion - not Gnostic but Dualistic

Marcion, it is said, posited two opposed "Gods": the biblical OT "god," and a previously unknown and "loving but (misunderstood) and unfamiliar" God, '*the Father*' of Christ. Marcion stated outright that a "lesser, judgmental and punitive god" haunted the OT text and realm (by which he meant the world and the Cosmos). He said this 'god' of the OT intended to preserve his autonomy and power over creation and over (human) beings. And this was to be too secured (in any way necessary)—wars, genocide, racial killing, and worse. But (part of) the NT "Unknown God," the Supremely Good, "God *the Father* and Jesus Christ" by his grace and compassion entered from outside into this localized, isolated, back-ward and "secluded Cosmos." He descended as Jesus Christ to help His children find their way back to "Heaven." And he came through the Savior's Incarnation and Resurrection as Christ. These oppressed human beings, according to Marcion, were under the sway of the OT's *inferior 'god.'* Note, Marcion labeled the OT God, not another "*God*" but an "*inferior god.*" And so, in fact, his theology was not "dualist with equally competing powers of Good and Evil or Light and Dark," but the Good, the One God of the NT, could easily conquer this "inferior god." The OT '*god*' was just a "demon." Two "Equal Gods" are a misunderstanding and misinterpretation of Marcion's claims.

Platonism

Claiming specific messianic titles would have immediately caused confrontation (and it did with the "Apocryphal" Simon Magus). Gnosticism or some Gnostic ideas intermingled within many early Christian communities surviving as part and parcel of Christianity until into the fourth century within the church (and in pockets of territories outside of the "canonically designated" churches much longer). Certainly, Gnostic ideas had a Platonic base, and philosophical 'Platonism' helped guide theology's elucidation (Christian and Gnostic) - and still does to this day.

Plotinus (turning back to Plato - and not to the later speculative writing and suppositions by some Platonists about an Evil Demiurge) states that the "Gnostics are wrong." In his treatise, *Against the Gnostics* Plotinus wrote a self-explanatory title for this book. "Against Gnosticism and Those Who Say The Creator of This World, and the World Itself, to be Evil." This definition of (really one strain only) of Gnosticism is a concept many modern (non-Gnostic) Christians have unknowingly taken aboard, especially today in this (current) age. Today's modern Gnostics have also pushed "*Knowledge*," especially over the last two hundred years. And the "importance of *Knowledge* (today) is lost on no one." Nobody in modern society denies the profound changes that have come about in modern nations because of the 'scientific and common sense' use of *Knowledge* (Moore, Edward. 2021). And Knowledge is the basis and requirement to conduct rational scientific research. I submit that I attempt to apply evidence-based science to my spiritual beliefs and practices. Unlike some who claim this has made them Atheists, it is just the opposite for me. Looking at the incomprehensible complexity of life and existence is transcendent for me. As the Psalmist (19:1) says: The heavens declare the glory of God, and the sky above proclaims his handiwork (ESV); "But ask the beasts, and they will teach you; the birds of the heavens, and they will tell you, or the bushes of the earth, and they will teach you, and the fish of the sea will declare to you. Who among all these does not know that the hand of the Lord has done this? (ESV). Many say "Gnosticism" is not interested in such views about '*God*' and the Universe as found in the OT. But, they say Gnosticism is hostile to it. I say look in the massive Gnostic text, '*Pistis Sophia*.'

The Logos

Furthermore, the *extreme* Gnostic emphasis on "*the Logos*" is correct, and its time has come. It is a term (and a concept) in Western philosophy, science, medicine, psychology, rhetoric, and religion derived from the Greek word meaning as applied, the "ground," "plea," "opinion," "expectation," "the word or Word," "speech," "account," "reason," "proportion," and "discourse." It also is a technical term meaning the principle of order and technical application of Knowledge (Freke, Tim., Gandy, Peter. 1997). Saint Jerome felt frustrated that he could not develop an equivalent "Latin" one-word designation. Though "The Word' is not (here) being demeaned in John's Gospel, it is beautiful and should not ever be changed. But, it is worth looking at how expansive the Greek term "the Logos" is (which is after all that John wrote). And is more applicable to science and the supernatural (or supernormal) we find today! I like the word Professor David Hart came up with (2017) to rival 'the Logos,' from Asia. He suggested the: Tao 道 or 'the Way.' And of course, 道 means a myriad of things similarly as does "the Logos."

Lastly, Christians did not assert no other "gods" existed. But these "*gods*" were such but with a small 'g,' and actually 'demons' and authentic. So that this ultimately leaves the "*lesser god*" of the OT demonic (though at times he acts "neutral.") Yet the last major "Gnostic group" actively growing before the modern era were the Cathars in Southern France. They did not beat around the bush, and the Cathars named the Demiurge the '*god*' of the OT "Satan." They claimed they were "Christians," but the Albigensian Crusade (of Catholic Christians) erased them from the face of the earth beginning in 1209–29; then again in 2013; and finally 'finished them off ' in 1217 and 1218. This bloody (and greed-fueled) crusade pitted the north's committed Catholics' aristocracy against the south. Southern France tolerated the Cathars (even their equally doomed Catholic brothers and sisters). Yet even after this Holocaust, a few lived on, even after all this!

Why Discuss "Gods, or a God or 'lesser gods" (and other beings of divinity)? One reason is because most scientists (but not all) believe in "the Block Universe." These scientists say it is a logical outcome of Einstein's Theory of Relativity and they are (actually) atheist openly or in a reserved way (and sometimes in a proselytizing way - like some modern physicists and philosophers). A Block Universe is a "Universe" in which everything (from the past, present and future) has already happened. So "free will" does not exist. Free will is only an *illusion*. Brave scientists will point out that this is (like the 'many worlds interpretation' and 'multiverses' - "are metaphysical" and) not proven by any significant, meaningfully testable, body of research.

It is funny (but ideas like this were deadly) in the way these "Mathematics" produce an "antinomian" freedom (or release to do anything you want as there are *no spiritual* consequences) for breaking man-made rules or laws.' But "certain man-made rules or laws, and crimes" will be punished *if detected* or seen and evidence demonstrates they occurred (against secular law enforcement). Similarly painful or difficult consequences often follow "adultery" or "cheating on one's spouse," *if caught* (God or no God)! Otherwise truly one can do anything they want (if you can get away with it).

It is how some interpreted the Apostle Paul's statement that "Christians" who *believed in Jesus* were released and "no longer under the Law," by under Grace. Misinterpreting teachings by Paul a small few went on to do things considered immoral believing they were no longer under the law or "Judaism or some forms of Pagan law - or earlier forms of religious practice" They thought they could sin yet would still be saved (by simply 'believing' in Jesus the Anointed.) They misunderstood both Pauls' (and Jesus') teachings which I discuss below..

So this "Block Universe derived from Einstein's Relativistic Mathematics" is believed by most who accept these mathematics has caused a 'block universe.' They posit it proves everything that happens (has already happened) and thus is predestined. And I note many especially Atheist scientists are pleased with the new research showing such things as nerve impulses to the muscles (such as are needed to grab a cup) "fire up" before the person "knows consciously" that they are about to grab the cup. This (for them) supports their belief that there is no "free will" in that decision. But free-will is (they assert) an illusion.

Now the Apostle Paul later corrected people who came to this ("spiritual" antinomian 'law-free') position by noting they were under the 'Law of Christ." What was the "Law of Christ?" Well as far as Theologians can tell, Christ did not say the 'Law, or Instruction or Torah' was abolished." But he pointed out that it was "misinterpreted at times" in a non compassionate way (when in fact there was scripture in the "Tanakh" or Torah (pre Talmud) that gave "license to 'break the law' in certain cases such as getting a child our of a well or getting a donkey or cow out of a ditch (or attending to a man just beaten by robbers. Like the Samaritan)" For Jesus said was OK to do so even on the Sabbath (when normally 'work' is not permitted) - as it is seen as breaking the "Law or Torah." It should be noted that today most observant Jews agree with this interpretation.

Otherwise he also gave the "Sermon on the Mount" that was in most ways a vigorous "strengthening" of many of the Ten Commandments found in the Torah. That he had talked to a "Samaritan women" at the well of Jacob (which anciently was about like… the equivalent of a committed "Nazi" or National Socialist befriending a Jew in Germany in the late 1930's) or healing a Roman Soldiers' servant (then an unacceptable "interracial or inter-ethinic" mingling). Many scholars today believe Jesus wished to include the Gentiles and other Nations in the worship of the "God of Israel."

James Brantingham PhD

6 15 2021

Thousand Oaks, CA

References to "Holy Wisdom and The Logos of God?"

Armitage, Robinson, Ed. (1920) Irenaeus Bishop of Lyon. The Demonstration of the Apostolic Preaching. The Macmillan Co. New York, NY

Attridge, Harold W., MacRae, George W. (2000). The Gospel of Truth. In Robinson, James M. Ed. The Coptic Gnostic Library. A Complete Edition of the Nag Hammadi Codices. Vol. 2. Koninklijke Brill NV, Leiden, The Netherlands

Bane, Theresa. (2012) Encyclopedia of Demons in World Religions and Cultures. McFarland & Co. Jefferson, NC

Barbelo or Barbēlō (2019) in: https://en.wikipedia.org/wiki/Barbelo (Accessed 4-19-2019)

Barnstone, William. (1984) The Other Bible. HarperCollins. New York, NY.

Barnstone, William., Meyer, Marvin. (2003.) The Gnostic Bible: Revised and Expanded 1st ed. Boston, Massachusetts, New Seeds Books.

Barnstone, William. (2009.) The Restored New Testament: A New translation with Commentary Including the Gnostic Gospels of Thomas, Mary and Judas. Publisher W.W. Norton & Co. New York, NY

Bauckham, Richard. (2006) Jesus and the Eyewitnesses: The Gospels as Eyewitness Testimony. Eerdmans Publishing, Grand Rapids, MI 2006

Beauchemin, Gerry. Reichard, Scott D. (2007, 2010, 2016; 2018). Hope Beyond Hell. The Righteous Purpose of God's Judgment. Malista Press. Kindle Edition. Olimo, Texas.

Beauchemin, Gerry. Reichard, Scott D. (2018) Hope For All: Ten Reasons God's Love Prevails (p. 19). Malista Press. Kindle Edition.

Beischel J, Boccuzzi M, Biuso M, Rock AJ. (2015) Anomalous information reception by research mediums under blinded conditions II: replication and extension. Explore (NY). 2015 Mar-Apr;11(2):136-42. doi: 10.1016/j.explore.2015.01.001. Epub 2015 Jan 7. PubMed PMID: 25666383.

Beischel, J. (2019) Windbridge Research Center. https://www.windbridge.org/ A List of Completed Research https://scholar.google.com/citations?user=rNejlNcAAAAJ&hl=en (Accessed 12 30 2019)

Bem D, tressoldi P, Rabeyron T and Duggan M. (2016) Feeling the future: A meta-analysis of 90 experiments on the anomalous anticipation of random future events version 2; referees: 2 approved F1000Research 2016, 4:1188 (doi: 10.12688/f1000research.7177.2)

Benko, Stephan. (1967). The Libertine Gnostic Sect of the Phibionites According to Epiphanius. Vigiliae Christianae, 21(2), 103-119. doi:10.2307/1582042

Bourgeault, Cynthia. (2008). The Wisdom Jesus. transforming Heart and Mind- A new Perspective on Christ and His Message. Shambala Publications Inc. Boston, MA

Bergman, James '19 (2017) "The Divine "Sofia": The Development of Jewish and Hellenistic Thought in the Christology of the New Testament," Furman Humanities Review: Vol. 29 , Article 29. Available at: https://scholarexchange.furman.edu/fhr/vol29/iss1/29 (Accessed 4 17 2019)

Brantingham, James. (2017) The Gospel of Philip. A New translation. Amazon Digital Services LLC. Seattle, WA. Paperback and Kindle. ASIN: B06XY2J951

Brantingham, James. (2019) Truth... What Is Truth. Holy Wisdom and the Logos of God. The Four Lost Apocryphal Christian Gospels: The Gospel of Truth. The Gospel of Philip. The Gospel of Thomas & The Gospel of Mary With the Secret Revelation of John. Pub. Amazon Digital Services LLC. Kindle. ASIN: B08R7Z8KXD

Brons, David. (2015) Valentinian Monism *in:* Gnostic Society Library, The. (2019). The Nag Hammadi Library. Available at http://gnosis.org/naghamm/nhl.html (Accessed 1/23/2019)

Brons, David. (2015.) The Demiurge in Valentinianism *in:* Gnostic Society Library, The. (2019)*.* The Nag Hammadi Library. Available at http://gnosis.org/naghamm/nhl.html (Accessed 1/23/2019)

Brown, T. Patterson. (2014) The Gospels of Thomas, Philip and Truth. Available from http://www.freelyreceive.net/metalogos/files/intro.html (Accessed 5 25 2014)

Gabriele Boccaccini and Carlos A. Segovia. Els. (2016) Paul The Jew: Rereading the Apostle as a Figure of Second Temple Judaism. Minneapolis: Fortress, 2016. Fortress Press, Minneapolis, MN

Boyarin, Daniel. (2012) The Jewish Gospels: The story of the Jewish Christ. New York NY, New Press

Bourgeault, Cynthia. (2008) The Wisdom Jesus. transforming Heart and Mind- A new Perspective on Christ and His Message. Shambala Publications Inc. Boston, MA

Brantingham, James. (2017) The Gospel of Philip. A New translation. CreateSpace Independent Pub. Amazon Digital Services LLC. Seattle, WA.

Chilton, Bruce. (2002) in Rabbi Jesus (Rabbi Jesus: An Intimate Biography). Publisher Double Day a Division of Random House, New York, NY

Conner, Miguel (2017) Apr 13, 2017 in How Did the Gnostics View the Crucifixion of Jesus. https://thegodabovegod.com/gnostics-view-crucifixion-jesus/

Couturier, Adam. (2021). Bible Study Magazine. What Were the High Places? https://www.biblestudymagazine.com/bible-study-magazine-blog/2017/10/10/what-were-the-high-places October 10, 2017. (Accessed 4 2 2021)

Davies, Stevan. (1996.) Mark's Use of the Gospel of Thomas. In The Journal of the New Testament Society of South Africa or Neotestamentica 30(2) 1996

Davies, Stevan. (2002) The Gospel of Thomas. Annotated & Explained. SkyLight Paths Paths Publishing. Woodstock, Vermont

Davies, Stevan. (2005) The Secret Book of John. The Gnostic Gospel Annotated & Explained. Skylight Paths Publishing. Woodstock, Vermont

Dawkins, R. (2006). The God Delusion. Bantam Books. New York, NY

Dawkins, R. (1986). The Blind Watchmaker. New York: W. W. Norton & Company.

DeConick, April D. (2005.) Recovering the Original Gospel of Thomas: A History of the Gospel and Its Growth. Publisher: T & T Clark. London, UK

DeConick, April D., J. Asgeirsson, J., Uro. R. (2005) "On the Brink of the Apocalypse: A Preliminary Examination of the Earliest Speeches in the Gospel of Thomas." In Thomasine traditions in Antiquity: The Social and Cultural World of the Gospel of Thomas. Nag Hammadi and Manichaean Studies 59. Leiden: E.J. Brill.

DeConick, April D. (2017.) The Gnostic New Age: How a countercultural spirituality revolutionized religion from antiquity to today. Columbia University Press. New York, NY

Delorme A, Beischel J, Michel L, Boccuzzi M, Radin D, Mills PJ.

(2013) Electrocortical activity associated with subjective communication with the deceased. Front Psychol. 2013 Nov 20;4:834. doi: 10.3389/fpsyg. 2013.00834. eCollection 2013. PubMed PMID: 24312063; PubMed Central PMCID: PMC3834343.

Dueholm, Benjamin J. (2019) A new canon, created by 19 people. A New New Testament. https://www.christiancentury.org/blogs/archive/2013-05/new-canon-created-13-people (accessed 5 9 2019)

Duggan M, tressoldi P. (2018) Predictive physiological anticipatory activity preceding seemingly unpredictable stimuli: An update of Mossbridge et al's meta-analysis. Version 2. F1000Res. 2018 Mar 28 revised 2018 Jan 1;7:407. doi: 10.12688/f1000research.14330.2. eCollection 2018. PubMed PMID: 30228876

Ecclesia Gnostica (Los Angeles. 2010) see below: Hoeller, Stephan A. (2002; 1998; 2010).

Ecclesia Pistis Sophia. (2019) https://www.sophian.org/index.html. Accessed 6/18/2019) The Fellowship.

Ehrman, Bart D. (2003) Lost Christianities: The Battles for Scripture and the Faiths We Never Knew. Oxford University Press. New York, NY. 2003

Ehrman, Bart D. (2003) Lost Scriptures: Books that did not make it into the New Testament by. Oxford University Press. New York, NY.

Ehrman, Bart D. (2011) Forged: writing in the name of god--why the bible's authors are not who we think they are. New York, NY: Harper Collins Publishers

Ehrman, Bart D. (2014). How Jesus Became God: The Exaltation of a Jewish Preacher. Publisher Harper Collins.

Eisenstadt, Peter. Fallen Angels. (2019) The Jewish Pluralist. https://thejewishpluralist.net/2014/04/fallen-angels/
Accessed 4 17 2019

Encyclopædia Britannica, Inc. (2021). Valentinus Gnostic Philosopher. Britannica Online". britannica.com. https://www.britannica.com/biography/Valentinus Corporate Site. (Accessed 27 January 2021)

Encyclopædia Britannica, Inc. (2021). Basalides Syrian Philosopher.. Britannica Online". britannica.com. https://www.britannica.com/biography/Basilides

Fiorenza, Elizabeth S. (1994) In Memory of Her: A Feminist Theological Reconstruction of Christian Origins. Crossroad Publishing, New York, NY

Freke, Tim., Gandy, Peter. (1997) The Hermetica. The Lost Wisdom of the Pharaohs. Publisher Timothy Freke. Kindle Edition.

Gnostic Society Library, The. (2015). The Nag Hammadi Library. Available at http://gnosis.org/naghamm/nhl.html (Accessed 2/7 2015)

Gnostic Society Library, The. (2015). Brons, David. Valentinians and the Bible in: The Nag Hammadi Library. Available at http://gnosis.org/naghamm/nhl.html (Accessed 2/7 2015)

Gnostic Society Library, The. (2019). Brons, David. Valentinian Theology in: The Nag Hammadi Library. Available at http://gnosis.org/naghamm/nhl.html (Accessed 1/23/2019)

Gnostic Society Library, The. (2019). Brons, David. Valentinian Monism in: The Nag Hammadi Library. Available at http://gnosis.org/naghamm/nhl.html (Accessed 1/23/2019)

Gnostic Society Library, The. (2015). James, M.R. The Apocalypse of Thomas *in:* The Nag Hammadi Library. Available at http://gnosis.org/naghamm/nhl.html (Accessed 2/7 2015)

Greyson, Bruce (2021). After: A Doctor Explores What Near-Death Experiences Reveal about Life and Beyond Saint Martin's Essentials Press ebook.

Grobel, Kendrick. (1960) The Gospel of Truth. The Valentinian Meditation on the Gospel. Publisher Abingdon Press. New York & Nashville TN

Grondin, Michael W. (2015) Coptic-English Interlinear translation.The Coptic Gospel of Thomas, saying-by-saying. http://gospel-thomas.net/sayings.htm (Accessed 1-2-2017)

Grondin, Michael W. (1996) Coptic-English translation of The Gospel of Thomas. http://users.misericordia.edu/davies/thomas/INTERLIN.HTM (accessed 2017)

Herbermann, Charles, ed. (1913). "Demiurge". Catholic Encyclopedia. New York: Robert Appleton Company.

Hanson, John Wesley. (1899) Universalism the Prevailing Doctrine of the Christian Church During Its First Five Hundred Years . Universalist Publishing House. Kindle Edition.

Hart, David B. (2017) The New Testament. A translation. Yale University Press. London, UK.

Hart, David B. (2019). That All Shall Be Saved: Heaven, Hell, and Universal Salvation. University Press. New Haven and London

Harris, Sam. (2004) The End of Faith: Religion, Terror, and the Future of Reason. Norton. New York, NY

Heiser, Michael S. (2015) The unseen realm. Recovering the supernatural worldview of the bible. Hexham Press. Bellingham, Wa.

Hitchens, Christopher (2007). God is Not Great: how religion poisons everything. Twelve Books; New York, NY.

Isenberg, Wesley, W., Layton, Bentley. (2000). The Gospel of Philip. In Robinson, James M. Ed. The Coptic Gnostic Library. A Complete Edition of the Nag Hammadi Codices. Vol. 2. Koninklijke Brill NV, Leiden, The Netherlands

Lange, Armin., De troyer, Kristin., Tzoref, Shani., David, Nora, Eds. (2012). Heger, Paul. Did Enochian Jews exist? *In:* The Hebrew Bible in Light of the Dead Sea Scrolls. Vandenhoeck and Ruprecht LLC. Oakville, CT. USA

Logan, Alastair, HB. (1996.) From Gnostic Truth and Christian Heresy. A Study in the History of Gnosticism. T&T Clark International. London, UK

Hoeller, Stephan A. (2002.) Gnosticism: New Light on the Ancient tradition of Inner Knowing. Publisher: Quest Books Wheaton, IL.

Hoeller, Stephan A. (1998 and 2010). Ecclesia Gnostica A Gnostic Catechism. Publisher: The Gnostic Society Press, Los Angeles, California. http://gnosis.org/ecclesia/catechism.htm (Accessed 5-5-2015)

Hoeller, Stephan A. (2016). Valentinus. A Gnostic for All Seasons. The Gnostic Society Library http://gnosis.org/valentinus.htm (Accessed 2/17/2016).

Isenberg, Wesley W. (1977) "The Gospel of Phillip (II3)," In: the Nag Hammadi Library, ed James M. Robinson Leiden: Brill

Isenberg, Wesley, W., Layton, Bentley. (2000). The Gospel of Philip. In

Robinson, James M. Ed. The Coptic Gnostic Library. A Complete Edition of the Nag Hammadi Codices. Vol. 2. Koninklijke Brill NV, Leiden, The Netherlands

Jenkins, Philip. (2008) The lost history of Christianity. The thousand-year golden age of the church in the Middle East, Africa, and Asia--and how it died. Publisher HarperOne. New York, NY.

Jenkins, Philip. (2015). The many faces of Christ. The Thousand - Year story and influence of the Lost Gospels. Publisher Basic Books. New York, NY

Jenkins, Philip. (2017). Crucible of Faith. Hachette Book Group. New York, NY

Jenkins, Philip. (2001). Hidden Gospels: How the Search for Jesus Lost Its Way. Oxford University Press. New York, NY.

Johannite Church, The Apostolic. (2019) Johannite Beliefs. https://www.johannite.org/ (Accessed 4/15/2019) See for the Gnostic Christian Church a statement of its' principle at: https://www.johannite.org/statement-of-principles/

Johnson, Paul. (1976) A History of Christianity. Published by Simon and Schuster. New York, NY.

Kelly, Edward F., Williams Kelly, Emily., Crabtree, Adam., et al. (2007.) Irreducible Mind: Toward a Psychology for the 21st Century. Publishers; Rowman & Littlefield. Lanham, Maryland.

Kelly, Edward F., Crabtree, Adam., Marshall, Paul., Eds. (2015.) Beyond Physicalism: Toward Reconciliation of Science and Spirituality. Publishers Rowman & Littlefield. Lanham, Maryland.

Kelly, Edward F., Williams Kelly, Emily., Crabtree, Adam., et al. (2007.) Irreducible Mind: Toward a Psychology for the 21st Century. Publishers; Rowman & Littlefield. Lanham, Maryland.

Williams Kelly, Emily., Greyson, Bruce., Kelly, Edward F. (2007) Unusual Experience Near Death Experience and Related Phenomena in: Williams Kelly, Emily., Kelly, Edward F. et al. Irreducible Mind: Toward a Psychology for the 21st Century. Publishers; Rowman & Littlefield. Lanham, Maryland.

Kilmon, Jack. (2019) Yeshua, the Enochian Jew. theurgic.com Posted November 7, 2008. (Accessed 4-19- 2019)

https://magdelene.wordpress.com/2008/11/07/yeshua-the-enochian-jew/

King, Karin., MacRae, R. George W., Wilson, McL., Parrot, Douglas M. (1978) The Gospel of Mary (BG 8502, 1) in: Robinson, James M. The Nag Hammadi library, ed. The definitive new translation of the Gnostic scriptures complete in one volume. Harper Collins, New York, NY

King, Karen L. (2003) What is Gnosticism? Harvard University Press. Cambridge, MA

King, Karen L. (2003) The Gospel of Mary of Magdala: Jesus and the First Woman Apostle. Published by Polebridge Press, Santa Rosa, California.

King, Karen. (2006) The Secret Revelation of John. Harvard University Press. Cambridge, Massachusetts (also see: Barbelo (2019) in: https://en.wikipedia.org/wiki/Barbelo Accessed 4-19-2019)

King, Karen. (2007). The Gospel of Mary with the Greek Gospel of Mary *in:* Meyer, Marvin. Ed. The Nag Hammadi Scriptures. HarperCollins 10 East 53rd St., NY, New York 2007

Layton, Bentley, (1987) The Gnostic Scriptures. A New translation with Annotations and Introductions. Publisher Doubleday & Company. Inc. Garden City, New York.

Min, Lee. (2010). The Conversion of Cornelius, seen against the Political and Social Background of the Roman Empire. Master's Thesis submitted to: The University of Birmingham (Accessed 2010) core.ac.uk./download/pdf/1631666.pdf

Leloup, Jean-Yves. (2002) The Gospel of Mary. Rochester, Vermont: Inner traditions.

Leloup, Jean-Yves. (2004) The Gospel of Phillip: Jesus, Mary Magdalene, and the Gnosis of Sacred Union.Rochester, Vermont: Inner traditions.

Leloup, Jean-Yves. (2005) The Gospel of Thomas: The Gnostic Wisdom of Jesus. Paris: Inner traditions. Rochester, Vermont

Martyn, James Louis (2003) First published 1968. History and Theology in the Fourth Gospel (3rd ed.). Westminster John Knox Press.

Matlock, James G. (2019) Bibliography of Reincarnation Resources Online. http://deanradin.com/evidence/Matlock%202012.pdf

Accessed 4 22 2019

Mattison, Mark M. (2013) The Gospel of Mary. Coptic-English Interlinear. http://gospel-thomas.net/MaryInterlinear.pdf Accessed 2 2018

Mead, G. R. S. (1921) Pistis Sophia. A Gnostic Gospel. A Gnostic Miscellany: Being for the most part extracts from the Books of the Savior, to which are added excerpts from a Cognate literature; (English). JM Watkins London. Kindle Edition.

Mead, G.R.S. (1899). Pistis Sofia. London: Theosophical Publishing Society. Mead, G.R.S. (1892). The Gnostic Society Library. gnosis.org (accessed 2015)

Meier, John P. (1991) A marginal Jew: rethinking the historical Jesus: the roots of the problem and the person, vol. 1. Publisher Double Day. New York, NY

Meier, John P. (2016) A marginal Jew: rethinking the historical Jesus: Probing the Authenticity of the Parables, vol. 5. Publisher Yale University Press New York, NY

Meyer, Marvin. (2005) The Gnostic Gospels of Jesus: The definitive collection of mystical gospels and secret books about Jesus of Nazareth. Publisher HarperOne, New York, NY

Meyer, Marvin W. (2007) The Gospel of Thomas and the Greek Gospel of Thomas *in:* Meyer, Marvin W.; Robinson, James M. The Nag Hammadi Scriptures. HarperCollins 10 East 53rd St., NY, New York 2007

Meyer, Marvin W., Thomassen, Einar. (2007). The treatise on the Resurrection *in,* Meyer, Marvin W., Robinson, James M. (2007) The Nag Hammadi Scriptures: The Revised and Updated translation of Sacred Gnostic Texts Complete in One Volume. HarperCollins. 10 East 53rd St., New York, NY

Meyer, Marvin., Madeleine, Scopello. (2007) Eugnostos the Blessed *in:* he Nag Hammadi Scriptures. HarperCollins 10 East 53rd St., NY, New York 2007

Meyer, Marvin., Madeleine Scopello. (2007). The Sofia of Jesus Christ *in:* The Nag Hammadi Scriptures. HarperCollins 10 East 53rd St., NY, New York 2007

Meyer, Marvin W., Robinson JM. (2007) The Nag Hammadi Scriptures. HarperCollins 10 East 53rd St., NY, New York 2007

Moore, Edward. (2021). The Internet Encyclopedia of Philosophy. Gnosticism. A Peer-reviewed Academic Resource. https://iep.utm.edu/gnostic/#SH5a (Accessed 3 31 2021)

Mossbridge JA, tressoldi P, Utts J., (2014) Ives JA, Radin D, Jonas WB. Predicting the unpredictable: critical analysis and practical implications of predictive anticipatory activity. Front Hum Neurosci. 2014 Mar 25;8:146. doi:10.3389/fnhum.2014.00146.

Ohlig, Karl-Heinz, Puin Gerd-R. Eds. (2009). The Hidden Origins of Islam: New Research into Its Early History. Publisher Prometheus Books, Amherst, New York

Omri (2021). New World Encyclopedia. Retrieved 23:15, April 2, 2021 Date first published: "Omri first published" (2018, December 17) from https://www.newworldencyclopedia.org/p/index.php?title=Omri&oldid=1016515.

Schaff, Philip., Ed. (2016) Origen. De Principiis In, The Complete Ante-Nicene, Nicene and Post-Nicene Collection of Early Church Fathers: Cross-Linked to the Bible. Toronto, Canada. Kindle

Philip Schaff. Origen. (2016). The Complete Works of Origen (8 Books): Cross-Linked to the Bible . Amazon.com. Kindle Edition.

Pagels, Elaine. (2003) Beyond Belief: The Secret Gospel of Thomas. Random House, New York, NY

Pagels, Elaine. (1973) Johannine Gospel in Gnostic Exegesis: Heracleon's Commentary on John. Abingdon Press, 1973. Nashville, TN

Pagels, Elaine. (1979) The Gnostic Gospels. Random House, New York, NY,

Pétrement, Simone. (1984). A Separate God. The Christian Origins and Teachings of Gnosticism. HarperCollins, Scranton, Pennsylvania

Pagels Elaine. (1992) The Gnostic Paul: Gnostic Exegesis of the Pauline Letters. Published by Continuum International Publishing Group. New York, NY

Parrott, Douglas. (1990) translation and introduction of "Eugnostos the Blessed" and "The Sofia of Jesus Christ" in The Nag Hammadi Library, James Robinson, editor. Publisher Harper, San Francisco 1990:220-243

Pope, Charles. (2021) Were the Pagan Gods Actually Demons? The Scriptural View and Why It Matters. http://blog.adw.org/2016/07/pagan-gods-actually-demons-scriptural-view-matters/ (Accessed 3 31 2021)

de Quillian, Jehanne. (2011.) The Gospel of the Beloved Companion: The Complete Gospel of Mary Magdalene. English Ed. Éditions Athara. ASIN: B0053HPQ2C

Quarles, Charles L. (2003) Jesus as Merkabah Mystic. Paper Delivered at The Evangelical Theological Society.

Quarles, Charles L. (2004) Jesus as Mamzer: A Response to Bruce Chilton's Reconstruction of the Circumstances Surrounding Jesus' Birth in Rabbi Jesus." Bulletin for Biblical Research 14.2 (2004) 243-55.

Radin, Dean. (2013) Supernormal: Science, Yoga, and the Evidence for Extraordinary Psychic Abilities. Crown Publishing House a division of Random House. New York, NY

Radin, Dean. (2018) Real Magic. Crown Publishing House a division of Random House. New York, NY

Radin, Dean. (2019) Selected Psi Research Publications

http://deanradin.com/evidence/evidence.htm (Accessed 2 1 2019)

Radin D. Electrocortical correlations between pairs of isolated people: A re-analysis. F1000 Res. 2017 May 15;6:676. doi: 10.12688/f1000research.11537.1. eCollection 2017. PubMed PMID: 28713556; PubMed Central PMCID: PMC5490474.

Robinson, James M. (1990) The Nag Hammadi library, ed. James M. Robinson. Harper, San Francisco

Robinson, James M., Hoffmann, Paul., Kloppenborg, John S., Moreland, Milton C. (2000) The Critical Edition of Q with Publisher Fortress and Peeters Press. Minneapolis.

Rohr, Richard. (2019) The Universal Christ: How a Forgotten Reality Can Change Everything We See, Hope For, and Believe. Random House LCC. New York, NY.

Runia, David T. (1990) Exegesis and Scripture: Studies on Philo of Alexandria, Variorum Collected Studies Series. Variorum, Aldershot, London

Saunders, Craig David. (2021). A Thesis submitted for the degree of Doctor of Philosophy. A Mediator in Matthew: An Analysis of the Son of Man's Function in the First Gospel. (Accessed 5 11 2021) https://core.ac.uk/download/pdf/83948986.pdf

Segbedji, Adama. The Book Of Enoch. (2019) Jesus Quoted It And So Did (The) Apostles by 'pastormustwacc'. Oct 21, 2012. https://www.nairaland.com/1080843/book-enoch-jesus-quoted-it#12643916 (accessed 4 17 2019). Or see 'Internet Sacred Text Archive: https://www.sacred-texts.com/bib/boe/boe051.htm *and:* 'Enoch'

Schaberg, Jane. (2002.) The Resurrection of Mary Magdalene. Legends, Apocrypha, and the Christian Testament. Publisher Continuum Int. New York, NY

Schaff, Philip., Ed. (2016) The Complete Ante-Nicene, Nicene and Post-Nicene Collection of Early Church Fathers: Cross-Linked to the Bible. Tertullian Chap. 4. Toronto, Canada. Kindle

Schoedel, William. 1980. 'Gnostic Monism and the Gospel of Truth' in The Rediscovery of Gnosticism, Vol.1: The School of Valentinus. edited by Bentley Layton. E.J.Brill. Leiden

Schneemelcher, Wilhelm., Wilson, Robert McLachlan., Hennecke, Edgar. Eds. (1991) New Testament Apocrypha I: Writings relating to the Apostles; Apocalypses and Related Subjects. Westminster John Knox Press. Louisville, KY. 1991

Schneemelcher, Wilhelm., Wilson, Robert McLachlan., Hennecke, Edgar. Eds. (2003) New Testament Apocrypha II: Writings relating to the Apostles; Apocalypses and Related Subjects. Westminster John Knox Press. Louisville, KY. 2003

Schwartz, Gary E. (2011). The Sacred Promise. Atria Books Division of Simon and Schuster. New York, NY.

Schwartz GE. (2010) Possible application of silicon photomultiplier technology to detect the presence of spirit and intention: three proof-of-concept experiments. Explore (NY). 2010;6(3):166-171. doi:10.1016/j.explore.2010.02.003

Schwartz GE. (2019). A computer-automated, multi-center, multi-blinded, randomized control trial evaluating hypothesized spirit presence and communication published online ahead of print, 2019 Nov 16. Explore (NY). 2019;S1550-8307(19)30552-X. doi:10.1016/j.explore.2019.11.007

Schwartz, Gary E., Woollacott Marjorie H., eds. (2019) Is Consciousness Primary? Perspectives from the Founding Members of the Academy for the Advancement of Postmaterialist Sciences (Advances in ... the Advancement of Postmaterialist Sciences). Copyright 2019 © by the Academy for the Advancement of the Postmaterialist Sciences www.aapsglobal.com

Simon, Bernard. (2004) The Essence of the Gnostics. Arcturus Publishing Limited 26/27 Bickels Yard, 151–153 Bermondsey Street, London SE1 3HA Copyright © 2017 Kindle Edition.

Smith, Andrew Philip. (2002). The Gospel of Thomas. Publisher Ulysses Books, Berkeley, CA

Smith, Andrew P. (2005) The Gospel of Phillip Annotated & Explained. Woodstock, Vermont: SkyLights Path Publishing

Smith, Andrew Philip. (2009) A dictionary of Gnosticism. Quest books. Wheaton, IL.

Smith Andrew P. (2015) The Secret History of The Gnostics. Their Scriptures and Beliefs and traditions. Published by Watkins Media Limited. London, UK

Smith, Geoffrey S. (2019) Valentinian Christianity. Texts and translations. University of California Press. Oakland, CA.

Smith, William., Wace, Henry. (1880) A Dictionary of Christian Biography. Literature Sects and Doctrines. William Vol. II. Pub. London, John Murry, Albemarle St. Google Books.

Stapp, Henry P. (2015) A Quantum-Mechanical Theory of the Mind/Brain Connection in: Kelly, Edward F., Crabtree, Adam., Marshall, Paul., Eds. (2015.)

Beyond Physicalism: Toward Reconciliation of Science and Spirituality. Publishers Rowman & Littlefield. Lanham, Maryland.

Stevenson, Ian. (2006). Half a career with the paranormal. Journal of Scientific Exploration, 20, 13–21.

Stökl, Jonathan. (2019) Priests and Levites in the First Century C.E., n.p. *cited 31 Oct 2019*. Online: https://www.bibleodyssey.org:443/en/passages/related-articles/priests-and-levites-in-the-first-century-ce

Thomassen, Einar. (2007) The tripartite tractate in: Meyer, Marvin. Robinson, James M. The Nag Hammadi Scriptures. HarperCollins 10 East 53rd St., NY, New York 2007

Thomassen, Einar. (2007). Interpretation of Knowledge *in,* Meyer, Marvin W., Robinson, James M. The Nag Hammadi Scriptures: The Revised and Updated translation of Sacred Gnostic Texts Complete in One Volume. HarperCollins. 10 East 53rd St., New York, NY

^Tillich, Paul. (1951) Systematic Theology, vol. 1: Reason and Revelation and Being and God. University of Chicago Press. Chicago, Il.

^Tillich, Paul. (1952) The courage to be. Yale University Press, Binghamton, New York

^Tillich, Paul. (1957) Systematic Theology, vol. 2: Existence and the Christ. University of Chicago Press. Chicago, Il.

^ '*God.*' There is One true (and Good) God (of Israel and Christianity). Tillich called this God, "*God Above God*" and for many other reasons that are beyond the scope of this Book, '*Holy Wisdom and The Logos of God*'. But, when I wish to make this point I will often use God with a capital "G" or 'G' with the entire word in Italics: '*God.*' *(or "God").* My definition of this God taken from Tillich is, **He** ('*God*') *must not be conceived as simply 'a god' or simply 'the god'; nor in any similar, mundane way. For He is 'God' (above every human conception of any god or 'gods').* He is

beyond human understanding and expression *(Brantingham, James. 2019).* This is also (for Gnosticism, correctly understood) the true God of Love that is *not* grasped by Judaism. And so He was (nearly two thousand years ago) misunderstood by Jews and non-Gnostic Christians as a: giver of death, judgment, punishment, and of genocide, with little compassion and, was not Universal but a tribal warrior god. This was not the "One '*God*" but a "demiurge,' and a '*lesser god.*'

Tucker JB. (2016) The Case of James Leininger: An American Case of the Reincarnation Type. Explore (NY). 2016 May-Jun;12(3):2007. doi:10.1016/j.explore.2016.02.003. Epub 2016 Mar 2. PubMed PMID: 27079216.

Turner, Martha L. (1996) The Gospel According to Philip: The Sources and Coherence of an Early Christian Collection (Nag Hammadi and Manichaean Studies). Publisher EJ Brill, Leiden, The Netherlands

Turner, John D. (2001), Sethian Gnosticism and the Platonic tradition (The History of the Sethian Movement, Sethian Gnosticism and the Platonic tradition). Presses Université Laval, Paris.

Turner, John., Meyer, Marvin W.; Robinson, James M. (2007) The Secret Book of John in: The Nag Hammadi Scriptures: The Revised and Updated translation of Sacred Gnostic Texts Complete in One Volume. HarperCollins. New York, NY

Turner, John D. (2016) trimorphic Protennoia; the Book of Thomas; Zostrianos; Marsanes; the Interpretation of Knowledge; Allogenes in: The Gnostic Society Library. http://gnosis.org/naghamm/trimorph.html (Accessed 2/17/2016)

Turner, John. (2019) Sethian Gnosticism: A literary History. https://archive.is/20121211123653/http://jdt.unl.edu/lithist.html (Accessed 5-8-2019)

Taussig, Hal. Ed. (2013) A New New Testament. A bible for the twenty-first century. Houghton Mifflin Harcourt. New York, NY

Valentinus. (2017) (Valentinus of Alexandria and Rome) Early Christian Writings. (Accessed 9 18 2017) http://www.earlychristianwritings.com/info/valentinus-wace.html

Van der Toorn, K. (1992). Anat-Yahu, Some Other Deities, and the Jews of Elephantine. Numen, 39(1), 80-101. doi:10.2307/3270076

Waldstein M., Wisse FW., In Robinson, JM., Klimkeit HJ. Eds. (1995.) The Apocryphon of John in: The Nag Hammadi and Manichaen Studies. EJ Brill. Leiden, The Netherlands.

Waldstein M., Wisse, FW., In Robinson, JM. (2000). The Apocryphon of John. In Robinson, James M. Ed. The Coptic Gnostic Library. A Complete Edition of the Nag Hammadi Codices. Vol. 2. Koninklijke Brill NV, Leiden, The Netherlands

Werth, Nicolas; Panné, Jean-Louis; Paczkowski, Andrzej; (1999) Bartosek, Karel; Margolin, Jean-Louis, Courtois, Stéphane, ed. (1999) The Black Book of Communism: Crimes, Terror, Repression. Harvard University Press, Cambridge, MA

Williams, Frank. (2008; 2009) The Panarion of Epiphanius of Salamis. Published by Brill. Herndon, VA (for electronic books and journals: (available: booksandjournals.brillonline.com;)

Wright, NT. (2008) Surprised by Hope: Rethinking Heaven, the Resurrection, and the Mission of the Church, SPCK, HarperOne

Wikipedia Church Fathers. https://en.wikipedia.org/wiki/Church Fathers. (Accessed 4 15 2019)

Appendix 1 (Holy Wisdom and The Logos of God)

See: Appendix A after references for The Gospel According to Mary of Magdala.

Reader, Appendix A is about Physics and Multiverses and is a discussion about the scientific evidence for a Multiverse. It is also about Physicist and Mathematician Edward Close's Grand Unified Theory, that unifies the Relativistic and Quantum Physics. It is not necessary to read these scientific materials or pages (and they may be skipped) to appreciate the rest of the "Gnostic Gospels or the Secret Revelation of John."

James Brantingham PhD

5 15 2021

Thousand Oaks, CA.

The Gospel of Truth

Introduction to The Gospel of Truth Today

Who wrote the Gospel of Truth (*Gtr*)? Many believe it was Valentinus (c. 100 – 180 CE) himself. Valentinus was the founder of Valentinian Christianity. Geoffrey S. Smith (2020) has published a book on "Valentinian Christianity." Better than anyone else, Smith has isolated (second and third hand "sayings of Valentinus") and the related primary Valentinian literature. Most of these "Church Fathers" are hostile toward Valentinus. But some (like Clement and Origen are at least neutral) while other scholars are hesitant to say Valentinus wrote it including G. Smith. It strongly accords with the "*tripartite tractate*" that Smith and other authors describe as a "Valentinian textbook of Theology." Other Valentinian disciples utilized the Theology from the *tritrac* and wrote what would come to be labeled 'other Valentinian books' such as, the '*treatise on the Resurrection*' (Meyer, Marvin W., Thomassen, Einar. (2007) or on the '*Interpretation of Knowledge*' (Thomassen, Einar. 2007). Sethian texts like the *Secret Revelation of John* or the *Holy Book of the Great Invisible Spirit* were also commonly utilized to write other "Valentinian texts," Including the *'Gospel of Truth' ('Gtr')* (Meyer, Marvin. Ed., Turner, John D. 2007).

Resurrection

Resurrection (of Christ) in the *Gtr* has been supported by some (Brown, TP 2014; JE Ménard, and Simone Pétrement) but not by all Scholars (Attridge, HW., MacRae, GW. 2000). Almost all translations from Coptic have something like this (or a very similar line): "the Spirit came quickly and grasped the hand of the one lying flat upon the ground lifting Him to His feet." Some have seen this as alluding to 'a prompt Resurrection' by Jesus. Their view is the 'Anointed' is 'lifted up' or 'resurrected' into immortality. One with the Father, He walks forth Immortal into the Age (which no power can take from Him ever again).

However, some posit this relates to the 'Primal Man,' 'Adam' (Heavenly *Adamas*) in the Highest Aeon if derived from Gnostic Theology such as in the *SRevJohn*. The "Primal Man" is made ('in Heaven') in the Image and Likeness of '*God*' (Attridge, Harold W., MacRae, George W. 2000). But if not so why, since the immediate the subsequent sentences have Jesus the Anointed as the subject which raised, "is real and palpable" (Brons, David. 2015). The Anointed does *not* appear (only) "like a human" (or docetically) in the *Gtr*. Attridge and MacRae say the Spirit raised Adam ('Adamas'), the 'Primal Man.' So it is also interpretable (that on earth it is) as 'earthly Adam' (Adam, *the Last Man*). But the "*Last Adam*" per Paul the Apostle is **Jesus the Christ** *the immediate subject subsequently discussed.* Even Attridge and MacRae (2000) note the symbolic references to the "resurrection." Later in the text (and most other translations), nearly all interpret this as the Anointed's Resurrection. And that "his resurrected body - is real, though not of flesh and blood." Yet it is seeable and palpable, akin to or similar to the "Resurrection Body" proposed by the Scholar, NT Wright (2008). But 'Resurrection in the flesh' (meaning before before death)," is Valentinian baptism that swallows up bodily death, so that at the body's 'fleshly death' there is Pneumatic Resurrection into the Age (Brown, TP. 2014; Wright, NT. 2008; Ménard, JE. 1972; Attridge, Harold W., MacRae, George W. 2000; Brons, David. 2015; Groebel, Kendrick. 1960; Pétrement, Simone. 1984; Peel, Malcolm L. 2000; NT Wright 2008.)

29 Blissfully the Spirit opened His eyes, He who had not yet stood up. Shed of mortality lying prostrate upon the floor, the *Spirit* quickly grasped He (*the last Adams'*) hand. Swallowing baptismal rebirth and death, by a pneumatic resurrection into immortality, He stood up and walked forth Immortal into the Age. For neither power nor life can ever again be taken from Him. '*Lifted up* He now lives 'an ever-enduring and mystical, 'life after death.'" Knowledge of the Father through living 'the Way' grants His children *experiential knowing...* ' so that *they too,* can see Him, hear Him, touch Him and blissfully experience Him - into the Age.'

A short excursus into Sethianism, Christian Supercessionist Dualism

Before looking at Valentinus and Valentinianism, there will be a short excursus into Sethianism. In Her PhD dissertation, Elizabeth A. Parton (2008) suggests that the first Gnostics were "Sethians." Gnosticism may have developed as a response by alienated Jews, especially after 115-117 CE and the "Jewish" calamities ending with the Bar Kokhba revolt in 132–136 CE. Left isolated and powerless in significantly depressed socioeconomic conditions, some Jews developed new religious innovations. That is, Parton suggests they wrote the earliest "Sethian texts and developed it into a religion," allowing these individuals to transcend their circumstances by finding a release through a "new theological system." But, *if* this revolt did indeed arise from within Judaism, its (paradoxical) but axiomatic effect once "Gnosticism" was present was the abandonment of Judaism! The first written Gnostic apocalypses like the *Apocryphon of John* (or the *Secret Revelation of John*) appear along with 4 Ezra or 2 Baruch. Or in the late 1st century CE following the destruction of the Second Temple.

But it is believed at this time in Alexandria, the *Epistle of Barnabas* was written. Some believe *Barnabas* was a reaction to the earliest Sethian Jewish gnostic texts. These Sethian texts were extremely anti-Cosmic world rejecting and demonstrated a mitigated dualism. Thus "the One God Most Hgh is Good," but 'Yatzevaot' or *Yaltabaoth* was, in fact, the Demiurge, a failed, weak, '*lesser god*' of the Old Testament or Tanakh (Bedard, Moe. 2016.) It was Yaltabaoth, the 'lesser god' that allowed near-total destruction of both "Judea, the Temple (where lived the "I AM") - and the devastation of Judaism and Jewish Ethnicity! This failure of a 'god' allowed nearly all of "Israel" to be crushed and scattered like dust!

Gnosticism may have developed (to some degree) from a response to the disappointing apocalyptic and messianic hopes of "Jewish roots" due partially to the calamities ending with the Bar Kokhba revolt in 132–136 CE. So Parton suggest that many have seen the "first Gnosticism or writing of the earliest texts as Sethian." And paradoxically if the source is Jewish, it is rejecting Judaism.

Dualism and the "Epistle of Barnabas"

In the writing of the *Epistle of Barnabas,* some see a "highly significant Gnostic-like anti-Cosmic Christianity vis-a-vis (compared to) Judaism. In "*the Epistle of Barnabas*" the letter should be divided into two parts. First, as a Christian spiritual or metaphorical (not literal) interpretation of the Old Testament. For example, "*the sacrifice God wants is that of a contrite heart,*" and "*the fasting God wants is not from food but injustice.*" Indeed the latter part of the "Letter" is similar to the Didache outlining "the Two Ways," or 1. the good or virtuous 'Way of Life' or 2. the bad or wicked 'Way of Death.'

Today many faithful observant Jews would read the OT with an "eye to both its literal and spiritual interpretations." But in the time of Jesus and the first few hundred years after, many Christians (and especially Gnostic-Christians) believed that only they understood and rightly practiced the 'OT law or instruction.' The OT's literal, non-metaphorical or non-spiritual practice of the "Law" by Jews (some Gnostics and non-Gnostic Christians *and even Jews* believed - erroneously) meant Jews were *in* "Darkness." This created a "dualism" in which the Good, Right, and Ethical OT action blessed by the Light' was by Christians. The Epistle of Barnabas never made it into the Christian Canon. Rightly concerned about Jewish-Christian relations, the Epistle of Barnabas was highly controversial (anti-Judaic) and an inflammatory exposition. Yet possibly a witness to (some) early Egyptian Christianity. The Church rejected Marcion (who tore out the OT and much of what he called "Jewish" scripture in the NT).

Allowing wholesale "rejection" of Judaism by such books as the "*Epistle of Barnabas*" or the *tearing out of the OT* and even what Marcion considered "Jewish-tainted NT material" eventually might have lead to an extensive questioning of the OT (and much of the NT). Had the Greater Universal Church agreed and ejected (all) this material from the Christian Bible, with loss of its crucial "Jewish OT scriptural credentials, bonafide ties to prophetic messianic revelations (and Jesus the "Jewish Messiah"), it would have been devastating. Christianity's claim to its 'Ancient Religious *Jewish* Provenance and 'the Anointed' stemmed from this same material. This loss *likely would have resulted in Christianity being labeled nothing more than a "new and novel Mystery Religion."*

Unlike Marcion, the top Intelligentsia of the Church realized the danger of inclusion of (over-the-top) violently "supercessionist" scriptures and anti-OT acts. Removal of OT and NT "so-called Jewish scripture" (like the extraordinary fulfillment of prophetic OT claims made in the *Gospel of Matthew* (and many other NT books) were gravely dangerous. If many unthinking and uncritical Christians had (resentfully) taken these actions, it likely would have destroyed the nascent Church. Fortunately, the leaders (of the Church) knew that the NT *could not actually "supersede the OT (or even Judaism)"* and maintain its claims to "prophecy, antiquity or about Jesus!

The History of The Gospel of Truth

The title "*Gospel of Truth*." is a modern title taken from the first few sentences in the Coptic *Gtr* given to the untitled third text from the Nag Hammadi codex I. It is true that ancient writer's book titles often were (but not always) taken from their incipit (or opening words). But nowhere is this title located in the two copies (another from Codex XII) of the *Gtr* from Nag Hammadi. The first sentence of the *Gtr* reads,

1. The *Gospel of Truth* is a joy and freely given, unmerited favor and a gift from the *Father* (Brantingham, James. 2019)

Who wrote the Gospel of Truth? Many believe it was Valentinus (c. 100 – 180 CE) himself. Valentinus being the founder of Valentinian Christianity. Geoffrey S. Smith (2019) has just recently published "Valentinian Christianity." Better than anyone else, Smith has isolated (second and third hand "sayings of Valentinus") and the related primary Valentinian literature. Most of these "Church Fathers" were hostile toward Valentinus. But some, like Clement and Origen (who were neutral), did not hesitate to ascribe it too Valentinus. It (the *Gtr*) strongly accords with the "*tripartite tractate*" that Smith and others describe as a "Valentinian textbook of Theology." Other Valentinian disciples utilized this books' choice of words and sentence or phrase construction in creating other "Valentinian texts." Including it appears the *Gospel of Truth*.

Irenaeus and Pseudo-Tertullian

Irenaeus claimed that the Valentinians had among them a "*Gospel of Truth*" and Pseudo-Tertullian contended that he wrote a "Gospel" of his own (Smith, Geoffrey S. 2020). No ancient writer explicitly states Valentinus wrote it himself.

Where is Valentinus Theology in Valentinian Works?

But this is part and parcel of the puzzle and mystery of Valentinus and Valentinian Christianity. For no agreed-upon, "Valentinian book" mentions Valentinus anywhere within its pages. It is a difficulty that what is considered a "Gnostic movement" (Gnostic in my book means "Gnostic-Christian" and Gnosticism, "Gnostic-Christianity") did not call themselves "Valentinians." This bothered the Church Fathers to no end. For when asked what religion they practiced, they answered "Christian." There are other Valentinian puzzles, 'accepted ideas' (that may have been Theologoumenon of Valentinians - but not Valentinus) such as, clear cut statements about achieving *Gnosis of the Highest, Unknown Father* (or of the God of Love; the Most High; '*God above God.*'). We see "Knowledge or to Know" (and but not even that tied to direct experiential "Gnosis" of '*God*' *Most High* (or, the Highest Unknown Father). And no unambiguous statement about the entity *"Divine Sophia"* or, of *'a Demiurge"* (particularly beyond "Wisdom" in the 'Valentinian texts'). Nor is there a clear and detailed description of a *Docetic Christ*. A 'Good' and even' Perfect' Christ ' (there is no religion without good and evil). But a phantom or apparent Christ no... *Yoking (or a similar term like androgynous mating; or brought together)'* between a man and an angel is apparent but not the word that theologically describes it (as it exists in other Gnostic texts) the, "syzygoi or syzygy."

And knowing the OT and NT thoroughly, they may have brought into the discussion their "special exegetical Gnostic understanding." But this was difficult to spot even by the unsympathetic Tertullian. They were called "Valentinians" solely by the Church Fathers. They called themselves "the Church," or as Geoffrey Smith (2020) points out, "the Spiritual Seed."

In an "excerpt of Valentinus" passed on by Theudas (a Gnostic who claimed to have been a disciple of the Apostle Paul) Valentinus said, Theudas wrote:

> 1 "Father," he says, "I commit into your hands my Spirit." Wisdom, he says, set forth the flesh for the Word, the spiritual seed; dressed with flesh, the Savior descended.

Or, again "a quote" by Theudas (paraphrased),

> 2 But the followers of Valentinus say that when the psychic body was molded, the Word implanted a "male" (or *spiritual* italics mine) seed into the elect soul while it was asleep ...brought forth separately by Wisdom. Adam's sleep ...maintained (it) lest the spiritual <seed> be dissolved.

So there are quite a few uses of this term, "Spiritual Seed," by Valentinus's disciples Smith notes (Smith, Geoffrey S. 2020.)

Gnostic Theological treatises

Here are 'similar terms' used in the *Tripartite Tractate* (*tritrac*)...*Spiritual emanations, spiritual offspring, spiritual word, and spiritual substance*. But most frequently used was "*the spiritual Logos...*" (Thomassen, Einar. 2007) And in the *Gospel of Truth* by William Barnstone and Marvin Meyer (2003; 2011) or in the translation of the *Gospel of Truth* by Harold W. Attridge and George W. MacRae (2000), the term *"Spiritual Seed"* is not present (but another term used like the above).

But in the *TriTrac* we find this about a threefold nature of humanity,

> Mankind came to be in three essential types: the spiritual, the psychic, and the material, conforming to the Logos' triple disposition, from which came the material ones and the psychic ones and the spiritual ones. Each of the three essential types is known by its fruit. And they

did not realize these divisions existed. Only at the Savior's coming did the saints reveal what each kind of person was (Thomassen, Einar. 2007).

Types of People, Corruption to Incorruption (Error and Wisdom of Knowledge) in the *Gospel of Truth*

Yet, these three types of people appear briefly and minimally in the *Gtr*. Nor does an actual (*'lesser god-like'*) 'Demiurge, Craftsman or Creator' (as found in the OT) make an appearance in the *Gospel of Truth*. Briefly, the '*Material ones*' appear and are associated with 'Matter' and various negative things such as "fleshly driven (bodies), foolishness, darkness, and death" in the *Gospel of Truth*. But suggestively as people without a mind or soul or a "soulless person." But a 'Psychic person '*with* a mind and soul' appears *once* in most translations of the *Gtr*. But no more than a minimal mention of a "Psychic" man (made of matter, mind, and soul) is found. Spiritual people arise after listening to the Savior. If they return (or listen) to the Source, the Root!

Yet, as Anthony Silva (2013) of today's modern *Johannite Church* would say, these three types of humanity or "three personalities or attitudes" appear briefly in the *Gospel of Truth*. But a genuine concern with dense, less spiritual "matter" appears. "Matter" in the *Gtr and the GThom, GPhil, GMary, and SRevJohn* can be used "neutrally." Or even (without the "Molders' or Fabricators'" understanding, be tricked) and used for "*the good*." Thus some ancient Gnostics and modern Gnostic scholars have propounded that Jesus' human body came forth first as 'psychic flesh' through the Demiurge (Mead, GRS. 2021; Herbermann, Charles, ed. 1913).

Now the Demiurge appears first to have been '*god'* found in the OT ("thus the Molder or Fabricator" who is most often called "Yaltabaoth or Yaldabaoth") but is ***not*** named nor mentioned in the *Gtr*. "Wisdom" *is* in the *Gtr*. But the divinity 'Sophia' (Greek for Wisdom) is not. However, "Knowledge" is frequently noted (and is a synonym for wisdom). In other Gnostic texts like the *SRevJohn,* the Demiurge bungles, messes up and mishandles and *abuses* the earth's aeon (and its local Cosmos). The Demiurge is *ultimately not* the true Creator. God the Father *allowed* the fabrication of the Cosmos and the world (by the Demiurge). But this *'lesser god'* does not understand the Cosmos is but a local backwater (of the Universe or "**the Vast Array of the Divine Fullness and the Universe**"). And just 'a part' of the whole, near-infinite Universe. This Fabricator creates humans, angels, fallen angels, and demons. For the physical body of Jesus in this Gospel is "made of matter," and *matter* is "corruption." But through *Error* "**He, was nailed to a cross; and fastened to a tree.** *And by this He caused to be published all of the Scriptures of the Word, Wisdom, and the Logos."* And after being hung, Jesus, "a human being," changes from corruption into "incorruptibility." Thus a "state" similar to the "Resurrection" is achieved.

Even better, it is the 'Resurrection into *'a Spiritual Body'*" identical to that described by the Apostle Paul (Wright, NT. 2008.) Though Wright cites 1 Corinthians 15 (to suggest Paul ultimately meant a future physical body (animated by God's spirit) when accurately understood. But on the face of it, it seems some "Spiritual body" comes first. And most English translations are akin to the KJV. There Paul says, "So also is the resurrection of the dead. It is sown in corruption; it is raised in incorruption!"

It is why *only* He, the **Logos** (the Incarnated Word) could "break the seals" and open that Book. ***Since He, Jesus knew His death meant life for the many.*** He knows that and that matter can be shaped or molded into bad things, used for doing wrongful, unacceptable, or evil things. And is how 'matter' became associated with various negative things such as "foolishness, darkness, and death." And people are made up of matter, in the *Gospel of Truth*. But a person "made of matter" seems to lack a mind or a soul. And is the unspiritual, "material form or a person *in the flesh*." This type of 'person' appears *infrequently* in most *Gtr* translations. Though it is assumed, no statement about a "soulless, mindless man" is found in the *Gtr*. But 'matter is deficient' in the *Gtr*. A note about a "Psychic" man (made of matter, mind, *and* soul) appears. But a "Spiritual or "Pneumatic" man or person is found throughout the *Gtr* As an example:

> And any who love the Sacred Spirit join themselves to these teachings from His *'tongue.'* So, by attaching themselves to these teachings from '*His mouth, and his tongue*' they receive the Father's Revelations… (Brantingham, James. 2019)

Error is 'an Adversary' or a *' proto-demiurge'* (even 'the deficiency')

In this Second Edition of Holy Wisdom and The Logos of God? I no longer equate **Error** with the "Demiurge." Strongly personified by others, *Error* has been seen (in the past) by others as the Demiurge. Similarly, with the Valentinian and Sethian Demiurges, the Sethians name Yaltabaoth, also called "Saklas," or the 'fool,' Samael, the 'blind' and with other various spellings for "Nebruel," the 'great demon.' But there is not as straightforward a Valentinian *Gnostic basis* for using *Error* in the same way as the Demiurge. "*Sophia*" is *not* obviously a part of this Gospel (for neither "Wisdom nor Knowledge" is a clear stand-in for *Sophia*). Yet *Error* acts like the Demiurge. And may best be seen as *an Adversary* (a devil or a demon but not "*The* Devil"). Or, *Error* can be seen as a kind of "*proto-demiurge* (even just '*the deficiency.*)' Thus Error is not entirely concrete enough nor personified sufficiently, to name it a divinity. For "She, Error" is sometimes 'just a mistake' and finds herself doing double-duty as an 'action' while being 'an entity' (Brons, David. 2015).

The Demi-urge, Error, Evil, Darkness, Demons and the Adversary in the GThom, GPhil, GMary and the SRevJohn

Valentinus may have been the possible author, but he was deeply involved in Roman politics, and using the (name of the) Sethian Gnostic' *lesser god*' for God found in the OT, "*Yaldabaoth*," might have been (politically) a bridge too far in 'the Bishopric of Rome (the future 'Vatican'). Nevertheless, *Error* is a feminine entity and emanation (unlike almost every other Demiurge, including Yaltabaoth) but, like Yaldabaoth, frequently is evil and hostile. In the included Valentinian books is the *GThom*. Though not known as a book written for Valentinian Christianity, they liked it and used it (Brons, David. 2015). The Demiurge is not called 'Yaldabaoth' in Valentinianism and (nameless) is sometimes good (even appearing to care) though he does evil. He, the Adversary *is* (in Valentinian Christianity) the '*lesser god*' of the OT! And the '*lesser god,*' (of the OT) is not the all-loving, all-knowing '*God Above God, "the Highest, the Father* (of Canonical Christianity)!

Evil or *wickedness* and "*poverty*" *is* in the *Gtr* and is similar to "*the Deficiency in Sethian texts.*" All of this is barely found or alluded to in the *GThom*. And though found in a "way or manner" in the *GPhil,* it is not clearly denoted nor strongly personified. In this text, the *Gtr* it says at verse 46 Cain, angry and jealous, is *the son of the serpent.* So, there is no mistaking the "son of the serpent." "*He is a murderer" and like 'the Adversary' or 'Satan' (does Evil). Yet even in this verse - it is still not an 'Ophitic-like* ascendant or awakening (to a more spiritual, knowing and loving consciousness) attained - as in other Sethian books - after speaking to the snake or serpent in the Garden of Eden. Here there are evil spirits and demons similar to those in the Valentinian *GPhil*. So in verse 50 in the *GPhil,* it says, "One who does not accept Rabboni Yeshua, might be an Israelite (even a Hebrew or God-fearer). But, these possess not His salvation… This is not a warning and not anti-Judaic but points out a "Psychic' individual (for it says the same thing about the Gentile (or "Whoever"). And, in the *GPhil,* there are many bad or evil people. And one can assume things like 'Bandits,' 'Dark enemies,' and the Darkness in the *GPhil*. For there is a general Adversary assumed in the *GPhil*. But in this text, the *GPhil* in "*Holy Wisdom and The Logos of God*" there is no "Yaldabaoth or Saklas or Nebruel." There are foolish men and women - yes, and men and women blind to Knowledge - yes. And in the *GPhil,* there are demonic forces; torments, terrors, and cravings (Brown, TP. 2014).

The *Secret Revelation of John* (*SRevJohn*) also know as the 'Secret Book of John' has them all! **But first and foremost the Demiurge (and Sophia) Yaldabaoth, Saklas, Samael, are all there.** But not Nebruel. Nebruel is found in the '*Holy Book of the Great Invisible Spirit*' (and other Gnostic texts but not in the *SRevJohn*.) And there are fallen angels, demons, evil, the Adversary and more (Davies, Stevan. 2005; Turner, John., Meyer, Marvin W.; Robinson, James M. 2007; Waldstein M., Wisse, FW., In Robinson, JM. 2000)

References

Attridge, Harold W., MacRae, George W. (2000). The Gospel of Truth. In Robinson, James M. Ed. The Coptic Gnostic Library. A Complete Edition of the Nag Hammadi Codices. Vol. 2. Koninklijke Brill NV, Leiden, The Netherlands

Bane, Theresa. (2012) Encyclopedia of Demons in World Religions and Cultures. McFarland & Co. Jefferson, NC

Barbelo or Barbēlō (2019) in: https://en.wikipedia.org/wiki/Barbelo (Accessed 4-19-2019)

Barnstone, William. (1984) The Other Bible. HarperCollins. New York, NY.

Bauckham, Richard. (2006) Jesus and the Eyewitnesses: The Gospels as Eyewitness Testimony. Eerdmans Publishing, Grand Rapids, MI 2006

Bedard, Moe. (2016.) The Gnostic Warrior. Yaldabaoth: https://gnosticwarrior.com/yaldabaoth.html (Accessed 7-29-2016)

Bem D, tressoldi P, Rabeyron T and Duggan M. (2016) Feeling the future: A meta-analysis of 90 experiments on the anomalous anticipation of random future events version 2; referees: 2 approved F1000Research 2016, 4:1188 (doi: 10.12688/f1000research.7177.2)

Beauchemin, Gerry. Reichard, Scott D. (2007, 2010, 2016; 2018). Hope Beyond Hell. The Righteous Purpose of God's Judgment. Malista Press. Kindle Edition. Olimo, Texas.

Beauchemin, Gerry. Reichard, Scott D. (2018) Hope For All: Ten Reasons God's Love Prevails (p. 19). Malista Press. Kindle Edition.

Beischel J, Boccuzzi M, Biuso M, Rock AJ. (2015) Anomalous information reception by research mediums under blinded conditions II: replication and extension. Explore (NY). 2015 Mar-Apr;11(2):136-42. doi: 10.1016/j.explore.2015.01.001. Epub 2015 Jan 7. PubMed PMID: 25666383.

Beischel, J. (2019) Windbridge Research Center. https://www.windbridge.org/ A List of Completed Research https://scholar.google.com/citations?user=rNejlNcAAAAJ&hl=en (Accessed 12 30 2019)

Bourgeault, Cynthia. (2008). The Wisdom Jesus. transforming Heart and Mind- A new Perspective on Christ and His Message. Shambala Publications Inc. Boston, MA

Benko, Stephan. (1967). The Libertine Gnostic Sect of the Phibionites According to Epiphanius. Vigiliae Christianae, 21(2), 103-119. doi:10.2307/1582042

Bergman, James '19 (2017) "The Divine "Sofia": The Development of Jewish and Hellenistic Thought in the Christology of the New Testament," Furman

Humanities Review: Vol. 29 , Article 29. Available at: https://scholarexchange.furman.edu/fhr/vol29/iss1/29 (Accessed 4 17 2019)

Brons, David. (2019) Valentinian Theology; Valentinian teachings in detail; and Valentinian on Sophia and Eve in: Gnostic Society Library (2015). The Nag Hammadi Library. Available at http://gnosis.org/library/valentinus/Brief-*Summary*Theology.htm (Accessed 1/23/2019)

Brons, David. (2015) Valentinian Monism *in:* Gnostic Society Library, The. (2019). The Nag Hammadi Library. Available at http://gnosis.org/naghamm/nhl.html (Accessed 1/23/2019)

Brown, T. Patterson. (2014) The Gospels of Thomas, Philip and Truth. Available from http://www.freelyreceive.net/metalogos/files/intro.html (Accessed 5 25 2014)

Brown, Raymond. (1979) The Community of the Beloved Disciple, New Jersey: Paulist Press, 1979

Brown, Raymond E. (1988). The Gospel and Epistles of John: A Concise Summary. The Liturgical Press. Collegeville, Minnesota.

Gabriele Boccaccini and Carlos A. Segovia. Els. (2016) Paul The Jew: Rereading the Apostle as a Figure of Second Temple Judaism. Minneapolis: Fortress, 2016. Fortress Press, Minneapolis, MN

Boyarin, Daniel. (2012) The Jewish Gospels: The story of the Jewish Christ. New York NY, New Press

Bourgeault, Cynthia. (2008) The Wisdom Jesus. transforming Heart and Mind- A new Perspective on Christ and His Message. Shambala Publications Inc. Boston, MA

Brantingham, James. (2017) The Gospel of Philip. A New translation. CreateSpace Independent Pub. Amazon Digital Services LLC. Seattle, WA.

Chilton, Bruce. (2002) in Rabbi Jesus (Rabbi Jesus: An Intimate Biography). Publisher Double Day a Division of Random House, New York, NY

Conner, Miguel (2017) Apr 13, 2017 in How Did the Gnostics View the Crucifixion of Jesus. https://thegodabovegod.com/gnostics-view-crucifixion-jesus/

Davies, Stevan. (1996.) Mark's Use of the Gospel of Thomas. In The Journal of the New Testament Society of South Africa or Neotestamentica 30(2) 1996

Davies, Stevan. (2002) The Gospel of Thomas. Annotated & Explained. SkyLight Paths Paths Publishing. Woodstock, Vermont

Davies, Stevan. (2005) The Secret Book of John. The Gnostic Gospel Annotated & Explained. Skylight Paths Publishing. Woodstock, Vermont

Dawkins, R. (2006). The God Delusion. Bantam Books. New York, NY

Dawkins, R. (1986). The Blind Watchmaker. New York: W. W. Norton & Company.

DeConick, April D. (2005.) Recovering the Original Gospel of Thomas: A History of the Gospel and Its Growth. Publisher: T & T Clark. London, UK

DeConick, April D., J. Asgeirsson, J., Uro. R. (2005) "On the Brink of the Apocalypse: A Preliminary Examination of the Earliest Speeches in the Gospel of Thomas." In Thomasine traditions in Antiquity: The Social and Cultural World of the Gospel of Thomas. Nag Hammadi and Manichaean Studies 59. Leiden: E.J. Brill.

DeConick, April D. (2017.) The Gnostic New Age: How a countercultural spirituality revolutionized religion from antiquity to today. Columbia University Press. New York, NY

Delorme A, Beischel J, Michel L, Boccuzzi M, Radin D, Mills PJ.

(2013) Electrocortical activity associated with subjective communication with the deceased. Front Psychol. 2013 Nov 20;4:834. doi: 10.3389/fpsyg. 2013.00834. eCollection 2013. PubMed PMID: 24312063; PubMed Central PMCID: PMC3834343.

Dueholm, Benjamin J. (2019) A new canon, created by 19 people. A New New Testament. https://www.christiancentury.org/blogs/archive/2013-05/new-canon-created-13-people (accessed 5 9 2019)

Duggan M, tressoldi P. (2018) Predictive physiological anticipatory activity preceding seemingly unpredictable stimuli: An update of Mossbridge et al's meta-analysis. Version 2. F1000Res. 2018 Mar 28 revised 2018 Jan 1;7:407. doi: 10.12688/f1000research.14330.2. eCollection 2018. PubMed PMID: 30228876

Ehrman, Bart D. (2003) Lost Christianities: The Battles for Scripture and the Faiths We Never Knew. Oxford University Press. New York, NY. 2003

Ehrman, Bart D. (2003) Lost Scriptures: Books that did not make it into the New Testament by. Oxford University Press. New York, NY.

Ehrman, Bart D. (2011) Forged: writing in the name of god--why the bible's authors are not who we think they are. New York, NY: Harper Collins Publishers

Ehrman, Bart D. (2014). How Jesus Became God: The Exaltation of a Jewish Preacher. Publisher Harper Collins.

Eisenstadt, Peter. Fallen Angels. (2019) The Jewish Pluralist. https://thejewishpluralist.net/2014/04/fallen-angels/
Accessed 4 17 2019

Fiorenza, Elizabeth S. (1994) In Memory of Her: A Feminist Theological Reconstruction of Christian Origins. Crossroad Publishing, New York, NY

Smith, Geoffrey S. (2019) Valentinian Christianity. Texts and translations. University of California Press. Oakland, CA.

Gnostic Society Library, The. (2015). The Nag Hammadi Library. Available at http://gnosis.org/naghamm/nhl.html (Accessed 2/7 2015)

Gnostic Society Library, The. (2015). Brons, David. Valentinians and the Bible in: The Nag Hammadi Library. Available at http://gnosis.org/naghamm/nhl.html (Accessed 2/7 2015)

Gnostic Society Library, The. (2019). Brons, David. Valentinian Theology in: The Nag Hammadi Library. Available at http://gnosis.org/naghamm/nhl.html (Accessed 1/23/2019)

Gnostic Society Library, The. (2019). Brons, David. Valentinian Monism in: The Nag Hammadi Library. Available at http://gnosis.org/naghamm/nhl.html (Accessed 1/23/2019)

Gnostic Society Library, The. (2015). James, M.R. The Apocalypse of Thomas *in:* The Nag Hammadi Library. Available at http://gnosis.org/naghamm/nhl.html (Accessed 2/7 2015)

Smith, Geoffrey S. (2019) Valentinian Christianity. Texts and translations. University of California Press. Oakland, CA.

Grobel, Kendrick. (1960) The Gospel of Truth. The Valentinian Meditation on the Gospel. Publisher Abingdon Press. New York & Nashville TN

Grondin, Michael W. (2017) Coptic-English Interlinear translation.The Coptic Gospel of Thomas, saying-by-saying. http://gospel-thomas.net/sayings.htm (Accessed 1-2-2017)

Hart, David B. (2017) The New Testament. A translation. Yale University Press. London, UK.

Hart, David B. (2019). That All Shall Be Saved: Heaven, Hell, and Universal Salvation. University Press. New Haven and London

Harris, Sam. (2004) The End of Faith: Religion, Terror, and the Future of Reason. Norton. New York, NY

Hitchens, Christopher (2007). God is Not Great: how religion poisons everything. Twelve Books; New York, NY.

Jawa, Daljit Singh. (2013) It Is the Same Light: The Enlightening Wisdom of Sri Guru Granth Sahib. An Interpretation. volume 4. XLibras LLC. (NY) USA

Johnson, Todd M. (2001) Christian martyrdom: a global demographic assessment in: World Christian trends. Barrett, DB. Johnson, TM. Pasadena, CA: William Carey Library, 2001.

Lange, Armin., De troyer, Kristin., Tzoref, Shani., David, Nora, Eds. (2012). Heger, Paul. Did Enochian Jews exist? *In:* The Hebrew Bible in Light of the Dead Sea Scrolls. Vandenhoeck and Ruprecht LLC. Oakville, CT. USA

Herbermann, Charles, ed. (1913). "Demiurge". Catholic Encyclopedia. New York: Robert Appleton Company.

Hart, David B. (2017) The New Testament. A translation. Yale University Press. London, UK.

Hart, David B. (2019). That All Shall Be Saved: Heaven, Hell, and Universal Salvation. University Press. New Haven and London

Hoeller, Stephan A. (2002.) Gnosticism: New Light on the Ancient tradition of Inner Knowing. Publisher: Quest Books Wheaton, IL.

Hoeller, Stephan A. (1998 and 2010). Ecclesia Gnostica A Gnostic Catechism. Publisher: The Gnostic Society Press, Los Angeles, California. http://gnosis.org/ecclesia/catechism.htm (Accessed 5-5-2015)

Hoeller, Stephan A. (2016). Valentinus. A Gnostic for All Seasons. The Gnostic Society Library http://gnosis.org/valentinus.htm (Accessed 2/17/2016).

Isenberg, Wesley W. (2017) "The Gospel of Phillip (II3)," In: the Nag Hammadi Library, ed James M. Robinson Leiden: Brill

Johannite Church, The Apostolic. (2019) Johannite Beliefs. https://www.johannite.org/ (Accessed 4/15/2019) See for the Gnostic Christian Church a statement of its' principle at: https://www.johannite.org/statement-of-principles/

Kelly, Edward F., Williams Kelly, Emily., Crabtree, Adam., et al. (2007.) Irreducible Mind: Toward a Psychology for the 21st Century. Publishers; Rowman & Littlefield. Lanham, Maryland.

Kelly, Edward F., Crabtree, Adam., Marshall, Paul., Eds. (2015.) Beyond Physicalism: Toward Reconciliation of Science and Spirituality. Publishers Rowman & Littlefield. Lanham, Maryland.

Kilmon, Jack. (2019) Yeshua, the Enochian Jew. theurgic.com Posted November 7, 2008 https://magdelene.wordpress.com/2008/11/07/yeshua-the-enochian-jew/ (Accessed 4-19- 2019)

King, Karin., MacRae, R. George W., Wilson, McL., Parrot, Douglas M. (1978) The Gospel of Mary (BG 8502, 1) in: Robinson, James M. The Nag Hammadi library, ed. The definitive new translation of the Gnostic scriptures complete in one volume. Harper Collins, New York, NY

King, Karen L. (2003) What is Gnosticism? Harvard University Press. Cambridge, MA

King, Karen L. (2003) The Gospel of Mary of Magdala: Jesus and the First Woman Apostle. Published by Polebridge Press, Santa Rosa, California.

King, Karen. (2006) The Secret Revelation of John. Harvard University Press. Cambridge, Massachusetts (also see: Barbelo (2019) in: https://en.wikipedia.org/wiki/Barbelo Accessed 4-19-2019)

King, Karen. (2007). The Gospel of Mary with the Greek Gospel of Mary *in:* Meyer, Marvin. Ed. The Nag Hammadi Scriptures. HarperCollins 10 East 53rd St., NY, New York 2007

Kleinman, Robert M. (2006) Four Faces of the Universe: An Integrated View of the Cosmos. Published by Lotus Press. Twin Lakes, WI. 2006.

Layton, Bentley, (1987) The Gnostic Scriptures. A New translation with Annotations and Introductions. Publisher Doubleday & Company. Inc. Garden City, New York.

Leloup, Jean-Yves. (2002) The Gospel of Mary. Rochester, Vermont: Inner traditions.

Leloup, Jean-Yves. (2004) The Gospel of Phillip: Jesus, Mary Magdalene, and the Gnosis of Sacred Union. Rochester, Vermont: Inner traditions.

Leloup, Jean-Yves. (2005) The Gospel of Thomas: The Gnostic Wisdom of Jesus. Paris: Inner traditions. Rochester, Vermont

Loftus, John W., Shermer, Michael., Hafer, Abner. (2019) Hyapatia Press The Case Against Miracles. USA

Martyn, James Louis (2003) First published 1968. History and Theology in the Fourth Gospel (3rd ed.). Westminster John Knox Press.

Matlock, James G. (2019) Bibliography of Reincarnation Resources Online. http://deanradin.com/evidence/Matlock%202012.pdf

Accessed 4 22 2019

Mattison, Mark M. (2013) The Gospel of Mary. Coptic-English Interlinear. http://gospel-thomas.net/MaryInterlinear.pdf Accessed 2 2018

Mead, G. R. S. (1921) Pistis Sophia. A Gnostic Gospel. A Gnostic Miscellany: Being for the most part extracts from the Books of the Savior, to which are added excerpts from a Cognate literature; (English). JM Watkins London. Kindle Edition.

Mead, G.R.S. (1899). Pistis Sofia. London: Theosophical Publishing Society. Mead, G.R.S. (1892). The Gnostic Society Library. gnosis.org (accessed 2015)

Meier, John P. (1991) A marginal Jew: rethinking the historical Jesus: the roots of the problem and the person, vol. 1. Publisher Double Day. New York, NY

Meier, John P. (2016) A marginal Jew: rethinking the historical Jesus: Probing the Authenticity of the Parables, vol. 5. Publisher Yale University Press New York, NY

Meyer, Marvin. (2005) The Gnostic Gospels of Jesus: The definitive collection of mystical gospels and secret books about Jesus of Nazareth. Publisher HarperOne, New York, NY

Barnstone, William and Meyer, Marvin. (2003; 2011). The Gospel of Truth in: Barnstone, William and Meyer, Marvin. The Gnostic Bible: Revised and Expanded 1st ed. Boston, Massachusetts, New Seeds Books.

Meyer, Marvin W. (2007) The Gospel of Thomas and the Greek Gospel of Thomas *in:* Meyer, Marvin W.; Robinson, James M. The Nag Hammadi Scriptures. HarperCollins 10 East 53rd St., NY, New York 2007

Meyer, Marvin., Madeleine, Scopello. (2007) Eugnostos the Blessed *in:* he Nag Hammadi Scriptures. HarperCollins 10 East 53rd St., NY, New York 2007

Meyer, Marvin., Madeleine Scopello. (2007). The Sofia of Jesus Christ *in:* The Nag Hammadi Scriptures. HarperCollins 10 East 53rd St., NY, New York 2007

Meyer, Marvin W., Robinson JM. (2007) The Nag Hammadi Scriptures. HarperCollins 10 East 53rd St., NY, New York 2007

Meyer, Marvin. Ed., Turner, John D. (2007). The Holy Book of the Great Invisible Spirit (The Gnostic Gospel of the Egyptians) in: The Nag Hammadi Scriptures. HarperCollins 10 East 53rd St., NY, New York 2007

Meyer, Marvin W., Thomassen, Einar. (2007). The treatise on the Resurrection *in*, Meyer, Marvin W., Robinson, James M. (2007) The Nag Hammadi Scriptures: The Revised and Updated translation of Sacred Gnostic Texts Complete in One Volume. HarperCollins. 10 East 53rd St., New York, NY

Meyer, Marvin. Ed., Turner, John D. (2007). The Holy Book of the Great Invisible Spirit (The Gnostic Gospel of the Egyptians) in: The Nag Hammadi Scriptures. HarperCollins 10 East 53rd St., NY, New York 2007

Min, Lee. (2010). The Conversion of Cornelius, seen against the Political and Social Background of the Roman Empire. Master's Thesis submitted to: The University of Birmingham (Accessed 2010) core.ac.uk./download/pdf/1631666.pdf

Mossbridge JA, tressoldi P, Utts J., (2014) Ives JA, Radin D, Jonas WB. Predicting the unpredictable: critical analysis and practical implications of predictive anticipatory activity. Front Hum Neurosci. 2014 Mar 25;8:146. doi:10.3389/fnhum.2014.00146.

Ohlig, Karl-Heinz, Puin Gerd-R. Eds. (2009). The Hidden Origins of Islam: New Research into Its Early History. Publisher Prometheus Books, Amherst, New York

Pagels, Elaine. (2003) Beyond Belief: The Secret Gospel of Thomas. Random House, New York, NY

Pagels, Elaine. (1973) Johannine Gospel in Gnostic Exegesis: Heracleon's Commentary on John. Abingdon Press, 1973. Nashville, TN

Pagels Elaine. (1975) The Gnostic Paul: Gnostic Exegesis of the Pauline Letters. Published by Continuum International Publishing Group. New York, NY

Pagels, Elaine. (1979) The Gnostic Gospels. Random House, New York, NY,

Parton, Elizabeth A. (2008) Apocalyptic and Sethian trajectories and Melchizedek Speculations in Late Antique Egypt the Melchizedek Apocalypse from Nag Hammadi (NHCIX,1) As a test case. PhD Dissertation. U. of Ottawa, Canada. (Accessed 3 31 2021).

Pétrement, Simone. (1984). A Separate God. The Christian Origins and Teachings of Gnosticism. HarperCollins, Scranton, Pennsylvania

Pagels Elaine. (1992) The Gnostic Paul: Gnostic Exegesis of the Pauline Letters. Published by Continuum International Publishing Group. New York, NY

Parrott, Douglas. (1990) translation and introduction of "Eugnostos the Blessed" and "The Sofia of Jesus Christ" in The Nag Hammadi Library, James Robinson, editor. Publisher Harper, San Francisco 1990:220-243

Quarles, Charles L. (2003) Jesus as Merkabah Mystic. Paper Delivered at The Evangelical Theological Society.

Quarles, Charles L. (2004) Jesus as Mamzer: A Response to Bruce Chilton's Reconstruction of the Circumstances Surrounding Jesus' Birth in Rabbi Jesus." Bulletin for Biblical Research 14.2 (2004) 243-55.

Quispel, Gilles. 1996). The Original Doctrine of Valentinus the Gnostic. *Vigiliae Christianae*, Brill. Vol. 50, No. 4 (1996), pp. 327-352. http://www.jstor.org/stable/1584312 (Accessed 7 5 2020)

Radin, Dean. (2019) Selected Psi Research Publications

http://deanradin.com/evidence/evidence.htm (Accessed 2 1 2019)

Radin, Dean. (2018) Real Magic. Crown Publishing House a division of Random House. New York, NY.

Radin D. (2017) Electrocortical correlations between pairs of isolated people: A reanalysis. F1000 Res. 2017 May 15;6:676. doi: 10.12688/f1000research.11537.1. eCollection 2017. PubMed PMID: 28713556; PubMed Central PMCID: PMC5490474. (*Vernacularly, 'Telepathy'* - italics my addition JB)

Radin, Dean. (2013) Supernormal: Science, Yoga, and the Evidence for Extraordinary Psychic Abilities. Crown Publishing House a division of Random House. New York, NY

Robinson, Armitage Ed. (1920) Irenaeus Bishop of Lyon. The Demonstration of the Apostolic Preaching. The Macmillan Co. New York, NY

Robinson, James M. (1990) The Nag Hammadi library, ed. James M. Robinson. Harper, San Francisco

Robinson, James M., Hoffmann, Paul., Kloppenborg, John S., Moreland, Milton C. (2000) The Critical Edition of Q with Publisher Fortress and Peeters Press. Minneapolis.

Robinson, James M. Ed. (2000) The Coptic Gnostic Library. A Complete Edition of the Nag Hammadi Codices. Vols 1-5. Koninklijke Brill NV, Leiden, The Netherlands

Rohr, Richard. (2019) The Universal Christ: How a Forgotten Reality Can Change Everything We See, Hope For, and Believe. Random House LCC. New York, NY.

Runia, David T. (1990) Exegesis and Scripture: Studies on Philo of Alexandria, Variorum Collected Studies Series. Variorum, Aldershot, London

Rouder JN, Morey RD, Province JM. (2013.) A Bayes factor meta-analysis of recent extrasensory perception experiments: comment on Storm, tressoldi, and Di Risio (2010). Psychol Bull. 2013;139(1):241–247. doi:10.1037/a0029008

Sarraf M, Woodley Of Menie MA, tressoldi P. (2020) Anomalous information reception by mediums: A meta-analysis of the scientific evidence published on-line ahead of print, 2020 Jul 3. Explore (NY). 2020; S1550-8307(20)30151-8. doi:10.1016/j.explore.2020.04.002

Segbedji, Adama. The Book Of Enoch. (2019) Jesus Quoted It And So Did (The) Apostles by 'pastormustwacc'. Oct 21, 2012. https://www.nairaland.com/1080843/book-enoch-jesus-quoted-it#12643916 (accessed 4 17 2019). Or see 'Internet Sacred Text Archive: https://www.sacred-texts.com/bib/boe/boe051.htm *and:* 'Enoch'

Schaberg, Jane. (2002.) The Resurrection of Mary Magdalene. Legends, Apocrypha, and the Christian Testament. Publisher Continuum Int. New York, NY

Schaff, Philip., Ed. (2016) The Complete Ante-Nicene, Nicene and Post-Nicene Collection of Early Church Fathers: Cross-Linked to the Bible. Toronto, Canada. Kindle

Schaff, Philip., Ed. (2016) Origen. De Principiis In, The Complete Ante-Nicene, Nicene and Post-Nicene Collection of Early Church Fathers: Cross-Linked to the Bible. Toronto, Canada. Kindle

Schoedel, William. 1980. 'Gnostic Monism and the Gospel of Truth' in The Rediscovery of Gnosticism, Vol.1: The School of Valentinus. edited by Bentley Layton. E.J.Brill. Leiden

Schneemelcher, Wilhelm., Wilson, Robert McLachlan., Hennecke, Edgar. Eds. (1991; 1992.) New Testament Apocrypha I and II: Writings relating to the Apostles; Apocalypses and Related Subjects. Westminster John Knox Press. Louisville, KY.

Schneemelcher, Wilhelm., Wilson, Robert McLachlan., Hennecke, Edgar. Eds. (2003) New Testament Apocrypha II: Writings relating to the Apostles; Apocalypses and Related Subjects. Westminster John Knox Press. Louisville, KY. 2003

Shaw, Gregory. (2015) Platonic Siddhas. Supernatural Philosophy of Neoplatonism in: Kelly, Edward F., Crabtree, Adam., Marshall, Paul., Eds. Beyond Physicalism: Toward Reconciliation of Science and Spirituality. Publishers Rowman & Littlefield. Lanham, Maryland.

Silvia, Anthony. (2013) Sanctuary of the Sacred Flame. A Guide to Johannite Spiritual Practice. Copyright ©Silvia, Anthony. Lexington, Kentucky

Simon, Bernard. (2004) The Essence of the Gnostics. Copyright © Arcturus Publishing, London, UK

Smith, Andrew Philip. (2009) A dictionary of Gnosticism. Quest books. Wheaton, IL.

Smith Andrew P. (2015) The Secret History of The Gnostics. Their Scriptures and Beliefs and traditions. Published by Watkins Media Limited. London, UK

Smith, William., Wace, Henry. (1880) A Dictionary of Christian Biography. Literature Sects and Doctrines. William Vol. II. Pub. London, John Murry, Albemarle St. Google Books.

Stapp, Henry P. (2015) A Quantum-Mechanical Theory of the Mind/Brain Connection in: Kelly, Edward F., Crabtree, Adam., Marshall, Paul., Eds. (2015.) Beyond Physicalism: Toward Reconciliation of Science and Spirituality. Publishers Rowman & Littlefield. Lanham, Maryland.

Stevenson, Ian. (2006). Half a career with the paranormal. Journal of Scientific Exploration, 20, 13–21.

Stökl, Jonathan. (2019) Priests and Levites in the First Century C.E., n.p. *cited 31 Oct 2019*. Online: https://www.bibleodyssey.org:443/en/passages/related-articles/priests-and-levites-in-the-first-century-ce

Storm L, tressoldi PE, Utts J. Testing the Storm et al. (2010) meta-analysis using Bayesian and frequentist approaches: reply to Rouder et al. (2013). Psychol Bull. 2013;139(1):248–254. doi:10.1037/a0029506

Storm L, tressoldi PE, Utts J., and Rouder et al. (2010; 2013) Testing the Storm et al. Meta-Analysis Using Bayesian and Frequentist Approaches: Reply to Rouder et al. (2013). Psychological Bulletin. 2013, Vol. 139, No. 1, 248–254

Thomassen, Einar. (2007) The tripartite tractate *in:* Meyer, Marvin., Robinson, James M. The Nag Hammadi Scriptures. HarperCollins 10 East 53rd St., NY, New York 2007

Thomassen, Einar. (2007). Interpretation of Knowledge *in,* Meyer, Marvin W., Robinson, James M. The Nag Hammadi Scriptures: The Revised and Updated translation of Sacred Gnostic Texts Complete in One Volume. HarperCollins. 10 East 53rd St., New York, NY

Tucker JB. (2016) The Case of James Leininger: An American Case of the Reincarnation Type. Explore (NY). 2016 May-Jun;12(3):2007. doi:10.1016/j.explore.2016.02.003. Epub 2016 Mar 2. PubMed PMID: 27079216.

Turner, Martha L. (1996) The Gospel According to Philip: The Sources and Coherence of an Early Christian Collection (Nag Hammadi and Manichaean Studies). Publisher EJ Brill, Leiden, The Netherlands

Turner, John D. (2001), Sethian Gnosticism and the Platonic tradition (The History of the Sethian Movement, Sethian Gnosticism and the Platonic tradition). Presses Université Laval, Paris.

Turner, John D. (2016) trimorphic Protennoia; the Book of Thomas; Zostrianos; Marsanes; the Interpretation of Knowledge; Allogenes in: The Gnostic Society Library. http://gnosis.org/naghamm/trimorph.html (Accessed 2/17/2016)

Turner, John. (2019) Sethian Gnosticism: A literary History. https://archive.is/20121211123653/http://jdt.unl.edu/lithist.html (Accessed 5-8-2019)

Valentinus. (2017) (Valentinus of Alexandria and Rome) Early Christian Writings. (Accessed 9 18 2017) http://www.earlychristianwritings.com/info/valentinus-wace.html

Waldstein M., Wisse FW., In Robinson, JM., Klimkeit HJ. Eds. (1995.) The Apocryphon of John in: The Nag Hammadi and Manichaen Studies. EJ Brill. Leiden, The Netherlands.

Waldstein M., Wisse, FW., In Robinson, JM. (2000). The Apocryphon of John. In Robinson, James M. Ed. The Coptic Gnostic Library. A Complete Edition of the Nag Hammadi Codices. Vol. 2. Koninklijke Brill NV, Leiden, The Netherlands

Werth, Nicolas; Panné, Jean-Louis; Paczkowski, Andrzej; (1999) Bartosek, Karel; Margolin, Jean-Louis, Courtois, Stéphane, ed. (1999) The Black Book of Communism: Crimes, Terror, Repression. Harvard University Press, Cambridge, MA

Williams, Frank. (2008; 2009) The Panarion of Epiphanius of Salamis. Published by Brill. Herndon, VA (for electronic books and journals: (available: booksandjournals.brillonline.com;)

Wright, NT. (2008) Surprised by Hope: Rethinking Heaven, the Resurrection, and the Mission of the Church, SPCK, HarperOne

Wikipedia Church Fathers. https://en.wikipedia.org/wiki/Church Fathers. (Accessed 4 15 2019)

5 19 2021

James Brantingham PhD

The Gospel of Truth

1 The *Gospel of Truth* is a joy freely given by the unmerited grace of the *Father*. It is the revelation of His Sacred Truth, through Knowledge of the Word from the Fullness. From His Pleroma, Paradise, the **Father** sends down His Logos, the *Savior*. A Savior to teach the Gospel and Plan of Redemption. He is bringing hope to those who seek Him and Truth to those grown ignorant about Him.

2 For, when human beings set out to find Him, whom they were already within, the Father, 'the One' was unimaginable and inconceivable. He is the author of Life and Light within and without. Indeed the Father, '*God Above God*' *is* the Incomprehensible, Unbelievable, Imperturbable and Unchangeable, **Source** and **Root** of All; of the Known and Unknown. But without knowing the Father, humans became filled with anxiety and terror, and life became meaningless, dark, and obscure.

3 Due to this increasing obscurity and darkness, '*Error*' grew confident. Confused and irresponsible, '*She, (Error)*' molded and fashioned humanity's aeon and Cosmos. Mimicking the Aeon and image of the One Most High 'it' became through delusion and fraud (and by terror and forgetfulness), a 'deceitful substitute' and 'a foolish Archon.' But it is a robust surrogate and 'deadly stand-in' for the Father with a cleverly concocted philosophy. Instructing in delusions, half-Truths, and unTruths, She created such a beautiful and seductive web of lies they served as a proxy *for* the 'Truth.' Thus, this '*counterfeit, false, and lesser spirit*' tricked everybody!

Yet, some are enticed by this Rootless one. Because of this, some wander into the 'intermediate or middle way.' And taken captive there, they become servants and slaves, worshippers of this ' *lesser spirit,* and *goddess.*' So by such machinations, *Error* prepares activity, loss of memory, and doubts which feel impossible to overcome, but the molded one's lies, chaos, and attacks are of no danger nor (even a) concern to the Father; 'the Good.' **So scorn Error!**

4*Error* induces 'Forgetfulness and Amnesia.' But these do **not** come from the Father or His Word. But forgetfulness and amnesia exist only *because He allows it*. Thus, with the revelation of Truth and Knowledge, gaps in memory vanish. No longer 'forgetful,' the Father is recognized and known (once) again. Such knowledge leads to understanding and becoming One (in Union) with the Father.

The Mystery, 'the Way' *and* 'the Truth'!

5 This, the *Gospel of Truth*, is the *Good* taught by the '*One who is*' and is 'the Word' of the Lord. Found by all who earnestly seek it, it is the perfecting of being through the mercies of the Father. Thus His hidden mystery **Jesus the Christ!**

set up His tent and dwelt among us. 'For He, the *Anointed*,' illuminates our path and shows each 'the Way' driving away darkness and revealing 'the Truth.'

6 But because of this, *Error* was enraged. Yet the Source of this anxiety and terror was not the Father (*nor "the Truth"*) but *Error* itself. Nonetheless, after a great struggle against the Father and the Son, all of Her machinations came to naught. So the Archons of Error (persecuting agents from the Valley of Hinnom) tortured and nailed Him to a tree. For *Lo,* they killed (and *cursed*) Him hanging Him from a tree! *But, 'Amēn, amēn, He had said,* only seeds that fall to the earth and "die," sprout a mighty tree!' And eating the "fruit" of this tree becomes the revelatory experiential knowledge of the Father. So those who do this, the ineffable, inconceivable Perfect Father they find within. And they are within the Father!

7 The Father, the '*One who is,*' created the Totality. But the Totality exists within Him, and the All exists within the Totality. Therefore, because of His Love of the One for the other, the Totality drew them to Himself. Therefore, if this generation had believed it already received its' completion and had achieved perfection, *Error* could have blocked them; and blocked them from 'becoming' One with the Father. But the Father withheld from them their perfection until their return to Him was complete! Then with joy, they entered into Holy Union with 'the One.' Because what does the Totality lack but the *"Inestimable Love, and Knowledge,* of the Father?" Nor does the Father envy them. For how could He envy children? Otherwise, if *Ignorance* and *Error* had prevailed, they would **not** have lost their deficiency nor gained a Perfect Knowledge of the Fullness.

The Teacher of the Torah and Word, Cautious Recognition

8 In a soft and calm voice, the Son lovingly expounded in Synagogues and Assemblies, guidance to understand Torah and the Word. Rabbi Jesus taught and illuminated *' the Way,'* revealing the **Truth**. But educated Scribes learned Pharisees, and Doctors of the Law - wise in their estimation challenged Him to no avail. Who are *You*? Yet He put them to shame, for they were not wise in the Truth of the Father. And they hated Him even more. For the '*One Who Sees*' revealed to the " little children" (of 'the Way') Imperishable, Authoritative Knowledge.' Without receiving instruction through the Word, how could one know right from wrong? Or first principles or the heart, mind, and thought of the Father! The One who laid the mysterious inscrutable foundation of 'All That Is.' But now "they know, and are known; grasped glory and gave it away!"

The Anointed Suffers, Bringing To All The Book of the Living

9 Thus, that despised and rejected man, *merciful, faithful* Jesus (knowing sorrow to the full) was tortured and beaten, enduring to the end. But He *and* the Father allowed it! For from 'the One,' comes *everything;* existence, non-existence, being, and unbeing, Life and Death and more! Alone out of all the people, the *Logos* could read the Father's testament (in this transitory place.) Then "breaking the seals" the Son received God's Instruction written upon his heart of flesh: the *Living Book of the Living*. **Since Jesus knew His death meant Life for many!** Lo, He delivered the Fathers' Word and Revelation to the Totality. And He gave it to all freely who seek the Full and Veridical Covenant.

10 Yet, He was nailed to a tree and hung upon a cross. His death publishing the Edict and Covenantal Scriptures of the Father. Bringing the Word, the Wisdom, and the Logos to all. O, such a glorious sacrifice! Such teaching! '*God*' the Father 'came down from Heaven.' And entered our aeon with "the mind of a fleshly human being." Becoming acquainted with our fears and terror, He emptied Himself (of immortality)! And after feeling what we feel (and fearing what we fear), passed downward into death (but backward into immortality) coming into 'being' as He passed away. Shedding himself of a corrupted and mortal body, he robed himself in righteousness and immortality into the Age. Risen, and with Perfect Knowledge, He lives "an ever-enduring and mystical resurrection!" He is deathless, now divine, and will never die again! **Lo, He went down past the Abyss and into the Pit!** There He preached Hidden Knowledge and Divine Salvation to any with ears to hear! And will teach it again and again, into the Age. For Jesus sits at the right hand of the Power, bringing us back, providing a path (and unveiling the true mind and heart of '*God*').

11 Those who listen to the Father are the living who reach for 'perfection,' those who He will inscribe in the "Book of Life." For, **though His will is that *all be saved*** because they lack knowledge, and what they lack is great, since what is lacked will perfect them. But only the Father can complete them *and* the Totality! Thus, the Totality must ascend to Him, and each receive one's own teaching. And as they rise to meet Him they become abundantly filled with that which each lacks, Perfected He accepts those whose hearts and minds *demonstrate metanoia*. No longer ignorant about themselves He draws the entirety to Himself.

12 Those who hear the call and choose the Father's way He sets apart. Those in unity with 'the One' *stand ready* when He calls their name. For '*God*' calls even those outside of time and space, near or far yesterday, today, *and* tomorrow! Because the Good Foresees — who (will) recognize their call 'into the Age' even from 'the time yet to come!' In the end, those called are those whose names the Father proclaims. But names unspoken leave some (in the mind of '*God*') without being. '*Amēn, amēn, if not called, how can one hear their name?* These are the un-

called creatures of oblivion. transitory, they dissolve and cease to be; nothing more than archetypes. Otherwise, why allow those who will not and choose not to listen (deluded, soulless wretches) any existence at all?

13 Like reprobates, they knew not (nor believed in) the Good. But purified and redeemed (even), they can start anew. Turning aside from *Error,* they learn *'the Truth'*. Though Evil, by nature, they found the Good. And said (*this time* when called), "Here I am!" Thus even these trouble-makers can recall from where they came and to where (from their beginning above) they go. Many have been brought "*Home*" this way and escaped *Error.* For the Father borders and penetrates all Aeons and Realms, even the Aeon of the Abyss (and Pit). Drawn to the Father through love (not coercion), these to understand they are '*Children of God!*' For it is His wish each receive what He prepared for them.

14 Going before them, He has helped many (asking for help) who were veering off track toward *Error.* For Error purposely leads them astray. Thus the Father explored every facet, life-choice, and viewpoint to which their hearts and minds had migrated. In and out of every Place or Realm they could go, they had gone *in the All in All*! It astonished them later when they finally recognized that they had already been with Him but knew it not. Even more surprising, they exited Him without being conscious in the slightest from Whom (and from Where) they had come. But the Father had not yet fully articulated His will. Especially for His creations (and emanations) to reunite in harmony with Him in Life (*and in Death*)!

A Psalm on the Perfect Book; the Living Truth 2

15 For this *is* 'the Word,' which is *not* just letters, vowels, and consonants. But the Knowledge and alphabet of the *Living Book.* Not just a language and grammar with clever syntax *that one might read and feel nothing just someone's secular conceit,* but Eternal Letters and a Sacred Alphabet of Truth.' Behold, It proclaims humanity's *Union* with the Father and contains no '*frivolous,*' or ' *meaningless sounds or words.*' Each letter is a *Holy sound* a *Holy symbol* that makes a *Holy Book.* That esoterically, metaphysically, and informatively imparts unity with 'the One.' Writings which those with *Knowledge* now (and in future) will understand. Words that outline who the Father is and His plan of salvation. Yet it is for those (*human and divine*) who have never known Him. Even for unbelievers that deny Him!

16

His Wisdom imbibes deeply, the *Word* of it,

His Sacred instruction *or Logos* is taught from it,

Its Hidden Knowledge gives *experiential exstasis* through it,

His Righteous restraint *crowns* it,

His Joy makes trivial anything *compared* to it,

For the Son exalteth the Father, and the Father *exalteth* the Logos.

And the Word made flesh is the *Ecclesia* of it.

And 'the Father's Repose' is the *Effect* of it.

Behold, *the Word*, and the *Totality:* the Father, Mother, and the Son are *embodied* by it.

For 'trust and Faith' come through *'reading and practicing 'the Way'* of it.

17 The Holy Father and Holy Mother revealed their hidden and most profound secret. Their gracious bestowal to Humanity and the Totality. The gift above *all* other gifts, Blissful *Jesus of Infinite Sweetness!* By revelation, a mystery kept secret from before time began. *Lo,* the Father uncovered His Bosom, and He (with the Holy Mother) brought to the ignorant, Hidden Knowledge of the Son,' the Savior in whom the All in All finds repose!

18 After filling the deficiency, He dissolved its matrix. The matrix of this world and cosmos. A defective place filled with jealousy and argument, anger and hatred, envy and strife. But the place where there is Unity is perfect. For those who no longer knew the Father caused the deficiency. When they recall the true Father, their deficit is no more. As Darkness scatters, Light shines—so Poverty ends when the Perfect One appears. Dissolved in a Unity with the One, the matrix and its' false reality is shattered. Within this Unity is the Truth about who we are.

19 **Look,** the Lord will rid the Totality of envy and dispute and bring tranquillity and peace. Because all such negative conceits must be wiped away and brought to naught. Speaking Truth relieves divisiveness Unifying all in fellowship. Look, the Savior's **inner fire** will burn away matter; and all selfish and empty time-consuming deficiencies. But thine household must be Holy. For He is found in *Silence* and, in that, the Totality will find *peace*.

Jars, Community and Judgment

20 The Kingdom is like someone who owns many jars (or vessels) of clay, supposedly filled with seed and 'anointed or sealed up.' One day these jars were moved and placed on ill-suited and unsteady shelves. Later many fell off these rickety, unstable shelves. The fragile pots or those with defective seals broke and caused a great disturbance. The spilled seeds and broken pottery made a terrible mess. Yet, the owner rejoiced! Now he knew which jars were strongest and best (and only kept those)— Inspecting them, He judged those poorly made against those appropriately constructed.

The Logos comes down

21 Yet in ignorance *Error* could not see that the *Logos*, the Word had become flesh. And he came amidst the disturbance, amongst the many fluctuating and unpredictable outcomes. For neither this one nor any decision (but indecision) reigned! Some jars were filled, but others empty. Some were clean, others filthy. Many had toppled over and broke. It shook up everything; and the Totality felt unstable, making decisions in a Fog! *Error,* deranged, demented, agitated and in anguish beat Her breast, not knowing what to do! For She was empty inside.

22 Salvation, Knowledge, and the Truth of the Holy Spirit came to the middle; (and) to all the Aeons and Realms to fill (up) beings both good and evil. Ultimately, and in fact, the Father *provides it all (the Source; and The Root of the All and All)*. If thou love the Sacred Spirit, attach thyself to His *'mouth'* and His *'tongue'* and learn the Truth! *Amēn, amēn, He sayeth,* 'whoever drinketh from My mouth becometh Immortal, like Me. And thou shalt divide My revelation rightly, with the hidden Word revealed.

23 Those, His children who come forth, do so (only) through *"That Which Is,"* through " *the One*," the Father. But He calls each by name, *His* sons and daughters—for each at first is without title or form. Out of the Father's mind, they proceed. At first, they do not recognize themselves or others, including *'God.'* But it is the Father who emanates and begets them into the earthly dimension and aeon and world below. Yet, *'God'* knows each intimately. Yet, when He gives them form, He gives them 'their name' and a unique designation But these come into existence ignorant about the Father and from whence they (really) came.

The Nightmares and Illusions of Life

24 Those who pre-exist, exist (at first) within the Conscious of 'the One.' And blissful are those who, ignorant before understanding 'it,' learn that before being, they were spirit. It is not that the Father rules those (in His Consciousness) not yet existing will never exist but, it is the Father that decides (inscrutably) when it is fitting, needed and whom He will manifest. He is like a farmer who picks the proper season for a chosen fruit. Thus up, down, sideways, and into the past, now and into the future (and from the future into the past). All exists which *'the Father Who Is,'* wills to exist! And so some exist beyond life or death; beyond *in and out or to and from, or into or out of* the Life to Come! **The Father shapes them and "names them" and sets them up on their feet (and sends them out)! He makes exist who before *did not* exist!**

25 But existence can be like a nightmare. For if not acquainted with the Father, one thinks, "I did not exist before so, why do I exist (now)?" For, *'into the Age,'* no one continues to exist! Sadly, such people live alongside others who are not (the Father's) fruit, and have no Root. Fearful of living, they are frightened of death. For many say that after, nothingness comes. *'Lo, they declare'* death, extinguishes body and mind, and *'that which is you'* vanishes like a mist! So what is it then that the Father's begotten, should know? It is this, *(fear not for), life is like shadows in*

the night and speculation without insight! Behold, the morning comes, and 'Light' comes, and the shadows and fantasies take flight!' The 'terror and fear' gripping thee was (but) a delusion!

26 Vulnerable, fearing retribution and conflict, *Life*, at times resemble a nightmare. Nightmares filled with terror, disturbance, delusions, uncertainty, doubt, senselessness, shocking immorality, and bloody violence. Hunted like an animal in these unpleasant dreams, one attempts to run away. Then someone is trying to murder you, and it makes you strike out and kill the other in a brutal fight to the death. Or it is also falling from a high cliff and suddenly, able to 'fly,' you fly away (like a bird). But all to no avail! Because as a follower of *'the Way'* thou waketh with the light.

27 When daylight breaks, one naturally wakes up. And casts off these bad dreams, fantasies, and illusions aware at last that they are 'nothing,' disturbances that have no reality and of no importance to be cast off like ignorance or sleep. So it is like to *trying* to believe compared to **having experiential knowledge** of 'the One' or, 'That Which Is!" And seeing reality for what it really is. Such nightmares were not real but unreal *horrors, and empty chimeras* not life! They were merely the "illusory fictions" of sleep (and life) and nothing more!

The Beatitude of Truth

28 Behold the most important and pivotal event (in history) is the advent and ministry of Jesus the Anointed. For before His resurrection the true God was unknown. Until that time only a defective and deficient image of the 'lawgiver,' *Error* (an imperfect image of God) was known. But those who gained knowledge do not deceive themselves. They know that *without effort* most gain no sacred knowledge or enlightenment "(or Rest)!" Thou must sacrifice time and effort, *in prayer or meditation* or even just, *digging a ditch!* Otherwise, (overall) transcendence is "wishful thinking," and fruitless! This is **'the Hidden Knowledge'** *and 'the* **Hidden Truth'** "from Above!"

29 Blissfully the Spirit opened His eyes, He who had not yet stood up. Shed of mortality lying prostrate upon the floor, the *Spirit* quickly grasped He (*the last Adams'*) hand. Swallowing baptismal rebirth and death, by a pneumatic resurrection into immortality, He stood up and walked forth Immortal into the Age. For neither power nor life can ever again be taken from Him. '*Lifted up* He now lives 'an ever-enduring and mystical, 'life after death.'" Knowledge of the Father through living 'the Way' grants His children *experiential knowing… '* so that *they too,* can see Him, hear Him, touch Him and blissfully experience Him - into the Age.'

'Hell' and 'Eternity'

30 After He spoke about the Father He breathed onto all of them and saith receive ye the Holy Spirit and Live!" Many followed, but some the worldly were unmoved. They did not see in Him the "image and likeness of the Savior *in the flesh.*" Yet nothing could stop the Savior's descent into Hell, even to save those who reject Him, for He will not abide endless suffering, death, or imprisonment! Therefore, He, the Light, and the *Logos* of the Father crieth out, 'this punishment and torture are to cease' and, 'cast off your fear of endless damnation.' For "Behold, *She, Error* leadeth thou astray. "Thus, through the Father's sweetness, He will have it - that all be Pardoned and Saved! And ascend back to the Root and Source (in the fullness of time)!

A Stray Sheep and The Shepard

31 He is like the Shepard looking for the *one* that has gone astray. But people, sheep, men, and women can lose their way and get lost (into the Age). But the Father and His Son (their Shepard) love unconditionally! Because if a person falls into the Pit, fallen angels and demons rejoice. But when a son or daughter falls is defiled and strays into the darkest Pit, the bottomless abyss, those that repent and change their mind (and heart) he brings up and out. Joyfully they mix again with family and flock. No longer unsteady, weak nor in need of support. They follow 'the Way' back and are restored to righteousness, and wholesomeness undefiled!

32 For the Sabbath is a day not merely to rest but a day to be restored. To join the 'One to the Many,' making complete that which was deficient, the ninety-nine sheep (counted on the left) becomes *one-hundred sheep* (adding that which strayed) counted on the right. Even *one* delivered out of the darkness is a celebration! Because He, the Father, is a refuge for all!

Salvation and on Keeping the Sabbath

33 Thus, the children of love, **Sons and daughters** *'of the Heart'* and of *'the Way'* lookout for the lost. And found, they restore them. Accordingly, *even on a Sabbath* do not neglect those fallen into a Pit or the Abyss. **Sons and daughters of God!** For those who grieve, lift them up! And those in darkness let in Light. For, make the Sabbath A Sabbath (yet answer a dire need as "spiritual response," and *not* 'labor' but religious observance, and an act of salvation). Then ye shall enter into a perfect night and perfect day when even the lost returneth too 'the Way.'

34 Proclaim from your hearts the Truth for, those who have ears will hear. But remind them of their many sins (but from ignorance and a) *lack of Sacred Knowledge, so Confusion* and *Error.* 'Amēn, amēn I say to you... *'thou who helpeth them helpeth Me. And thou who rescue them rescue me! And, when thou cureth the sick, thou cureth me! So in feeding the hungry, thy feedeth me! But raise them* up *and teach them, that which will set them free!*

35 If through mine strength thou act, My grace is sufficient for thee. And thout shalt becometh stronger still. But leave behind *'that'* which thee cast off, it beeth already moth and worm-eaten vomit and retch. For thou *already* cast off such foul things. Listeneth not to the Adversary. Who *Lawlessly* and through *Error* returneth like a dog and eateth its' own dung! Fortify **not** 'those' (the unrighteous) that maketh ye stumble and fall. But *seek Divine Knowledge, and do the will of the Father through Spirit. Then shalt thou blissfully find - Life (Into the Age)!* For wisdom leadeth to Truth and Uprightness!

36 Beware, *Error*, the '**god**' (the Ruling Archon, *goddess*, and the Adversary) is the 'Mother' *of* this earthly aeon and world. A fallen angel, she proselytizes others into believing her *'false and counterfeit spirit'* then wills them to violate Torah. And so they do, ignorantly wicked things! *This* daemon rules others by duplicity, iniquity, and death. Therefore be not the stumbling block nor a false witness for her (leading others to *Error*). For 'the true, the Highest' *is* **a Loving** *God*. Look, the Good, the Father, desires all to be kind and loving, caring and giving! For, if the tree is good, its fruit is good. Yet, a tree is known by its fruit. Thus shall others see their actions and know they are sons and daughters of 'the One.'

They Whom Are Here, Are Yours in the Silence, Light and Fragrance

37 The Father is sweet and knows those who restrain themselves. Women and men who stand in holiness before His Countenance. Blissful are 'these sons and daughters of *God Above God.*' Everyone sees them caring and attending others *the fruit' of the Father.* Who mixes his aromatic ambiance with matter the world and even with the light. And they rest savoring ' *His intoxicating, otherworldly fragrance.*' For it is a healing, and aromatic salve. It encircles, surrounds, and restores everything: matter, flesh, ' *Lo,'* even sound, and light! *For it is written…* spiritual love is intoxicating and a balm. Those the anointed are drawn in by His Spiritual Fragrance and Character and 'baptized'! For they perceive what is, and it *is* the *Breath of God!*

38 A miasma escapes from this fragrance grown 'old and cold.' The odor 'weakens' (like a body losing it soul) brings the smell of damp and unstable earth. Like mud caused by cold water running over rocky soil, it compels the ground to move, making everything it touches dirty. But later (playing with one's grandchildren), the warm (and fragrant) breath of the Father, His Fullness and Love, comes again, melting away and abolishing loss and fear. Yet it all will dissolve again. And return to the Root. But step forward (now) in trust and faith, for He will raise us! And purified to a ' *new life, the Life to Come' we live; every deficiency and doubt wiped away!* Because Love drives out the cold in unity with His 'perfect thought.'

39 Despite this, most were taken unaware by what came next. Who can comprehend the Father? For He the 'Holy Bythos,' 'the One,' *'the Physician'* went to the illness, the insufficiency. Though unfathomable, He the *'One Who Is '*arrived with insight and caused in the one with deficit, Metanoia. And with an understanding of incalculable experience; with *Knowledge* and factual, veridical skill He ended the confusion! **Lo,** He (who needed curing) was in Unity with 'the One' *within and without.* **For the Father possesses infinite knowledge,** and without Error or doubt. It is unlimited Divine Knowledge giving Him *irrevocable* **cognizance** of what the problem is and what to do. And with this …He stood Him back up upon His feet (then lying prostrate, and lifeless) even after death itself!

40 This is why some (now enduring and imperishable and without lack) *remain.* They put off entering the Father's Pleroma and 'The Life to Come.' For, they seek out those still in darkness and ignorant of their transgressions. They bring them the Light and Knowledge of the Logos. Even though the *Logos* (already!) absolved and forgave them! It fills them because they lack a *spirit-filled, peaceful, repose.* '**Lo**,' people laugh at them and cry out '*Doctor!,*" *'heal thyself'!* Yet, He with fullness and the Light of Sacred Knowledge has no deficiency. His only desire is to replenish those who lack.

Anointment, Chrism and Baptism by Fire

41 The Perfect Man gave of himself entirely, so *that those who lack the Grace of Knowledge* could receive it and receive Fullness. But in Grace and Fullness, the deficient one finds *the Truth and the Logos, and sees the Covenant fulfilled!* Seek and keep on seeking, says the Father. Because thou shalt find Him in the Fullness and Perfection. He will be doing that which is in 'the image and likeness of the Christ!' In Him is Truth, and no Deceit! He will anoint thee and baptize thee. ***And thou will enter into the light and the Age and the Life to Come!***

42 Filled jars when ' *sealed*' or *' anointed'* 'do not leak.' Loaded with good seed *sealed* jars appear dependable. But (like some followers) a number of jars are *'sealed or anointed imperfectly'*. Stressed beyond "mechanical integrity" they break. Yet, the Father waits patiently. For the ' God' of love is ready to 'anoint ' and 're-seal any, even the broken,' into the Age. And because some (now) observant walk away, the Father's open door lets others take their place!

The Logos

43 The Father is good and kind. And He knows those who are His, For, *before the beginning* He assigned them their roles in Paradise. Yet in that Aeon of Perfection is rest and repose. And the Father knows their thoughts and ways, and their most likely acts, but their will is their own. Why? Because the logoi are 'within His mind' and therefore *free!*. For before any pre-existed, they existed within Him. And will exist and live into the Age. And can share, *'Being One with the Father.'* 'For like *that* which the Father shares with the Son He will share with all. So

He will give to any of His Children, especially those who become logoi!' Since the **'Son'** is the Father's name, He, the Lord is "the Father." Thus, the Father wills any or all to exist. But at the right time (in the right place) when He wills it from Above!

The Will of the Father

44 For when He wills it, it is by His Grace and Volition that what exists, exists *only* by His will. **Behold!** He is unknowable, ineffable, and is *beyond human* understanding. All that will be will be only because He wills it! And the Father cannot be controlled by the creation He created. But it will be as He deems it even if it does not please them who live in it! For He is the beginning and the end (the Alpha and Omega). And knows their start, their future, and their return, so that upon dying, He will review their lives. Yet, for purification, not damnation, and to be questioned face to face. He, "That Which Is, The One," did not just predestine but gave all free will imparting this through *Knowledge*, Holy Scripture, *and* Revelation. This Divine Knowledge leads to '*Gnosis,* and experiential unity' (*or union with*) 'the One' (either at once or gradually). Since the Father created them in His likeness and image, male and female, He created them, *God Above God* is *neither a man* nor *a woman! For He alone is self-begotten and brought forth the Heavens the "Aeons" above (and below)! The many Aeons must learn the Father's Name,* "the Lord," **and His real Name in Truth!** (See "Purification or Correction below").

The Name Above All Names

45 He, the Father shares His Sacred name with 'the One,' He who begot Himself as 'the Son,' emanating out and away from Him. He brought forth His Son and gave Him '*this,*' the Holiest of names: *the Name Above All Names*. For His name, the '*Son*' is His name in Truth, Strength and represents the Love and Compassion of '*God*' **the Father**! As the name of the Father is the Son! So the name of the Son is the Father! *He, the 'One,' a Mystery, and a Spirit and the transcendence above it all! And as a result, His transcendent names that are a mystery of 'the One,' the invisible, are made visible!* And the *Logoi*, or all the sons and daughters of '*God*' have spiritual aptitude, intellect, reason *and* knowledge. And in conjunction with the soul or psyche translates each of 'the children' into those endowed with the light. *For Wisdom knoweth the Father and seeth the face of 'the Most High'*.

46 Names of the Father are a source of confusion. For whatever way one describes the '*One Who Is,*' it does **not** (*in Truth*) explain how or what He is nor why He exists. Nor why He does **not** exist. But the Son knows the Truth and revealed

the Sacred Name of the Father. Which, *is* ' the Son!' *He, the 'One,'* is a Mystery, a Spirit *and the* **transcendent One** *above it all*! As a result, these ethereal transcendent names make up the invisible mystery made visible! In light of that, the *Logoi,* the sons and daughters of *'God,'* have a spiritual aptitude, intellect, reason *and* knowledge. Therefore Rejoice! For He bestows His name upon those, who belong to Him, 'the children of *God Above God'*!

Being Itself

47 Indeed the Son, 'He Who Is,' 'the Father,' *is* **Being-Itself, Ground of Being, Power of Being, and the Bythos and Abyss of God's Bottomless Depth even,** *He Who (Will Be) Their After 'Our Being' Becometh, 'Non-being'!* For, before the Origin He begat the Universe, His Pleroma, Spirit, the Son, the first Aeons, and finally matter, materialism and the flesh. Thus began: *being*, in the Age of Creation, unto the Age, into the Ages to Come. But His Name and all such names or words in the Cosmos *like*, 'Father, Son, the Holy Mother or Spirit, Life, Light, Resurrection, Congregation and Assembly' are *mere facades*! Their true meaning and reality is found only in the Life to Come.

The *Name*

48 The Highest is: unnamable, unutterable, *and* ineffable. For that reason, it is fitting to understand how He received His Name. **That… *'it,' is His*** Name indeed! Thus 'the Son' is *the* name given Him by the Father. But *'the Son'* **is** the Name of the Father. For, no-one has seen the Father (except the Son) for *'the One'* is invisible and his name a mystery and 'not shown.' Yet when the time came, the Father (alone) uttered it and said, "He Who Is the Compassionate One, My Beloved…" Today I begot Thee, ***Thou*** my Son! For after all, who but "*That Which Is*" could give a name to someone who existed before **He Himself existed?** As if He had lived *before* He lived, and given birth to Himself 'before *He Himself* was birthed!' Thus before the self-generated gave "birth" to the self-generated Father Himself! ***Behold,*** He will live but not as you live; and will die but not die as you die (and become dead)! Because He is Me and I am He, and We are free, secure, perfect, and complete in power! *'Lo'* the riddle of the Son, and His secret is, His Name is *the* Name of 'the LORD' and *it* is the ' *Mystery Beyond All Mysteries!*

49 So it is that the name above all names was bestowed upon the unnameable, the ineffable, He who is Perfect, the Son. The Son is the name of the Father (and the Fathers' name). For *'He Who Is,'* ' *God Above God,'* ***is*** the First and the Last, the Beginning and the End,' the Son. Out of His mouth, He speaks about Hidden Things. He tells them of the Father's Aeon, *Paradise Above.* And the complexity and scheme, 'of the Entirety, of the All in All.' For He has the Father's Spirit,

Power, and Name, *and is the Perfect Son, the Anointed, and Savior for all humanity and the Cosmos.* His will is that *all* return to that place where he received his Name, His Aeon (our Heaven) of Fullness and Rest.

50 Through the benevolence of the Father, His secrets were made known. So He brought forth His Son to speak for Him. For the Son has the power to say his name and see him openly; since the Father is Good, without Evil, and is Kind. So then the Anointed came forth on behalf of *all* the sons and daughters of *'God Above God'*. And the Son, 'the One,' taught each (and all who seek it) the Father's will. So seeketh it, *and* thine shalt find it: (Sacred Salvational Knowledge) and experiential unity with the Highest! It is the place (one day) to which *all* return. So share about this blissful eternal realm, from which all come. That place, the place of the Father's Rest, Peace, and Repose! And glorify Its' Fullness and Celebrate the Infinite Sweetness of the Most High!

All Will Return to the Source

51 *All* beings and their Aeons are emanations from the Root, *the true Source;* the **Father.** And emanated from Him, the Highest is at Rest. For from the fullness of the Father's **Heavens above Heaven** and the highest degree of the entirety comes His *Logos* (the *Word*). And His uncountable *Logoi* (His faithful speaking His words and doing His will). So when the time is right, He bestows upon each *'the Way'* back through meditation and by giving up wrong action; so that they can learn to do what is right and reach their destiny! Then they finally rejoin the Father in His Silent and Peaceful Repose! Thus to the **true Source** which lifts them above the highest *Heaven above Heaven.* To dwell with the 'Lord of Spirits' in Paradise! Drawing near to him, they "hold his face" and over and over give Him the kiss of peace. *Consider!* They are not exalted because they exalt Him and are not glorified, for they Glorify Him! Look! Like Him, they are not petty and not embittered nor angry. **Behold,** He (with the Mother and Son) is without evil and infinitely sweet, serene, and undisturbed. Not jealous or unclear about what He wants, it is this: the Father will have it that *all* ascend back to the Source, *to Heaven and Paradise* and *'the All in All!'*

52 This is 'the Way' for those who possess His revelation and illumination. They await the Father from above, the Blissful *'One Who Is.'* Because they do *not* go down into Gehenna (the Valley of Hinnom) *of death;* which no longer exists within them. No longer envious of the young and healthy, they groan no more, nor do they get sick or suffer. Instead, they rest within Him *He who is Always at Rest 'into the Age!'* For, the Father is in them, and they are in the Father! Blissful and *revived* they lack nothing! They are neither anxious nor duplicitous but complete and Perfect dwelling with the Root and Source of the All! No longer ensnared by or confused about the Truth, they can extend toward the Fa-

ther and Spirit. Because their Heart and Mind their Nous is free! Undivided, they work on their (own) Root and Source; in this place of blessing!

The Sacred Fathers' After-Thought and Aeon

53 As for the rest of humanity whatever realm or place they lie in wait for, I Jesus the Anointed await them here in Heavenly Repose. Therefore I need not keep talking about it. Yet, from this Aeon, *of Paradise*,' I remain dedicated to '*God*,' and to His faithful sons and daughters below. For He poured out His love upon them, and they are no longer deficient. Yea, He has made them His "Descendents!" Worthy and perfect, they speak of the Light, of the Father's Love, His Word, and of the Fullness! For, 'spiritually,' they have entered 'the Life to Come into the Age.' The Father rejoices, for they glorify 'the One' who spoke the Word and Sacred Knowledge; He is Good. And these Perfected Sons and Daughters of '*the Way*' are the children the Father loves!

James Brantingham PhD ©

6 15 2021

Thousand Oaks, California

Footnote and Other Commentary

I highly recommend Dr. David Hart's *'A New translation'* (2017) in the references andI cited below (*'That All Shall Be Saved,'* 2019). In my opinion, he has written a New Testament that rivals (in need) the Greek text (and interpreted rightly the ancient early Theology of Jesus and the Early Church Fathers) that may save Orthodox Christianity. His translations are as important for Christians now as Erasmus' were (no Greek reading) European and English readers (in the middle ages). Hart is 'The Erasmus' for our Age and His New Testament (and text, 'That All Shall Be Saved') is needed just now if Christianity - under attack like never before - is to be saved!') For He brings out all the nuances and restores the interpretation of the oldest and best Greek translations and insights of the earliest Church Fathers. Such correct translations and theology is desperately needed now; a blessing indeed! Other Orthodox Christians such as Gerry Beauchemin and Scott Reichard (2007, 2010, 2016; 2018) have also presented profound texts such as *'Hope Beyond Hell'* and *'Hope For All,'* also support a similar "new" (but anciently the most correct) interpretation of the OT and NT scriptures similar to, *'That all will be saved.'* And while supporting virtually all of the scriptures currently found both in the OT and NT. Beauchemin's books (ad Kindle's) are at the Kindle Amazon site and He is giving them away at no cost (as this is written.)

The Logos and 'the Way'

David Hart directly and strongly influenced my thinking about the ideas in these sayings from, his above referenced book. His influence along with Beauchemin's and Reichard's could bring people back into the pews. For example he gives the more accurate and correct reading of the English term 'Word' (John) which *is* explicating the Greek word 'Logos' used by the Apostle John. The Apostle (or his Johannine 'community') actually wrote in Greek and, used the term 'Logos'. This word meant far more than the term *'Word'* means in English. Hart strikingly suggests that, instead of the English term, *'Word'* that the Asian word *'Tao'* ('the Way') comes closer too the concept of *'the Logos.'* And Late Antiquity of Christianity understood the Logos' to have a very broad meaning; even beginning with nascent Christianity (even by the incipient beginnings of Rabbinic Judaism). Yet the broad definition of *'religious or spiritual'* practice first describing the practice of Jesus (morally and ethically) was described as 'the Way.' Hart suggests that the 'Word' (or actually the Greek term the 'Logos') is better understood as similar to the Doaist asian word *'Tao* or *Dao.'* 'Taoism, or Daoism,' Hart reflects, covers all the 'new' philosophical, religious and technical ideas found within the earliest New Testament or for, *'the Logos'* as delineated by the Great Jewish writer, *Philo* of Alexandria. Especially as it was meant in the first century and probably what the Apostle John probably meant to convey at that time.

So John's term was not a near equivalent Greek idiom or expression for the English term: 'Word' (in Greek ῥῆμα; or rhema). But John chose 'Logos'. ***Now, (as Dr. Hart points out) there is nothing wrong with the term 'Word' nor must it be changes (it is a beautiful translation of the Greek into English scripture);*** But many today have come to understand its' broader meaning by the study of John's use of the Greek term, the 'Logos.' And though one meaning for Logos is the 'Word' (and so by definition, 'the Word of God,' thus this would cover for all Christians - today - all the information and knowledge in 'the Logos' of antiquity). But (at the time of Jesus) it, anciently the Logos was more often used in Greek philosophy (but became Christian scripture in the earliest Gospels such as that of John's and it should be noted that 'the Logos' was already used by Jews in their Greek Tanakh that would become *the* Christian Old Testament.) Thus was it found in both the earliest full and complete OT and NT Christian bibles such as Septuagint LXX) *and* in the Hebrew bible in their Greek the Septuagint LXX; where the LXX dealt with 'religious, philosophical, or ethical issues. Thus it is also a Judeo-Christian term.

The term 'Word' today (meaning for Christians, 'the Word of God' (and the Incarnation of the Word: Jesus Christ) was simply not expansive enough for the way *'Logos'* was meant overall in 'Second Temple Judaism.' 'Second Temple Judaism' is sometimes easily recognized by Christians as the time period "between the writing of the Old and New Testaments" and called by Christians in the past the 'intertestamental period.' Yet the earliest Christians read many important biblical works from that time period before the Canonization of the current NT like: *Enoch, Jubilees, The Wisdom of Solomon, Sirach also called Ecclesiasticus, Psalms of Solomon, 1 Maccabees, 2 Maccabees, 3 Maccabees, 4 Maccabees, Judith, Tobit, and Odes of Solomon*. And some writers such as Donald Akeson (2000, 2001) would include as "Second Temple" work (or 'intertestamental') Jewish literature, the *'New Testament'* (and many of the writings of the Church Fathers) such as Clement I and II, Ignatius of Antioch, Polycarp of Smyrna, Origen, Justin Martyr, Irenaeus of Lyons, Clement of Alexandria, and many others (to controversially name but a few). Thus, as the Great Gnostic Gospels and texts are reviewed in the light of this modern age (with its profound scientific studies and research) I would suggest including the Great Gnostic Christian texts and writers) within the previously unacceptable 'works of the Church Fathers.' Such texts from (communities representing), Doubting Thomas, Philip, Mary of Magdala (a Church Mother!) and Valentinus (from his cited and his disciples writings found in the refutations of the already included Church Fathers) and in texts He is believed to have written (such as the Gospel of Truth) or influenced (like the Gospel of Philip) as part of the larger body of the 'Christian' Church Fathers as a whole.

Gnostic-Christian Church Fathers (pseudepigraphic or a real, people or community… such as around Valentinus, or Mary Magdalene)

But this is *my* suggestion and, not that of Drs. Hart, Beauchemin and Reichard; that is, including within the 'Christian Church Fathers' the pseudepigraphic works of these Gnostic-Christian texts and 'their books and scriptures' as the work of the 'Gnostic-Church Fathers' (and at least it appears Mary of Magdala). For many of the writings of the Father's texts extended up into the Fifth and even a few important theological treatises that still changed the final translation of the Christian Bible 'playing out' up to the Seventh century. Thus many Gnostic, and 'Christian Gnostic' texts (produced by such writers as Valentinus or his Disciples; or Sethian writers and so on…); and other Pseudepigraphic 'Christian Gnostic' writings in this material should be denoted as 'Christian Paracanonical or Apocryphal' texts such as (this very text 'the *Gospel of Truth*') and others such as: The *Gospels of Thomas, Philip, and Mary* along with, *the Secret Revelation* (or Apocryphon) *of John*.

Even if it is only recognizing their use as counter-point in final formulation and concrete writing of what is the current modern (NT) theological stance. Accepting them as constituting 'Para-canonical Christian' writings would give them obliquely, the importance they played in the development of the 'proto-canonical' scriptures of the past. But, this is not an accepted mainstream view under Biblical Scholarly consideration at this time. Still, even in the time of Jesus most of those who could write and read Greek in 'Late Antiquity' were acquainted with a broader meaning for (many other) terms like the '*Logos*.'

Reading these 'Para-canonical Christian Gnostic texts' alongside the modern "Canonical texts" could bring about the immense and monumental, the inclusive, erudite and profound understandings needed for today. it's farseeing, prophetic strength makes it almost impossible to see Jesus as anything other than equal to God ('the One') at least "*in Spirit*" and foresees and allows the ecumenical reach needed to "learn from and usefully use" material from other religions or religious practices; even to remain at peace with science, even using 'the methods of science' linking 'logos' to such concepts as the scientifically (now) robust peer-reviewed and published evidence demonstrating the reality of psi (See below).

The Logos, Truth, Science, Psi and Religious Practice and Revelation

Linking the 'logos' to 'psi' there is evidence for telepathy, precognition or foreknowledge, telekinesis; even mediumship and more… see Dean Radin PhD's research at http://deanradin.com/evidence/evidence.htm (2019). And Julie Beischel PhD's (research at) https://scholar.google.com/citations?user=rNejlNcAAAAJ&hl=en

Radin lists science that satisfies falsifying the null hypothesis and the required quantity of replication by using the full length (and abilities) of extraordinary, extended methodologies (already known) in science such as (multiple blinding; blinding - in fact for example by Radin and Beischel - up to five times, and on 'both sides,' (as one example) to rule out bias! This demonstrates to: *a scientist* (one) that will **honestly look at and read fully** the research *'scientifically,'* which demonstrates the reality of telekinesis, healing at a distance, telepathy and ESP, Precognition & Presentiment, Mind-Matter Interaction; Potential (Therapeutic) Applications of the scientific use (and research into) mediums and much, much more. Scientists that have rejected this work often have not read it claiming in a circular statement Psi does not exist and since it does not there is no valid scientifically evidenced paranormal or parapsychological research. They should take the time to read Patricia Utt's the Head of the Statistical Department from the University of Irvine in California and a renown Statistician (Utts J, Patricia. 1996). Many ignorantly pass judgement (for example that failure in such research is hidden) when in fact it is a stronger requirement to publish non-significant research in this field than it is in non-psychic or non-paranormal science (Radin, Dean. 2013; 2018).

Today *even*, Survival of Consciousness *now* (*more than ever before*) has developed some solid scientific evidence. So much so that there are desperate and extremely dishonest debunkers (and haters of all views that suggest there is anything other than matter, time and space)! These angry men and women go to great efforts to produce fake data, twisting or deleting data (from already peer-reviewed and published psi research) and "live" (and get paid) to debunk psi and psi researchers (such I assert was done against Bem D. et al) see: https://skeptiko.com/daryl-bem-responds-to-parapsychology-debunkers/

Aeon, Aeons and 'Eternity' (in) Hell as opposed to: Purification and Correction

But Hart also clears up and addresses (again) the Greek terms for time: **'Aiōn and Aiōnios'** (commonly written as 'Aeon or Aeons' in English) which are usually translated as meaning 'eternal, or forever' throughout the Gospels and Pauls' letters. But in fact, **Aiōn and Aiōnios'** almost *never* meant 'eternal' but, for a very few exceptions. 'Aiōn and/or Aiōnios' actually meant 'a long time' or, emphasized and written repeatedly (equivalent to writing, for Ages upon Ages) or by the use of adjectives with 'Aiōn and/or Aiōnios' such as an 'ever enduring' Age and similar. So with a number of *adjectives* and *with repetitions* the term could come to essentially mean (but, rarely did) 'the, or a' word for: 'eternal'. Hart gives some examples: For instance, εἰς τὸν αἰῶνα (eis ton aiōna) is often translated as "forever" but literally means "unto the age" or "until the age" or "into the age" or "throughout the age" (and was the equivalent of the Aramaic 'le-alam' or Hebrew ad-olam ("unto the age" or "until the age"). Nevertheless, Hart points out that, this is very rare in the New Testament. So logically this has significant import as to just what the term meant in Greek then and of course what it means today! especially in regards 'to time' in *both* Heaven and 'Hell'. Heaven - was a term (in Hebrew) described as the 'heights,' 'elevations,' the 'Sky' or even: a 'whirlwind' (and above as the 'firmament') or, in the New Testament, the 'Father's house,' 'Paradise,' 'The heavenly Jerusalem,'; or 'in Abraham's bosom.' In fact, this is found in one of the most famous NT prayers: 'our father who art in Heaven... (the land of the 'Sky-God'). Understanding these matters changes significantly the way Hell and Heaven should be described or defined.

So these less definitive words seem to point to a different sense for definitions of time in heaven. And some have decided that, 'Hell' (which is *not* a word used in the Greek NT) but its many loan words (such as Hades and Gehenna) should actually rightly define various and periods of time (being rarely used for meaning "forever" or "eternally." Being purified or corrected prior to entrance into Heaven appears to occur for many outside of "Hell" (or for a small number in 'Hell' or somewhere else) before being made "clean or purified." For some that have been horrific (like Hitler, Mao, Stalin or Pol Pot) time (even a very long time) may be required for a few as, "Correction even Punishment," 'into the Age unto the Ages and Ages to come'. However in the New Testament (and many Gnostic Christian texts like the Secret Revelation of John (see in this book) a very small number of people who are undergo something essentially akin too 'Eternal Damnation' and 'Punishment' by various combinations of adverbs and suffixes merged with 'Aiōn and/or Aiōnios' to reasonably suggest eternity or a near eternity. Certainly an 'Eternal Damnation' would seem appropriate for such genocidal murderers of Christians such as Stalin and other Communists (authoritarian socialists) or the Jews by Hitler and his (authoritarian) National Socialists. But I must finally note that it was through the study of the *NHL* Gnostic Scriptures that I was led to and found Dr. Hart's NT; and it has led to an educational and partial *'Gnosis'* for me! (Panné, Jean-Louis., Paczkowski, Andrzej., Bartosek, Karel., 1999).

Hart (2017) makes in his 'NT' translation makes an argument for essentially Universalism (and he confirms this in his book published in 2019); but accepts that some form of 'Purification or Correction' is required periodically by a few. But, this great Orthodox Scholar (David Hart) does not define exactly what 'this' is (in this text)but denies it is simply a "hell-like" 'Purgatory' for the few. Thus he certainly seems to make an argument for the 'God of Jesus Christ,' and what *His*Loving, 'Father' actually does or would do. What Hart suggests is based on his more accurate Greek (correctly rendered translations) - many of which are opposite to dogma taught (for over a millennium) in much of Western Christianity.

References for "The Gospel of Truth"

Aeon Gnosticism (2018.) A description of Logos in Gnosticism. https://en.wikipedia.org/wiki/Aeon_(Gnosticism) Accessed 9 23 2018Akenson,

Akenson, Donald H. (2000.) Saint Saul a skeleton key to the historical Jesus. Oxford University Press. New York, NY

Akenson, Donald H. (2001.) Surpassing Wonder: The Invention of the Bible and the Talmuds. Chicago: University of Chicago Press

Attridge, Harold W., MacRae, George W. (2000). The Gospel of Truth. In Robinson, James M. Ed. The Coptic Gnostic Library. A Complete Edition of the

Nag Hammadi Codices. Vol. 2. Koninklijke Brill NV, Leiden, The Netherlands

Barnstone, William. (1984) The Other Bible. HarperCollins. New York, NY.

Barnstone, William., Meyer, Marvin. (2003, 2009, 2011) The Gnostic Bible: Revised and Expanded 1st ed. Boston, Massachusetts, New Seeds Books.

Barnstone, William. (2009.) The Restored New Testament: A New translation with Commentary Including the Gnostic Gospels of Thomas, Mary and Judas. Publisher W.W. Norton & Co. New York, NY

Barron, David. (2017.) God and Christ: Examining the Evidence for a Biblical Doctrine. Wisdom, Jesus Christ and the New Testament. http://www.scripturalTruths.com/articles/ology/firstbornwisdom/. (Accessed 1-31-2017)

Barr, Stephen M. (2003) Modern physics and ancient faith. Notre Dame, Indiana: University of Notre Dame Press

Barrow, John., Tipler, Frank. (1986) The Anthropic Cosmological Principle. Oxford University Press Inc. New York, NY

Barton J., Ed. (2016.) The Hebrew Bible . A Critical Companion Princeton University Press. Princeton NJ

Bauman, Lynn. (2012) The Gospel of Thomas, Wisdom of the Twin 2nd Ed. Ashland, Oregon: White Cloud Press

Bauckham, Richard. (2006) Jesus and the Eyewitnesses: The Gospels as Eyewitness Testimony. Eerdmans Publishing, Grand Rapids, MI 2006

Bem D, tressoldi P, Rabeyron T, Duggan M. Feeling the future: A meta-analysis of 90 experiments on the anomalous anticipation of random future events. F1000Res. 2015;4:1188. Published 2015 Oct 30. doi:10.12688/f1000research.7177.2

Bem DJ. (2011) Feeling the future: experimental evidence for anomalous retroactive influences on cognition and affect. J Pers Soc Psychol. 2011;100(3):407–425. doi:10.1037/a0021524

Beischel J.(2015) Boccuzzi M, Biuso M, Rock AJ. Anomalous information reception by research mediums under blinded conditions II: replication and extension. Explore (NY). 2015 Mar-Apr;11(2):136-42. doi: 10.1016/j.explore.2015.01.001. Epub 2015 Jan 7. PubMed PMID: 25666383.

Bem D, (2016) tressoldi P, Rabeyron T and Duggan M. Feeling the future: A meta-analysis of 90 experiments on the anomalous anticipation of random future events version 2; referees: 2 approved F1000Research 2016, 4:1188 (doi: 10.12688/f1000research.7177.2)

Beischel, J. (2019) Windbridge Research Center. https://www.windbridge.org/ A List of Completed Research https://scholar.google.com/citations?user=rNejlNcAAAAJ&hl=en (Accessed 12 30 2019)

Betty, Stafford. (2011) The Afterlife Unveiled: What the Dead are Telling Us About Their World. O-Books John Hunt Pub. Ltd. Alresford, Hants UK.

Betty, Stafford. (2014) Heaven and Hell Unveiled. Updates from the World of Spirit. White Crow Books. Guildford, UK.

Beauchemin, Gerry. Reichard, Scott D. (2007, 2010). Hope Beyond Hell. The Righteous Purpose of God's Judgment. Malista Press. Kindle Edition. Olimo, Texas.

Beauchemin, Gerry. Reichard, Scott D. (2018) Hope For All: Ten Reasons God's Love Prevails (p. 19). Malista Press. Kindle Edition.

Brantingham, James. (2017) The Gospel of Philip. A New translation. CreateSpace Independent Pub. Amazon Digital Services LLC. Seattle, WA.

Brantingham, James. (2019) Truth... What Is Truth. Holy Wisdom and the Logos of God. The Four Lost Apocryphal Christian Gospels: The Gospel of Truth. The Gospel of Philip. The Gospel of Thomas & The Gospel of Mary With the Secret Revelation of John. Pub. Amazon Digital Services LLC. Kindle. ASIN: B08R7Z8KXD

Brown, T. Patterson. (2014) The Gospels of Thomas, Philip and Truth. Available from http://www.freelyreceive.net/metalogos/files/intro.html *Accessed 5 25 2014*

Brown, T. Patterson. (2003) The Gospel of Truth. Available from http://www.freelyreceive.net/metalogos/files/intro.html (Accessed 5 25 2014; listed as published 1992; 2003) Also: https://web.archive.org/web/20031030132950/http://www.metalog.org/files/valent.html

Bauman, Lynn. (2012) The Gospel of Thomas, Wisdom of the Twin 2nd Ed. Ashland, Oregon: White Cloud Press

Brons, David. (2015.) Valentinians and the Bible in: The Nag Hammadi Library. Gnostic Society Library, The. Available at http://gnosis.org/naghamm/nhl.html (Accessed 2/7 2015)

Brown, Thomas Patterson. (2014) The Gospels of Thomas, Philip and Truth. Available from http://www.freelyreceive.net/metalogos/files/intro.html (Accessed 5 25 2014)

Bauckham, Richard. (1978) "Universalism: a historical survey", Themelios 4.2. theologicalstudies.org.uk/article_universalism_bauckham.html (Accessed 8-23-2016)

Bauckham, Richard. (2006) Jesus and the Eyewitnesses: The Gospels as Eyewitness Testimony. Eerdmans Publishing, Grand Rapids, MI 2006

Bourgeault, Cynthia. (2008). The Wisdom Jesus. transforming Heart and Mind- A new Perspective on Christ and His Message. Shambala Publications Inc. Boston, MA

Boyarin, Daniel. (2012) The Jewish Gospels: The story of the Jewish Christ. New York NY, New Press

Cornell, Jim A. (1995) From The Alpha and the Omega - Introduction ALL THE HOST OF HEAVEN. http://www.mazzaroth.com/Introduction/AllTheHostOfHeaven.htm Accessed 5-9-2018

Davidson, Gustav. (1967). A dictionary of angels: including the fallen angels. The Free Press Simon and Schuster. New York, NY

Davies, Stevan. (2005) The Secret Book of John. The Gnostic Gospel Annotated & Explained. Skylight Paths Publishing. Woodstock, Vermont

DeConick, April D. (2017.) The Gnostic New Age: How a countercultural spirituality revolutionized religion from antiquity to today. Columbia University Press. New York, NY

Ecclesiasticus; The Wisdom of Ben Sira

Fiorenza, Elizabeth S. (1994) In Memory of Her: A Feminist Theological Reconstruction of Christian Origins. Crossroad Publishing, New York, NY

Smith, Geoffrey S. (2019) Valentinian Christianity. Texts and translations. University of California Press. Oakland, CA.

Gnostic Society Library, The. (2015). The Nag Hammadi Library. Available at http://gnosis.org/naghamm/nhl.html Accessed 2/7 2015

Grobel, Kendrick. (1960) The Gospel of Truth. The Valentinian Meditation on the Gospel. Publisher Abingdon Press. New York & Nashville TN

Grondin, MW. (2017) Coptic-English Interlinear translation.The Coptic Gospel of Thomas, saying-by-saying (Linked to: Andrew Bernhard's presentation of the

Greek POxy fragments). http://gospel-thomas.net/sayings.htm (Accessed 1-2-2017)

Harris, Sam. (2004) The End of Faith: Religion, Terror, and the Future of Reason. Norton. New York, NY

Hart, David B. (2017) The New Testament. A translation. Yale University Press. London, UK

Hart, David B. (2019). That All Shall Be Saved: Heaven, Hell, and Universal Salvation. University Press. New Haven and London

Heiser, Michael S. (2015) The unseen realm. Recovering the supernatural worldview of the bible. Hexham Press. Bellingham, Wa.

Hoeller, Stephan A. (2002.) Gnosticism: New Light on the Ancient tradition of Inner Knowing. Publisher: Quest Books Wheaton, IL.

Hoeller, Stephan A. (1998 and 2010). Ecclesia Gnostica A Gnostic Catechism. Publisher: The Gnostic Society Press, Los Angeles, California. http://gnosis.org/ecclesia/catechism.htm (Accessed 5-5-2015)

Jenkins, Philip. (2008) The lost history of Christianity. The thousand-year golden age of the church in the Middle East, Africa, and Asia--and how it died. Publisher HarperOne. New York, NY.

Jenkins, Philip. (2015). The many faces of Christ. The Thousand - Year story and influence of the Lost Gospels. Publisher Basic Books. New York, NY

Jenkins, Philip. (2017). Crucible of Faith. Hachette Book Group. New York, NY

Jenkins, Philip. (2001). Hidden Gospels: How the Search for Jesus Lost Its Way. Oxford University Press. New York, NY.

King, Karen L. (2003) The Gospel of Mary of Magdala: Jesus and the First Woman Apostle. Published by Polebridge Press, Santa Rosa, California

King, Karen L. (2000) Images of the Feminine in Gnosticism (Studies in Antiquity & Christianity) Published by trinity Press, Harrisburg, Pennsylvania

King, Karen L. (2003) What is Gnosticism? Harvard University Press. Cambridge, MA

King, Karen. (2006) The Secret Revelation of John. Harvard University Press. Cambridge, Massachusetts

Keener, Craig S. (2011) Miracles. The credibility of the New Testament accounts volumes 1 & 2. Baker Publishing Group. Grand Rapids, MI

Irenaeus Bishop of Lyon, Robinson, Armitage Ed. (1920) The Demonstration of the Apostolic Preaching. The Macmillan Co. New York, NY

Johnson, Elizabeth (1993). "Wisdom Was Made Flesh and Pitched Her Tent Among Us" Reconstructing the Christ Symbol: Essays in Feminist Christology. Paulist Press. New York, NY

Johnson, Todd M. (2001) Christian martyrdom: a global demographic assessment *in:* World Christian trends. Barrett, DB. Johnson, TM. Pasadena, CA: William Carey Library, 2001.

Layton, Bentley, (1987) The Gnostic Scriptures. A New translation with Annotations and Introductions. Publisher Doubleday & Company. Inc. Garden City, New York.

Leloup, Jean-Yves. (2004) The Gospel of Phillip: Jesus, Mary Magdalene, and the Gnosis of Sacred Union. Rochester, New York: Inner traditions.

Logos (2018) https://en.wikipedia.org/wiki/Logos A general description of Logos. Accessed 9 23 2018

Mark M. Mattison. The Gospel of Truth. (2017) The following translation has been committed to the public domain and may be freely copied and used, changed or unchanged, for any purpose. It is based on the Coptic text of NHC I, 3. https://www.gospels.net/Truth/ Accessed 9 25 2017 This exhibit reproduces the text of NHC I,3. (Coptic to English line by line and near interlinear Accessed 2021).

Martyn, James Louis (2003) First published 1968. History and Theology in the Fourth Gospel (3rd ed.). Westminster John Knox Press.

Mattison, Mark M. (2017) The Gospel of Truth. Notes On The translation. Coptic Text of NHC I, 3. https://www.gospels.net/Truth/ Accessed Accessed 9 25 2017.

Menard, J.E. (1972) L'Evangile de verite NHS 2; Leiden: Brill, quoted *in*, Attridge, Harold W., MacRae, George W. (2000). The Gospel of Truth. In Robinson, James M. Ed. The Coptic Gnostic Library. A Complete Edition of the Nag Hammadi Codices. Vol. 2. Koninklijke Brill NV, Leiden, The Netherlands

Meier, John P. (1991) A marginal Jew: rethinking the historical Jesus: the roots of the problem and the person, vol. 1. Publisher Double Day. New York, NY

Meier, John P. (2016) A marginal Jew: rethinking the historical Jesus: Probing the Authenticity of the Parables, vol. 5. Publisher Yale University Press New York, NY

Meyer, Marvin. Ed. (2007). The Nag Hammadi Scriptures. HarperCollins 10 East 53rd St., NY, New York 2007

Meyer, Marvin. (2005) The Gnostic Gospels of Jesus: The definitive collection of mystical gospels and secret books about Jesus of Nazareth. Publisher HarperOne, New York, NY

Meyer, Marvin W., Einar, Thomassen. (2007) The Gospel of Truth in, Meyer, Marvin W., Robinson, James M. The Nag Hammadi Scriptures: The Revised and Updated translation of Sacred Gnostic Texts Complete in One Volume. HarperCollins. 10 East 53rd St., New York, NY

Origen. De Principiis (2016) In, Schaff, Philip., Ed. The Complete Ante-Nicene, Nicene and Post-Nicene Collection of Early Church Fathers: Cross-Linked to the Bible. Toronto, Canada. Kindle

Pagels, Elaine. (2003) Beyond Belief: The Secret Gospel of Thomas Random House, New York, NY

Panné, Jean-Louis., Paczkowski, Andrzej., Bartosek, Karel., Margolin, Jean-Louis., Werth, Nicolas., Courtois, Stéphane., Kramer, Mark. (Editor, translator), Murphy, Jonathan (translator). (1999) The Black Book of Communism: Crimes, Terror, Repression. Harvard University Press. Cambridge, Mass.

Peel, Malcolm L. (2000) treatise on the Resurrection *in*, Robinson, James M. Ed., et al. The Coptic Gnostic Library. A Complete Edition of the Nag Hammadi Codices. Vol I. Koninklijke Brill NV, Leiden, The Netherlands.

Pétrement, Simone. (1984). A Separate God. The Origins and Teachings of Gnosticism. HarperCollins, Scranton, Pennsylvania

Pew Research Center. (2013) Religion & Public Life. A Portrait of Jewish Americans. http://www.pewforum.org/2013/10/01/chapter-4-religious-beliefs-and-practices/ (Accessed 2018)

Polkinghorne, John. (1998) Science and Theology: An Introduction Fortress Press Box 1029 Minneapolis, Minnesota

Polkinghorne, John T. (2002) The God of Hope and the End of the World. Yale University Press. Published by RR Donnenlly and Sons, Harrisonburg, Virginia

Polkinghorne, John T. and Beale, Nicholas (2009) Questions of Truth. Published by Westminster John Knox Press, Louisville, Kentucky

Polkinghorne, John and Beale, Nicholas. (2010) Testing Scripture: A Scientist Explores the Bible by John Brazos Press a division of Baker Publishing Group. Grand Rapids MI

Polkinghorne, John. (2014) http://www.franciscans.org.uk/franciscan/franciscan-september-2012/a-destiny-beyond-death-heaven-john-polkinghorne *Accessed 4-9-2014

Polkinghorne, John. (2012) God and the Scientist: Exploring the Work of John Polkinghorne edited by Fraser N. Watts, Christopher C. Knight. Ashgate Publishing. Burlington, VT

Radin, Dean. (2019) Selected Psi Research Publications

http://deanradin.com/evidence/evidence.htm (Accessed 2 1 2019)

Radin, Dean. (2013) Supernormal: Science, Yoga, and the Evidence for Extraordinary Psychic Abilities. Crown Publishing House a division of Random House. New York, NY

Radin, Dean. (2018) Real Magic. Crown Publishing House a division of Random House. New York, NY.

Robinson, James M., Hoffmann, Paul., Kloppenborg, John S., Moreland, Milton C. (2000) The Critical Edition of Q with Publisher Fortress and Peeters Press. Minneapolis

Robinson, James M. Ed. (2000) The Coptic Gnostic Library. A Complete Edition of the Nag Hammadi Codices. Vols 1-5. Koninklijke Brill NV, Leiden, The Netherlands.

Schaff, Philip., Ed. (2016) Origen. De Principiis In, The Complete Ante-Nicene, Nicene and Post-Nicene Collection of Early Church Fathers: Cross-Linked to the Bible. Toronto, Canada. Kindle

Philip Schaff. Origen. (2016). The Complete Works of Origen (8 Books): Cross-Linked to the Bible . Amazon.com. Kindle Edition.

Saunders, Craig David. (2021). A Thesis submitted for the degree of Doctor of Philosophy. A Mediator in Matthew: An Analysis of the Son of Man's Function in the First Gospel. (Accessed 5 11 2021) https://core.ac.uk/download/pdf/83948986.pdf

Schoedel, William. 1980. 'Gnostic Monism and the Gospel of Truth' in The Rediscovery of Gnosticism, Vol.1: The School of Valentinus. edited by Bentley Layton. E.J.Brill. Leiden.

Schwartz, Gary E. (2011). The Sacred Promise. Atria Books Division of Simon and Schuster. New York, NY.

Schwartz, GE. (2011) Photonic Measurement of Apparent Presence of Spirit Using a Computer Automated System. Explore: The Journal of Science and Healing 7(2) 100-109 DOI: 10.1016/j.explore.2010.12.002

Schwartz GE. (2019). A computer-automated, multi-center, multi-blinded, randomized control trial evaluating hypothesized spirit presence and communication published online ahead of print, 2019 Nov 16. Explore (NY). 2019;S1550-8307(19)30552-X. doi:10.1016/j.explore.2019.11.007

Smith Andrew P. (2015) The Secret History of The Gnostics. Their Scriptures and Beliefs and traditions. Published by Watkins Media Limited. London, UK

Stapp, Henry P. (2015) A Quantum-Mechanical Theory of the Mind/Brain Connection in: Kelly, Edward F., Crabtree, Adam., Marshall, Paul., Eds. (2015.)

Beyond Physicalism: Toward Reconciliation of Science and Spirituality. Publishers Rowman & Littlefield. Lanham, Maryland.

Stark, Rodney. (2016.) Bearing false witness. Debunking centuries of anti-Catholic history. Templeton Press. West Conshohocken, PA

Tillich, Paul. (1951) Systematic Theology, vol. 1: Reason and Revelation and Being and God. University of Chicago Press. Chicago, Il.

Tillich, Paul. (1952) The courage to be. Yale University Press, Binghamton, New York

Tillich, Paul. (1957) Systematic Theology, vol. 2: Existence and the Christ. University of Chicago Press. Chicago, Il.

Turner, John., Meyer, Marvin W.; Robinson, James M. (2007) The Secret Book of John in: The Nag Hammadi Scriptures: The Revised and Updated translation of Sacred Gnostic Texts Complete in One Volume. HarperCollins. New York, NY

Utts J, Patricia. (1996). An assessment of the evidence for psychic functioning. J Sci Explor. 1996;10(1):3-30.

Waldrop, Mitchell M., Computer modelling: Brain in a box. Nature 482, 456–458 (22 February 2012) doi:10.1038/482456a)

Waldstein M., Wisse FW. The Apocryphon of John. (1995). In Robinson, JM., Klimkeit HJ. Eds. The Nag Hammadi and Manichaen Studies. EJ Brill. Leiden, The Netherlands.

Waldstein Michael., Wisse Frederik., Robinson, JM., Klimkeit HJ. Eds. (1995.) The Apocryphon of John Nag Hammadi Codices 11,1; 111,1; and IV,1 with BG 8502,2 in: The Nag Hammadi and Manichaen Studies. EJ Brill. Leiden, The Netherlands.

Waldstein, Michael., Wisse, Frederik. Ed. Owens, Lance. Gnostic Society Library, The. (2018). The Secret Book of John - The Secret Revelation of John (The Short Version) from the: Berlin Codex (BG 8502, 2) & Nag Hammadi Codex III, 1 in: The Nag Hammadi Library. Available at http://gnosis.org/naghamm/nhl.html Accessed 7 18 2018 The Nag Hammadi Library

Waldstein, Michael., Wisse, Frederik. Ed. Owens, Lance. Gnostic Society Library, The. (2018). The Secret Book of John - The Secret Revelation of John (The Long Version: Nag Hammadi Codex II, 1 & Nag Hammadi Codex IV, 1) from the: Berlin Codex (8502,2) & Nag Hammadi Codex III, 1 in: The Nag Hammadi Library. Available at http://gnosis.org/naghamm/nhl.html Accessed 7 18 2018 The Nag Hammadi Library

Wilson R.McL., MacRae, George W. (2000) The Gospel According to Mary in, Robinson, James M. Ed., et al. The Coptic Gnostic Library. A Complete Edition of the Nag Hammadi Codices. Vols 3. Koninklijke Brill NV, Leiden, The Netherlands.

Wisse, Frederik. Gnostic Society Library, The. (2018).The Secret Book of John - The Secret Revelation of John in: The Nag Hammadi Library. Available at http://gnosis.org/naghamm/nhl.html (Accessed 7 18 2018)

Wikipedia Church Fathers. https://en.wikipedia.org/wiki/Church Fathers. (Accessed 4 15 2019)

The Gospel of Philip

Introduction To The Gospel of Philip

The *Gospel of Philip* and Valentinian Christianity

The Codices of the Nag Hammadi Library (and associated literature like the GMary)

The Gospel of Philip (GPhil) is one of four Gnostic-Christian Gospels from the codices of the NHL found in my book "*Holy Wisdom and The Logos of God*" (*WisdLogos*). I added to this collection of Codices *WisdLogos* a Sethian text of theology, the *SRevJohn*. It is clear in the *GPhil* that it uses some of this theology. I first published the *Gospel of Philip* (*GPhil*) in 2017 and 2019. But the first verse is now restored from the 2017 Gospel of Philip. This second edition and publication makes a few minor changes to several 'verses' as seen in the *Gospel of Philip* and the 2020 *WisdLogos* (Brantingham, James. 2017; 2020).

The *Gospel of Philip* was an ancient **Christian** *Apocryphal Gnostic Gospel* found in the great archeological discovery of 1945 in the codices of the Nag Hammadi Library. It is not a "narrative" Gospel, telling the story of Jesus Christ, but instead similar to a 'Sayings Gospel.' It is like the better known *GThom* or the hypothetical '*Sayings Gospel Q*.' Many early Church fathers treated the *Gospel of Philip* as a heretical, Gnostic text. The Church Father Epiphanius (d. 403 CE) and others discussed an *Evangelium Philippus*. There are possibly additional independent attestations of this book mentioned by Timotheus of Constantinople and Leontius in the sixth century (or from the fifth century) by Psuedo-Leontius of Byzantium; and mentioned when they discussed the *Gospel of Thomas*.

Yet this book, the *Gospel of Philip* was ignored by Iraeneus and other Heresiologists. It simply was unknown until it appeared in the *NHL* cache physically attached to and a part of the last page of the *Gospel of Thomas*! Found 'intact' for the first time in 1945 after nearly two thousand years as part of the horde of *unknown* ancient manuscripts discovered at Nag Hammadi, Egypt, the *Gospel of Philip* is available to us today for the first time after near two thousand years *in* this archeological triumph. Yet, It is not clear that the *Gospel of Philip* found at Nag Hammadi is a redacted version of the book '*Evangelium Philippus*' described by these church fathers and so this remains uncertain. (Gnostic Society Library, The. 2015; Schneemelcher, Wilhelm., Wilson, Robert McLachlan., Hennecke, Edgar. Eds. Vols I & II 1991; 2003; Smith, William., Wace, Henry. 1880.)

The title '*Gospel of Philip*' is believed to have been applied because he is the only 'Apostle' named within the text. Whether this is one of the *original* 'twelve Apostles' or Philip the (Greek) Disciple (from outside of Jerusalem), often called *The Evangelist*, is not explicit. Philip the Evangelist was one of the initial Seven Greek Disciples chosen for a specific task in the New Testament (see Acts 6). The

Seven were to care for the *Greek* poor in the original Jerusalem Christian community.

Conflation and confusion of these two "Philips" have occurred since then repeatedly, and it is outside the scope of this text to disentangle. Still, it is worthwhile for the reader to know that more than one possibility exists as to which Philip the book was named after (Brown, T. Patterson. 2014.)

(See Addendum A and B after the References for the *GPhil* (2021) on Chokhmah, Wisdom, Σοφία or Sofia/Sophia and Barbēlō in scripture, with other associations through - canonical and non-canonical scripture related to 'Wisdom' etc.)

The Hebrew Bible, Tanakh, or Jewish Scriptures were translated by Jews (into Greek.) These were translated around the second century BCE and are pre-Christian Greek translations of the "word." So I have looked at this massive data and accept 'Wisdom' *was*, for all extents and purposes, as David Hart points out (at least to some Jews) 'a divinity' (Hart, David. 2017). Yet, 'Wisdom,' is '*Sophia or Sofia*' as first transliterated from the Greek. As 'Sophia' in the Wisdom (or Writings) literature (in the OT) She is personified divinity.' And She is "Wisdom" mentioned (and lightly personified) in the New Testament Letter of James. Paul makes direct statements that associate Jesus Christ and Wisdom together such as "Yeshua is the Wisdom of God" or *Christ,* the Wisdom of *God.* So, (Wisdom) or Sophia was (at least minimally) very early a part of '*the Way*' and was utilized in Yeshua's instruction to live the Torah. 'Lady Wisdom' (*Prov. 8*) or Sophia was a divinity (and worshipped) by Gnostics and many in the earliest Christian associations or ecclesia. She still so today.

In the Tanakh, or the Septuagint LXX (the Greek OT), 'Sophia' is the' living gift of or, 'expression of, the feminine presence of God Most High.' Wisdom' as *God Above God's* 'first thought' (or Forethought who is also Barbēlō needs to be explained.) Barbēlō is not found in the *Gospel of Philip* or any other text in this collection (except in the '*SRevJohn.*') But …His, God's first emanation of Spirit (the Proarchē, before the beginning) *is* Sophia (and includes Barbēlō in at least eight other Gnostic texts). Barbēlō in these many other texts is presented in diverse ways such as in the '*Pistis Sophia*'and the '*trimorphic Protennoia*' But many Gnostic texts often (with some form of equality) present Sophia, Barbēlō and or 'the Holy Spirit,' also called *the* 'Holy Mother' (or simply 'Mother') which precede the earthly incarnation of the Logos. For, it is written… She, 'Sofia,'…was, before the beginning (Prov. 8) with Me ('*God*') (Prov. 8:2) …beside 'the Way, the word' and before and during Creation (*and*) …*before* the start of the Cosmos ('even before the Universe'). And She was …with Me from before time, space and matter … before My works of old; …before I prepared the heavens.

For *Lo,* She was there in the Beginning, during the Hē Archē; before I, the Highest, established the clouds above; before I 'the One' made the fountains of the deep. And with the Logos from before time …and 'in the Beginning or Hē

Archē' when God created time, space, matter and life, into the age. And from the ages and ages past unto the Age. And will be with Me Into the Ages and Ages and Ages to Come ('unto eternity')! She, is **'Yoked'** to the Son (*the Logos*) as a Syzygy. And is the 'hidden Wisdom of Christ.' As it is written... She 'is the revelation of a mystery kept secret since the Age, into the Ages and Ages. A special messenger and **an** *'Archangel "* (Schwartz, Gary E. 2011; 2011; 2019) Sophia is a 'Light' and a teacher (the daughter of God)! For She is a 'goddess', like-*too* a devout and pious Jew or Christian (all the 'sons and daughters of God'). Confirmed an Archangel (by Sophia) herself She brings to humanity: comfort, counsel, guidance, Truth, perception, healing, and wisdom! Many later will call Her *'the Shekhinah.'* Yet as a companion and helpmate to the Father, and His muse who helped to bring forth creation. Sophia has inspired sacred revelation. But until the Logos, she *was* a Mother without a Son. Yet is Yoked to Jesus Christ (the *'Wisdom'* of Christ)! **(see: Addendum A and B after References: covering Chokhmah, Wisdom, Sofia, Barbēlō, and Shekhinah)**.

The Codices of the NHL

The *Gospel of Philip* (GPhil) is one of four Gnostic-Christian Gospels from the codices of the *NHL* found in my book *Holy Wisdom and the Logos of God*

(*WisdLogos*). I added to this, the Sethian text of theology, the *SRevJohn*. I have already published The *Gospel of Philip* (*GPhil*) in 2017. This publication makes a few minor changes to several 'verses' in the *GPhil* (Brantingham, James. 2017; 2019).

The *Gospel of Philip* was an ancient **Christian** *Apocryphal Gnostic Gospel* found in the codices of the Nag Hammadi Library. It is not a "narrative" Gospel, telling the story of Jesus Christ, but instead similar to a 'Sayings Gospel.' It is like the better known *GThom* or the hypothetical *'Sayings Gospel Q.'* Many early Church fathers treated the *Gospel of Philip* as a heretical, Gnostic text. The Church Father Epiphanius (d. 403 CE) and others discussed an *Evangelium Philippus*. There are possibly additional independent attestations of this book mentioned by Timotheus of Constantinople in the sixth century and by Leontius (or from the fifth century) and by Psuedo-Leontius of Byzantium; and mentioned in discussing the *Gospel of Thomas*.

Yet this book, the *Gospel of Philip* was ignored by Iraeneus and other Heresiologists. **It simply was unknown** until it appeared in the *NHL* cache physically attached to, and a part of the last page of the *Gospel of Thomas*! Found 'intact' for the first time (in 1945) after nearly two thousand years as part of the horde of *unknown* ancient manuscripts discovered at Nag Hammadi, Egypt in 1945. The *Gospel of Philip* is available to us today but was only read for the first time after almost two millennia *in and after* this archeological triumph! It is not clear that the *Gospel of Philip* found at Nag Hammadi is a redacted version of the book *'Evangelium Philippus'* described by these church fathers and remains uncertain (though the "idea or concept" they read about *is* in the 1945 text). (Gnostic Society Library, The. 2015; Schneemelcher, Wilhelm., Wilson, Robert McLachlan., Hennecke, Edgar. Eds. Vols I & II 1991; 2003; Smith, William., Wace, Henry. 1880.)

The title '*Gospel of Philip*' is believed to have been applied because he is the only 'Apostle' named within the text. Whether this is one of the *original* 'twelve Apostles' or Philip the (Greek) Disciple (from outside of Jerusalem), often called *The Evangelist*, is not explicit. Philip the Evangelist was one of the initial Seven Greek Disciples chosen for a specific task in the New Testament (see Acts 6). The Seven were to care for the *Greek* poor in the original Jerusalem Christian community.

Conflation and confusion of these two "Philips" have occurred since then repeatedly, and it is outside the scope of this text to disentangle. Still, it is worthwhile for the reader to know that more than one possibility exists as to which Philip the book was named after (Brown, T. Patterson. 2014.)

A note about the *Gospel of Philip* in relation to the *NHL*

Unlike other Gnostic books, the Gospel of Philip lacks many classical "Gnostic ideas." For example, there is no clear or named evil demiurge, nor a lesser and 'evil God' of the Old Testament. As the Scholar AP Smith noted (2005) about the Gospel of Philip — "God is One!" And, the resurrection is real (in "flesh and blood," or at least as 'resurrection flesh'). As in Canonical Christianity, Jesus (or Messiah Yeshua) returns and resurrects after death. It even seems there is an agreement between the Gnostic Scholar Stephan Hoeller (2002) and New Testament Scholar NT Wright (2003). Both discuss "Christs' resurrection body" and Jesus returning alive. Both believe it was "palpable body" and both say it was not (normal human) "flesh and blood." So Paul said, "Now I declare to you, brothers, that flesh and blood cannot inherit the kingdom of God." (Berean). And they all agree that Jesus (after his death) inherited the Kingdom of God!

Similarly, in the Gospel of John, "In the beginning was the Word and the Word was with God…" Thus, there is very little contradiction between the *Gospel of Philip* and the canonical NT. But since it is not a 'history,' the Holy Spirit entering Jesus is only mentioned taking place at his Baptism. (Turner, Martha L. 1996; Bourgeault, Cynthia. 2008; DeConick, April D. 2001.)

The Gospel of Philip (the Gnostic Gospel)

1 Israelites beget Israelites. But untutored proselytes convert no one. Yet some simply know it and live it. They live the Word and Wisdom. Others see and hear and they convert.

2 Without freedom, a slave does not seek the wealth nor knowledge of their Master. But these are sought by a Son. Because the Son receives everything from His Father. Only the Son is given All. Thus the Son turned to His disciples saying, all authority in the heavens and on earth has been given to me.

3 Those who inherit the Word without Spirit, the Word is dead. And the people are dead. But, if they find the Living One and inherit Spirit then, Wisdom will raise them up and they will Live. But the living inherit the living and the dead. The dead inherit nothing. Yet if those who are dead become heirs of the Living One, they will inherit Spirit and never die.

4 Unbelievers cannot die. They are not living so, how can they die? One who finds the Messiah through faith, trusting in the Truth of His divine salvational knowledge has found 'the Way'. Yet you fear death and do not want to die. Because as Messianics now, you live. Finally living and in fullness, abundantly and in repose eternally.

5 He showed us the Kingdom. The City of God, decorated with light, filled with compassion and love. It is the Heaven above Heaven and the paradise in the All in All. In that place death is no more; life is eternal and in repose, and we look upon the face of God.

6 When we were Israelites, knowing only Torah, we were orphans. But we were turned and brought around by the Mother (or Holy Spirit). Then we became Messianic. Now we also have the Father, the Son, and the Mother.

7 Sow in winter's darkness. Reap a bountiful summer harvest. Winter is life: meaning existence here, below. Summer is finding Gnosis and Rest, living fully now then entering the Heaven above Heaven into the Life to Come. But if gathered too soon, a harvest is lost. Then neither summer nor Sabbath give fruit.

8 The Messiah came. He ransomed us, forgave and atoned for us. To those who sought him He found them. He released them from illness, from possession; even the unclean and corrupt.

The first Adam came as a man with soul; then children with souls. Yet Yeshua already pledged himself their ransom! Yet, even before the advent of Adam, God's gift of Spirit, Love and Choice was free.

After crucifixion, He entered Hell. And delivered souls; the souls of Patriarchs, Saints, Prophets and believers. Those held captive in Gehinnom, or Sheol he freed. The Savior revealed the power of God to the living and the dead and to the souls imprisoned below. He took them back and, brought goodness into their hearts, even to the wicked dead in the Abyss of Shadows. Yet he saved creation; redeemed it all - Good and Evil, Right and Wrong.

9 Light and darkness, life and death, left and right are like brothers and sisters; they are inseparable. That is why good is not always Good; evil, Evil; nor life, Living; Nor death, the final Death.

Yet, all created will decompose, returning to the source; but, those awake to the Truth know: life is without beginning or end; uncreated & eternal.

10 Words and names are a source of confusion. They turn us from the Real to the Unreal. He who hears the word God does not perceive what actually exists but, only an image or shadow of what does not exist. So too for other words. Like: Father, Son, and Holy Spirit, Life, Light, Resurrection and the Church.

These words are masks, simulations, facades of their true reality and veracity in Eternity. And so death comes to us all. Then we will know their meanings. But for now, words and names, here, and in the world — deceive us: coming from the realm of the Spirit, the wholly Other, words attempt to express the inexpressible. Not understood here they will be there. Their purpose and meaning lies in eternity. Beyond, they will be clear, and understood completely in the Heaven above Heaven.

11 There is a Sacred name the Father shares with the Son. The Holiest name — yet they do not speak it. But, the Son of God is the Father and, the Father is the Son; both Lord and God of Israel.

12 The One is singular while being many! So it is that without the Father, the Son would be unknown; and unknowable. Truth is One, but its names are many. The Holy Mother teaches us this: that the One through love is many.

13 The Adversary, fallen angels and demonic leaders deceive humanity. They take the good from these Archons and label good, evil. This Malevolent Spirit, was a hypostasis (or creation) from Sofia. But since Sofia received from the Father, Breath or Spirit she ultimately caused the breath to pass into the Earthly Adam. This gave Adam life, soul and a spark of (God's) Spirit; a spark of light. Thus spirit was finally transferred to the last Adam — the living Yeshua, filling him with the Holy Spirit, making him the Anointed One. Then the Son of Man lived among us.

Yet, the Chief Archon, and his angels, mis-appropriated names for themselves: Savior, Redeemer as did the (fallen) angels and demons. The Adversary and his angels applied these names to what was not good. Putting words into the Anointed's mouth that were deceitful. These words were joined to that which is without Truth or Goodness. And the Fallen mislead people. Even unknowing Clerics mislead with his lies and simulations, making free people slaves.

14 Angels, demons and their ideas, enslave Humanity. Because they do not want them saved. To gain freedom, humanity sacrificed living animals or precious possessions.

Yeshua was offered up dead. His Disciples scattered with his failure, or so it seemed.

But this dead man, God resurrected in glory. This confirming act of power filled his followers with *unspeakable* Hope and Joy. And *instantaneous 'Gnosis'* thus, they understood that Death is not the end — Yeshua is the Messiah, the Anointed, The One.

15 Before the coming of Christ many lacked the Bread of Life. In paradise, animals fed on plants. But for humanity there was no bread; neither the bread of life nor the bread of heaven. But then the bread of heaven even the bread of life was sent by the Holy One. He is the Bread of life, the Messiah. Yeshua is the Logos, and the knowledge of the Word and Wisdom. He is the Bread of Salvation: Gnosis for all.

16 Priests and rulers thought their power would spread Wisdom, the Word or Gnosis. Gnosis is divine knowledge and spiritual Truths, essential to salvation. Beguiled, it was not them but the Holy Mother (through them) spreading the Spirit in secret.

17 Truth is sown everywhere; but only by Grace may be discerned. But few see it early; even less at harvest.

18a Some say Mary conceived by the Holy Spirit. They misinterpret these words: a woman does not impregnate another Woman. But, by the Spirit of Holiness the Sacred Spirit (the Father) and the Holy Spirit (the Mother) conceived. Thus sanctified, they effected the conception of Yeshua within the Virgin.

Thus the Virgin was with child. Therefore Mary, no man or adulterer debased and no evil defiled. She is unbearable too many followers of "the Way".

Unstained, enduring insults, she abideth with Joseph — a compassionate, loving, and Godly man. This was incomprehensible to the Apostles, Apostolic Disciples, Israelites, and more.

Yet, some claim it otherwise; but they merely dishonor themselves. Thus the miraculous birth of Yeshua, fulfilled the scriptures. The Breath of the Father overshadowed the Holy Mother and conceived. Messiah therefore came through God Most High. And Mary was with child.

Mary gave birth to the Anointed, the Living One, Yeshua Son of God Most High.

18b Rabbi Yeshua would never blasphemy and say, My Father (meaning God) in Heaven Most High. Unless He, the One, had truly been His Father.

19 He said: Enter Heaven, the house of Our Father. But, do not ascend to boast of forbidden mystery. And returning, do not attempt to bring anything nor anyone out.

20a Yeshua *is* the hidden name: bestowed through divine revelation and including the Fathers Name (*Yeh-ua*). The Messiah in Hebrew is Mashiach. He is the Anointed or the Chosen One. But the Messiah has near equivalents in all tongues (such as the Christ, Khristós, M'sheekha; the Consecrated, the Blessed; the Hallowed One; Lord Christ). Yet all must transliterate The Name "Yeshua". In Hebrew Yeshua; in Archaic Aramaic Eashoa,'^ or in Greek Ιησούς^^

> ^(Eashoa' is transliterated as yəšwʿ but sounds like or similar to, "EEH-SHO") with the 'long E' sound of English
> ^^Greek Ιησούς for Jesus is (phonetically "Iisoús") which sounds similar to the Aramaic but is (ee-ay-sooce')!

20b The revealed name was the Nazarene. Jesus of Nazareth was the unknown; and Nazareth His secret name.

21 The Messiah has everything. He is: Man, Messenger, Mystery, and Fire.

22 Those who say the Lord died and then resurrected are confused. First he resurrected, then he died so first, you be resurrected, then you cannot die. If first resurrected, you will live as God lives.

23 No one hides a money or things of great value in a clearly visible, jeweled or pretty box. treasures are hidden in inconspicuous pots. So it is with the precious soul; Incarnated and placed in a human being, made of clay.

24 Some fear death, being revived without a body. As incorporeal spirits without flesh. Then they will be seen for what they really are. And to be fully revealed is to be terrified. They know they are neither pure, simple, holy, nor good. Neither are all sure they are truly spirit or light. They do not remember they have become spirit and when brought to Heaven, will be welcomed in; welcomed as spirit and as light. They are no longer ignorant and are therefore forgiven. Thus in their garment of light they will enter the Kingdom of God.

25 I pity and rebuke those who deny resurrection of the flesh. Who claim no flesh can inherit eternal life. Neither human flesh nor blood can inherit the Kingdom; the Life to Come. Then what is unable? Yeshua said it: he who eats not my flesh and drinks not my blood, has no eternal life within him.

What is his flesh? It is the Bread of Being (the Logos, Torah, and Gnosis). And what is his blood? (the wine) the Holy Spirit and Life. Those who have this, have spirit and life now and, in the Life to Come.

Whoever welcomes these has received real food, real drink, and a garment. But remember…

What you are — you are in a body;
What you do — you do in a body.
Arise thou now — in this body, in this life!
For everything exists in it.
Death awaits us, but God will remember.
Remember your body, soul and spirit.
And the Breath of the Blessed One
will knit you back together.
His divine gnosis and power will bring us back. And the
Logos resurrect and animate us and we will become light.

26 In this world souls wear a garment of provisional, fragile flesh. Yet, our resurrection is dependent on this fallible, corporeal body. Our soul is bound to this garment through all life: love and sorrow, health and disease, life and death. But, in the Kingdom, the Heaven above the Heavens the true God remembers us. Remembers our garment and all that the body, mind and soul was, thought, did and experienced. The God of Love raises up our garment but as a tangible garment of light. And He gives us our imperishable, purified, precious and resurrected body; and we live.

27 Revelations purify: that which is visible becomes visible; That which is secret remains hidden; Yet, if indispensable, secrets may be revealed.

28 Living Water, used in Baptism must be running water; But the Sacred, or Baptismal Fire comes from the Chrism, or Anointing.

29 Yeshua did not reveal himself as he is, but, according to the capacity of those who seek Him. He is unique to all. Yet to the great he appeared great; to the small, small; to angels as an angel and to human beings as a man.

Yet the Incarnation *is* the secret. The Word, the Logos walked and talked, lived in our skin and walked in our shoes. Yeshua, made of flesh and blood and a human being was Emmanuel living among, and with us. But high on a Holy Mountain, in Glory above Glory he appeared. The most perfect, greatest prophet, he made his disciples perfect as well, so they too could see: the face of God.

30 In an act of grace during the Lord's Supper, Yeshua prayed: Thou hast brought us together, Word and Wisdom as one. In the union of the Father's Light and the Sacred Spirit, He anointed me! The disciples pleaded, Lord guide us and guide our guardian angels too.

31 Do not despise the Shepard, the gift of God. His Wisdom leads us to the door. Through that door we enter Life and, the Life to Come. Yet one cannot approach this gate without a garment of Light. So one gains their garment through trust, piety, prayer and sacramental attainment of *Gnosis*.

32 Humanity are many, but weak and mortal. Yet those made free of spiritual blemish by the Perfect Man Yeshua, never die. Gnostic Christians know rebirth and, are reborn anew each day.

33 The Father begat a Son, but the newly born cannot Beget. Still, being birthed in the world makes one a creature. But, imparting Gnosis and Wisdom Begets a Brother; so trust, study, practice, and perform the sacraments, then You will beget spirit. God begat Yeshua, and if we trust in his Divine Salvational Knowledge He will beget us all sons and daughters of God.

34 All begotten in the world, are begotten by nature. Christian Gnostics are begotten by the Spirit and the Word. Born again through Pneuma, a Brother or Sister enters thy Realm.

35 Those nourished by the Word, from the mouth of Yeshua, gain Gnosis. From the prophet's mouth he taught and made us Perfect. We who have this rebirth are raised anew and greet each other with a kiss; the kiss of peace. We have established this construct, the ecclesia, so that the Perfect may grow.

36 There were three who always walked with the Lord. Miriam, his mother. Miriam the sister of his mother and Miriam of Magdala, his companionc and disciple. So for Yeshua, Mary was a sister, mother, companion *and* disciple.

37 We call on the Father and the Son; and the Holy Spirit which is everywhere. She is above and is below; is in the Father and the Mother and, in the hidden and revealed. The Spirit of Holiness, the Mother manifests to all; bringing Holy revelations to the world.

38 Prophets make use of spirits: demons can be blinded by the Holy Spirit and used by the wise, and by spiritual Messengers. Double crossed and deceived they are forced to help us. Because a disciple heard this he asked the Rabbi a question.

Rabbi Yeshua answered: ask the Spirit, the Holy Mother. She will answer and guide you.

39 The Apostles said to the congregation, may our offering contain His salt. And embody the Wisdom of Sofia.

40 'Wisdom' or 'Chokhmah' in the Tanakh, is called 'Sofia' in the Septuagint a 'being of divinity'. 'Sofia' is a special messenger of the 'Word and Wisdom' and like the 'son of God' is a... 'daughter of God' too. For it is written, '...*your eyes shall be opened, and ye shall be as 'gods'*. So Sofia '...who understands the all,' is like-to Elohim, and a 'goddess,' as well. *Inspiring His disciple...(Mary of Magdala)* She became a messenger, to the rest! His companion and *beloved*; a Partner, to the last. But, however viewed... Sophia is the Wisdom, and the Knowledge and, the Salt of scripture too. Void without the Son, 'the Logos' yet, found in the fullest covenant together and everywhere! Yet, the Truth! 'Wisdom, the Holy Spirit, or the Mother...' was from the first thought(s) of 'the One'. And 'She, the Holy

Spirit,' gave birth to angels, prophets and the Word, for the children of God Above God! Halleluia!

> *(see for Verse 40 the Addendum A & B on: Chokhmah, Σοφια Wisdom, Sofia, etc., after the References)*

41 What belongs to the Father belongs to the Son. But in the fullness of time, the All in All is entrusted to the Perfect Man, His Son: the Son of Man.

42 Those who are born up by the spirit know not where they go. The same Breath lights, flares and extinguishes the flame.

43 Hokhmah is the Wisdom of life. Yet Wisdom (Sofia; Ekhamoth) is the higher wisdom. A Wisdom learned that brings *Gnosis*. Therefore everything needed for salvation becomes known. It is God's Pillar of Mercy. But Ekhmoth is the Wisdom of death, the lesser Wisdom. This, *Ekhmoth* informs us all because, first you must learn this hidden Truth and then you may attain Wisdom and experience Life.

44 Some animals obey but others (wild animals) do not. Humanity works with tame animals; feeding them and themselves. So it is with Gnostic Christians; they work creatively with life and accept things as they are. Thus all things have meaning — and play their part. Good and evil, light and darkness, right and left, peace and war.

Yet, the Spirit controls, guides and tames it all as the ultimate ground of being; whether obedient or chaotic, good or evil.

45 Adam with Eve, both were created, bred, made, but not begotten. They gave birth to sons: (of flesh and blood). Adam's mortal sons begot the perishable and weak. But Cain was created through Eve's adultery, and he murdered Abel.

46 Cain, angry and jealous, is the son of the serpent, and like his father a murderer too. His father was beautiful an unearthly, human-like archangel of light. This archangel was Anointed to protect the true God and His creation. But he rebelled. He desired to be greater, more powerful than, and worshipped like God and Man. Thus he was thrown down, into the bottomless pit. For, without remorse first he lured, then raped Eve. This rape bore Cain who as a half-breed, was the son of Perdition and a Man who killed his brother.

47 God is a dyer. His royal dyes fuse with us when we are immersed below living water — and baptized. They permeate us with good and behold, sin and death is washed away.

48 It is impossible to see Reality, the Truth as it really is without becoming part of it. It is not so, living in the world.

Here you see the sun but do not become it; see the sky, the earth, or anything, but do not become it; you are separate from what you see.

But in the Other World, that hidden place; when you see something there, you becomes part of it. So,

If you see the Spirit, you become Spirit.

If you see the Christ, you become Christ.

If you see the Father, you become the Father.

In that Place one becomes all things and see themselves no more. Yet, within that world becoming all, you do not cease to be.

49 With trust, one learns how to receive; and with love, to give. In spite of that, none receives nor properly gives without love. Know and trust, then believe. Believe, then give in faith and love. You do so by the Grace of God. But, if giving in animosity this may cause a loss of faith.

50 One who does not accept Rabboni Yeshua, may be an Israelite (even a Hebrew or God-fearer). But, these possess not His salvation nor Messiah's blessed Gnosis.

51 The apostles called him Yeshua of Nazareth; Messiah. Yeshua first, Messiah last …the Nazarite and Nazarene. But Messiah can have two meanings: the anointed one or the interpreter of Truth and Law. Yet in Hebrew, Yeshua means freedom, Nazara means Truth. And thus the Nazarene is a provider of Law, Liberty, and Truth.

52 A pearl thrown in the mud does not lose its value. Anointing it with oil does not increase its value. In the eyes of its owner, its value is unchanged. So it is with the children of God; whoever or whatever, they are all just as precious to the Father.

53 If you say, I am a Jew, no one is amazed. If you say, I am Roman, no one is startled. If you say, I am a Greek, a pagan, a barbarian, or a slave, it will trouble no one. But, say: I am Christian, then (even today) immediately people come at me angry, incoherent with rage, red hot with offense, suspicious and quick to do violence. Why is this?

For we wrestle not against flesh and blood, but against principalities, against powers, against the rulers of the darkness of this world, against spiritual wickedness in high places. The entirety of Hell breaks forth upon us. Lord Messiah, when this happens, may I bear up under this attack with grace and, honor.

54 Adam, the son of Man was a sacrifice for God; God was a man-eater. After this, the sons and daughters of Man sacrificed animals. But, sacrifices, burnt offerings, the blood of bulls and lambs — what are they to Me? Says the Lord of Spirits: worship in Truth and Spirit …and let justice roll down like a river, a never-failing stream.

What is right sacrifice? A broken, repentant heart and spirit. *Not* useless human and animal sacrifice says the God above God. Do not sacrifice to ignorance and sin; which is *no* sacrifice. A loss to fallen archons, angels and empty, inconsequential 'gods'.

55 Glass and clay vessels, both pass through fire. Glass vessels may break but can be restored; shaped with spirit and breath. Discarded clay vessels, made without breath (nor even artistic exhalation) are tossed into the rubbish.

56 A donkey hitched to a mill wheel can travel hundreds of miles. But when you untie it, it is standing in the same place. There are people who walk, work or study and never get anywhere. When evening falls, these people see nothing. They see nothing on the horizon; no village, no creature, no God, no Spirit, no Higher Power, not even a messenger. They have suffered, and suffered very much, and in vain.

57 Yeshua, our Holy Communion; He is the Saving Grace of the Most High God. From Syria they call him: Yeshua, He who was spread out. The Messiah, the Logos was crucified and stretched out to the four corners of the world. Therefore, …the earth and everything evil done within it… will be crucified too.

58 The Teacher went to Levi's works; he took seventy-two nations – different skin colors, different hair colors, different eyes; and threw them all into the same vat. When he took them out they were all the same. So, the Son of Man, the Lamb without blemish shows us, we are all — human beings.

59 Sofia or Wisdom called barren (void), was in fact the Mother of Prophets and Angels. Many women disciples followed Yeshua but of those, Mary Magdalene was His closest disciple and, companion. Some Disciples felt Rabbi Yeshua loved her the most. They noted, He often kissed her . When the other disciples saw this, they asked: Why do you love her more than us? The Teacher answered: How can it be that I do not love you as much as I love her? Well, listen and understand…

60 Yeshua says: when a blind man and one who sees both walk in the dark, there is no difference between them; but when they come into the light, one sees, the other does not.

61 Yeshua says,

Blessed are you who recognize where your eternal spirit came from before you were born. For those who perceive this, may know rebirth again. So in the beginning, will it be in the end.

Look, in Paradise you will find five trees that do not change in summer nor lose their leaves in winter. And if you listen to my words these very stones beneath your feet will minister to you. Verily, verily I say, if any of you understands my words, you will not taste death.

62 The superiority of humans is not apparent - but hidden; They dominate, raise and use animals bigger and stronger than themselves. But, if humans abandon these animals they kill and eat each other. Animals do not cultivate crops (write books, music or domesticate animals). But humans do, and both eat and live.

63 If you go beneath the water and emerge with no new knowledge or faith then, you might claim you are raised from the dead. Yet, if you have not learned nor changed, and proclaim you are a Messianic, the name above names was just taken on loan. But you who have received the gifts, the Word and Wisdom of the Lord you will not be deprived of the name. But you, who have taken these on loan, must pay them back.

64 When two unite in Sacred Marriage it is transcendent. Marriage is a mystery. Joyful and ecstatic, without it, the world could not exist. Mating in marriage is therefore powerful. A sacred rite; though it may appear a debasement it is the opposite. This is the enigma.

The construct, substance, and creation of the entire system (civilization) is dependent on marriage. The stability of life and the world depend on betrothal (kiddushin) and its' consummation or sexual intercourse (called nisu'in). In fact the complexity and scheme of "the Entirety" (the Universe) was created for Anthropos; for the children of God. So, for a loving, intimate, enduring relationship in marriage and the family calls for a healthy worship the true God. This system holds great power and such intimacy is not defilement. The prophets affirm marriage is good. It is a profound, sacred rite without which the world could not survive.

65 Some Unclean Spirits are masculine, others feminine. Masculine spirits unite with females; feminine spirits mate with males. But when such spirits are uncontrolled and unopposed none are safe nor free except those united beyond, in the Bridal Chamber. In this Holiest Chamber Men, Women and God Wed together.

So, a young man or women sees the other, alone. They hunger for, seduce, and take the other. But, if a couple meet, those who trust in the teaching of Yeshua Messiah and wed, they grow together in Gnosis, and men and women will leave them in peace. Because their image is in the image of God. Such likeness no one disturbs.

Whoever is free of this world is no longer a slave. Above attraction and repulsion they master their nature, and are free of envy and live. But, if the Adversary sees such a person it will attempt to seize them. How, then, can we be free and pass by this demonic force; with its torment, terrors and cravings; for the people and things in this world? How can one escape?

(see: Gospel of Philip Verse 3 and Verse 66 below as potential answers)

66 Do not condescendingly say: We are believers, and have no fear. Do not say you are beyond contamination either in this world or, another. You say, No unclean spirits or base, daemonic desires are within us!

Yet without Yeshua and His divine salvational knowledge or Gnosis, you cry out, Save us. Hide us! The Adversary and his demonic angels stalk us! In Truth, if you possess His Word, Wisdom, Spirit and Gnosis within, no daemon can bother you.

67 Do not fear the flesh nor be thee captivated. If thou fear it, it will rule you. If thou love it, it will paralyze and devour you.

68 One is either in the world, or resurrected. If not, be baptised into rebirth now and the resurrection of your soul today. Otherwise you may be lost and end up in the middle way. Let me not be lost to the middle way! It is a place of loss, a place of fog and shadows. There, one is neither dead nor alive. And certainly not in repose.

Therefore in this world there is good and evil. But what seems good may not be good, nor evil truly evil. But, in the intermediate world, you, your memories and being are lost in shadows.

While we are yet in this world trust Yeshua Messiah. Make haste, be baptised and resurrect now. Study the Word. Gain divine salvational knowledge now; and attain it in this world. So, when free of the flesh, we will find repose and peace; and the true resurrection.

Then, we will no longer be ignorant and full of sin. With knowledge, we will not wander into the intermediate way. Without this many are lost seeking and looking for the Way; and for the Light. Thus it is good to awake now, before we go astray.

69 You, not of this world, covet neither people nor things! Stop the act, stop the sin, before sinning. Some do whatever they want, and pay no penalty… at least outwardly it seems. Some indeed desire to stop, but cannot. And they lie and seem virtuous.

Others who wish to do these things do not, and do not do the sin — at first. But, they do not benefit. Because, they yearn for it, crave it and their minds are possessed by it… a dark, unceasing impulse and desire. They feign control. It will break them.

Yet sin begins in the mind. So, first be not ignorant.

Change your thoughts then stop the sin. Change your thoughts then covet not. Coveting people, things, money, this is the source of sin. This is the true source and root of the pain. Yeshua gives you divine salvational knowledge. And so, no longer ignorant, stop the sin.

You crave, so drink Wisdom and stop your thirst. Ask for knowledge. Do not feign righteousness. Otherwise, good intentions are not enough. Find those who have this Wisdom.

Tell them anonymously your problems. Did Yeshua not say, knock and keep on knocking until you find? The answer may disturb and astonish you. But He will bring it; then knowing what to do, do it. You can become righteous and know salvation and find repose.

70 In the Spirit, the Apostle Philip had a vision: he saw people locked up in a house of worship. The house was on fire. And the people, just apparitions really — cried out in terror throw water on the fire. And they begged and begged but, the Archons would not allow it.

In the Spirit, the Apostle understood. He saw into those locked inside. Sons (and daughters) of Perdition they had made their choice. The outcome of their choice *is* the final death. Then the Archons cast their ash into the Outer Darkness.

71 The soul and the spirit are born of water and fire. And with water, fire, and light, the Son enters the Bridal Chamber manifesting to all. The fire is His anointing, His Chrism, wrapped in Light.

This is not a formless fire. But, fire whose form is stunning, unearthly and ethereal. From God's burning bush; a white light, and a Chrism from the Savior who saves your soul and life.

72 Truth did not come into the world naked and understandable. But through types and images, allegory and symbol. The world cannot receive it any other way.

There is rebirth, and an image of rebirth. Rebirth through image alone is not enough. Without trusting in His divine salvational knowledge, attaining Spirit, and undergoing rebirth, literally being born again, no one will enter the kingdom of God. Flesh gives birth to flesh, but only the Spirit gives birth to a being with spirit; flesh with spirit. Through this, the bridegroom enters the Bridal Chamber, and becomes the image of Truth.

By this rebirth we rise again, to act and live; so as to imitate His image and likeness. Accepting death of the old life, we arise and resurrect anew. Born again we are renewed, and live!

Yet some will not or cannot accept this. Nor accept baptism or the sacraments. They deny the old and the new. They publicly profess belief in nothing. To them God is no Father. Nor does God have a Son, nor is there a Spirit of Holiness. They are not believers; and certainly not Messianics.

Yet, one acquires the name Christian through the power of the cross. The Apostles called it the power of good and evil, right and left, of life and death; the union of opposites. For one who by the grace of God, trusts in the Word and Wisdom… you may turn back (and at any time) and become a believer or a Messianic again; then you are not just a Christian, but a Christ.

73 The Lord performed each sacrament as a mystery: Baptism, then Chrism, Redemption through remembrance and the Eucharist with Atonement in, the Holy Bridal Chamber.

74a The Teacher said, I come to make earthly realities like heavenly realities. The outer like the inner. And the outside like the inside, as it is in the Other, showing it by images and symbols.

74b Messianics who have received these hidden, revealed words are beyond all opposites. Beyond confusion; and enlightened.

74c Those who say there is a Man above in-the-sky are mistaken. For He who declares Revelation, the Word and Wisdom is the Lord of Heaven; the Hidden one, the One from Heaven above heaven.

Rabbi Yeshua said, My father lives in secret. So you, enter your chamber, close the door, and pray to The Father in secret. Pray from your innermost being: and know you this, Heaven is within.

Yet the Ineffable, the All in All, the Fullness, the Unknown God Most High, the One Who Is; the Beginning is the indescribable, inexpressible and incomprehensible One. He, the One Who Is does not exist as we exist, nor live and we must live nor die as we must die. The Hidden, Everlasting, and Most High Lord of Spirits is beyond time and space, life and death, being and non-being and more. Nor is He any one thing that we can describe. And, though indescribable, yet all existence, all creation, the universe and all being is reliant on the One Who Is. He *is* the primary non-dependent necessary ground of being and uncaused cause. 'For in him we live and move and have our being.' In apprehending fullness "out of nothing" one must understand the profundity and hidden wisdom of the Fecund Silence. So the Sages said. The One Who Is, who was before the beginning, spoke a Word. And, with a *single* Word created — the World, the Cosmos and the Heavens above. By His Word, the fullness filled everything: above, below, in and out and the in-between.

Then is it right to say, the inner and the outer are one?

Yet, what is outside the outer? Nothing; outside the outer nothing exists. It is the outer darkness and annihilation.

75 Before Messiah Yeshua, other messengers came forth. Yet, they could not return from whence they had come neither could they leave. They need His

help. So, those who were in Gehenna, he brought out; and some inside the Kingdom, he took to another place.

76 When Eve and Adam united, there was no death, no sin; nor original sin. Absent God's Word and Wisdom, Eve listened to the Serpent, the Liar. And expulsion and death followed. But if they Eve, Adam and God re-unite in the Bridal Chamber, death will be no more.

77 My God my God, why, O Lord, have thou forsaken me? Crucified, **He hung on the cross**. Yeshua's spirit departed. But in passing away, He came into being, at the right hand of The Father.

78 *The Teacher rose beyond death and resurrected; becoming more than he was before death. His resurrection body is whole and is the true body, our mortal body is transient;* a pale image of the incorruptible, perfect body beyond. Then we will be raised from the dead by our Savior in, the life to come.

79 The Bridal Chamber; Baptism. It is union in the Holy of Holies with God. And it is not for beasts, the habitually lawless, or those who remain constantly impure. It is for people who wish to liberate themselves from slavery to the impure; from too much covetousness or materialistic or harmful desires. And it is for those who wish to grow in humility, modesty, quietness and peace.

80 From His Breath we experience re-birth and through Messiah, He unites us with the Most Holy God. Yet, we are reborn in the ecclesia and in kinship two by two. In His Spirit we experience a new embrace; no longer are we a duality, but one in unity.

81 None can see themselves as they really are, in water or a mirror without Light. Yet, none can enter the Light without the Word. The Word is God's mirror or wisdom to reflect you as you are. So you are immersed in His Light, and then you are anointed by the Logos.

82 There were three places to Sacrifice in Jerusalem. Baptism occurred in the West called the, Holy. Resurrection and Redemption took place in the South called the, Holy of Holy. But in the third room, open to the East, was the Holy of Holies. Their, if Baptized, Resurrected and Atoned for, one enters the Holy of Holies with the High Priest. There, Sacred Marriage and Union with God was sacramentally performed in The Bridal Chamber.

83 Those who pray for the Heavenly Jerusalem, pray for the New Jerusalem. These Saints pray in the Holy of Holies, the Bridal Chamber. What is this Bridal Chamber, the New Jerusalem, but a place of trust and faith in God? It is an Icon of our union beyond understanding; here the veil was torn from top to bottom, here the dead arise and awaken.

84 The temple veil though torn from below, was ripped apart from top to bottom; where the low and the dead arise and awaken. So from below they rose up

and entered the Bridal Chamber. And seeing into it, they recognized and glimpsed their true image. In the Heavenly Chamber, in the Temple of Heaven Most High; in the Holy of Holies dwelt their icon, image and likeness. There their true spirit resides with the true God.

85 The Adversary and his Powers can not see nor restrain those clothed in the spiritual garment of perfect Light. One shall enter the life to come, invisible through this light. Leaving darkness, they will cross the threshold to the Lord of Spirits. And in the mystery of God's Love enter into Union and in a Sacred Embrace with the Truth Above.

86 Eve was separated from Adam and, no longer yoked together she united with him in the Garden but, not in the Bridal Chamber; and so without the blessing of God. This separation was the true origin of death and is why Adam and Eve and their progeny die. For dust thou art, and unto dust shalt thou return.

But when Messiah comes wounds will be healed. The Way back to the Highest Heaven taught by Eve to Adam. Eve, as the Epinoia of God (His "after thought") brings Wisdom to Adam. She brings the divine salvational knowledge from the Messiah. Thus if one consummates a hallowed marriage in the Bridal Chamber this yoking and union is protected by guardian angels. And you, married in the Holy of Holies — through divine salvational knowledge will never die.

87 Adam's soul was animated by his Mother (through the Holy Breath). But when his soul and spirit reunited with his Mother he had not yet heard the Logos. Yet, Adam did unite with his wife Eve; with Wisdom in the Bridal Chamber, then he spoke the Word. The powers and principalities recognized immediately that this man was superior to them all. Yet in Hell demonic Shadows, Archons, and the demiurge Satanael began to plot. Jealous, they plot violence to the sons and daughters of Man.

88 On the banks of the Jordan River, Yeshua manifested His life, the Sacred Spirit and the Kingdom of YHWE and the fullness of God in Heaven Most High. Yet, even before creation the One manifested His love, anointing His Son Yeshua, who made atonement who gives us his Word and Wisdom. Then we are baptized, sinless, and at last fully conscious and aware. We know that Messiah Yeshua and his Word and Wisdom eternally offers salvation for all. The only Son, Begotten not created redeems us all.

89 Can we speak about the hidden mystery? The mystery of the Virgin Mother with child; yet Mary knew not Joseph nor any man. How can this mystery be understood? Here is how:

Ruah Elohim, the breath of God, hovered over creation. Then the Spirit of Holiness, the Father's Pronoia or forethought became His will and He emanated the Holy Mother. She, the Mother and Holy Spirit was providentially wise and is the benevolent Spirit of God. She hovered above the deep.

The Father then descended to the Bridal Chamber, the Holy of Holies. *There the Bridegroom and the Bride, the Holy Father and Holy Mother brought Messiah into being as the Logos and Wisdom of God. That day, the Son of God was begotten.* The One was begotten by his true Father. And by Wisdom He was conceived by the Virginal Spirit and Holy Mother, and grew in the womb of Mary. Through this, the Word became flesh and dwelled among us. And we have seen his glory, the glory of the one and only Son, who came from the Father and the Mother, full of grace and Truth.

Mary could not conceive alone nor from another woman. No one has heard of that. But, the Sacred Spirit as the Holy Father with the Holy Mother cast a veil over her. That day Mary conceived: and Yeshua, who would be Messiah, came into the world. That day the Anointed became flesh.

90 Adam was born of two virgins; from the Breath of the Virginal Holy Mother and the virgin earth. He, Adamah was named and made, dug out from the first dust taken and molded by God. Therefore in time, the Logos was given flesh and born from that virginal spirit and dust. This will put right Adam's sin and fall; it will be wiped clean by the divine salvational knowledge brought by Yeshua Messiah.

91 In Paradise grow two holy and sacred trees. Adam ate from the tree of good and evil and begat bestial humans. These men came to worship animals; and sin increased.

But when Adam ate from the tree of life he begat humans, and they, they worshipped humans.

92 In the beginning, God created man. Then, men created gods. This is the way of the world; humans create gods and worship them. These gods, idols made of gold, silver and precious stones; are but merely images of men. They should worship the humans that made them.

93 The works of Humanity are powerful; they seem divine like signs. Yet we do not see it. You create children in His likeness and image; a miracle rightly understood. Yet this, this seems as nothing, a simple act from pleasure; a sign and a treasure. Here is the profundity of this the vision: you create in repose His image and likeness!

94 In this world slaves serve those who are free; In the Kingdom the free will serve slaves. Those who are baptized will, through re-birth here, be resurrected there. They rest in Union with the Chosen. They contemplate in tranquility, marriage in the Bridal chamber. They live now and will then in Paradise, in extraordinary and stunning peace and joy.

95 Contemplation of the Holy image, Holy things, and Heavenly glories is by reflection on the Light. Meditation can move one into the Heaven above Heaven. Then with the Hidden, Holy Saints the Perfect will feel ecstasy and bliss. In the

Bridal Chamber above is the unutterable, ineffable experience of being in the presence of God. In the Heavenly Bridal Chamber one sees God, and lives. Beyond suffering and death, they will dwell in the All in All without deficiency and in fullness.

96 One immersed below water, she the Messiah will ransom. Her ignorance and her sins forgiven. As a Messianic, and Israelite when baptized, she will not go through the second and final death but, will be raised up to a rebirth. Raised to the true "resurrection" her soul will resurrect while still in this world; in this life. We were buried therefore with him by baptism, in order that… by the glory of the Father, we too may arise anew and walk in a new way of life…

One who trusts in Messiah Yeshua, the Redeemer, is rightly led and will attain to divine salvation and knowledge. The Lord will make her Righteous. And Justified, her penance paid in glory… she will throw off all deficiency, and through Gnosis enter Paradise now, and the true Resurrection in the Life to Come.

97 Those who say we must first die and then resurrect are misguided. First, our souls must be raised up in this life, now. If not, then after death we receive nothing at all; but those who go under the water know a re-birth. They are reborn by baptism, and resurrect from death like Yeshua. Then beyond mere human experience begins our spiritual and messianic life. Yet after death, we will live — as God lives!

98 The Apostle Philip says Joseph, father of Yeshua grew trees in his garden; a grove for carpentry and work. Yet in horror and shock, they hung his son on a tree. And made the Cross — from Joseph's own grove. Yeshua was nailed to that tree but He became the precious fruit of God's proclamation; the Word and Wisdom of the One true God. Then the Hidden was revealed.

After His resurrection Yeshua Messiah's word was published; a book of His oracles to show us the Way; the way to the Messiah, Yeshua of infinite sweetness. He taught the way, and His Way is the Truth: that the Father is in us and we are in him.

In paradise this tree is the tree of Life. And the Chrism from that tree anointed Messiah Yeshua before His death; but after death came the Resurrection. The Messiah raised from the dead and alive again, resurrected in Power by the mighty hand of God.

99 Our world is an eater of souls. Though Lord Messiah and we, are not of this world, yet it is here we will be consumed. Consumed by the loss of others, by age, disease and darkness and finally we too will die. So feed on the Truth, and, fed by Truth: you will live.

Yeshua came from that realm that is not of this world. His disciples cried, Lord, we don't know where you are going, so how can we know the way?

Yeshua said to him: I AM the Way and the Truth and from me comes divine salvational knowledge, *Gnosis*, and life eternal...

100 God created a Paradise. Humanity lived in that Garden as an image of God. There, there were trees of 'Good and Evil' and of 'Knowledge and Wisdom'. Yet the immortal Adam and Eve were instructed, you may eat from any tree but, not from The tree of Knowledge. Even in Paradise Adam and Eve were divided; then in disobedience ate from the tree of Knowledge. They followed the Serpent's advice who said, you will be like gods; you will know all things, and surely you will not die! In the end, haven eaten from the tree of Knowledge (as Solomon said) the tree of Happiness and Unhappiness, they were expelled from paradise and Adam would die.

Yet outside of Paradise, this tree helped regain divine salvational knowledge. It opened doors to comprehension, and spurred the Oracles of the Torah; and brought the Word and Wisdom through all of revelation and inspiration by the New Covenant of the Logos.

Yet, this did not prevent evil nor guarantee good. Eating from it exposed them to guilt and to the fear of death for those who read, mis-use or misunderstand the tree of Knowledge. For when God said, eat this, but not that, this began free will and all of its' consequences. With choice, they disobeyed. And that led them to expulsion and to their graves.

One must be guided when eating from the tree of knowledge. Only then may it help gain the true Word and the true Wisdom; then those who do this will attain to divine salvation. Finally with knowledge they will learn that, no human can avoid all evil nor establish everlasting good; only Messiah.

101 Anointing with oil is even more important than baptism. When anointed, we receive Chrism. That is, we become fully Christian or Messianics. Christ (the Messiah) means the Anointed one. The Father gave unction, the sacrament of Chrism when He anointed the Son. The Son anointed the Apostles; the Apostles anointed us. Thus whoever is anointed already partakes in the Fullness, and is allowed into the Bridal Chamber and the Realm of Heaven.

Resurrected now, they find rebirth and live. In life after death, that is when entering the Life to Come, their spirits will be hidden, protected and secure. Under the arms of the Cross and in the Light of the One, they will ascend to the Sacred Spirit, and to the God of Love.

102 The Father is in the Son, the Son is in the Father; Such is the Kingdom of Heaven.

103 The Lord said it rightly; some enter heaven laughing. Because, after baptism a Christian (even more so the Gnostic Christian) sees this fallen world and death, so feared as the small transitions that they really are. And sees to what they are not, and laughs. One cannot fix this Fallen World, so remember who,

what and where you came from and, to who, what and where you hope to return!

104 Likewise, do not mock the Bread, the Chalice, or the Chrism. Yet the Bridal Chamber (union with God in the Holy of Holies) is the highest Sacrament of all.

105 The world came into being through the ignorance of an Adversary. He created Adam and meant to make him imperishable and immortal. Yet he failed for, neither Adam nor the world are imperishable nor incorruptible. What we call the world — is not the Real world. If we could see it with the eyes of God, the Eternal who sustains it, we would see the things of this world as they really are. The fall consists in missing this vision for, this ignorance is the cause of sin: because the world has always been transient, perishable and corruptible. The Heaven above Heaven and the true God above God cannot receive corruptibility. Therefore, one must be grounded in Yeshua, His divine salvational knowledge and in all the scriptures and sacraments. Only these sons and the daughters of the Son of Man are imperishable (as the true children of God). But if one cannot receive the Truth here, how much more will they not receive it there?

106 The Cup of Christ contains wine and water. These are symbols of blessing and prayerful thanksgiving. We give thanks, over the wine (His blood) and the water in the wine (the Holy Spirit). It is shared in prayer with the Perfect Man (Messiah). To drink of this, ends our thirst for Spirit. Then we can become Perfected (a Spiritual Messianic) too.

107 *The water of life moves in and over a body. We must be baptized in water (and by Fire) or Chrism. Then, given our garment and clothed by The Perfect Man, Yeshua,* the Living One, we are baptized naked. That is we confess secretly and privately to another, what and who we really are. Thus are we clothed immediately in a Perfect and Resurrected Body even then, in the Bridal Chamber.

108 A horse begets a horse, a human begets a human, a God begets a God. The Bridegroom and Bride, sons and daughters of God are the children of God. And they are the body of the Congregation — reborn in the Bridal Chamber. The law says, a Jew cannot be born of a "Greek" mother. Nor can a man convert to Judaism (without full circumcision). Yet both are Israelites and chosen; Messianic and Jew.

Israelites descend through Abraham. But Messianics are adopted as the children of Abraham, yet ancient Gnostic revelations say, the chosen also descend through Seth. Thus the seed of Adam's third son were chosen too. Like Abraham and his family, Sethians were an earlier community of the elect. Noah gave birth to Seth and through him to Shem, Shem to Arpachshad, Arpachshad to Abraham, Abraham to Isaac, Isaac to all of Israel and all Israelites though Jacob. Through them both (Seth *and* Abraham) came Yeshua Messiah. Lord Messiah, the Logos and Wisdom of God.

Seth too was anciently a God Fearer, before Abraham and from the beginning. They too, Sethians, strove with God and men, and prevailed. They were called by God and the Holy Spirit to worship, and worship in spirit and in Truth. They came forth by the Wisdom of the Sacred Spirit and were anciently the Chosen Ones. Called the Unshakable People, and the true and Faithful, later, Sethians became Christians; and, as with Jews, a part of Israel. Sethians are sons and daughters of the Perfect Man (God); and (as Christics) through Yeshua… sons and daughters of the Son of Man. They came from the First *and* the Last Adam; and through an Immortal Perfect Man. All from God; and all, like Yeshua called to love.

109 Christian men and women, metaphorically but physically are seen as strength and weakness and are blessed in mating. Mating, marriage, in the Holy in the Bridal Chamber brings *their* strengths and weaknesses together; but in the Holies of Holies in the Temple Space.

It is Holy too in the Other realm, in the Life to Come. There exists, a likeness or *image* of union, of mating, but it is far superior to carnal mating below. Ordinary, commonly spoken words cannot suffice to give an explanation of this extraordinary union in Heaven above.

But there is a type of union in Heaven, transcendent even above mating above or below. This is the union that can change destiny. So here and above you will no longer be one but two; but paired as one in Heaven. This transcendent pairing and intimacy is like the yoking of Yeshua and Sofia; the Son of Man yoked with the Wisdom of the Holy Spirit is beyond all human comprehension.

110 This one believes, that one does not; even so they live together and are unified. Though no longer two but one, yet Flesh and blood cannot enter the Kingdom.

111 Though they possess everything they want, *they do not know themselves.* In this way they are deficient. In fact, they have everything and more than they need. Yet, despite this they enjoy little, or nothing in life. Why? Because… they do not know Wisdom nor the Word and for that reason, themselves. Yeshua said it, You shall know the Truth, and the Truth shall make you free.

112 Clothed in a garment of Perfect Light, one becomes undetectable and imperceptible. Cloaked in this Perfect light, the Elect, Anthropos or Spirituals are invisible and may return to the Upper Highest Aeon and to Heaven in the Kingdom of God. Clad in this garment, they cannot be seen. For if seen, the Fallen would grasp them, hold and imprison them.

But by His Word and Wisdom they have found peace and upon death leave in assurance they will dwell with Yeshua. They will repose in spiritual union. Thus shall they come forth after death, ascending to the Pleroma; up and out of the world. Perfected sons and daughters of the Bridal Chamber.

113 Before leaving this life, we must receive His Breath, the Spirit of God. Yet, if Perfection is received here, then we will rest in peace there. There, is the Perfect light, the Invisible Spirit; yet some persist and reject this. Yeshua (only) knows their end.

114 Blessing bread, consecrating wine. *All that the Holy Saints' touch is purified. Their Holiness sanctifies everything, when performing a Thanksgiving or the Eucharist.*

115 Yeshua blessed the living water of baptism and *death* was poured away. After baptism, one is raised to life anew. The spirit of the world and our old life is poured out and away. But the wind of the world blows cold in winter and reminds one of death. But the Holy Breath of the Father, like the warm breeze of summer is *life*.

116 Whoever has attained Salvation through divine Knowledge is enlightened. Enlightened by the Wisdom and Truth of Yeshua, Messiah. They are perfected and free. No longer ignorant they are declared spiritual; not guilty, and justified before God as Israelites who follow 'the Way'. They are followers of the divine Word and Wisdom (*Gnosis*) of Lord Christ. These will return from where they began: from the Heaven above Heaven and to the true God above.

Christian Gnostics (who stop study, fellowship and prayer) may forget and slip back into ignorance and sin. They can descend into serious transgression, becoming slaves of sin again through ignorance.

Some Elect or Spirituals, even having gained Gnosis before death, linger. They could ascend to Heaven and Repose but through compassion, though already free and liberated, choose to remain here and help those enslaved to ignorance.

What should those who return to ignorance do? Yeshua said it, You who seek, must keep seeking until you find. When you find, you will be disturbed. Disturbed you will be astonished. Then you will be lifted up by the Spirit and find life. Then you will attain and know divine salvation and peace. He said it, ... wake sleeper, arise from the dead, and let the glory of the Lord shine upon you.

117 Finding real love, as bond-servants to Truth we remain to help others enslaved to ignorance (and therefore to sin). We must trust in His salvational knowledge: then we can love, give, serve and free others and ourselves, from hatred and fear. The Messiah said, all that I have *is* yours, and all that you have *is* mine; and glory comes to me through you, the Elect.

118 Spiritual Love is intoxicating and, a balm; those so anointed rejoice. And, even those who do not believe yet who live aside this community, rejoice. For they benefit from proximity. But, if the Anointed, the Perfect depart, so too does their Holy peace. Then the community is filled with unbelievers and natural law.

No more wine and oil for the wound, nor binding up the broken. No longer is their civility and peace; nor the love that heals a multitude of sin.

119 A woman's children resemble the man she loves; from her husband, they resemble him; from another, the lover. If married, and a man or a woman unites out of obligation, their heart may be with another. Yet, even if conception comes from duty alone, renewed vows of faithfulness and love may lead and teach real, spiritual love.

After all, the children conceived are an image and likeness (the Icons) of God. If the parent is a believer and spiritual, but yet cares for their unfaithful spouse, there is a choice. The best choice may be an obedient act of loving reconciliation which may teach their children and their grandchildren, even their spouse real love.

Yet, as you who love the Son of God, do not love the world (nor the affair) but rather love the Lord (and your family), so what is begotten resembles the Lord.

120 Humans mate with humans, horses with horses, donkeys with donkeys, each species with its own. But, if you behave like an animal instead of a human being…

You will be incapable of union with another rather human, or with that which is spiritual and beyond. Nor with the Lord whom is within you. One cannot unite with any of these unless you become like them.

Likewise, our intelligence seeks intelligence beyond; clarity seeks light. If you become more human, humans will love you; if thou become more spiritual, Spirit unites with you, and if you increase in Gnosis and Faith, the Logos will unite with you. Become open, and open minds will seek you out. Enlightened by *Gnosis* this transcendence will bring peace.

121 A slave made against their will when released is free. But you are free by the grace of God. However, if you choose again to sell yourself there may (ultimately) be no way back.

122 The harvest from the world is made from four elements: Earth, Wind, Water and Light. God cultivates four attributes within humanity: Faith (Pistis), Hope (Elpis), Love (Agape), and Wisdom (Sofia).

Humanity is the Earth in which Faith grows. Living Water is the Word that gives us hope; the hope we will flourish. The Breath of God, and the Love of God was implanted in us through Wisdom. And God's unconditional Love lights 'the Way'. With desire, and with fire in our breasts, we increase in divine salvational knowledge and long to return to Him and to our true home.

123 Grace was transmitted through the Logos, by the Word of Yeshua who would be Messiah. His humbleness and obedience to God made Him the Lord of Heaven above Heaven, and of all the Earth.

Beyond this, his authoritative and honest words show us who He is. Acts of love and compassion, and His signs, confirm His identity. He healed the sick, fed the multitudes, and neither harmed nor hurt anyone. Such a life could only be lived by the Perfect Man, the One like the Son of Man. He, the Logos became a human child, flesh and blood and a man who lived among us. In this world of darkness and separation, He lived and walked among and alongside us down every road.

124 Blessed is he, Messiah Yeshua. He burdens no one. His Words are life; and the hope of life! He came to the world as it is. Ask and He will come to you and will give you salvation as you are; He is the Last Man, the Perfect Man; He is the Son of Man. The Logos and the Word *and* the Wisdom of God.

125 His disciples begged, 'tell us Rabbi, how to free ourselves from blindness and sin. How can we be Holy like you? How can we know the will of Heaven and have the strength to carry it out? And Like you Lord, teach us how to be unselfish; and like you Lord, to love; and Like you Lord, to do as you do to imitate you and to trust in you Lord, Messiah Yeshua of infinite sweetness. Give us and divine salvational knowledge and, teach us to be spiritual like you Oh Lord 'on the Last Day'.

126 Above all, if it is possible for you, make no other person sad or hopeless. No matter whether they are: great or small, faithful or unfaithful. Praise and welcome those who love God and wish to do good.

Yet some do not believe and we might wish such people would find Yeshua Messiah, Salvation and Gnosis. Yet salvation is between them and God. To impart the peace of Yeshua Messiah and *Gnosis* is a gift of grace from our Savior and Redeemer. Love and belief in Yeshua Messiah… is beyond us to impart. This must come from the one who listens and learns; and listening they may turn; and turning they may hear and be saved. They must seek and keep seeking. He said it, if you seek me you will find me when you seek me with all your mind and all your heart.

Christians or Israelites are the happier people. They no longer oppress, causing others to suffer. Yet others are jealous and angry and strike out. They loathe your peace. They loathe you and, think you a fool. They covet your contentment and your happiness which to them is hateful; and they lash out. But, it is not because you are Israelites. trusting God and Yeshua and finding freedom from ignorance fills one with faith, knowledge and joy and …the peace of God, which passeth all understanding. This becomes your nature and who you are. The Lord's gift of grace to all who seek it and ask for it.

127 A great landowner had sons, servants, livestock, dogs, pigs, wheat, barley, hay, bones, meat and acorns. In his wisdom he gave to each what was appropriate. To his children, bread, olive oil, and meat. To his servants, oil and wheat; to

his livestock barley, hay and grass; bones to the dogs, acorns and bread crumbs to the pigs.

So it is with the disciples of God, when wise, they perceive the needs of each. They are not misled by outward appearance; they consider the disposition of each soul. Then attune their words accordingly.

Yet there are many humans that behave like animals; outwardly human inwardly Hylic, without a soul. The wise give acorns to pigs, barley and hay; grass to livestock, bones to dogs. But to Servants basic moral lessons, and to the Landowners' children they teach the Torah, Word and Gnosis in its entirety.

128 The Son of Man is the Son of the sons and daughters of Man, the children of God. So, the Messiah, the Son of Man who being in His very nature God, did not consider equality with God something to be used to his own advantage… Thus he came to us. As a man He walked beside us.

Messiah Yeshua, the Word, was One with God. And only a God may beget a God. But Yeshua, the Son of Man, by incarnating the very nature of a human being as a human being could, as a human create.

But he begat sons and daughters of the Son or God; that is, children of God. They, the children of God can and do create. But they also can teach and persuade by divine salvational knowledge and *beget* brother and sister Messianics, Israelites and Gnostics that are one with God. That is, people made in His Image and likeness. Imitating His Word and Wisdom; and acting out of love with care and compassion in the likeness and image of God.

129 He who creates is a creature; he who begets is a Son; He who creates cannot beget; but he who begets can create. Yet people say, He who creates, begets but a creator cannot beget a God. Only God can beget a God.

130 The Son of Man creates, breeds and, makes lower animals exist. But the son and the daughter of the Son of Man beget in privacy. If you are begotten as his children then act like and mimic Him. This is right to do openly and visible to all. Then you are not just a creature, but one who acts, loves and helps others as His Spiritually Begotten children of God.

So God created the World. But, when you, as Gnostic Christians beget, conceive in secret; hidden from the visible. And your children, will be the real children of the Son of Man.

131 None know the day when a man or woman will mate. Holy marriage should not be equated with carnal lust. It is a normal and sacramental desire. Yes, but it is a mystery: why her with him, or him with her? Why? Because society and the world are complex but no people can exist without it. Though the act appears defiling, it is not. And yet, it is only a shadow of a much stronger union and true love in Heaven above. Yet it is pure, it is a sacrament and, it is good.

A sacramental marriage must display public decorum and it should not thoughtlessly, indifferently or overtly display strong carnal affection. Even sacramentally married, such open display may cause them to be judged fornicators. Carnal-like public intimacy resembles dissolution and impurity; and if with other than the spouse, a cruel and harmful theft.

A bride may only show themselves naked or undressed to the father, mother, family or a close friend only. Others may not see nor hear the voice of the Lovers. Nor hear and see the beloved couple entwined. Nor will they breathe the perfume of their embrace.

They may imagine, long to know, and one day experience the same sacred embrace they covet. But now, though they wish to see it, or hear it they are like dogs who eat any morsel that falls from the table.

However, a Messianic marriage and union is a sacrament; a sacrament of the Bridal Chamber. Outside of this it may be no more than prostitution. Only Israelites are given this sacred marriage.

Such marriage is not only for selfish desire; nor for fleshly delight, nor only to experience joy. It is certainly not to prove ascetic ideals! But, when appropriate it may be all this and more. It is a sacrament and one of the Blessed Five Seals. It is consummated in the light, and may not be taken by force. It is not of darkness and night but rather of the daytime and the Light!

132 *Abraham rejoiced!* Blessed by the Lord he grasped the hand of the Eternal, the true, the Ultimate One. trusting he became a follower, 'one who crossed over' to follow the transcendent, Ineffable Unknown God. In the Spirit and in ecstasy and attaining Gnosis he received future revelation. ***So by God's command, and in exultation he obediently circumcised himself, his family and his tribe to show: Spirit and Wisdom come before flesh.***

133 Certain realities live if hidden; when visible, they die. People's entrails must remain inside; if exposed they die. So with the mighty Oak tree. As long as its roots are hidden, it grows and can flourish. But if it's roots are laid open this will kill it.

Thus for all things born in the world there are visible and invisible realities. If the root of evil is hidden, it grows. Thus the Baptist said… The axe has been laid to the root of the trees, and every tree that does not produce good fruit will be cut down and thrown into the fire.

The Messiah removed the root of evil in His world and took away our ignorance and fear. But, for our good, He exposed only a part. The rest we must dig out and uproot ourselves. And we must face these things and thoughts and deeds and our refusal to see and accept evil; and the unhappiness it makes in our life and, the poison in the lives for our loved ones. Yet you can only remove what you recognize is wrong.

Thus is it true for all who are born in this world. For them there are things visible and invisible. If the root of evil is hidden, it may grow and even kill. Confess it to Yeshua and another Messianic in private, then it may be controlled or destroyed. So scripture tells us to do.

If ignorance is hidden, sin will dominate. And make us its slaves. And we too shall say... for I desire to do what is good. But, I do not do the good I want, but evil I do not want to do, this I keep on doing. Like the Apostle we cry out, who will rescue me from this body of lies and death?

134 Ignorance is the mother of evil. Its' power comes from our refusal to see it. If present, it works against us. Evil is born from ignorance. Study the Holy through scripture and prayer. This alone leads to happiness when real Truth is revealed. But none can become Perfect nor find Salvation until the Word, Wisdom and the Truth are revealed.

Hidden Truth, like Ignorance, helps no one. Yet when Truth is revealed, it prevails over ignorance. Truth glorifies Wisdom. Wisdom is divine salvational knowledge, the *Gnosis* and the Logos of God. More powerful than ignorance or error, it brings joy, freedom and peace. So it is written, know the Truth and the Truth will set you free.

Ignorance is slavery, Knowledge is freedom. If we recognize Truth we realize the fruits of the Sacred Spirit. These, as it is written are... love, joy, peace, forbearance, kindness, goodness, faithfulness, gentleness and self-control. So recognize the Truth and taste real love and live.

135 Phenomenal creation reveals a world of things real and visible. Such real things seem strong and worthy. But that which is not visible, or that which appears unreal and unseen (the thing in itself, the noumenal) can be decidedly more powerful. Even that which seems unreal, weak and unworthy. Such insensible, ethereal entities like the Spirit, or God, look pitiful, illusory and inadequate. Yet, as Elijah heard and learned, the 'still small voice,' may hold the power of Almighty God; a still small voice and a 'whisper' that has won wars, toppled governments, created mighty and lasting empires.

Yet, the reality of the supernatural seems illusory, poor, deficient and even to some, a fraud. Yet, the very opposite is true.

136 Hidden, this sacrament of marriage is a metaphor or symbol of the Greatest Mystery enacted in the Temple of the true God. It is so explained and carried out in the Temple, the Holy of Holies by the High Priest, Yeshua of the true God; God alone. This Holiest of sacraments, one from the Five Seals remains a mystery. Carried out solely in the Bridal Chamber it is here that the Sacrament of Union takes place. Where Lover and Beloved (that is, Messiah and Messianics; Israelites now) vow holy matrimony, to each other and to God forever.

137 The Temple Veil concealed God and the Host of Heaven for He said, you cannot see my face and live. The veil obscures the Lord of Spirits, how He governs, and how He maintains the stability and survival of the world. He maintains the very ground of being; yet out of that silence comes a voice speaking to those below…

Today, through observation humanity peers behind the veil and sees an infinitesimal part of nature. A tiny part of the activity, the labor of the Creator.

But scripture gives divine salvational revelation. Once, much later a son of man split the least of it, an atom… and he said,

"Now I am become death, the destroyer of worlds". So at that moment he understood the power of God and, what he saw. The Creator unveiled, and revealed, and unleashed His destructive might and power. Thus he understood how things hold together. But those who saw the light unleashed… understand.

Yet, God is everywhere; here, there, up and down, in and out; and with the living and the dead. Yet He is pure Spirit and Light. He *is* the fullness with no deficiency. ***But even more so, the Lord must be worshipped in Spirit and Truth beneath the Cross.***

138 This ark will be our rescue, when the raging waters of chaos overtake us. A maelstrom is coming; and Hell itself will break out, destroying everyone and everything in its path. But the Wisdom and the Word will save us.

139 Christians, Israelites, be a nation of priests. Go within and beyond the veil; go in with the High Priest Messiah Yeshua.

Enter the Holy of Holies. Where the veil was not torn just from above nor, torn just from below but, torn from above to below so that all may view the hidden Word and Wisdom, and worship in Spirit and Truth.

With such fragile images and symbols we penetrate to the very essence of being; to the heights of Heaven above Heaven. And we find protection under the arms of the Cross. Then we too enter into the Bridal Chamber, the Holy of Holies by divine salvational knowledge and, in Wisdom and in Truth. Enter the Kingdom, and be filled with His love and power.

140 The realities of life are trivial before, the Lords' dominion and sovereignty over life, the world and the universe; His is sovereignty over every realm and over everything in the All in All.

Thus, it appears we enter the Kingdom through fragile and contemptible religious images and symbols. Yet, in the Kingdom the Pleroma, the Realm above Realms, Heaven most High…

There, is revealed the Hidden Secrets of All Truth…

There, is Glory beyond glory, and Power beyond Power…

There, is the Kingdom of God, and Heaven above the Heavens…

There, We will dwell with God in fullness in, the All in All.

The Spiritual Elect, the Pneumatics, The Perfect, the Elect passed on to us the Hidden and Divine Salvational Knowledge of Yeshua Messiah. They gave us His Words and His Truth and His Wisdom, *Gnosis*. Thus we too were invited into the Bridal Chamber — into the Holy of Holies to dwell in Repose.

141 If the Word, Gnosis remains hidden and covert. If oppression is tolerated within and without. Then unhappiness and cruelty prevails. Everything is poisoned. Malevolence scatters and divides. But, when manifest, the Word and Light from the Perfect One envelops all. Then all receive Chrism and, the God of Love frees us all; slaves and prisoners, rich and poor.

142 Any plant rooted in the earth but not consecrated by the Father, will easily pull out. In the young, passion burns by night but in the morning — the blaze is not in sight. Separated, they enter the Bridal Chamber but blessedly

there, they will again unite. Then they too may kindle the Light.

143 If one becomes with the son of Man a child of God, they may enter the Bridal chamber and receive their garment of Light. But if they do not receive *Gnosis* here, they will not receive it there, in the Life-to-Come.

Yet one who receives this light, is not visible nor can they be seized. Moreover, when they die they leave this world knowing that Truth is but an image. Neither evil daemons, fallen angels nor any being will disturb their journey Home. Today, even as you dwell in the flesh, you mix joyfully in the world. Yeshua said it… I have come that you may have life, and have it abundantly… but, be in the world but not of the world.

For these Messianics, here is a Holy Place; now, is a Holy Time. As children of God you too will enter the Bridal Chamber and there become whole, healed and at peace. In this world His Kingdom has begun; and you have already entered the Heaven above Heaven, into the Fullness, and are part of His All in All.

Freed, you no longer live in shadow but in the light. No longer trapped and hiding in darkness nor by the night; instead you are concealed in a Perfect Day and by His Holy light.

James Brantingham PhD

5 19 2021

Thousand Oaks, California

References for "The Gospel of Philip"

Akenson, Donald H. (2000.) Saint Saul a skeleton key to the historical Jesus. Oxford University Press. New York, NY

Akenson, Donald H. (2001.) Surpassing Wonder: The Invention of the Bible and the Talmuds. Chicago: University of Chicago Press

Bauman, Lynn. (2012) The Gospel of Thomas, Wisdom of the Twin 2nd Ed. Ashland, Oregon: White Cloud Press;

Barbelo or Barbēlō (2019) in: https://en.wikipedia.org/wiki/Barbelo (Accessed 4-19-2019)

Barnstone, William. (1984) The Other Bible. HarperCollins. New York, NY

Barnstone, William., Meyer, Marvin. (2003, 2009, 2011) The Gnostic Bible: Revised and Expanded 1st ed. Boston, Massachusetts, New Seeds Books.

Barnstone, William. (2009.) The Restored New Testament: A New translation with Commentary Including the Gnostic Gospels of Thomas, Mary and Judas. Publisher W.W. Norton & Co. New York, NY

Bohlig, Alexander; Wisse, Frederik. (2015) Gospel of the Egyptians in: Gnostic Society Library, The.

Bourgeault, Cynthia. (2008). The Wisdom Jesus. transforming Heart and Mind- A new Perspective on Christ and His Message. Shambala Publications Inc. Boston, MA

Brantingham, James. (2017) The Gospel of Philip. A New translation. CreateSpace Independent Pub. Amazon Digital Services LLC. Seattle, WA.

Brown, T. Patterson. (2014) The Gospels of Thomas, Philip and Truth. Available from http://www.freelyreceive.net/metalogos/files/intro.html (Accessed 5 25 2014)

Brown, Patterson Thomas. Hypertext interlinear of the Gospel according to Philip. (Coptic to English.) http://www.freelyreceive.net/metalogos/files/ph*interlin.html* (Accessed 5 25 2014)

Brown, Raymond. (1979) The Community of the Beloved Disciple, New Jersey: Paulist Press, 1979

Brown, Raymond E. (1997) An Introduction to the New Testament. Publisher Doubleday, New York, NY 1997

Brown, T. Patterson., Isenberg, Wesley W. (2015) Gospel of Phillip translations online Available at: http://gospelofthomas.nazirene.org/philip.htm *Accessed* 7-19-2015

Caruana, Laurence. (2015) The Gnostic Q Glossary of Gnostic Terms. Available at: http://www.gnosticq.com/az.text/glos.af.html *Accessed* 3 18 2015

Charles, RH. (1913) The Apocrypha and Pseudepigrapha of the Old Testament. Oxford: University Clarendon Press, New York, NY. Also available at: http://wesley.nnu.edu/sermons-essays-books/noncanonical-literature/non-canonical-literature-ot-pseudepigrapha/

Davies, Stevan. (2005) The Secret Book of John. The Gnostic Gospel Annotated & Explained. Skylight Paths Publishing. Woodstock, Vermont

Davies, Stevan. (2005) The Gospel of Philip. Skylight Paths Publishing. Woodstock, Vermont

DeConick, April D. (2001.) Brill. The true Mysteries: Sacramentalism in the "Gospel of Philip". *Vigiliae Christianae* Vol 55. No. 3 (2001) 225-261

DeConick, April D. (2017.) The Gnostic New Age: How a countercultural spirituality revolutionized religion from antiquity to today. Columbia University Press. New York, NY

DeConick, April D. (2005.) Recovering the Original Gospel of Thomas: A History of the Gospel and Its Growth. Publisher: T & T Clark. London, UK

Ehrman, Bart D. (2003) Lost Christianities: The Battles for Scripture and the Faiths We Never Knew. Oxford University Press. New York, NY. 2003

Ehrman, Bart D. (2003) Lost Scriptures: Books that did not make it into the New Testament by. Oxford University Press. New York, NY.

Ehrman, Bart. (2004) Truth and Fiction in The Da Vinci Code: A Historian reveals what we really know about Jesus, Mary Magdalene and Constantine. Oxford University Press. New York, NY.

Gnostic Society Library, The. (2015) The Nag Hammadi Library. Available at http://gnosis.org/naghamm/nhl.html (Accessed 2-7 -2015)

Hart, David B. (2017) The New Testament. A translation. Yale University Press. London, UK.

Hoeller, Stephan A. (1989) Jung and the Lost Gospels. Publisher: Quest Books Wheaton, IL.

Hoeller, Stephan A. (2002.) Gnosticism: New Light on the Ancient tradition of Inner Knowing. Publisher: Quest Books Wheaton, IL.

Hoeller, Stephan A. (2016) CG Jung and Gnostic tradition: Gnosis, Gnosticism and Jungian Psychology. The Gnostic Society Library http://gnosis.org/gnostic-jung/ (*Accessed 2/17/2016*).

Hoeller, Stephan A. (1998 and 2010). Ecclesia Gnostica A Gnostic Catechism. Publisher: The Gnostic Society Press, Los Angeles, California. http://gnosis.org/ecclesia/catechism.htm (*Accessed 5-5-2015*)

Isenberg, Wesley W. (1977) "The Gospel of Phillip (II3)," In: the Nag Hammadi Library, ed James M. Robinson Leiden: Brill

Isenberg, Wesley, W., Layton, Bentley. (2000). The Gospel of Philip. In

Robinson, James M. Ed. The Coptic Gnostic Library. A Complete Edition of the Nag Hammadi Codices. Vol. 2. Koninklijke Brill NV, Leiden, The Netherlands

King, Karen L. (2003) The Gospel of Mary of Magdala: Jesus and the First Woman Apostle. Published by Polebridge Press, Santa Rosa, California

King, Karen L. (2003) What is Gnosticism? Harvard University Press. Cambridge, MA

King, Karen. (2006) The Secret Revelation of John. Harvard

University Press. Cambridge, Massachusetts

Leloup, Jean-Yves. (2004) The Gospel of Phillip: Jesus, Mary Magdalene, and the Gnosis of Sacred Union. Rochester, New York: Inner traditions.

Leloup, Jean-Yves. (2005) The Gospel of Thomas: The Gnostic Wisdom of Jesus.Paris: Inner traditions*

Mead, G.R.S. (1892). Simon Magus. London: Theosophical Publishing Society. Mead, G.R.S. (1892). The Gnostic Society

Library. Gnosis.org

Mead, G. R. S. (1921) Pistis Sophia. A Gnostic Gospel. A Gnostic Miscellany: Being for the most part extracts from the Books of the Savior, to which are added excerpts from a Cognate literature; (English). JM Watkins London.

Mead, George Robert Stow. (2021). Fragments of a Faith Forgotten: A Contribution to the Study of the Origins of Christianity in, The Gnostic Society Library. gnosis.org (Accessed 2021) Theosophical Publishing Society: London (1900; 1906).

Meyer, Marvin (2003) The Secret Book of John *in:* Barnstone, William., Meyer, Marvin. The Gnostic Bible: Revised and Expanded 1st ed. Boston, Massachusetts, New Seeds Books.

Meyer, Marvin. (2005) The Gnostic Gospels of Jesus: The definitive collection of mystical gospels and secret books about Jesus of Nazareth. Publisher HarperOne, New York, NY

Meyer, Marvin. Ed., Turner, John D. (2007). The Holy Book of the Great Invisible Spirit (The Gnostic Gospel of the Egyptians) *in:* The Nag Hammadi Scriptures. HarperCollins 10 East 53rd St., NY, New York 2007

Meyer, Marvin. Ed., Turner, John D. (2007). The Holy Book of the Great Invisible Spirit (The Gnostic Gospel of the Egyptians) *in:* The Nag Hammadi Scriptures. HarperCollins 10 East 53rd St., NY, New York 2007

Meyer, Marvin W., Poirier, Paul-Hubert. (2007) Thunder, Perfect Mind *in:* The Nag Hammadi Scriptures. HarperCollins 10 East 53rd St., NY, New York 2007

Meyer, Marvin W.; Robinson, James M. (2007) The Nag Hammadi Scriptures: The Revised and Updated translation of Sacred Gnostic Texts Complete in One Volume. HarperCollins. 10 East 53rd St., NY, New York 2007

Pagels, Elaine. (1979) The Gnostic Gospels. Random House, New York, NY,

Pagels Elaine. (1992) The Gnostic Paul: Gnostic Exegesis of the Pauline Letters. Published by Continuum International Publishing Group. New York, NY

Pagels, Elaine. (2016) "Ritual in the Gospel of Philip". (2016) Princeton University" http://ww3.haverford.edu/religion/courses/222a/PagelsGPhil.pdf *Accessed* 6 30 2016)

Pagels, Elaine. (2003) Beyond Belief: The Secret Gospel of Thomas Random House, New York, NY

Pétrement, Simone. (1984). A Separate God. The Origins and Teachings of Gnosticism. HarperCollins, Scranton, Pennsylvania

Pistis Sophia. (2019) Wikipedia https://en.wikipedia.org/wiki/Pistis_Sophia

Accessed (11/23/ 2019)

Robinson, James M. (1990) The Nag Hammadi library, ed. James M. Robinson. Harper, San Francisco

Robinson, James M., Hoffmann, Paul., Kloppenborg, John S., Moreland, Milton C. (2000) The Critical Edition of Q with Publisher Fortress and Peeters Press. Minneapolis.

Rupp, Joyce. (2019) Desperately seeking Sofia. The biblical Sofia is more than metaphor; she is an expression of the presence of God.

US CATHOLIC: Accessed (3 21 2019)

Shekinah in: (2019) Wikipedia, the free encyclopedia https://en.wikipedia.org/wiki/Shekhinah#In_Judaism (accessed 23 21 2019)

Schipper, Bernd., Teeter, D. Andrew Editors. (2013) Wisdom and Torah. The Reception of 'Torah' in the Wisdom Literature of the Second Temple Period. Vol 63; 2013

Schneemelcher, Wilhelm., Wilson, Robert McLachlan., Hennecke, Edgar. Eds. (1991) New Testament Apocrypha I: Writings relating to the Apostles; Apocalypses and Related Subjects. Westminster John Knox Press. Louisville, KY. 1991

Schneemelcher, Wilhelm., Wilson, Robert McLachlan., Hennecke, Edgar. Eds. (2003) New Testament Apocrypha II: Writings relating to the Apostles; Apocalypses and Related Subjects. Westminster John Knox Press. Louisville, KY. 2003

Schneemelcher, Wilhelm., Wilson, Robert McLachlan., Hennecke, Edgar. Eds. (1991; 2003)

Schwartz, Gary E. (2011). The Sacred Promise. Atria Books Division of Simon and Schuster. New York, NY.

Schwartz, GE. (2011) Photonic Measurement of Apparent Presence of Spirit Using a Computer Automated System. Explore: The Journal of Science and Healing 7(2) 100-109 DOI: 10.1016/j.explore.2010.12.002

Schwartz GE. (2019). A computer-automated, multi-center, multi-blinded, randomized control trial evaluating hypothesized spirit presence and communication published online ahead of print, 2019 Nov 16. Explore (NY). 2019;S1550-8307(19)30552-X. doi:10.1016/j.explore.2019.11.007

Smith, Andrew Philip. (2002). The Gospel of Thomas. Publisher Ulysses Books, Berkeley, CA

Smith, Andrew P. (2005) The Gospel of Phillip Annotated & Explained. Woodstock, Vermont: SkyLights Path Publishing

Smith, Andrew Philip. (2009) A dictionary of Gnosticism. Quest books. Wheaton, IL.

Smith Andrew P. (2015) The Secret History of The Gnostics. Their Scriptures and Beliefs and traditions. Published by Watkins Media Limited. London, UK

Smith Andrew P. (2015) The lost history of the Cathars. Their Scriptures and Beliefs and traditions. Published by Watkins Media Limited. London, UK

Taussig, Hal. Ed. (2013) A New New Testament. A bible for the twenty-first century. Houghton Mifflin Harcourt. New York, NY

Tillich, Paul. (1951) Systematic Theology, vol. 1: Reason and Revelation and Being and God. University of Chicago Press. Chicago, Il.

Tillich, Paul. (1952) The courage to be. Yale University Press, Binghamton, New York

Tillich, Paul. (1957) Systematic Theology, vol. 2: Existence and the Christ. University of Chicago Press. Chicago, Il.

Turner, Martha L. (1996) The Gospel According to Philip: The Sources and Coherence of an Early Christian Collection (Nag Hammadi and Manichaean Studies). Publisher EJ Brill, Leiden, The Netherlands

Turner, John D. (2016) trimorphic Protennoia; the Book of Thomas; Zostrianos; Marsanes; the Interpretation of Knowledge; Allogenes in: The Gnostic Society Library. http://gnosis.org/naghamm/trimorph.html (Accessed 2/17/2016)

Vincent, Martine., Godet, Frederic., Mackintosh, Hugh.,Campbell John. (2019) The Meaning of 'Logos' in the Prologue of John's Gospel. (Accessed 3 21 2019) http://www.bible-researcher.com/logos.html

Williams, Frank. (2008; 2009) The Panarion of Epiphanius of Salamis. Published by Brill. Herndon, VA (for electronic books and journals: (available: booksandjournals.brillonline.com;)

Williams, Michael A (1999) and Rethinking "Gnosticism": An Argument for Dismantling a Dubious Category. Princeton, N.J.: Princeton University Press

Wright, NT. (2003) The Resurrection of the Son of God. Fortress Press. Minneapolis, MI

Wikipedia: Barbelo

Addendum A on Chokhmah, Wisdom, Σοφία or Sofia/Sophia and Barbēlō in scripture, with other associations (canonical and non-canonical scripture related to 'Wisdom' etc.)

The Hebrew Bible, Tanakh, or Jewish Scriptures were translated by Jews (into Greek.) These were translated around the second century BCE and are pre-Christian Greek translations of the "word." So I have looked at this massive data and accept 'Wisdom' *was,* for all extents and purposes, as David Hart points out (at least to some Jews) 'a divinity' (Hart, David. 2017). Yet, 'Wisdom,' is '*Sophia* or *Sofia*' as first transliterated from the Greek. As 'Sophia' in the Wisdom (or Writings) literature (in the OT) She is personified divinity.' But as She is "Wisdom" mentioned (and lightly personified) in the New Testament Letter of James. But Paul makes direct statements such as "Yeshua is the Wisdom of God" (or *Christ* the power of *God*). So, Sophia is part of '*the Way*' and was utilized in Yeshua's instruction to live the Torah. Lady Wisdom or Sophia was a divinity (and worshipped) by Gnostics from their earliest Christian association. She still is today.

In the Tanakh, or the Septuagint LXX (the Greek OT), 'Sophia' is the' living gift of' or, 'expression of, the feminine presence of God Most High.' Wisdom' as *God Above God's* 'first thought' (or Forethought who is also Barbēlō) …His first emanation of Spirit (before the beginning) and *is* in Gnostic texts 'the Holy Spirit,' also called *the* 'Holy Mother' (and the term 'Holy Mother' precedes the earthly incarnation of the Logos). For, it is written…' She, 'Sofia,'…saith that, Proarchē, (Prov. 8) was with Me (Prov. 8:2) …beside 'the way, the word' before Creation (*and*) …*before* the beginning of the Cosmos ('the Universe'). And She was …with Me before time …before My works of old; …before I prepared the heavens.

'*God*' says, for *Lo,* She was there; before I, the Highest, established the clouds above; before I made the fountains of the deep. And with the Logos from the Proarchē …*before* the beginning. And from the ages past into the Age. Into the Ages and Ages and Ages to Come ('into eternity'). She is **'Yoked'** to the Son (the Logos) as a Syzygy. She is the 'hidden Wisdom of Christ.' *As it is written…* She 'is the revelation of a mystery kept secret since the Age out of the Ages and Ages. A special messenger and **an Archangel** (Schwartz, Gary E. 2011; 2011; 2019). And is a 'Light' and a teacher (a daughter of God). Or a '*goddess'*, like-*too* a devout and pious Jew or Christian. *Confirmed an Archangel (by Sophia) herself* (see Gary E. Schwartz below)' bringing to humanity: comfort, counsel, guidance, Truth, perception, healing, and wisdom! Many will later call Her 'the *Shekhinah*.' Yet as a companion and helpmate to the Father, His muse who helped to bring forth creation. Sophia has inspired sacred revelation. But until the Logos, she *was* a

Mother without a Son. Yet is Yoked to Jesus Christ (the '*Wisdom*' of Christ)! (see: Addendum A and B after References: Chokhmah, Wisdom, Sofia, Barbēlō, and Shekhinah)

The 'altered verse':

59 …Some Disciples felt Rabbi Yeshua loved her the most. They noted, He often kissed her… ('mouth or lips' removed; it is not in in the Coptic) but used by J-I Leloup (2004) and TP Brown (2014) and others b When the other disciples saw this, they asked: Why do you love her more than us? The Teacher answered…

See: Addendum B below for Chokhmah, Σοφια, Sofia or Sophia, Wisdom, Barbēlō and the Shekhinah in GPhil (as well as the original verses in 2017)

References see: Introduction to tr?

Union

Saving this relationship is Jesus's "Sacred Union or Yoking" (the most intimate merger or Syzygy) in the Bridal Chamber with Mary of Magdala. In fact Geoffrey Smith (2019) used the word "Union" to describe Jesus' and Mary's relationship (although Smith leaves it at that). Some suggest memorizing Verse 73 (and when asked to, to be able to repeat the essence of this saying in or outside of the Bridal Chamber).

73 The Lord performed each sacrament as a mystery: Baptism, then Chrism, Redemption through remembrance and the Eucharist with Atonement in, the Holy Bridal Chamber (Brantingham, James. 2017)

Geoffrey Smith (2019) agrees about that this verse is important and says,

> "The focus on ritual is particularly striking in the Gospel of Philip, where as many as five rituals are discussed: baptism, chrism, the Lord's Supper, redemption, and the bridal chamber.

And Others suggest this verse (or the essence of it) be memorized too:

112 Clothed in a garment of Perfect Light, one becomes undetectable and imperceptible. Cloaked in this Perfect light, the Elect, Anthropos or Spirituals are invisible and may return to the Upper Highest Aeon and to Heaven in the Kingdom of God. Clad in this garment, they cannot be seen. For if seen, the Fallen would grasp them, hold and imprison them.

But by His Word and Wisdom they have found peace and upon death leave in assurance they will dwell with Yeshua. They will repose in spiritual union. Thus shall they come forth after death, ascending to the Pleroma; up and out of the world. Perfected sons and daughters of the Bridal Chamber.

And possibly "live" this and be able to demonstrate it (the essence of which is): "Know Thyself." (see Verse 111)"

111 Though they possess everything they want, *they do not know themselves.* In this way they are deficient. In fact, they have everything and more than they need. Yet, despite this they enjoy little, or nothing in life. Why? Because... they do not know Wisdom nor the Word and for that reason, themselves. Yeshua said it, You shall know the Truth, and the Truth shall make you free.

Mary Magdalene (or the Apostle Mary of Magdala) is found mentioned twelve times in the New Testament (Bauckham, Richard. 2006) Richard Bauckham notes this is extraordinary even for the other Apostles! But Mary Magdalen is in a great many Gnostic texts (such as the Gospel of Thomas, the Gospel of Mary, this Gospel of Philip, in the Secret Revelation of John and in Pistis Sophia: here is a paraphrase of Mary from the Pistis Sophia

From the Pistis Sophia A *dynamic paraphrase* of Pistis Sophia (*After* GRS Mead 1921;

Mary (of Magdala) said: "My Lord, 'Grace and Truth met together,'--'grace' then is the Spirit of Thee... And Mary drew nigh unto him, fell down, adored his feet and kissed his hands and said: "Yea, my Lord, reveal unto us: What is the use of the ways of the midst?

Jesus answers regarding the 'midst' and ...outlines five realms of purification, correction or punishment (the 'Midst' is one place where these actions take place). After that, He discussed with them his "Incarnation" as the Word and, administered the "baptism of the first offering" to his disciples in the Bridal Chamber.

...when thou didst receive the baptism from John. 'Grace' then was the Spirit which came upon thee; for the Father hath mercy on the race of men, and hath sent down and given thee the power of Sabaōth, 'the Good,' ...And Thou Christ, proclaimeth the Truth!

And the Father hath Thee say: 'Righteousness and Peace kissed each other,' --'righteousness' then is the Spirit of the Light, which came upon Thee and brought Thee the Mysteries of the Height and Breadth, to give unto the race of men. And thy gave them 'Peace' through, Sabaōth, the Good, (or *'God'*) which is *in* Thee. Thou who baptize and washeth clean the race of men,—for it filleth them with peace as it did for the sons of the Light Above.

...'Truth sprouted out of the earth,'--the power of the Good... with 'Righteousness.' And the Father and all the sons and daughters of Light looked down,' (and) saw Thee bring the mysteries of the Height and Breadth to the Christ, and Christ gave it to them, the race of men and women; so that they too may becometh righteous and good, and inherit the Kingdom of *'God'*" And it came to pass, when Jesus had heard Mary speak these words, he said: "Well said, Mary, inheritress of the Light!" (*After* Mead, G. R. S. 1921).

Addendum A continued for: Chokhmah, Wisdom, Sofia, Barbēlō and the Shekhinah:

'Wisdom' in the **Tanakh** (in Hebrew is: *Chokhmah*) is in the Greek *'Sofia'*. In English the word is 'Wisdom' to represent both (Jewish) and Greek' Scriptures. This Hebrew 'Sapiential literature' was translated by the Jews into Greek and found in the **Septuagint LXX.** This **'LXX'** was adopted by those who followed Yeshua the Anointed and (some of) His later disciples using the Septuagint LXX (later *calling it the* **Old Testament** or *'OT')* and some reading this literature became devoted to *'Sofia'*. Sofia *is simply the Greek word for 'Wisdom'*. 'Wisdom' as God Above God's Forethought, was with Him at the beginning, *and… in Truth God said…* **'Wisdom …(was) with Me** before *time …and before My works of old; …before I prepared the heavens,* **Lo,** before I, *the Most High,* established the clouds above; the fountains of the deep below… For She… *'Wisdom,'* was there from the Ages past unto the Ages into the Ages, and upon the Ages and Ages to Come.

And Wisdom or Sofia came early in Gnostic-Christianity from the OT, the Deuterocanonical and Apocryphal scriptures *(also from the: SRev-John)* as Barbēlō; so John said in the *Secret Revelation* (and Barbēlō is also found in): The *Holy Book of the Great Invisible Spirit*, the *trimorphic Protennoia, Gospel of Judas,* the *Three Steles of Seth, Zostrianos, Marsanes, Melchizedek,* and *Allogenes*.

Arising (self-generated with the Father, the Son and the Logos) She (Barbēlō) arose within the Father's *'nous'* or in and from His mind and in His heart. Barbēlō was with *God Above God* and the *Logos, before creation and before it all…* For, like the incarnation of the Son, She was already in *His* Mind, in *His* Image and, in *His* likeness and had (and has) the Power of God Most High! For it is written Moses even in *Genesis…* (coming from the Talmud wrote, She (Chokhmah) *is* the 'Word yoked to righteousness' of the LORD' Prov. 8:8) *and he said it:* 'Wisdom *is* the Holy Spirit…' and further, She *was that* which hovered over the formless, chaotic void… the murmuring deep! So to the prophet Enoch noted… 'Wisdom took her seat… next to God… She, Wisdom or *'Sofia'* was and is the feminine emanation of *God Above God,* the *Shekhinah*. For the spirit of the Lord shall rest upon the Anointed and upon Wisdom, and, upon the spirit of knowledge! For 'Wisdom' in the *Secret Revelation of John,* (as *Sofia*) was the first thought of the One (true) and, Most High God appearing first in Her alter Persona of 'Barbēlō;' *the* Holy Spirit *(and* 'Holy Mother') who *is* the 'Wisdom' of God Most High. And, as the Holy Spirit sits at the left hand of *Power…* So Barbēlō ('Wisdom' or 'Sofia') *all* emanate from the Wisdom of *God*.

Barbēlō is often depicted as the supreme female principle, with the name "Holy Mother" (or feminine Holy Spirit or "ruach ha-kodesh"), or simply 'Mother,' and even the androgynous "Mother-Father" (among other names). She is the Father ('*God's*') first-thought and co-creator of all other emanations including Yeshua. What her name means is unclear. William Barnstone mentions that, 'Barbēlō' may mean Bar- ba-Elo, 'The Deity-in Four' associated with the Tetragrammaton or YHWE (Barnstone, William and Meyer, Marvin. 2003.) Even the "son of El" has been proposed. But I like Alastair H. B. Logan's proposal (1996) that 'Barbēlō' is from the Hebrew: '*barah ba 'lo,*' daughter of the Lord.

Addendum B continued for Chokhmah, Σοφία, Sofia, Wisdom, Barbēlō and the Shekhinah (as well as the original verses in 2017)

For **'Wisdom,'** (*Sofia*) helped bring about God's plan for creation, salvation and Israel. She is spoken of by the prophets, even Moses first in *Deuteronomy* or 'Deut' 4:5–8 16:19–20; Job; (also see from Torah *Jer 8:8, Ecclesiaticus* (or Qohelet); *Psalm* 19; 119 and Ezra 7:25. And some believe that 1 Enoch (and the Temple Scroll from the Dead Sea Scrolls) are derived at least partially from: *Jubilees* (*1 Enoch* 91:1–10, 92:3–93:10, 91:11–92:2, 93:11–105:3) making it a Sapiential or Wisdom text; and it has remained so as part of Ethiopian Orthodox Churches (and for Judaism solely by the Beta Israel Jews formerly of Ethiopia) in each canon (Charles, RH. 1913).

…But the Rabbi's explicitly state this through the Oral Torah or Talmud; and clearly express that " **Wisdom is the Spirit of God or the Holy Spirit…**" which hovered over the deep, the formless, chaotic and murmuring void… so said Moses (*Gen 1:2-3*) and Enoch (*1 Enoch 42.1-2*) 'Wisdom' (or in Greek 'Sofia'). And so says 'Edem' (from *Baruch* by Justin) and by David (in *Prov. 8:22*). And in Solomon (*Wis in:* LXX), and Baruch (Bar *in:* LXX) *and* Ben Sirach (*Sir in:* LXX) and, the Apostle Paul who saith, 'Christ *is* the… Wisdom of God (*1 Corinthians 1:24*) and *John* who saith 'He *is* the Word (the Logos) and both: He *is* 'One with God and in God' (the Most High; the One Good God of Love and Truth). Therefore it *is* the 'Spirit' of God and it is *the* Wisdom of God; the Only Begotten Son through whom all things were created; and Jesus sends the Holy Spirit (Wisdom or Sofia both emanating as a persona from Barbelo) who follow 'His Way' and are filled up with the 'Spirit' (*John*). For the *Talmud* or Oral Torah see: King K. 2003; and Torah and Sapiential or Wisdom Literature (Schipper, Bernd., Teeter, D. Andrew Editors. 2013). Therefore it is even in the non-Gnostic books that we find these "Yokings" and associations of '*God*,' with Sophia (or in SRevJohn) with

(Original Verses 1, 40 and 59 from the 2017 edition below)

The first verse is changed back to that found in the 2017 text:

1 Israelites beget Israelites. But untutored proselytes convert no one. Yet some simply know it and live it. They live the Word and Wisdom. Others see and hear and they convert.

40Wisdom in the Old Testament, the Tanakh, is not an incarnation. There, Sofia is but a non-being, a personification of sacred revelation yet a Mother without a Son. She is the wisdom and knowledge, the salt, of scripture. In the Tanakh she is divinity in potentiality but is void without the Son. Yet, in the new covenant, the Logos and through all its scriptures she became real; the Holy Mother of God giving birth to angels, prophets, and to the children of the Son.

> (Note: Like Sirach; or in full Shimon ben Yeshua ben Eliezer ben Sira *or* Yeshua Ben Sirach; and the Enochian Jews I now accept **Sofia** as a real divinity.)

59

Sofia or Wisdom called barren, void, was in fact, the Mother of Prophets and Angels. Women disciples followed Yeshua. Mary Magdalene was His close disciple and companion. Some Disciples felt Rabbi Yeshua loved her the most. They noted, He often kissed her… When the other disciples saw this, they asked: Why do you love her more than us? The Teacher answered: How can it be that I do not love you as much as I love her? Well, listen and understand.

> In this second publication I have lightly changed three verses:
> Verses 1, 40 and 59 are slightly changed from my 2017 *Gospel of Philip*. Note: there is nothing wrong with the word 'Jew or Hebrew'; these are correct and proper translations; even more so, my 2019 translation honors these terms.)

Instead of, 'A Jew makes a Jew (or 'Hebrew') whom we call a convert (Meyer, Marvin, Barnstone, William 2003) or (taken from the Coptic) a 'Hebrew makes a Hebrew' I broadly defined the word 'Jew' or 'Hebrew' reflecting the words from the OT… 'Those who have struggled with man and God in trying to be better; to please God…' as this was a text written for Gnostics (Christian-Gnostics) and Jews who had also become Christians (or, as we would see it today) Gnostics in late antiquity but reconsidering I feel "Israelite" represents all inclusively and makes the verse closer to the Coptic. I have removed the 2019 first verse and reverted to the 2017 verse in the *GPhil*.

Wisdom, Σοφία or *Sophia* (1st Verse 2019 in the first edition below has been removed; and the 2017 verse added back to the 2021 update)

The 2019 verse *is removed* for the Second 2021 Edition:

1 Those who have struggled with man and God to do better please 'the One,' the Most High. They change toward goodness, restoring - not harming others; helping, not hurting them. And, more loving they are no longer filled with hate. They strive and live a better life. '*Sons and daughters of God*' that endeavor to live 'the Way,' (and the Good!) So living it, they 'beget' others by Wisdom (not oppression). Yet, many lost souls are naive or arrogant 'know-it-alls'. Dogmatic converts or novitiates who *repel*… but do not persuade… Still, some (unfairly) appear blissful from birth; intuitively living and knowing 'the Way'. They live

the Word and Wisdom. However, some see it and hear it but later (and from the one or, from another) blissfully follow finding Life (at last)! (REMOVED)

40 'Wisdom' or '*Chokhmah*' in the Tanakh, is called '*Sofia*' in the Septuagint a 'being of *divinity*'. '*Sofia*' is a special messenger of the 'Word and Wisdom' and like the '**son of God**' is a... '**daughter of God**' too. For it is written, '…your eyes shall be opened, and ye shall be as 'gods'. So Sofia '…who understands the all,' is like-to Elohim, and a 'goddess,' as well. For she was the beloved disciple… (and messenger to the rest!) His companion and His Partner, to the last. But, however viewed… **She is** the Wisdom and the Knowledge, and the Salt of scripture too. Void without the Son, 'the Logos' yet, found in the fullest covenant together and everywhere! Yet, the Truth! 'Wisdom, the Holy Spirit, or the Mother…' was from the first thought(s) of 'the One'. And 'She, the Holy Spirit,' gave birth to angels, prophets and the Word, *for the children of God Above God!* Halleluia!

59 Sofia or Wisdom called barren (void), was in fact the Mother of Prophets and Angels. Many women disciples followed Yeshua but of those, Mary Magdalene was His closest disciple and, companion. Some Disciples felt Rabbi Yeshua loved her the most. They noted, He often kissed her… (lips). When the other disciples saw this, they asked: Why do you love her more than us? The Teacher answered: How can it be that I do not love you as much as I love her? Well, listen and understand…

'Wisdom' in the Tanakh (in Hebrew: Chokhmah) is 'Sofia or Sophia' in the (Jewish) Greek' Scriptures (who is also in the SRevJohn and much Sethian literature is also Barbēlō . This Hebrew 'Sapiential literature' was translated by the Jews into Greek and found in the Septuagint LXX. This 'LXX' was adopted by those who followed Yeshua the Anointed and (some of) His later disciples using the Septuagint LXX (calling it the Old Testament or 'OT') and some reading this literature became devoted to 'Sophia'. Sophia is simply the Greek word for 'Wisdom'. 'Wisdom' as '*God Above God's*' Forethought, was with Him at the beginning, and… in Truth God said… 'Wisdom …(was) with Me before time …and before My works of old; …before I prepared the heavens, Lo, before I, the Most High, established the clouds above; the fountains of the deep below… For She… 'Wisdom,' was there from the Ages and Ages past unto the Age and into the Ages and Ages to Come.

And Wisdom or Sofia came early in Gnostic-Christianity from the OT, the Deuterocanonical and Apocryphal scriptures (also from the: *SRevJohn* as Barbēlō); so John said in the Secret Revelation (and Barbēlō is also found in): *The Holy Book of the Great Invisible Spirit,* the *trimorphic Protennoia, Gospel of Judas,* the *Three Steles of Seth, Zostrianos, Marsanes, Melchizedek,* and **Allogenes.**

Barbēlō is often depicted as the supreme female principle, with the name "Holy Mother" (or feminine Holy Spirit or "ruaḥ ha-kodesh"), or simply 'Mother,' and even the androgynous "Mother-Father" (among other names). She is the Father (*'God's'*) first-thought and co-creator of all other emanations including Yeshua. What her name means is unclear. William Barnstone mentions that, 'Barbēlō' may mean Bar- ba-Elo, 'The Deity-in Four' associated with the Tetragrammaton or YHWE (Barnstone, William and Meyer, Marvin. 2003.) Even the "son of El" has been proposed. But I like Alastair H. B. Logan's proposal (1996) that 'Barbēlō' is from the Hebrew: *'barah ba 'lo,'* daughter of the Lord.

Associations with Mary of Magdala

Thus Yeshua the Anointed said… to Mary His companion and disciple, thou art *'the **wisdom** and knowledge, and the salt, of scripture.'* For He told Mary, *'Mary, thalt shalt do the will of God, and be My Apostle who exceleth all the rest; a Disciple and, 'the first Disciple to the other Disciples'.* For, she, Mary is one who **knows** the All! And, she *'is the One'* who will reveal **'the Greatness of the Son**,' and *be* a Revelator too! For she hath inherited the Spirit's Light; and is a Privileged Interlocutor; **Lo,** seen as 'One' always *with* the Lord; she will be the One whom *many call* His Companion, even more and the Chosen One of women! Mary thou hath the '***Wisdom***' of scripture and both *Holy Wisdom* and *Spirit* within thee! For thou Daughter of Man, hath insight, intelligence and wisdom like-*too* that of the Son of Man.

And as the Apostle said regarding Mary's mentor… 'Christ (*is*) the Wisdom and the Logos of God with us… So the Apostle John said… He *is* the *logos* (the word and wisdom; and so much more…) For the **Logos is:** discourse; skillful and practiced speaking; and developed doctrine; and narrative; and a matter, affair or case in law under discussion; inward thought and the faculty of thinking and reasoning and of regarding or considering a subject; and of reckoning or taking something into account; and of determining a cause or reason… and *Wisdom* (here, as Jesus the Logos) became flesh and dwelt among us; the Word (or Logos) as of God among us… denoting the Ten Commandments or 'decalogue'; and as the Ten 'Words or Logoi' it was Moses who wrote of Joseph, the 'Word (from out of the Talmud, the Hebrew word for 'LORD' was translated equally as the 'Word' or: Memre) and it was with Joseph in prison…'.

Citations of Wisdom

All these citations are all derived from prophecy, knowledge and wisdom and from the Prophets and the Apostles and books and texts from throughout the history of Judaism and Christianity: Enoch, Seth; Moses; David; Solomon; Baruch; Daniel; Isaiah; Paul; John; Luke; and James. (See: *1 Enoch; Genesis 39:91; Proverbs; Psalms; the Wisdom of Solomon; Job; Song of Solomon; Ecclesiastes; Isaiah 11:2(!); Daniel; Baruch; Sirach or Ecclesiasticus; 1 Corinthians; the Gospel of John; Revelation; Secret Revelation of John; this book or gospel (of Philip); and in the Origin of the*

World; in Baruch by Justin; in the Pistis Sofia; the Three Steles of Seth; and see Acts; and the Gospel of John, the Revelation; the Letter of James and the Tanakh, Talmud; Septuingint LXX and the New Testament. See also: Vincent, Martin., et al. (2019) The Meaning of 'Logos' in the Prologue of John's Gospel; also see Shekinah in: Wikipedia, the free encyclopedia https://en.wikipedia.org/wiki/Shekhinah#In_Judaism (accessed 23 21 2019) and see Strong's #4633: for 'skene' or 'skēnē' at: https://www.bibletools.org/index.cfm/fuseaction/Lexicon.show/ID/G4633/skene.htm So the *Shekinah* is most likely derived from 2 Maccabees 14:35 '*a temple for your habitation,*' where the Greek text (Koine Greek: ναὸν τῆς σῆς σκηνώσεως) suggests a possible parallel understanding, of... skēnōsē "a tent-building" (the verb shakan and terms coming from the root škn, which do occur in the Hebrew Scriptures even before the later *rabbinic literature* using *Shekhinah* or שכינה in the English transliterated as, 'Shekhinah'; and are or is, a variation on an early loanword from Phoenician (the Ancient Greek word for the: ἡ σκηνή or skēnē "tent" or dwelling tent, or a tabernacle, (made of green boughs, or skins or other materials).

For all of this indicates the 'Presence' or 'dwelling' of the Spirit of God (in Christianity 'the Holy Spirit') but in the Hebrew the noun for the 'Holy Spirit' being 'skēnē' a *feminine* noun (from which Shekinah is believed to have been developed). And it is deliberately used to represent the original Hebrew or Aramaic term. Thus the 'background for feminine characterization of the Holy Spirit as feminine and how that was meant to be brought out in the term *Shekhinah* as often used in Kabbalah, (Christian) Cabbala and the *NHL* and Associated texts (like *Pistis Sofia*). But it was taken seriously by those who would later be called 'Gnostics' or *Gnostic-Chiristians*. For it appears to be the basis of the naming of the 'Holy Spirit' as 'a woman' in the *Gospel of Philip* verse 18 (per Brantingham and others see: T. P. Brown the Gospel of Philip).

Appendix A, Barbēlō and Consorts

She (Barbēlō) is the 'first thought' of the true God (in this collection of books *only in the Secret Revelation of* John but is brought up here for any allusion to Sophia must take Barbēlō into account. She is his image. But importantly she becomes the womb of everything (of all creation). The Very Womb of the All. For she is prior to creation and prior to tit all. Barbēlō is explicitly described as giving birth to Sophia (thus Wisdom). Of course this associates her with Wisdom (canonically). Wisdom or "Sophia" is canonically a co-creator (as Sophia) with God. So this is one of Barbēlō's direct association's with Sophia. And of course Messiah Yeshua is associated with the exact same "Wisdom". As Paul said, *"Jesus is the Wisdom of God."*

It must be remembered that Gnostics and Gnostic Christians considered themselves Christians. As Christians they also used the proto-canonical "catholic" scriptures (though they interpreted them through Gnostic eyes and texts). Since "Wisdom or Sophia" became clearly associated with Yeshua, this associates Yeshua and Barbēlō. All of these complex associations leads too descriptions of Barbēlō as androgynous. Or even described as a male. For example she is... the Mother-Father, the first man; the Holy Spirit, the thrice-male, thrice-powerful, thrice-named, the androgynous eternal realm (or Aeon) outside of all, outside of the realms of time, space and matter among the invisible ones, and the first to come forth (After Davies, Stephan. 2005)

However Isenberg an early translator gives a hypothesis that the entire Gospel of Philip derives from a single comprehensive Gnostic Christian text and that most of its excerpts derive from a single book a "harmony" (possibly like the Diatessaron). It certainly is a Gospel that transmits many of the words of the Lord (Yeshua) who is a bringer of Salvation. It appears that it was probably commonly transmitted with the *Gospel of Thomas.* And given it weight to its metaphors, dynamic spirit, boldness of spirit and images, and a palpable greatness (that is) both mysterious and enigmatic. This being the probable reason for its' popularity and its' being placed next to the *Gospel of Thomas* (Schneemelcher, Wilhelm., Wilson, Robert McLachlan., Hennecke, Edgar. Eds. 2003)

Thus Yeshua the Anointed said... to Mary of Magdala His companion and disciple, thou art *'the **wisdom** and knowledge, and the salt, of scripture.'* For He told Mary, *'Mary, thalt shalt do the will of God, and be My Apostle who excelleth all the rest; a Disciple and, 'the first Disciple to the other Disciples'*. For she, Mary is one who *knows* the All! And, she *'is the One'* who will reveal **'the Greatness of the Son,'** and *be* a Revelator too! For she hath inherited the Spirit's Light; and is a Privileged Interlocutor; **Lo,** seen as 'One' always *with* the Lord; she will be the One whom *many call* His Companion, even more and the Chosen One of women! Mary thou hath the *'**Wisdom**'* of scripture and both *Holy Wisdom* and *Spirit* within thee! For thou Daughter of Man, hath insight, intelligence and wisdom like-*too* that of the Son of Man.

And as the Apostle said regarding Mary's mentor… 'Christ (*is*) the Wisdom and the Logos of God with us… So the Apostle John said… He *is* the *logos* (the word and wisdom; and so much more…) For the **Logos is:** discourse; skillful and practiced speaking; and developed doctrine; and narrative; and a matter, affair or case in law under discussion; inward thought and the faculty of thinking and reasoning and of regarding or considering a subject; and of reckoning or taking something into account; and of determining a cause or reason… and *Wisdom* (here, as Jesus the Logos) became flesh and dwelt among us; the Word (or Logos) as of God among us… denoting the Ten Commandments or 'decalogue'; and as the Ten 'Words or Logoi' it was Moses who wrote of Joseph, the 'Word (from out of the Talmud, the Hebrew word for 'LORD' was translated equally as the 'Word' or: Memre) and it was with Joseph in prison…'.

The Gospel According To Mary

Introduction to The Gospel According To Mary (of Magdala)

A Reflection and A New Interpretation

by James Brantingham PhD

John 20:15

He asked her, "Woman, why are you crying? Who is it you are looking for?"
    Thinking he was the gardener, she said, "Sir, if you have carried him away, tell me where you have put him, and I will get him."
    Jesus said to her, "Mary." She turned toward him and cried out in Aramaic,
    "**Rabboni!**" (which means "Teacher")… (After NIV)

A Note About Gnostic Theology and 'Missing Scriptural Terms' in the 'Gospel According to Mary'

A Brief History about this "Gnostic" Gospel, the *Gospel According To Mary of Magdala* (abbreviated *GMary*) and most commonly called the *Gospel of Mary* follows. I have written earlier that Gnostics, Gnosticism, and 'Gnostic Theology' would be highly likely found in the missing pages that underline the infrastructure, source, and inspiration behind this Gospel. If the *Gospel of the Beloved Companion: The Complete Gospel of Mary Magdalene* translated by Jehanne de Quillian (2011) is accepted by Scholars as legitimate, I was correct. However, I wish to make it clear I take **no** stand (in this book, *Holy Wisdom and the Logos of God*) on the provenance or dating of de Quillian's "*Complete GMary*."

From what I have read (in de Quillian's) *Gospel of the Beloved Companion: The Complete Gospel of Mary Magdalene* its verses appear similar to the structure found in the Canonical Gospels (especially John). But immediately, quotations from the *Gospel of Thomas,* the *Gospel of Mary,* (and as I assess it) from the *Gospel of Philip* and the *Gospel of John* are evident. These verses then would have **preceded** there later placement in the above Gnostic Gospels (and at least a part of Thomas) and (*maybe*) even before John, based on the dates given for the writing of the *Gospel of the Beloved Companion: The Complete Gospel of Mary Magdalene* by de Quillian (2011).

Finding the Coptic *GMary*

The *NHL*-associated Coptic *GMary* was purchased in Cairo in 1896 by German diplomat Carl Reinhardt. Archaeologists Grenfell and Hunt dug up two other Greek fragments of the Gospel of Mary sometime between 1897 and 1906. That Cairo codex is called the Akhmim Codex because Reinhardt was told it had come from that part of Egypt. It contained the *SRevJohn* (also called the 'Apocryphon of John') and other Gnostic texts like, *The Sophia of Jesus Christ* and the '*Act of Peter.*' In the *SRevJohn* Wisdom (Sophia or Barbēlō) *is* the 'Holy Spirit.' Or She is portrayed this way in 'Sethian' texts and theology;' and portrayed that way in some Valentinian texts. But allusively as "Wisdom," in the *Gospel of Philip*) along with the *SRevJohn*. This 'theology' has a central place in Gnostic cosmogony and holds not just for Sethians but for Valentinians too. Yet, there is another term we will look at below (Schaberg, Jane. 2002; King, Karen L. 2003; Davies, Stevan. 2005; Smith, Andrew P. 2005; 2015).

But... in the *NHL*-associated Coptic *GMary* the term 'Holy Mother or just Mother' is missing. And since 'Valentinus' is credited by some with being 'the first' to describe God as a Triune God or 'Trinity' (and to publish it) it seems a grave loss. Stevan Marshall (2019) points out that in the 'Valentinian' *Gospel of Philip* 'we see written...' the name of... 'the Father and the Son and the Holy Spirit.' But, except for the 'Son' the other two are not mentioned in the extant *GMary*. So the words 'Holy Spirit' or 'Mother' are not found in the Coptic GMary, anywhere; nor is God the Father, or just 'Father' or even 'god,' and so on. Be that as it may, I judge that the use here of the title 'Son of Man' is, (in the *GMary*) meant to reflect the 'Danielic Messianic' figure (no matter whether as the proto-canonical 'Son of Man,' the Messiah) or, as a human being or the 'son of Man'). A "human son of Man" (like a 'human son of God') was or could have been a highly devout and extraordinarily Spiritual Jewish man and, in this case - a high or even the highest, prophet. Either could have been the Messiah of Israel, human or divine (or both). Nevertheless, the 'Danielic title 'Son or Man' was fraught with seditious under-tones. And this was heard by the Romans to mean, 'the leader of a rebellion,' this Jesus (to the Romans) was a dangerous pretender as 'King of the Jews or Israel'.

The Marian community

Like *John*, the *GMary* was likely written by a "Marian community." A community that venerated and followed the "teachings" of the 'Apostle Mary.' If so, the Scholar Karen King believed (2003; 2007) and wrote (before de Quillian's publication) that the Gospel of Mary had a 'life' even in *some* early proto-canonical churches. The *Complete Gospel of Mary* certainly has "Canonical-like" verses throughout but (and there is no doubt) many "Gnostic verses" too. Unfortunately, the *"Greek"* from which Jehanne de Quillian (2011) translated the *Gospel of the Beloved Companion: The Complete Gospel of Mary Magdalene* is not available at this time. But before this publication Dr. King suggested the greater proto-canonical community ultimately ruled out the Gospel of Mary and its way of worshipping.

Because, she believes "leadership was accorded women in the Coptic *GMary.*" And such leadership by women is confirmed in the *Gospel of the Beloved Companion: The Complete Gospel of Mary Magdalene* (King, Karen. 2007; de Quillian, Jehanne. 2011).

There is no apparent Gnostic theology in the Coptic *GMary*, (or in the Greek fragments) and none is 'cited.' But either an Orthodox (or Gnostic) "theology" could (and was) construed. Yet the *GMary* makes better sense (if seen as once containing either Canonical and Gnostic theology (or both). In the (2011) de Quillian *Complete GMary* there are clear "Canonical verses" (*and many "Gnostic" verses*) and so it contains both "Canonical and Gnostic Theology" as presented in the *Secret Revelation of John*. It is certainly possible to read the entire (*Coptic* and Greek Fragments) of the Coptic *GMary* without resorting to any "Gnostic Theology." And seeing it as a proto-canonical Gospel. The Coptic *GMary* is neither clearly Gnostic nor Canonical. But de Quillian's *Complete GMary* has both. Yet there was "one thing that differentiated the Coptic *GMary* from all other Canonical literature." And that is the evident importance and equality of Mary as a "Disciple" ('an Apostle') of Jesus Christ; otherwise alongside the Twelve Apostles (King, Karen. 2007). In the *Complete GMary* Mary she is both. After this paragraph I will not bring up de Quillian's *Complete GMary* (2011). The following literature will only address the Coptic (with Greek fragments) *Gospel According to Mary of Magdala* - which will also use the contraction *GMary*).

Wisdom (or the Wise) *in* (the *NHL*-associated) Coptic GMary, no "Sophia (or Barbēlō) is found.

'Wisdom' in the Hebrew *Tanakh* (which are the same scriptures in the Christian OT) is 'Chokhmah,' and in Greek: 'Sofia' spelled in English as 'Wisdom or *Sophia*'. Gnostic texts in English spell it 'Sophia'. Gnostic theology states that after Aeons and Aeons of Silence, God's 'first thought' emanated forth as 'Wisdom' and in some texts (like the *Secret Revelation of John*) as 'Barbēlō.' Barbēlō and Sophia (are named outright in *the Secret Revelation of John* as the '*Holy Spirit*'). And this was His ('*God*' the Father's) 'First Thought,' (see the *SRevJohn* and more below). 'Wisdom,' Sophia (and Barbēlō) '*is*' a complex religious figure. The existence and growth of Gnosticism (or 'Christian-Gnosticism') though, just like "non-Gnostic Christianity" *had to* (at this time) *maintain monotheism* too. Otherwise without a claim to being derived from (Jewish) antiquity no one would have taken a seriously look at it, including at any Gnostic books or Gnosticism. A nascent trinitarian understanding is clearly found in both Valentinian and Sethian texts. And it is clear that Jesus (in the Canonical Gospels) took the "Holy Spirit" seriously in including it in so many of His prayers and in their Baptism. Here is where the importance of Barbēlō and Sophia (also Wisdom) being named the "Holy Spirit" is made clear. This maintains monotheism in Gnosticism and as I see it also in the GMary (though all the implications of trinitarianism would not be worked out yet for hundreds of years).

Valentinian Christians (or Gnostics)

Certainly in the first few hundred years *Valentinus and Valentinians, or Valentinian Christians"* (today, Valentinian Gnostics) successfully accomplished being considered Christian (which they called themselves) and a part of Christianity for about two hundred years (Smith Andrew P. 2015). So, the much ballyhoo'd "Two Gods" of Gnosticism is, I believe wrongly understood and wrongly described (especially in the past and today by non-Gnostics). Valentinus and "Valentinian Christians" (and their books: the *Gospel of Truth* and, *Philip*) and their presentation of other "Gnostic" books such as (the *Gospel of Thomas*, the *Secret Revelation of John* and the *Gospel of Mary*) **had to have been initially explained in a monotheistic way.** It was impossible for the God of the OT and another God of the NT to be equal in power and to remain a part of Christianity (and Gnosticism). This allowed them to claim the ancient roots of Judaism. The OT 'God' was (and had to be explained by Gnostics as a *'lesser ' god or archangel or similar*). And explained by *'non-Gnostic Christians'* as being misunderstood but rightly explained and demonstrated by Jesus the Anointed. Non-Gnostic Christians believed that the Jews did not understand who the "real OT *'God'*" was. Jesus the Anointed explained that the *'God' of the OT* was *a God of Love and Compassion* (and therefore an 'unknown, but not unknowable God' to most Jews and Gentiles).

Jesus and the God of the Old Testament

This is why there was a need to write the "New Testament" to clarify how "Jesus" explained the *'God' of the OT* ! For Jesus the 'God' of the OT was His Father. And tied the God of Israel (and Judaism) to 'the Way.' The need to maintain Monotheism was a brutal fact for the first Jewish-Christians (and later all 'Christianity' including Gnostics). But I assert Gnosticism (and its scriptures) were and are primarily derived from "Christianity" as did the Gnostic Scholar, Simone Pétrement (1984). Today many other influences (such as Platonism) also have been recognized. But Christianity claimed to be the 'true and Ancient Religion' extending from the OT and Judaism (and the Hebrew Bible or the Septuagint or Greek Jewish Bible or Tanakh, the Christians OT) and the NT. Without this Gnosticism too, would have been kaput!

Did Valentinus demand two Gods?

If the Valentinians had (*really*) demanded that "Wisdom," (Sophia and particularly 'Barbēlō') be accepted as an equivalent (Second) God or even Consort (or Wife and equally powerful God) this would have caused a theological explosion. I believe the "Gnostics" would have been immediately and forcefully ejected out of the Christian Community." This is not saying anything here about Mary Magdalene and Jesus (but associations between Jesus and Sophia or 'Barbēlō.'

A True Religion

Two thousand years ago a "true Religion" *had to have* a primeval pedigree. Without a *primitive* claim extending (often even) into prehistory a "Religion" was labeled an innovation. Or labeled a mystery cult and rejected (by most). Christianity (and so *by extension*) "Gnosticism" claimed to be the continuation of the Judaism, the Jewish scriptures (and of Jewish religion). Of course this was because Jesus *was* Jewish and taught from the Jewish OT (and possibly, other ancient Jewish scriptures.) Called *the 'Second Temple' ("or intertestamental period") revelations or scriptures they included such books as Enoch, Jubilees and the Assumption of Moses* used by the Apostle Jude. And the *Wisdom of Solomon, Sirach or Ecclesiaticus, 4 Ezra*

used by the Apostle Paul). Clearly without this direct tie to the Jewish Tanakh or Christian Old Testament (and the required ethical practice from the OT or Hebrew Bible or Jewish Greek Septuagint (such as "the Ten Commandment's") which Jesus clearly indicated were to be practiced neither Christianity nor Gnosticism would not be here today.

Observation

Thus this claim to antiquity - **required not just belief, 'but practice'** ("or as Jews would say today, *'Observation'*") of 'the Way,' (and so for Christians as much as Jews) ***doing*** the Ten Commandments **was** observation of Jewish Bible, or the OT (was part of the primeval religion of 'the Way' or Christianity). *It was far more important to the ancients that a religion be Ancient! Than for todays' "religious practice" based upon what academic, scientific 'textual criticism" has signed off on (as OK).*

However, Christianity would have probably (and immediately) died off *(for Jews)* after the Death of Jesus if it had been proclaimed (then) that there were "two" equal gods (Jesus and the Father)! This was *not* claimed by Jesus though it took a difficult and complex development of 'trinitarian' Christian theology so as to allow the Apostle Paul to exhort "God is One!" Many Jews (and Muslims) then and now assert that claiming Jesus (along with the Holy Spirit and Father) 'is God,' was "Pagan then, and still is now." But this is not the place to go into a discussion of trinitarian theology. Today much more can be interpreted metaphorically or allegorically (and in light of the ever growing "body of research" of the World and the Laws of Nature.

Gnosticism, with its massive Christology will remain a part of Christianity and as part of Christianity makes Christianity the largest Religion in the Modern World. I believe 'Gnosticism' is "of the Christian Faith" and a part of 'the larger Christian body' (Hoeller, Stephan A. 2010). Though of course there are some today who see "Gnosticism as its own religion or practice (and not a part of Christianity.") So be it. Maybe that is best for today. But in antiquity (and thus its justification as part of Christianity) it was seen as more an exegesis explaining the arrival of the Jewish Messiah. Many Jews accepted (but again many more) Jews did not. Paul claimed that the Jewish Jesus was the Messiah (often quoting from OT scripture) but was (both a Jewish) and a Universal Messiah! So Peter claimed! So John claimed! So Thomas claimed! I believe that the Apostle Mary claimed Jesus was the "Resurrected Jewish and World's Messiah too." But, Christianity was tied to the Jewish scriptures which of course Jesus taught from *and* believed in. (Johnson, Paul. 1976; Jenkins, Philip. 2001; 2008; 2015).

Marcion claimed that the OT 'god' could not be the same as the loving and compassionate true God of Jesus Christ. But in the process Marcion pushed that there were "two Gods." One of the OT (evil, bad and overly concerned with "justice" rather than forgiveness and compassion) instead of God the Father of Jesus Christ (Johnson, Paul. 1976; Jenkins, Philip. 2001; 2008; 2015). And Marcionism flared and survived for a few hundred years but ultimately died being wiped off the face of both the Middle East, Europe and the Earth (2001; 2008; 2015).

Ancient Christianity

All can read the OT and NT and see clearly that there were (and are) other "divinities or divine beings in both Judaism and Christianity." Both faiths had to take the reality of these "beings" into account. There are many "named gods, angels, and demons in the books of the Hebrew Bible, Septuagint and OT, and NT Apocrypha, *as well as the New Testament and patristic literature (including the Gnostic NT Apocrypha* Heiser, Michael S. (2015). Long before Christianity Judaism had dealt with Other Gods like "Baal, Beelzebub, Amun, Asherah, Belial, Bel (or 'lord' for a number of different gods), and Marduk, and Moloch. Marduk, and Moloch (were supposedly 'gods' that had required 'child sacrifice' in *Gehenna* or the Valley of Hinnom). And so this is how 'Gehenna' became a metaphor for Hell!'. Of course there were also Archangels, angels (good and bad) demon's and other divinities. About two and a half thousand years ago these were rebranded by Judaism as (at most) lesser, ineffectual, nearly powerless *lesser gods* or angels, demons along with good and bad angels and so on (Heiser, Michael S. 2015).

Christianity took these Jewish definitions over lock, stock and barrel! So there was the overwhelming need for the Councils (to maintain the ancient roots of Monotheism in Christianity) and define just how Jesus and the Holy Spirit fit in with the One God (Johnson, Paul. 1976). So I assert that Christianity (whatever the particular ancient sect, proto-canonical or other, etc.,), would not have accepted an equal second God. So the "Borborites" who apparently worshipped 'Barbēlō' as 'God' or (really) the "Goddess." They said Barbēlō' reigned in the eighth heaven, the mother of the living; the Goddess of All, the supreme God. This signed the Ophites death warrant (and Ophites died off). To some Gnostic groups Jesus was divine but not human, and had only "appeared to have been human" (or 'docetic'). This docetism alone (or usually in conjunction with other theological difficulties) like renouncing the God of the Old Testament ultimately caused Gnostic and non-Gnostic Christians to split. Some church fathers accused Gnostics of holding and carrying on orgies. So it was written by the heresy hunter and Church Father, Epiphanius of Salamis. But we do not actually have their the ("Borborites") side of it. In fact they were plagued much more by asceticism rather than libertinism. Yet most scholars think (the Ophites - a small isolated group) were beyond the pale for the Christianity - at that time (Smith, AP. 2015; Schaff, Philip., Ed. 2016.)

Christianity (the OT and NT) were and still are generally masculine in their expressions about God (so it is even today most often: 'God the Father') but not completely so. God 'the Father' was the most (or one of the most) commonly used words in Gnosticism for 'God Most High' (and a common term in Christianity as a whole). Indeed it appeared in Jewish scriptures first: ...God says too David and to his offspring, "I will be his father and he will be my son" (2 Sam 7:14; 1 Chron 17:13). And, Moses spoke to Pharaoh... "This is what the Lord says: Israel is my firstborn son, and I told you, 'Let my son go, so he may worship me'. In Deuteronomy 32 we find another explicit statement about God being the Father of Israel. Moses presents a sharp contrast between God and his people. He praises God and scorns Israel with... "Is he not your Father, your Creator, who made you and formed you?" (Medved, Goran. KAIROS 2021; *After* NIV). Though the proto-canonical and orthodox also frequently used this term (Father) for *'God.'* But the Gnostic-Christians more strongly and more often emphasized the term Father than anything else (but not excluding *'God'*).

Mary and Close Canonical Variants

Mary says many "ideological canonical variants to the other disciples. Jean-Yves Leloup (2002) has some suggestions

John 14:27

"I leave you my peace,

I give you my peace,

I do not give it to you as the world gives it."

Mary,

"May My peace be with you and fulfill you and, He who gives us peace, be with you all, Amen."

Lk 24:36;

"Peace be with you"

Mary,
"..peace be with you"

Mt 24:4-5

"See that no one leads you astray. For many will come in my name, saying, 'I am the Christ,' and they will lead many astray (ESV)

Mark 13:5

Jesus said to them: "Watch out that no one deceives you. Many will come in my name, claiming, 'I am he,' and will deceive many.

Luke 17:23

People will tell you, 'Look, there He is!' or 'Look, here He is!' Do not go out or chase after them.

Mary,

Yet, beware. Do not be mislead by anyone who says, *'Lo, here it is* or *Lo, there He is* the Savior!

Luke 17:20-21

Now when He was asked by the Pharisees when the kingdom of God would come, He answered them and said, "The kingdom of God does not come with observation; nor will they say, 'See here!' or 'See there!' For indeed, the kingdom of God is within you." (NKJV)

Mary

Yet, beware. Do not be mislead by anyone who says, *'Lo, here it is* or *Lo, there He is* the Savior! 'Rather, **The Kingdom of the Blissful One, the Son of Man** (ⲱ ⲡ·ϣⲏⲣⲉ ⲅⲁⲣ ⲙ·ⲡ·ⲣⲱⲙⲉ)^ **is within**; and there thee shall find the peace that passeth all understanding *in* and, *all about you!*

Mt 7:7 7 "Ask, and it will be given to you; seek, and you will find; knock, and it will be opened to you.

Mary

trust 'the Way' and seek the Good! And you will find Him!

God the Father, 'the Way,' and Monotheism (and 'Lady Wisdom')

But the point of this is that in the time just before and just after Jesus both Jews and Christian Theologians understood that, Numbers 23:19 God is not a man, that He should lie, or a son of man, that He should change His mind… and God (I would add) is not just a woman… This was fully understood by the Pharisees like Gamaliel or Theologians like Origen! So (some part of) Judaism first (as is obvious in Ecclesiasticus) worshipped 'Lady Wisdom' or "Sophia," as a divinity (or a 'good demiurge,' or as an angel) clearly recognizing she had been God's Demiurge in Proverbs 8 as one of many examples. And of course as "Wisdom" She is found in Ecclesiaticus, Ecclesiastes and in the NT Epistle of James! (Schaff, Philip., Ed. 2016; 2016).

The problem with positing two equal Gods (like Barbēlō and Yahweh as Consort and Husband) leads to the loss of "Monotheism." And Christianity could not lose that two thousand years ago, if it were to grow and prosper. The average person (then) might not understand this but Christian (and Jewish) Theologians did. In effect in accepting "God is not just a man…" leaves conceiving of God with feminine attributes to be described as 'Barbēlō' or the 'Holy Mother ' as the 'One God' or even the 'One Goddess' theologically possible; and was so understood even for Origen two thousand years ago. Though others differ it is still crucial to maintain Monotheism today (lesser divinities such as the ineffectual Demiurge Yadabaoth (a divinity or *'lesser god'*) of the Secret Revelation of John do not threaten core monotheism (nor does a *'goddess'*).

Intellectually this maintained monotheism (and maintains it today). Separate

but equal (and of the same powerful) *'Gods'* destroys Monotheism (and will cause the Gnostic scripture to be laid aside and forgotten). And this "cleaves off" the NT from the OT. Christianity could be wounded maybe lost (even in these modern days). However the same problem exists in the opposite direction (of a "Matriarchal Goddess or Matriarchy") and if there is an insistence on Barbēlō,' the 'Holy Mother,' the One 'Goddess' being held as the only way to represent "God or Goddess Most High." I believe (and I may be wrong) that holding an equally powerful God and a Goddess in "Gnosticism" cleaves it from the OT and NT or (Christianity) and will destroy it.

Sophia

But the word 'Wisdom' in Greek is 'Sophia'. And (Greek) 'Sofia *or* usually in English texts is spelled Sophia.' David Hart (2017) notes, Sophia was virtually 'deified' by Jewish writers many hundreds of years before Jesus walked the earth. This is explicit in the Jewish scriptures such the books of Psalms as in Psalm 8, and 'Ecclesiasticus'. I would note that emanation of "Wisdom or Sophia" (also called 'Barbēlō') this happened "before time and before the Aeon of the Earth and creation of the Cosmos (or Universe)." Thus such Gnostic Theology describes God's 'first thought' "Wisdom or Sophia 'Barbēlō' who immediately emanate 'Christ') do so, since time does not yet exist, 'concurrently.' In essence this is the emanation of the "trinity" before time (in the vernacular before the big bang). So, though it appears that "Wisdom or Barbēlō" (called the 'Holy Spirit') in the Secret Revelation of John - what will later come to be known as the "trinity" is at least hinted at in the beginning in Gnostic Theology.

Tripartite Tractate and Gnostic Theology

Indeed in the "Valentinian book of Theology" (in addition to the *SRevJohn*) is the Valentinian *Tripartite Tractate* or '*TriTrac*' discusses the self-generated 'First Principles" which are the "Father, Son, and 'the Church of the Aeons' (Thomassen, Einar. 2007). It appears here at the "passion of the youngest Aeon, Sophia (or Wisdom) comes "after" the Son. And it is *not* the "demiurge or Yaltabaoth" or the "lesser god of the OT" that is the Ruler or Chief Archon but "the Logos" (or Word) that plays a similar role in the aeon and Cosmos of earth.

The '*TriTrac*' outlines the three different types of Human beings - the spiritual, psychical, and material - each "known by its fruit "(Thomassen, Einar. 2007). But are only recognized when the Savior (Christ Jesus) descends to them with this Knowledge. In this text the "Spiritual or Pneumatic" already "know" and are already "saved." But the "psychical" people must "choose" and can descend or remain wrapped up with 'matter, materialism and the fleshly life' or ascend through Knowledge and become "Spiritual" and saved. "Material" ("Hylic or Choic') people in the *TriTrac* come near to being "demonic" and are simply "lost" to evil. It is notable that the Modern Johannite "Esoteric-Gnostic-Christian" church sees these (all three 'types of people') as stages or expression of a modern human being manifested at different times within their lifetime, and that "none are necessarily lost." Certainly no group is labeled "just material" and automatically damned (Johannite Church, The Apostolic. 2018.) However the *TriTrac* allows for some people to eventually be annihilated "unto destruction."

Associations with Mary of Magdala Jesus and Wisdom; *and* Jesus and Mary Magdalene)

Thus Yeshua the Anointed said… to Mary His companion and disciple, thou art '*the **wisdom** and knowledge, and the salt, of scripture.*' For He told Mary, '*Mary, thalt shalt do the will of God, and be My Apostle who excels all the rest; a Disciple and,* '*the first Disciple to the other Disciples'*. For she, Mary is one who **knows** the All! And, she '*is the One*' who will reveal '**the Greatness of the Son**,' and *(like John)* be a Revelator too! For she hath inherited the Spirit's Light; and is a Privileged Interlocutor; **Lo,** seen as 'One' always *with* the Lord; she will be the One whom *many call* His Companion, even more the Chosen One of women! '*Mary thou hath the* 'Wisdom' *of scripture and both* **Holy Wisdom** *and* **Spirit** *within thee!* For thou *Daughter of Man*, hath insight, intelligence and wisdom like-*too* that of the Son of Man.

And as the Apostle Paul said regarding Mary's mentor… 'Christ (*is*) the Wisdom and the Logos of God with us… So the Apostle John said… He *is* the *Logos* (which is: the word and wisdom; and so much more…). For the **Logos is:** discourse; skillful and practiced speaking; developed doctrine and narrative; and, a matter, affair or case in law under discussion; and inward thought and the faculty of thinking and reasoning in regarding or considering and solving a problem or dealing with a question; and, it is reckoning or taking everything possible into account and of determining a cause or reason… and taking a stand and going forward with the solution. *'Wisdom'* (here, as… Jesus *'the Logos'*) became flesh and dwelt among us and the Word of God came among us… Giving and showing us how to practice the 'Ten Commandments; the 'decalogue; the Ten 'Words or Logoi' written by the 'finger of God' and given to Moses… Jesus (and Mary Magdalene) tell us how to carry out or 'observe' the Ten Commandments (and much, much more). And they do this in a loving and deeply compassionate manner. For Moses wrote about Joseph, as the *'Word* (retro-cognitively in the Talmud, using the Hebrew word for 'LORD,' and the Word - of God - *'Memre'* as a synonym for the Logos.) So he wrote about Joseph in prison…'.

Citations of Wisdom (or 'Sofia') in "Canonical Scripture." And the Jewish feminine Spirit of Holiness (or the Holy Spirit) the, Shekinah

All these citations are all derived from prophecy, knowledge and wisdom and from the Prophets and the Apostles and books and texts from throughout the history of Judaism and Christianity: Enoch, Seth; Moses; David; Solomon; Baruch; Daniel; Isaiah; Paul; John; Luke; and James. (See: *1 Enoch; Genesis 39:91; Proverbs; Psalms; the Wisdom of Solomon; Job; Song of Solomon; Ecclesiastes; Isaiah 11:2(!); Daniel; Baruch; Sirach or Ecclesiasticus; 1 Corinthians; the Gospel of John; Revelation; Secret Revelation of John; this book or gospel (of Philip); and in the Origin of the World; in Baruch by Justin; in the Pistis Sophia; the Three Steles of Seth; and see Acts; and the Gospel of John, the Revelation; the Letter of James and the Tanakh, Talmud; Septuingint LXX and the New Testament.* See also: Vincent, Martin., et al. (2019) The Meaning of 'Logos' in the Prologue of John's Gospel; also see 'Shekinah' (2019) and see Strong's (2019) for 'Shekinah.' So the *Shekinah* is most likely derived from 2 Maccabees 14:35 *'a temple for your habitation,'* where the Greek text (Koine Greek: ναὸν τῆς σῆς σκηνώσεως) suggests a possible parallel understanding, of… skēnōsē "a tent-building" (the verb shakan and terms coming from the root škn, which do occur in the Hebrew Scriptures even before the later *rabbinic literature* using *Shechinah* or שכינה in the English transliterated as, 'Shekhinah'; and are or is, a variation on an early loanword from Phoenician (the Ancient Greek word for the: ἡ σκηνή or skēnē "tent" or dwelling tent, or a tabernacle, (made of green boughs, or skins or other materials).

For all of this indicates the 'Presence' or 'dwelling' of the Spirit of God (in Christianity 'the Holy Spirit') but in the Hebrew the noun for the 'Holy Spirit' being 'skēnē' being a *feminine* noun (from which Shekinah is believed to have been developed). And it is deliberately used to represent the original Hebrew or Aramaic term. Thus the 'background for feminine characterization of the Holy Spirit as feminine and how that was meant to be brought out in the term Shekhinah is often used in Kabbalah, (Christian) Cabbala and the NHL and Associated texts (like *Pistis Sophia*:see below). But it was taken seriously by those who would later be called 'Gnostics' or *Gnostic-Christians*. It appears to be the basis of the naming of the 'Holy Spirit' as 'a woman' in the Gospel of Philip verse 18 (per Brantingham; and others see: T. P. Brown the Gospel of Philip).

Valentinus and various "trinities"

Now this is not to say that this is the same "trinity"(then or now) as developed over time by the Catholic, Orthodox and Protestant Churches. But many writers have noted that Valentinus may have been the first to strongly posit a trinity of the "Father, Son and Holy Spirit"(more often called something like "The Father (God), Mother (the Holy Spirit, Wisdom, Barbēlō or Sophia) and the Son (the Word and the Logos, the Savior and the "Christ."). But Valentinus died long before the "trinity was developed as we have it today" starting with the first Council of Nicaea in 325 C.E. Valentinus died in around 160 CE.

In like manner the philosophical 'Word,' or 'Logos' was called 'the son of God' by Philo Judaeus (Grosso, Michael. 2015) an Alexandrian (Platonic philosopher) and highly educated, very devout Jewish man (who lived concurrently in the time of Jesus Christ). Philo wrote extensively about the 'Logos' and probably influenced the Apostle John. Philo also said that, 'God is the mind of the Universe' as each of us is the 'god' (*or mind*- italics mine) of our bodies! Mankind Philo noted, is the image and likeness of 'God' figuratively, as our personal individual minds *intelligibly a subliminal consciousness* are part of the *greater mind or supreme consciousness*. Thus the mind or consciousness of a human being makes up part of the overall universal superconsciousness he labeled 'the One' or, God (Grosso, Michael. 2015).

But I strongly emphasize **none of these missing "terms" or beings or "hypostases"** (or theological persons, particularly who would later be part of the Christian trinity) **are found in the** *GMary* (from the Nag Hammadi) and, neither is the "Demiurge" there or as the most common hypostases of the Demiurge or Yaldabaoth, the *'lesser god'* of the Old Testament. None are found in the *GMary*(from the *NHL*) but there are vague allusions only.

Classical Gnosticism

Classical Gnosticism is heavily concerned with the dueling natures of spirit and matter (Good and Evil, Light and Darkness). But unlike other dualist faiths, it was a form of a mitigated dualism or 'Monism' (Brons, David. 2015). This means both the One true God (historically the Monad) is Good and much stronger and greater than Evil (Yaldabaoth).

I today use an even simpler definition for 'Gnosticism' for, the public has spoken and the general academy agrees: these texts will be 'called' Gnostic Christian Apocrypha'. After that point each book can be taken on its exegetical merits. So though I am in agreement with Thomas Patterson Brown that the 'The Gospel of

Thomas, Philip and the Truth are actually 'Christian' (and minimally - and with almost no effect, use the 'Gnostic Theological Story and Exegesis, as found in the *SRevJohn* to the very minimum; (without hindering there otherwise Orthodox Christology) yet I call them 'Gnostic' as that is how they are described almost by all. At least they were found with many Classic texts that utilized the full Gnostic Theology.

'Classical Gnosticism' sees the world of matter as being in a fallen, lesser state to the world of spirit. In classical Gnosticism, the universe begins with an unknown 'Good' God (the Monad). He (the One Good God) creates a series of divine beings. One of the first 'created or emanated' is divine Sophia (or Wisdom) that at times appears to be designated as the Higher or Greater Sophia. This is the 'Sophia' or 'Wisdom' found in the OT Sapiential literature (such as in Proverbs 8), where She is personified as 'Wisdom' *and* the 'Holy Spirit' (who is called and identical to the 'Holy Mother').

Sophia seeks to prove her worth, and becomes 'Sophia the Lesser' when She attempts to create a divine being by herself. Her efforts, undertaken alone (without the Good, Holy Father) produce a flawed divine being, a 'lower, inferior *god*'. This divinity is described in the Apocryphon of John as 'Yaldabaoth'. But he is often described or referred to in classical Gnosticism as the Demiurge. The term *'Demiurge'* is derived from the classical Greek term for a craftsman. Neither a name nor definition is included for the 'demiurge' in these Gnostic Gospels. But, the name of Sophia's demiurgic creation, 'Yaldabaoth' is, in the SRevJohn.

The true Fall

The Demiurge Yaldabaoth believes he is the only god. And sets about creating our flawed and fallen material world. Later both he and Sophia will interact with it. But he declares that he is the only true god.

Yaldabaoth creates a host of petty rulers (known as Archons) to rule over humanity. Gnostic Christians believed the failed creation of 'Yaldabaoth' by Sophia was a catastrophe, and that his later molding of the world and of 'matter' was and *is* the 'true Fall'.

These 'Gnostic' Christians asserted that 'matter' is a dense, darker material… that it is less ethereal, and thus less 'spiritual and against what would be the true wisdom of the Spirit…' and that the 'spirit and spiritual… would not become entangled with matter and 'its' materialism and fleshly outcomes.' (DeConick, April D. 2017; Davies, Stevan. 2005; Hoeller, Stephan A. 2010; Gnostic Society Library, The. 2015).

Classical Gnosticism from around the beginning of the second century viewed the Demiurge as the God (or '*god*') of the Old Testament. This '*god*' created a world of matter, and out of that a world, all and every form of materialism and fleshly desire. Yet unknowingly he (Yaldabaoth) passed along a spark of the 'divine spirit' (of the One Most High and Good God) when breathing upon humanity. When he breathed into Adam and Eve the 'breath or spirit' of the Good God entered them and they lived. Why? Because Yaldabaoth had inherited that spirit from his mother Sophia (as She had when emanated from *God above God*, the Father).

So if a human attains wisdom and enlightenment they grow closer to the spiritual world and closer and experientially know and become 'one' with the true God. This final 'becoming one with, and attaining experientially knowing about *the true One God*' is the attainment of '*Gnosis*'.

With 'Gnosis' they have attained salvation. However, the Demiurge does not wish to see humans ascend above him. So he seeks to keep humanity away from divine wisdom and knowledge. Thus, the events of the Garden of Eden in Genesis have an inverse significance in the Gnostic point of view.

To Gnostics, eating the fruit of the tree of Knowledge by Adam and Eve (in defiance of the '*god*' of this world) was good. Instead of being seen as a fall from Grace it was rather the first step towards wisdom. And, towards a piece of greater spiritual knowledge and existence leading to heaven.

In 1945 CE, peasant farmers digging for fertilizer struck a sealed jar. The buried (and hidden) jar was found near Nag Hammadi in Egypt. The large number of books found at Nag Hammadi will be denoted as 'the Nag Hammadi Library' or the '*NHL*'. Inside the jar was a cache of ancient Gnostic Christian manuscripts. Thirteen leather-bound codices (collections of books, texts or treatises), twelve of them complete, with the thirteenth incomplete.

Before this find in 1945, scholars had found a few other Gnostic codices. Purchased in 1896 through the Cairo 'antiquities market' was the *Secret Revelation of John*. Also called the *Apocryphon of John*, this Codex contained the *Gospel of Mary* and a few other texts.

Later in 1945, scholars found the full text of the *Gospel of Thomas*. And beginning on its last page (and 'attached to it') was the *Gospel of Philip*. The *Gospel of Thomas* is today, the most popular and most studied Gnostic Gospel in history.

'The Gospel of Philip' has been unknown in the West for approximately the last 1,500 years. Only Eastern Byzantine or Orthodox Church Fathers briefly mentioned a *Gospel of Philip*. Surprisingly, they noted that *Thomas and Philip* were always found together! Today these same two Gospels are the most "popularly purchased". Being "read and cited" more than all other Gnostic Gospels (Smith Andrew P. 2015; Bourgeault, Cynthia. 2008)

The Codices

These codices were ancient, handwritten books in the Coptic language. And approximately fifty-two, mostly 'Gnostic' treatises were found (Meyer M., Robinson, J. 2007.)

This book, *'Holy Wisdom and The Logos of God'* (*WisdLogos*) is presenting four of the lost Christian Apocryphal Gospels - the *Gospel of Truth* (*Gtr*), the *Gospel of Philip* (*GPhil*), the *Gospel of Thomas* (*GThom*), and the *Gospel of Mary* (*GMary*) - along with one of the most important texts of Gnostic Christian theology, the *Secret Revelation of John* (*SRevJohn*). The *Gospel of Mary* (*GMary*) was **not** found with the *NHL* books, but crucially the *SRevJohn* was found with both the *GMary and with* the Nag Hammadi finds. *The* SRevJohn (also called the *'Apocryphon of John,'* or the *'Secret Book of John'*) ties the *GMary* (by its literary structure and content) strongly to the *NHL* corpus (Stevan Davies 2005; Karen King 2006).

Pistis Sophia

There are a number of Clearly, 'Gnostic texts' that were found hundreds of years before the 1986 purchase of the *GMary* and the *SRevJohn*. The text that may be most interesting in relation to the *GMary* is *'PistisSophia'*

(*PS*). The *PS* MSS was found around 1770 to 1773 (in Coptic) by Anthony Askew, and being a 'book collector' in an antiquarian bookshop in London. How it ended up there is unknown. Scholars have dated it to between the third and fourth centuries. The British museum bought it from Anthony Askew, an English physician or his family 'and the entire Askew Codex' in about 1785. It was in Coptic and only translated and published first in 1896 (though there were, GRS Mead informs us even earlier translations into Latin (1851) and French (1856). GRS Mead gave his final translation in 1921. Carl Schmidt did a German translation that Mead held in high regard. Schmidt had the German translated into English later by his wife, Violet McDermot Schmidt in 1978.

Old Testament in the Pistis Sophia

In the Pistis Sophia it is a post resurrection revelation of Christ to all the disciples in Mary Magdalene plays a very prominent role. Others have pointed out that Out of the 46 questions asked in the *PS* Mary asks fully 39 of them, the majority of all the many questions put to Jesus about 'Sophia and her full repentance for creating the Chief Archon (or lesser *'god'*) of the aeon of earth. And, about all sorts of other mundane and esoteric matters. It is striking that there are many Old Testament or Jewish scriptures (primarily taken from the Psalms) in the Pistis Sophia there are many of the *Psalms of Solomon* in the *PS* which goes directly against the common belief that 'Gnostics and Gnosticism' wanted nothing to do with the 'Old Testament'. There are also the *Odes of Soloman* in the *PS* (which would be found as a separate text almost two thousand years later. Mary is praised in The *Pistis Sophia* as 'one whose heart is more directed to the Kingdom of Heaven than all her brothers' (Hooper Richard J. 2008)

My definitions of 'Gnostic and Gnosticism'

Hereafter in this book, the term 'Gnostic' text will mean a Gnostic-Christian text, and the term 'Gnostic' or 'Gnosticism' will mean either a Gnostic-Christian or, 'Gnostic-Christianity'. Gnostics in late antiquity called themselves 'Christians,' *not* 'Gnostics'.

I today use a simpler definition for 'Gnosticism' for the public has spoken and the general academy agrees: these will be 'called' Gnostic Christian Apocrypha. After that point each book can be taken on its exegetical merits. So though I am in agreement with Thomas Patterson Brown that the 'The Gospel of Thomas, Philip and the Truth are actually 'Christian' (and minimally - and with almost no effect, use the 'Gnostic Theological Story and Exegesis, as found in the *SRevJohn* to the very minimum; (without hindering there otherwise Orthodox Christology) yet I call them 'Gnostic' as that is how they are described almost by all. At least they were found with many Classic texts that utilized the full Gnostic Theology.

Clearly, there is much controversy about what the term 'Gnostic' means. So, this is what is meant by the terms 'Gnostic and Gnosticism' in this book unless otherwise noted. Pre-Christian Jewish, Platonic, Egyptian or, other sources for Gnosticism are not being denied. (King, Karen L 2003; 2006; DeConick, April D. 2017.)

Classical Gnosticism

Classical Gnosticism is heavily concerned with the dueling natures of spirit and matter (Good and Evil, Light and Darkness). But unlike other dualist faiths, it was a form of a mitigated dualism or 'Monism' (Brons, David. 2015). This means both the One true God (historically the Monad) is Good and much stronger and greater than Evil (Yaldabaoth).

'Classical Gnosticism' sees the world of matter as being in a fallen, lesser state to the world of spirit. In classical Gnosticism, the universe begins with an unknown 'Good' God (the Monad). He (the One Good God) creates a series of divine beings. One of the first 'created or emanated' is divine Sophia (or Wisdom) that at times appears to be designated as the Higher or Greater Sophia. This is the 'Sophia' or 'Wisdom' found in the OT Sapiential literature (such as in Proverbs 8), where She is personified as 'Wisdom' *and* the 'Holy Spirit' (who is called and identical to the 'Holy Mother').

Sophia seeks to prove her worth, and becomes 'Sophia the Lesser' when She attempts to create a divine being by herself. Her efforts, undertaken alone (without the Good, Holy Father) produce a flawed divine being, a 'lower, inferior *god*'. This divinity is described in the Apocryphon of John as 'Yaldabaoth'. But he is often described or referred to in classical Gnosticism as the Demiurge. The term '*Demiurge*' is derived from the classical Greek term for a craftsman. Neither a name nor definition is included for the 'demiurge' in these Gnostic Gospels. But, the name of Sophia's demiurgic creation, 'Yaldabaoth' is, in the *SRevJohn.*

The true Fall

The Demiurge Yaldabaoth believes he is the only god. And sets about creating our flawed and fallen material world. Later both he and Sophia will interact with it. But he declares that he is the only true god.

Yaldabaoth creates a host of petty rulers (known as Archons) to rule over humanity. Gnostic Christians believed the failed creation of 'Yaldabaoth' by Sophia was a catastrophe, and that his later molding of the world and of 'matter' was and *is* the 'true Fall'.

These 'Gnostic' Christians asserted that 'matter' is a dense, darker material… that it is less ethereal, and thus less 'spiritual and against what would be the true wisdom of the Spirit…' and that the 'spirit and spiritual… would not become entangled with matter and 'its' materialism and fleshly outcomes.' (DeConick, April D. 2017; Davies, Stevan. 2005; Hoeller, Stephan A. 2010; Gnostic Society Library, The. 2015).

Classical Gnosticism from around the beginning of the second century viewed the Demiurge as the God (or '*god*') of the Old Testament. This '*god*' created a world of matter, and out of that a world, all and every form of materialism and fleshly desire. Yet unknowingly he (Yaldabaoth) passed along a spark of the 'divine spirit' (of the One Most High and Good God) when breathing upon humanity. When he breathed into Adam and Eve the 'breath or spirit' of the Good God entered them and they lived. Why? Because Yaldabaoth had inherited that spirit from his mother Sophia (as She had when emanated from *God above God*, the Father).

So if a human attains wisdom and enlightenment they grow closer to the spiritual world and closer and experientially know and become 'one' with the true God. This final 'becoming one with, and attaining experientially knowing about *the true One God*' is the attainment of '*Gnosis*'.

With 'Gnosis' they have attained salvation. However, the Demiurge does not wish to see humans ascend above him. So he seeks to keep humanity away from divine wisdom and knowledge. Thus, the events of the Garden of Eden in Genesis have an inverse significance in the Gnostic point of view.

To Gnostics, eating the fruit of the tree of Knowledge by Adam and Eve (in defiance of the '*god*' of this world) was good. Instead of being seen as a fall from Grace it was rather the first step towards wisdom. And, towards a piece of greater spiritual knowledge and existence leading to heaven.

An Additional Note About the 'Missing Scriptural terms' in the *'Gospel According to Mary'*

Later Christians, in theologically defining 'the trinity,' (the Father, Son and Holy Spirit) eventually turned away from *'God'* defined though the term 'the Monad'. But it appears they had not done so at the time of the writing of the *GMary*. And this was true too in proto-canonical circles. Other favorite *'Gnostic'* terms for *'God'* are missing in the *GMary*. Number one, of course, is ***'the Father,'*** and also, ***'the One'***. Yet 'the One' is used of Jesus and I thus use it more loosely. **But frequent use of 'Son of Man'** (ⲡ·ϣⲏⲣⲉ ⲅⲁⲣ ⲙ·ⲡ·ⲣⲱⲙⲉ **or** ⲛϣⲏⲣⲉ ⲙⲡⲣⲱⲙⲉ) **is** *in* **the GMary (- a 'Danielic and Enochic' term that relates Jesus both to** *God* **and to being 'the Messiah.')** And in canonical use of the 'son of Man,' He and the Father are One. So it is justified to use 'the One' for God, the Father. Also not used of God, but were for Jesus was 'Lord and/or Savior'. I equate Christ as 'one with the Father and the Father one with the Son'. So in this case, *God* is also LORD and Savior. And, therefore a justification to use the term *'God'* a few times which otherwise is not found in the *GMary*. There is no 'Most High,' but still at that time 'the Monad' was contemporaneously understood. And at that time used by both Judaism and nascent Christianity. So, 'Most High' is certainly derived from the Greek definition of 'the Monad' (also often denoted as the 'One'.)

Strikingly nowhere in the *GMary* is 'Holy Spirit or Holy Mother' used. While both 'blessed' and 'spirit,' are ('blessed' is a synonym for 'holy'). These justify by (*my*) liberal exegesis throughout this text, use of the term 'Holy Spirit' (and its associations with the Holy Mother). We will see in the *Secret Revelation of John* (or *SRevJohn*,) *God* Most High or '*God Above God*' (see below) first emanated 'Wisdom' as found in *Proverbs 8* (Wisdom in Greek being: 'Sophia'.) Wisdom and Sophia are also given the name '*Barbēlō*' in Pistis Sophia (or PS) and especially in the *SRevJohn* (also called the '*Apocryphon of John*').

> Hereafter, singular notations of *'God'* with a capital 'G' and in Italics are meant to express this title: 'God Above God'. *God* in the nascent practice of '*the Way*' and into late antiquity was often defined still as the Monad or, the Unknown (Good) God Most High. 'God' (in italics) means the God Above God or... (the) '*God*' above, every human conception of any 'God' (or 'gods'.)

Other missing Terms In The *GMary*

In the *GMary* these and other missing terms does not mean these terms were not used. We have ten missing pages and Gnostic scripture often used these terms (or their equal). Whatever the case may be, I judge the title 'Son of Man' (in the *GMary*) the 'Danielic Messiah'. Whether He came as the proto-canonical 'Son of Man' fully human and fully divine. Or, as human but, one like Moses, somehow divine and human, this being the 'son of Man'. Either way, he was a highly devout and extraordinarily spiritual Jewish man.

Jesus Signs and Wonders

Jesus came with 'Signs and Wonders' or what we call 'abilities and power or, powers'; and which today are labeled as 'paranormal or parapsychological abilities' (along with nature 'miracles' and psychokinesis as great or greater than those of Moses). Reading minds, healing through a touch or a word or sending his thoughts into the minds of others; seeing others or events far outside of his or normal human vision; and, seeing into the future; even, raising the 'dead' (like Elijah or Elisha). And like a 'quantum' particle 'tunneling through a solid 'wall' He (the Savior or Christ) could simply pass through a solid door into a room with locked doors'. Significant support for such heightened abilities now has a large body of scientific evidence supporting the validity of such abilities as Telepathy (the Samaritan woman at the well) Clairvoyance (seeing something far outside of normal human visual capability as in the Anointed's seeing Nathaniel studying scripture under the tree) prophecy or precognition (this temple will be destroyed; or 'my hour has not yet come') healing (making a man born blind see or, getting a paralytic of many years get up and walk) are now accessible greater than any other time in the history of humankind, science and history itself (Radin, Dean. 1997; 2013; 2014; 2016; 2019; Bem D, tressoldi P, Rabeyron T and Duggan M. 2016; Krippler, Stanley., Rock, Adam J., Beischel, Julie., et al. 2013; Betty, Stafford. 2011; 2014; 2016; Beischel J, Boccuzzi M, Biuso M, Rock AJ. 2015; Beischel J, Boccuzzi M, Biuso M, Rock AJ. 2015; Beischel, J 2019; Delorme A, Beischel J, Michel L, Boccuzzi M, Radin D, Mills PJ. 2013; Keener, Craig S. Miracles 2011).

Mary's Vision of the Resurrected Christ

After death (as he did in the *GMary*) He came back, exalted and alive. For, He came back in clearly overwhelming 'experiential visions' or greater. Perceived 'alive' He showed himself to Mary, Thomas, Peter, Paul, John, James and more. He was, without doubt, a high or even the highest, Savior and prophet. And in those with 'eyes to see' the Messiah of Israel and of the world, human or divine (or both). Nevertheless, the 'Danielic title, 'Son of Man' was fraught with seditious undertones. When the Romans heard he was being called The 'Son of Man' they did not hear simply that he was a 'prophet' but a rebel. This *Enochic, Danielic* title meant he was 'the leader or King of Israel. Leader (in their eyes) of a rebellion'. Jesus the Anointed (to the Romans) was a dangerous pretender to being 'King of the Jews or, of Israel' (and since the Emperor was the 'true and legal' King of the World and Jerusalem) this sealed His fate. He must be put to death and, He was.

Ultimately, it seems this is the reason the Romans crucified and killed Jesus (this seditious 'King of the Jews'). So what did the Gnostics mean by *their* use of the title, 'son of Man'? It appears they held various and different positions (not unlike ancient proto-canonical Christianity and modern Christianity with Catholicism and Protestantism - not to mention the Western Orthodox and Eastern, or 'Oriental, Orthodox' churches today); along with this are the non-trinitarian Christian churches like the Church of Jesus Christ of Latter Day Saints and other groups originally derived from Christianity such as the Unitarians. Yet it appears to me there is another growing body 'Ecclesia's' (or Churches) of 'Christians' (many members who today no longer call themselves 'Christians' but 'Gnostics,' Esotericists or by other names - but not 'Christian'.) However some Gnostic churches often boldly state that they are 'Gnostic-Christian' (such as the Ecclesia Gnostica church or the Ecclesia Pistis Sophia. But unmistakably *all* identifying partially as 'Christian' or no Jesus Christ in some sacred and High manner as for example, *one of or, the highest prophet and*, the Messiah. And like the 'non-Gnostic' Christian churches these 'Gnostic-Christian Ecclesia' have and hold various positions regarding Jesus divinity and humanity. These vary from his being only a man an 'ascended master' and/or a the 'Highest Prophet' to an*Incarnation*(similar to the mainstream) of *God* Himself. Yet most of these 'Ecclesia or Churches' agree that Jesus was at the least, 'One with God (in Will), as God was One with (Him) the Son' and a great spiritual teacher. As a Prophet at least *similar-too* and like *or above* Moses his teaching in the Old and New Testaments is revered (along with for example the Nag Hammadi and similar scriptures). And so likewise held His 'true Father' (real, or *spiritually*) was 'God the Father' and that made him and makes him 'a,' or *the* 'Messiah of God Most High' with or without the incarnation.

Yet though the 'Incarnation' is not clearly spelled out in the *GMary* (which we will return to visit below). Surprisingly it is *certainly so* in the *Gospel of Philip (GPhil)*:

> GPhil 25 I pity and rebuke those who deny resurrection of the flesh. Who claim no flesh can inherit eternal life. Neither human flesh nor blood can inherit the Kingdom; the Life to Come. Then what is unable? Yeshua said it: he who eats not my flesh and drinks not my blood, has no eternal life within him.
>
> What is his flesh? It is the Bread of Being (the Logos, Torah, and Gnosis). And what is his blood? (the wine) the Holy Spirit and Life. Those who have this, have spirit and life now and, in the Life to Come. Whoever welcomes these has received real food, real drink, and a garment. But remember...
>
> What you are — you are in a body; What you do — you do in a body.
> Arise thou now — in this body, in this life!
> For everything exists in it.
> Death awaits us, but God will remember.

> Remember your body, soul and spirit.
> And the Breath of the Blessed One
> will knit you back together.
> His divine gnosis and power will bring us back. And the Logos resurrect and animate us and we will become light.*(Brantingham 2017; 2019)*

And the 'Incarnation' is clearly spelled out in the profound work of Valentinus himself in his *Gospel of Truth (Gtr)*

Gtr 16 …Incarnation becomes the Word and the ecclesia and the Logos of it. … His love, the Logos embodies it…

Gtr 21 Yet in ignorance Error could not see that the Logos was the Word; nor understand that the Word had become flesh, and a Man… the 'One' and, the 'Truth'. And so the Logos walked alongside humanity, the people of this earthly aeon…

The great scholar Thomas Patterson Brown (2014) noted that in the *GThom* 28 or verse 28 Jesus says,

I stood in the flesh ('sarc,' was used as a 'loanword' for the Coptic), incarnated in their world revealing myself a man and Messiah, to all. But I found everyone drunk and intoxicated…

Wisdom (Sophia) and Barbēlō in *Pistis Sophia*

And, What are we to make of this verse in the *Pistis Sophia* (another 'Gnostic text' in which Mary Magdalene is a full Apostle and referenced more often than any other Apostle including all the well known male Apostles).

So we see Jesus himself say, in GRS Mead's (1916; 1921) translation of *Pistis Sophia*… in which both the Most High God and Jesus are identified as 'the First Mystery' that hints at the 'incarnation' being a 'reincarnation,' a concept that harkens toward 'Righteous Seth' who was head of the steadfast and immovable congregation and community 'the unbreakable Ones' (or the 'Seed of Seth') found in the *SRevJohn* (GRS Mead's 1916; 1921)

> 'And Jesus continued again in the discourse and said: "It came to pass then thereafter, that at the command of the First Mystery I looked down on the world of mankind and found Mary, who is called 'my mother' according to the body of matter. I spake with her in the type of Gabriēl, and when she had turned herself to the height towards me, I cast thence into her the first power which I had received from Barbēlō— that is the body which I have borne in the height. And instead of the soul I cast into her the power which I have received from the great Sabaōth, the Good, who is in the region of the Right.'

Strikingly we see in the *Secret Revelation of John (SRevJohn)* these words regarding (Brantingham, James. *SRevJohn* 2019)

> Yet even before the foundation, His (the Most High's) Protennoia (or earliest thoughts) and Pronoia (His Providence or, plan of salvation) had become real. One of the first thoughts appeared before Him, Perfect in Purity and Power. Look! She, Barbēlō is His luminescence and manifests as the Holy Spirit and 'Mother,'. For He, the Holy Father; with Her (together) are Perfect in Power. Thus arising in and from His 'nous' (His mind and heart) and, in His likeness, image and power is the Mother who 'is one' with the Father in will. She, with the Logos and as Wisdom completes the Word. Therefore they are the Providence of the plan of salvation for those who will have need of it…
>
> Barbēlō is: Holy Spirit And,
> Thrice male,
> Thrice Powerful,
> Thrice named
> (the Father, Mother and Son) for…

The Unbegotten Father brought forth Wisdom; revealing the sacred name of 'Barbēlō,' 'the Mother,' who comes from out of His pure light. Behold the Father (the Virgin Invisible Spirit) looking back and into Her, caused Her to conceive the light (of life); for She had received the 'the Spark' of the Fathers's Light.

…This brought forth the only-begotten, the Logos… the Son who would descend into and become the Anointed.

…And the Word incarnated and became Christ the Man, the Divine Self-Generated One (on earth).

(Brantingham, James. *SRevJohn* 2019)

Holy Mother a Gnostic Substitution for the Holy Spirit

Though the term 'Mother' is also nowhere to be found in the *GMary* it too (like 'the Father') can be *derived* from 'the Son'. **So, one or more of these terms is highly probable in the missing 10 pages or other half of the book.** But the 'Holy Spirit' as the 'Holy Mother' should not be confused with the canonical 'Holy Mary' his 'earthly mother' (and Mary his earthly mother is canonically called… in Catholicism, the 'Holy Mother'). Furthermore, in the *GMary* 'Mary Magdalene' speaks of 'his Kingdom'. And as in Daniel, so in *1 Enoch* (as accepted by many Jews like the Essenes, or other so-called 'Enochian Jews' some of whom may have become 'protofollowers' of Jesus (an 'Enochian Jew,' as Jack Kilmon makes the case (2019). What some today believed became (as 'Enochian

Jews') followers of, 'the Way'. These texts (Daniel and Enoch) are believed by some to have 'primed' Jews (by prophecy) to later become **followers** of Jesus Christ. Not only Daniel but also Enoch, or *1 Enoch*. *1 Enoch* has been found in extant Septuagint LXX's, the first and most popular Jewish 'Greek translation' of their bible, or the Greek Tanakh; later called by 'the Way or Christians' the 'Old Testament'.

Enoch's *inclusion of the Messiah* was found in both *Daniel* in the Tanakh and in *Daniel* and *Enoch* in the LXX. One of these LXX's *without doubt* contained *1 Enoch*. And there is further proof of this in *1 Enoch's* inclusion by the Ethiopian Orthodox Churches in their complete Old Testament (derived from one of the most ancient Septuagint's and translated into their tongue 'Ge'ez' (and because for them as Christians) like Daniel, Enoch had 'the Messiah and Son of Man' too. For *Enoch* or *1 Enoch* was written before the birth of Jesus and is dated to about 100 BCE. In, *1 Enoch* (as in *Daniel*), the 'Son of Man' **is** the highly exalted 'King' of Heaven and 'King' *spiritually* of the earth and, therefore is the 'Messiah' of Israel (and of the world) protected by the One, **Good** God Most High (Brown, Thomas P. 2014; Barnstone, William. 1984; Kilmon, Jack. 2019)

Son of Man, Son of Humanity and the Messiah

However, the term 'Son of Man or, son of Man' was found originally in the Coptic (see Mattison, M. 2013; Leloup J-I. 2002; King, Karen. 1978; 2003; 2007; MacRae, George W., Wilson., Robert. McL. 2000) 'ⲡ·ϣⲏⲣⲉ ⲅⲁⲣ ⲙ·ⲡ·ⲣⲱⲙⲉ' (*and*, in the Greek). It is true that this can mean Son of Humanity since the term for "human" is 'ⲣⲱⲙⲉ' but since so much is missing from the Coptic *GMary* clearly the Choice of 'Man' (and thus the Christological title) ties this work by *"the Apostle Mary Magdalene or the 'Marian community'"* to the "proto-canonical and the chosen Canonical Scriptures" prior to the Council of Nicea. As Karen King suggested, the *GMary* might have been part of (for a while), the early Canon up to Constantine (and not *'just'* a Gnostic Gospel - *no offense intended toward Gnosticism or Gnostic texts*). As David Saunders (2021) points out, even in the twenty-first century there is no consensus among all the Biblical (including Gnostic scholars) about how "The Son of Man" (using the Coptic above) should be interpreted. And the first (and many after 1945, and up to the current day) offer translations using the title 'the Son of Man' (Leloup, J-I 2002; MacRae, George W., Wilson., Robert. McL. 2000). However other modern scholars like King and Mattison choose the 'Son of Humanity.' Jehanne de Quillian in 2011 published "The Gospel of the Beloved Companion. The Complete Gospel of Mary Magdalene. de Quillian uses (I believe) only the 'Son of Humanity.' It seems there is a very broad agreement about this title and its place for saying "myself," or, "myself and my community." But even the majority of Jewish scholars agree that

For some reason I have only just recently come to know about this, Jehanne de Quillian's translation of "The Gospel of the Beloved Companion. The Complete

Gospel of Mary Magdalene." de Quillian claims that she translated it from the original Greek (and that it was probably brought from Alexandria to the Languedoc (Southern France, or Roman Gaul) in the early to middle part of the first century and whoever received it eventually translated it into Occitan around the 12th century, the language of the Languedoc. "Her spiritual community" (which she does not name) has preserved it since that time for nearly a millennia. Who had it before that time? It appears from what she writes that some part of the early or what would become the Cathar movement had it and it was in there with them in the Languedoc. She speaks of the Albigensian Crusade and Genocide by the then Catholic church (and associated "countries" beginning in 1209). Of course this was another of the real "genocides," and is well documented (along with those by Stalin, Hitler, Mao and Pol Pot) see: Werth, Nicolas; Panné, Jean-Louis; Paczkowski, Andrzej; et al. (1999). I cannot take a position about this book as I have not yet purchased and read it. Kaufmann Kohler notes (2021) that "ben enosh," is used only once in Psalm 144… "Jehovah, what is man, that thou takest knowledge of him? Or the son of man, that thou makest account of him? But "ben adam" is used extensively throughout the Tanakh or OT for the "Messiah" (including much Second Temple literature such as Enoch. Kohler notes that "bar enash" has a peculiar use in Daniel:

Son of Man

> There is no dispute among commentators that Israel is thereby meant; but they differ as to the question whether the "son of man" depicted is merely a personification of the people, or whether the writer had in mind a concrete personality representing Israel, such as the Messiah or Israel's guardian angel, the archangel Michael. The latter interpretation, proposed by Cheyne and adopted by others, has little in its favor compared with the older opinion that the person of the Messiah is alluded to—a view shared by the Rabbis.

So more Rabbis and Academic Scholars of Judaism look toward an individual Messiah than "one like a son of man" being Israel. But it is no different in Christianity (Biblical and Gnostic Scholars included). Some say "Son of Man" means the Messiah, Jesus the Anointed and some suggest it means "the church, as a whole" or "the Anointed and His followers - first the Twelve Apostles, then the Apostle Mary (of Magdala) and all of those directly around Jesus during and just after His mission including those who became followers after the resurrection.

However in one review it is stated that in this "Gospel of the Beloved Companion…" a decision was made to translate the "Son of Man" into the "Son of Humanity." Son of Man in Jewish is "ben adam" or, "ben enosh." In Aramaic it is "bar enash," "bar nasha," or "bar nash" (Kohler, Kaufmann. 2021)

Son of Man. In Mattison and King

The Son of Man in Mattison's Coptic to English interlinear translation is: 'ⲡ·ϢⲎⲢⲈ ⲅⲁⲣ ⲙ·ⲡ·ⲣⲱⲙⲉ' and the Coptic means: ' the-Son For of-the-Human.' And King probably used (ⲡ·ϢⲎⲢⲈ ⲅⲁⲣ ⲙ·ⲡ·ⲣⲱⲙⲉ) but, since there is a "lacuna" (or a hole) in the Greek text (she noted by using Brackets) translated the Greek Manuscript as the, 'child or humanity.' For me the Coptic is virtually everywhere else the: 'Son of Man,' and so also by MacRae, ⲛϢⲎⲢⲈ ⲙ·ⲡ·ⲣⲱⲙⲉ the: **'Son of Man'** as found in Daniel. **'Child of humanity'** (a genderless) Messiah is not acceptable to me (though I know King's intention was to be 'inclusive'). So we also have in the *GThom*:

GThom 106 (Coptic) Sons of Men in *GThom*

The Sons of Men: N̄·ϢⲎⲢⲈ M̄·ⲡ·ⲣⲱⲙⲉ (Coptic)

Greek for **Son of Man** is: γιος του ανθρώπου and the *Koine* Greek, "ὁ υἱὸς τοῦ ἀνθρώπου," which again is = *the* **Son of Man.** Or on occasion is found as: υἱὸς τοῦ ἀνθρώπου, which is also the **Son of Man** for υἱὸς means the "son"!

Then in the *GThom* 28 **"Sons of Men"** can be used as the "children," or the **sons** of humanity" (Koine Greek): υἱὸις τῶν ἀν(θρώπ)ων

Hebrews 2:6-9 states:

But one testified in a certain place, saying: "What is man that You are mindful of him, or the **Son of man** that You take care of him?" Some say the Christological connection is unlikely due to this being a quotation of Psalms; Really? Does Hebrews discuss the Messiah?

So, the **Son of Man** in Hebrew, Aramaic, Greek literature (and Coptic) could be used for: the "Son of Man and Israel," or 'One like a Man and Israel.' Or similarly, 'One like a Man and the followers of Jesus and 'the Way.' Or, One like a Man and Christians.' But today many scholars deny it means more than Israel alone, or Christianity or the Church, alone. So "one like a son of man coming on the clouds of heaven seated next to the Power," is like: Israel, or the Followers of Jesus and the Way,' or Christianity," coming on the clouds - seated next to the Power ('*God*')." Yet. there is **no doubt** that it was also used for 'the Messiah' (in Hebrew, Aramaic, Greek *and* Coptic). Most Jewish Scholars - not all, but most, think that the Danielic "one like a Son of Man" means the "Messiah." *Their* Messiah (the Jewish Messiah for 'Judaism") who for them has not yet showed up! Virtually the same could be said for Christianity: One like the Son of Man can just mean 'the Church' (or 'Christians') or the "Son of Man and His followers of Jesus," or, 'the Anointed' sitting next to the Power. And of course Christians two thousand years ago (and today) decided it *did mean the (Jewish) - but also, the Messiah for the world had come.*

Though God is more than a man (or a woman), Jesus ***did not come*** as a **genderless child** but (*and without shame or embarrassment*) came as a Man! And the *GMary* also denotes this… *as it is also found* in 1 *Enoch* and in the '*Danielic title*'!

He was the... '**Son** of Man,' and so (*in these texts*) in the *GMary*, He is the (male) 'Messiah'! This takes nothing away from the Apostle Mary of Magdalene nor from the *GMary*!

Women in the Gospels

Another issue found (somewhat less) in Gnostic but clearly in the Canonical Gospels (and texts), is that most women (except for Mary) are rarely mentioned (we have the Apostle Junia mentioned by Paul) and other women in Jesus' inner circle so, Priscilla and her husband Aquila, and Mary and "the beloved Persis" and Julia, and Nereus' sister, who worked and traveled as missionaries (and there were more). So I have added the Apostle Junia in, for inclusiveness and historical accuracy (since it is now known that women disciples accompanied Jesus and that some of these 'disciples were recognized as Apostles' such as Junia, and labeled so by Paul - and Mary (and apparently by Jesus). Thus here, the 'followers' (or disciples) are 'Brothers and Sisters' *the* 'followers of Jesus' (instead of *just* 'Brothers or Male Followers' alone). Also Mary Magdalene (and Junia) are outright, Apostles (which she was technically always, but only now officially, and fully recognized as such today by the Catholic Church). Previous translations of the Gospel of Mary referred only obliquely to 'followers' (not even using the term 'disciples'). Yet the context (of his 'followers') is clearly about the 'Twelve Disciples and/or other 'following Apostles'. However, today we celebrate that Mary Magdalene fully belongs to 'the Apostolate,' and is so recognized 'officially' (within the Catholic Church) ...and that: into the Age, unto the Ages to come, World Without End...! (King, Karen L. 2003; 2007; Pederson, Rena. 2006; Holy See Press Office 2016.)

No 'Named Demiurge in the GMary'

There are common names for the 'demiurge' in the Nag Hammadi Library. And, in Valentinian but especially Sethian texts. In the *NHL*, he is 'son' of Sophia and *some* manner of Deity. But in actions, he appears the 'lesser *god*' of earth; or as Yaldabaoth the '*god* of this world' in the *Secret Revelation of John*. The term 'demiurge,' is a word borrowed from 'platonism'. There it means 'a helpmate or craftsman serving God in fabricating creation'. Sophia (Wisdom) in *Proverbs 8* fills this role. But it is term never used in the *GMary* or in any *other* Gnostic book. It is the term used academically to describe 'Yaldabaoth, 'son of Chaos,'. And Yaldabaoth is called elsewhere Saklas the 'fool' or Samael 'the blind'. 'Yaldabaoth' in particular, is used in the *SRevJohn*. Though he is not found 'explicitly' (it is possibly implicitly) in the dark or negative personified attributes in the *GMary*. Looking at the *GMary* in Mary's ascent of Her spirit to 'heaven' she is assaulted and assailed. These negative 'Personifications' such as: 'forbidden desire' attack her. And, 'Evil and Darkness, and notably 'Ignorance,' pummel Mary while apparent depression gives her again a 'Zeal for Death, or to escape through 'Pleasure' and 'the Flesh'. These certainly are not uncommon emotions or thoughts and for many today are part of the human condition.

But I conjoin all these terms in the *GMary* and label them together as either *the* 'False Spirit' or *the* 'Evil One'. These easily are construed as aspects of a demiurge. However, this is uncertain. Though the 'Gnostic demiurge' (or lesser '*god*') is all these things and more.

The Problem of Evil

Though 'he, Yaldabaoth would be denoted much later as *'ha satan,'* ('a devil' in *Pistis Sophia,* and 'Satan' with the Cathars) his divinity, even before that time *was* one significant *'Gnostic* answer' to the problem of Evil or, Theodicy (Mead, G.R.S. 2016; 1921; Smith Andrew P. 2015.) This demiurge though does not appear by any of his common names (see above) in the extant pages of the *GMary*. Even though, the *GMary* (with the *SRevJohn*) was first purchased on the Antiquities Market in Cairo in 1896 long before the discovery of the 1945 Nag Hammadi Library (or *NHL*) cache of texts, the *GMary* was **not** found with the NHL's copies of the *SRevJohn*. The *GMary* was not found in the NHL. With so much of the book missing, and without clear 'Sethian or Valentinian' key words or redaction (or any other obvious 'school's' characteristics) Karen King suggests it is simply (and essentially) 'Christian' with no clear contradictions to canonicity. She posits it could have been part of a Christian community that was maintaining the 'traditions of Mary Magdalene and based on their foundation by her or on another female Apostle like Junia. King suggest these communities allowed women to participate fully even at the top in clerical posts such as a Bishop or Deacon (King, Karen 2003; 2007.)

References for *"The Gospel According to Mary of Magdala"*

Akenson, Donald H. (2000.) Saint Saul a skeleton key to the historical Jesus. Oxford University Press. New York, NY

Akenson, Donald H. (2001.) Surpassing Wonder: The Invention of the Bible and the Talmuds. Chicago: University of Chicago Press

Bauckham, Richard. (2006) Jesus and the Eyewitnesses: The Gospels as Eyewitness Testimony. Eerdmans Publish- ing, Grand Rapids, MI 2006

Barbēlō (2019) in: https://en.wikipedia.org/wiki/Barbelo Accessed 4 -19 -2019

> I prefer Alastair Logan's (1996) explanation of this name, Barbēlō as from the Hebrew *'barah ba 'lo,'* or "daughter of the Lord"

Barnstone, William. (1984) The Other Bible. HarperCollins. New York, NY.

Barnstone, William. (1984) *1 Enoch* (Book of Parables or Similitudes) *in:* The Other Bible. HarperCollins, New York, NY., 1984.

Barnstone, William., Meyer, Marvin. (2011) The Gnostic Bible: Revised and Expanded 1st ed. Boston, Massachusetts, New Seeds Books.

Barnstone, William. (2009.) The Restored New Testament: A New translation with Commentary Including the Gnostic Gospels of Thomas, Mary and Judas. Publisher W.W. Norton & Co. New York, NY

Beischel Julie. (2013) Among Mediums: A Scientist's Quest for Answers. Publisher: Windbridge Institute. Tucson Arizona

Beischel Julie. (2014) From the Mouths of Mediums Vol. 1: Experiencing Communication (From the Mouths of Mediums: Conversations with Windbridge Certified Research Mediums). Publisher: Windbridge Institute. Tucson Arizona

Beischel J, Boccuzzi M, Biuso M, Rock AJ. (2015) Anomalous information reception by research mediums under blinded conditions II: replication and extension. Explore (NY). 2015 Mar-Apr;11(2):136-42. doi: 10.1016/j.explore.2015.01.001. Epub 2015 Jan 7. PubMed PMID: 25666383.

Beischel Julie. (2019) Investigating Mediums : A Windbridge Institute Collection. Publisher: Windbridge Institute. Tucson Arizona

Bem D, tressoldi P, Rabeyron T and Duggan M. (2016) Feeling the future: A meta-analysis of 90 experiments on the anomalous anticipation of random future events version 2; referees: 2 approved F1000Research 2016, 4:1188 (doi: 10.12688/f1000research.7177.2)

Bernhard, Andrew (10, 11, 2012). "How The Gospel of Jesus's Wife Might Have Been Forged" (in PDF). gospels.net. Archived from the original (PDF) on March 5, 2016. Accessed and Retrieved June 4 2018.

Betty, Stafford. (2011) The Afterlife Unveiled: What the Dead are Telling Us About Their World. O-Books John Hunt Pub. Ltd. Alresford, Hants UK.

Betty, Stafford. (2014) Heaven and Hell Unveiled. Updates from the World of Spirit. White Crow Books. Guildford, UK.

Betty, Stafford. (2016) When did you become less by Dying? After Life: the evidence. White Crow Books. Guildford, UK

Brantingham, James. (2017) The Gospel of Philip. A New translation. CreateSpace Independent Pub. Amazon Digital Services LLC. Seattle, WA.

Brantingham, James. (2018) The Gospel of Thomas: Authors' own translation.

Brantingham, James. (2018) The Gospel of Mary: Authors' own translation and interpretation.

Brown, T. Patterson. (2014) The Gospels of Thomas, Philip and Truth. Available from http://www.freelyre- ceive.net/metalogos/files/intro.html Accessed 5 25 2014

Bauckham, Richard. (2006) Jesus and the Eyewitnesses: The Gospels as Eyewitness Testimony. Eerdmans Publishing, Grand Rapids, MI 2006

Caruana, Laurence. (2015) The Gnostic Q Glossary of Gnostic Terms. Available at: http://www.gnosticq.com/az.text/glos.af.html Accessed 3 18 2015

Charlesworth, James H. (1973) The Odes of Solomon. Oxford University Press. . Oxford, UK (Charlesworth, James. Odes Sol 1973)

Close, ER and Neppe, V. (2015) Putting Consciousness into the Equations of Mathematics: the third substance Gimmel and trUE IQ Nexus J 7:4; 7.119, 2015 v4 160111 © ECAO

Close Edward R., Neppe, Vernon M. (2015) translating Fifteen Mysteries of the Universe by Applying a Nine Dimensional Spinning Model of Finite Reality: A Perspective, the Standard Model and triadic Dimensional-Distinction Vortical Paradigm, Part I. NeuroQuantology June 2015 Volume 13, Issue 2; 205-217

Close Edward R., Neppe, Vernon M. (2015) translating Fifteen Mysteries of the Universe by Applying a Nine Dimensional Spinning Model of Finite Reality: A Perspective, the Standard Model and triadic Dimensional-Distinction Vortical Paradigm, Part II. NeuroQuantology June 2015 Volume 13, Issue 3; 348-360

Close Edward R. Mathematical Unity of Space, Time, Mass, Energy & Consciousness in: Schwartz, Gary E., Woollacott Marjorie H. (2019) Is Consciousness Primary?: Perspectives from the Founding Members of the Academy for the Advancement of Postmaterialist Sciences (Advances in ... the Advancement of Postmaterialist Sciences). Copyright 2019 © by the Academy for the Advancement of the Postmaterialist Sciences www.aapsglobal.com

Davies, Stevan. (2005) The Secret Book of John. The Gnostic Gospel Annotated & Explained. Skylight Paths Publishing. Woodstock, Vermont

Davidson, Gustav. (1967). A dictionary of angels: including the fallen angels. The Free Press Simon and Schuster. New York, NY

Delorme A, Beischel J, Michel L, Boccuzzi M, Radin D, Mills PJ. (2013) Electrocortical activity associated with subjective communication with the deceased. Front Psychol. 2013 Nov 20;4:834. doi: 10.3389/fpsyg. 2013.00834. eCollection 2013. PubMed PMID: 24312063; PubMed Central PMCID: PMC3834343.

DeConick, April D. (2001) Voices of the Mystics: Early Christian Discourse in the Gospel of John and Thomas and Other Ancient Christian Literature. Publisher T&T Clark, New York, NY

DeConick, April D. (2017.) The Gnostic New Age: How a countercultural spirituality revolutionized religion from antiquity to today. Columbia University Press. New York, NY

Ehrman, Bart. (2004) Truth and Fiction in The Da Vinci Code: A Historian reveals what we really know about Jesus, Mary Magdalene and Constantine. Oxford University Press. New York, NY.

Ehrman, Bart D. (2006.) Peter, Paul and Mary Magdalene: The Followers of Jesus in History and Legend. Oxford University Press. New York, NY.

Emmel, Stephan. (2021). The Dialogue of the Savior. The Gnostic Society Library. gnosis.org (Accessed 4 19 2021)

Funk, Wolf-Peter. (2007.) The First Revelation (Apocalypse) of James, in: Meyer, Marvin W.; Robinson, James M.. The Nag Hammadi Scriptures. HarperCollins. New York, NY.

Funk, Wolf-Peter. (2007.) The Second Revelation (Apocalypse) of James, in: Meyer, Marvin W.; Robinson, James M.. The Nag Hammadi Scriptures. HarperCollins. New York, NY.

Friedman, Richard E. (2017.) The Exodus. HarperCollins. New York, NY.

Gnostic Society Library, The. (2015) The Nag Hammadi Library. Available at http://gnosis.org/naghamm/nhl.html Accessed 2/7 2015

Grant, Robert McQueen. (1967.) Gnosticism. Columbia University Press. New York, NY

Greyson, Bruce (2021). After: A Doctor Explores What Near-Death Experiences Reveal about Life and Beyond Saint Martin's Essentials Press ebook.

Grobel, Kendrick. (1960) The Gospel of Truth. The Valentinian Meditation on the Gospel. Publisher Abingdon Press. New York & Nashville TN

Grosso, Michael. (2015) The transmission Model of Mind and Body, a Brief History in: Kelly, Edward F., Crabtree, Adam., Marshall, Paul., Eds. Beyond Physicalism: Toward Reconciliation of Science and Spirituality. Publishers Rowman & Littlefield. Lanham, Maryland.

Heiser, Michael S. (2015) The unseen realm. Recovering the supernatural worldview of the bible. Hexham Press. Bellingham, Wa.

Hart, David B. (2017) The New Testament. A translation. Yale University Press. London, UK

Holy See Press Office (10 June 2016). "The liturgical memory of Mary Magdalene becomes a feast, like that of the other apostles, 10.06.2016". The Holy See. Retrieved 29 March 2018.

Hoeller, Stephan A. (1998 and 2010). Ecclesia Gnostica A Gnostic Catechism. Publisher: The Gnostic Society Press, Los Angeles, California. http://gnosis.org/ecclesia/catechism.htm Accessed 5-5-2015

Hooper Richard J. (2008) The Crucifixion of Mary Magdalene: The Historical tradition of the First Apostle and the Ancient Church's Campaign to Suppress It. Sanctuary Publications. Sedona, AZ

James, Montague Rhode. (1924) The Apocalypse of Thomas *in*,

The Apocryphal New Testament. Oxford, UK. Clarendon Press

"Lord of Spirits" (God the Father),

"Hear thou, O Thomas, for I am the Son of God the Father and I am the father of all spirits." Clearly "Lord of Spirits" could be drawn from The Apocalypse of Thomas (and other Revelations as it is taken from granted that the reader understand this term: the "Lord of Spirits" is meant to be "God," (or the Father, 'the One,' the 'Most High,' and similar.

Jenkins, Philip. (2001). Hidden Gospels: How the Search for Jesus Lost Its Way. Oxford University Press. New York, NY.

Jenkins, Philip. (2008) The lost history of Christianity. The thousand-year golden age of the church in the Middle East, Africa, and Asia--and how it died. Publisher HarperOne. New York, NY.

Jenkins, Philip. (2015). The many faces of Christ. The Thousand - Year story and influence of the Lost Gospels. Publisher Basic Books. New York, NY

Johannite Church, The Apostolic. (2018) Johannite Beliefs. https://www.johannite.org/

Keener, Craig S. Miracles. The credibility of the New Testament accounts volumes 1 & 2. Baker Publishing Group. Grand Rapids, MI 2011

Kilmon, Jack. (2019) Yeshua, the Enochian Jew. https://magdelene.wordpress.com/2008/11/07/yeshua-the-enochian-jew/Posted November 7, 2008 (Accessed 4-19- 2019)

King, Karin., MacRae, R. George W., Wilson, Robert McL., Parrot, Douglas M. The Gospel of Mary (BG 8502, 1) in: Robinson, James M. (1978) The Nag Hammadi library, ed. The definitive new translation of the Gnostic scriptures complete in one volume. Harper Collins, New York, NY

King, Karen L. (2003) The Gospel of Mary of Magdala: Jesus and the First Woman Apostle. Published by Polebridge Press, Santa Rosa, California

King, Karen. (2007) The Gospel of Mary With The Greek Gospel of Mary *in:* Meyer, Marvin W.; Robinson, James M. The Nag Hammadi Scriptures: The Revised and Updated translation of Sacred Gnostic Texts Complete in One Volume (p. 737). HarperCollins. Kindle Edition.

King, Karen L. (2003) What is Gnosticism? Harvard University Press. Cambridge, MA

Kloppenborg, John. (1987.) The Formation of Q. trinity Press International. Harrisburg, PA.

Kloppenborg, John S., Marvin W. Meyer, Stephen J. Patterson, Michael G. Steinhauser, eds. (1990.) Q Thomas Reader. Sonoma, Ca.: Polebridge Press.

Krippler, Stanley., Rock, Adam J., Beischel, Julie., (2013) Friedman, Harris L., Fracas, Cheryl L. (Eds). Advances in Parapsychological Research 9. McFarland & Company, Inc. Pubs. Jefferson, NC and London.

Leloup, Jean-Yves. (2002) The Gospel of Mary. Rochester, Vermont: Inner traditions. (Coptic to English line by line, interlinear included with English).

Leloup, Jean-Yves. (2004) The Gospel of Phillip: Jesus, Mary Magdalene, and the Gnosis of Sacred Union.Rochester, Vermont: Inner traditions. *Leloup in Thomas per Logion 55 …Whoever cannot free themselves from their brother and sister and does not bear their cross as I do is not worthy of me.*

Leloup, Jean-Yves. The Gospel of Thomas: (2005) The Gnostic Wisdom of Jesus. Inner traditions/Bear & Company. Kindle Edition.

Logan, Alastair, HB. (1996.) From Gnostic Truth and Christian Heresy. A Study in the History of Gnosticism. T&T Clark International. London, UK

MacRae, George W., Wilson., Robert. McL. (2000) The Gospel According to Mary. In Robinson, James M. Ed. The Coptic Gnostic Library. A Complete Edition of the Nag Hammadi Codices. Vol. 3. Koninklijke Brill NV, Leiden, The Netherlands. (Coptic to English line by line, interlinear included with English).

Marshall, Stevan. (2019.) A Homily for trinity Sunday in: Gnostic Society Library, The Nag Hammadi Library. Available at http://gnosis.org/naghamm/nhl.html Accessed 10 3 2019 http://gnosis.org/ecclesia/homily*trinity.htm*

Mattison, Mark M. (2017) The Gospel of Mary. gospels.net http://www.gospels.net/ and http://www.gospels.net/mary.html. (The following translation is public domain and may be freely copied and used, changed or unchanged, for any purpose. It is based on the Coptic text of BG 8502). Accessed Jan 2, 2017.

Mattison, Mark M. (2013) The Gospel of Mary. Coptic-English Interlinear. http://gospel-thomas.net/MaryInterlinear.pdf Accessed 2 2018

Mead, G.R.S. (1899; 2016). Pistis Sophia. London: Theosophical Publishing And The Gnostic Society Library. gnosis.org (Accessed 2016.)

Mead, G. R. S. (1921) Pistis Sophia. A Gnostic Gospel. A Gnostic Miscellany: Being for the most part extracts from the Books of the Savior, to which are added excerpts from a Cognate literature; (English). JM Watkins London. Kindle Edition.

Medved, Goran. KAIROS (2021). The Fatherhood of God in the Old Testament - Evangelical Journal of Theology / Vol. X No. 2 (2016), pp. 203-214 file:///Users/jamesbrantingham/Downloads/4Medved.pdf (Accessed 4 20 2021)

Meyer, Marvin W; Turner, John D. (2007.) The Book of Thomas in: Meyer, Marvin W.; Robinson, James M.. The Nag Hammadi Scriptures. HarperCollins.

Meyer, Marvin. (2005) The Gnostic Gospels of Jesus: The definitive collection of mystical gospels and secret books about Jesus of Nazareth. Publisher HarperOne, New York, NY

Meyer, Marvin with De Boer, Esther. (2004) The Gospels of Mary: the secret tradition of Mary Magdalene, the companion of Jesus. HarperCollins 10 East 53rd St., NY, New York

Meyer, Marvin W., Scopello, Madeleine. The Dialogue of the Savior in: Meyer, Marvin W.; Robinson, James M.. The Nag Hammadi Scriptures: The Revised and Updated translation of Sacred Gnostic Texts Complete in One Volume (p. 297). HarperCollins. Kindle Edition. (139, 11– 13).

Meyer, Marvin W., Scopello, Madeleine. (2007) Eugnostos the Blessed *in*, Meyer, Marvin W., Robinson, James M. The Nag Hammadi Scriptures: The Revised and Updated translation of Sacred Gnostic Texts Complete in One Volume. HarperCollins. 10 East 53rd St., New York, NY

Meyer, Marvin W.; Robinson, James M. (2007) The Nag Hammadi Scriptures: The Revised and Updated translation of Sacred Gnostic Texts Complete in One Volume. HarperCollins. New York, NY Kindle Edition.

Meyer, Marvin. Ed., Turner, John D. (2007). The Holy Book of the Great Invisible Spirit (The Gnostic Gospel of the Egyptians) in: The Nag Hammadi Scriptures. HarperCollins 10 East 53rd St., NY, New York 2007

Meyer, Marvin W.; Robinson, James M., Scopello, Madeleine (2007) The Dialogue of the Savior in: The Nag Hammadi Scriptures: The Revised and Updated translation of Sacred Gnostic Texts Complete in One Volume. HarperCollins. New York, NY

Monad. see Wikipedia: https://en.wikipedia.org/wiki/Monad (Monad in Gnosticism)

Neppe, Vernon M., Close Edward R. (2012) Reality Begins with Consciousness: A Paradigm Shift that Works. Brainvoyage.com http://www.brainvoyage.com/RBC/perspective.php Accessed 4 27 2020

Neppe VM. (2020) Consciousness, science and spirituality: the broad conceptualization of consciousness through the prism of extending to the new physics Beyond EPIC applying the mnemonics PIERCED MOCKS. J Psychol Clin Psychiatry. 2020;11(1):18–38. DOI: 10.15406/jpcpy.2020.11.00666

Neppe VM. (2019) Meaningful Evolution ('ME'): triadic Dimensional Vortical Paradigm (TDVP) And Consciousness: A Refutation Of Darwinian Evolution ('DE') and a scientific addition or alternative to Intelligent Design ('ID'): Part 3 In Meaningful Evolution, abiogenesis and life solved through gimmel: translating from the infinite continuity to the discrete finite by applying the Neppe-Close triadic Dimensional Vortical Paradigm (TDVP). IQNexus Journal. 2019;11(2):20–25.

Olson, Roger E. (1999) The Story of Christian Theology: Twenty Centuries of tradition & Reform. Inter Varsity Press, Downers Grove, Il.

Pederson, Rena. (2006) The Lost Apostle: Searching for the Truth About Junia. Published Jossey Bass A Wiley Imprint. San Francisco. CA.

Pétrement, Simone. (1984). A Separate God. The Christian Origins and Teachings of Gnosticism. HarperCollins, Scranton, Pennsylvania

Pick, Bernhard. (1911) The Attack of Celsus on Christianity. The Monist 21(2): 223-266

Price, Robert M. A Complete translation of the Gospel of Mary. At: https://thegodabovegod.com/a-complete-translation-of-the-gospel-of-mary/. Accessed: May 2017

Radin, Dean. (1997) The Conscious Universe: The Scientific Truth of Psychic Phenomena. HarperCollins Pub. New York, NY.

Radin, Dean. (2013) Supernormal: Science, Yoga, and the Evidence for Extraordinary Psychic Abilities. Crown Publishing House a division of Random House. New York, NY

Radin D. (2014). Getting comfortable with near death experiences. Out of one's mind or beyond the brain? The challenge of interpreting near-death experiences. Missouri medicine, 111(1), 24–28.

Radin D. (2017) Electrocortical correlations between pairs of isolated people: A reanalysis. F1000Res. 2017 May 15;6:676. doi: 10.12688/f1000research.11537.1. eCollection 2017. PubMed PMID: 28713556; PubMed Central PMCID: PMC5490474.

Radin, Dean. (2018) Real Magic. Crown Publishing House a division of Random House. New York, NY.

Radin, Dean. (2019) Selected Psi Research Publications

http://deanradin.com/evidence/evidence.htm (Accessed 2 1 2019

Robinson, James M. (1990) The Nag Hammadi library, ed. James M. Robinson. Harper, San Francisco

Robinson, James M., Hoffmann, Paul., Kloppenborg, John S., Moreland, Milton C. (2000) The Critical Edition of Q with Publisher Fortress and Peeters Press. Minneapolis.

Roche, Arthur. (2016) Mary Magdalene, apostle of the apostles (Congregation for Divine Worship and the Discipline of the Sacraments) 10.06.2016.

Romanoff, Katia. (2016) Sophia: Goddess of Wisdom & God's Wife. http://www.northernway.org/Sophia.html (*Accessed* 7-30-2016)

Schaberg, Jane. (1990.) The Illegitimacy of Jesus: A Feminist Theological Interpretation of the Infancy Narratives. Continuum Int. Press

Schaberg, Jane.(2002.) The Resurrection of Mary Magdalene. Legends, Apocrypha, and the Christian Testament. Publisher Continuum Int. New York, NY

Schaff, Philip., Ed. (2016) The Complete Ante-Nicene, Nicene and Post-Nicene Collection of Early Church Fathers: Cross-Linked to the Bible. Toronto, Canada.

Philip Schaff. Origen. (2016). The Complete Works of Origen (8 Books): Cross-Linked to the Bible . Amazon.com. Kindle Edition.

Schwartz, Gary E. (2002). The Afterlife Experiments. Breakthrough Scientific Evidence of Life After Death. Pocket Books (Simon and Schuster) New York, NY.

Schwartz, Gary E. (2006) The G.O.D. Experiments: How science is discovering God in everything, including us. Atria Books. New York, NY

Schwartz, Gary E. (2011). The Sacred Promise. Atria Books Division of Simon and Schuster. New York, NY.

Schwartz, GE. (2011) Photonic Measurement of Apparent Presence of Spirit Using a Computer Automated System. Explore: The Journal of Science and Healing 7(2) 100-109 DOI: 10.1016/j.explore.2010.12.002

Schwartz GE. (2019). A computer-automated, multi-center, multi-blinded, randomized control trial evaluating hypothesized spirit presence and communication published online ahead of print, 2019 Nov 16. Explore (NY). 2019;S1550-8307(19)30552-X. doi:10.1016/j.explore.2019.11.007

Schwartz, Gary E., Woollacott Marjorie H., eds. (2019) Introduction to the Primacy of Consciousness Hypothesis In: Schwartz, Gary E., Woollacott Marjorie H. (2019) Is Consciousness Primary?: Perspectives from the Founding Members of the Academy for the Advancement of Postmaterialist Sciences (Advances in ... the Advancement of Postmaterialist Sciences). Copyright 2019 © by the Academy for the Advancement of the Postmaterialist Sciences www.aapsglobal.com

Shoemaker, Stephan J. (2012.) The Life of the Virgin by Maximus the Confessor. Yale University Press, An MPG Books Ltd, Bodmin, Cornwall, UK

Schmidt, Carl., Schmidt, Violet MacDermot. Schmidt (VM MacDermot translator). Pistis Sophia. (1978) Volume 9. Leiden, Belgium. Brill

Smith, Andrew P. (2005) The Gospel of Phillip Annotated & Explained. Woodstock, Vermont: SkyLights Path Publishing.

Smith Andrew P. (2015) The Secret History of The Gnostics. Their Scriptures and Beliefs and traditions. Published by Watkins Media Limited. London, UK

Smith Andrew P. (2015) The Secret History of The Gnostics. Their Scriptures and Beliefs and traditions. Published by Watkins Media Limited. London, UK

Stevenson, I. (2006). Half a career with the paranormal. Journal of Scientific Exploration, 20, 13–21.

Thomassen, Einar. (2007) The tripartite tractate in: Meyer, Marvin. The Nag Hammadi Scriptures. HarperCollins 10 East 53rd St., NY, New York 2007

Throckmorton, Burton H. (1992.) Gospel Parallels. Fifth Edition. Publisher Thomas Nelson. Nashville, TN

Stevenson, I. (2006). Half a career with the paranormal. Journal of Scientific Exploration, 20, 13–21.

Throckmorton, Burton H. (1992.) Gospel Parallels. Fifth Edition. Publisher Thomas Nelson. Nashville, TN

Turner, John D. (2001) Sethian Gnosticism and the Platonic tradition (The History of the Sethian Movement, Sethian Gnosticism and the Platonic tradition). Presses Université Laval, Paris.

Turner, John. (2019) Sethian Gnosticism: A literary History. https://archive.is/20121211123653/http://jdt.unl.edu/lithist.html (Accessed 5-8-2019)

The Gospel According to Mary of Magdala (the Coptic Gnostic Gospel)

A New Interpretation (of the Extant pages 7-11)

The Eternal Perspective and Contentment

Page 7

1Peter asks the Savior. 2 'Lord, will *this*, this world of matter (its materialism, and flesh), be destroyed or not?' 3But the Savior said, 4 'Peter, "every object, all entities are intertwined one with the other. Humans too each other 5 and the *All in All to the Universe.* 6 Earth, wind, fire, and water are linked.* So Breath is yoked to Life, Life to Death, Good to Evil - in and throughout nature and the Cosmos. 7Ultimately things disintegrate, dissolving into their constituent parts, 8 returning 9to their Root. 10Those who have ears to hear, let them hear! 11Peter then asked, 'Lord, you've illuminated everything 12 prophesying how things will go into the Age. Please, then tell us one more thing 13 what is the *greatest* sin of this 'materialistic and fallen world preoccupied with sin?' Mary pointedly asked, 'Lord, are you Master over this deficiency or not?' 14Then the Anointed said to Peter and Mary, 'you are both right to ask these questions.' *For 'amēn, amēn, I say,'* 15 **'Sin does not exist!'** There is no Sin!'

16You create Sin when you commit immoral deeds. And do so despite the consequences. 17 *Lo,* you justify them by your deceitful practice and 18 adulterous, unfaithful ways. And you say *'a false and counterfeit spirit'* 19 is the cause of your lawless acts.

The Nature of Good, The *'Imageless, Deficient Spirit'* and Contentment

20**Yet, this is why the Good** (*the 'Lord of Spirits'*) came among you. 21 So that through His teaching and instruction, you will seek a 'better path and the road home, to enlightenment.' 22 For though you are far from the Light, with a corporeal body and a garment of flesh, *if you seek it, you can find it;* 'thy Way' to 'the One', the 'Good Who Is.' Then thou may entwine with your true Source and Root! 23 *'truly,'* 24 this is why you become 25sick and die! 26Because you live in a material and a carnal world 27 that takes you away from the Light. 28 Thus it is written. Anyone who has ears to hear should hear!

Page 8

1 *'For, so the Truth is, and, I say it to you now,'* 'In Life there is always trouble, and suffering.' 2 To relieve this you search out flesh and blood, carnal and material pleasure. 3 'This Intoxicates you' and impels uncontrollable passion with agony throughout the body; conversely *escape by alignment with the Blissful One!'* 4 'This is why I told you, 5 let your heart be satisfied, even content.' 6 'For, when disappointed or discouraged, 7 take comfort and serenity in 8 observing the myriads of living things, and the beauty in nature, and all the different forms of creation. For, *in spite of it all* life is astonishing, even beautiful! 9 Anyone who has ears to hear 10 should hear! 11 And after this, He said, 12 May My peace be with you and fulfill you and, 13 He who gives us His peace, 14 be with you all, Amen.

The Good News of The Gospel

15 'Yet, beware. Do not be mislead by anyone who says, 16 *'Lo, here it is* or 17 *Lo, there He is* 18 the Savior! 19 'Rather, The Kingdom of the Blissful One, 20 **the Son of Man** (ⲡ·ϣⲏⲣⲉ ⲅⲁⲣ ⲙ·ⲡ·ⲣⲱⲙⲉ)^ is within; and there thee shall find the peace that passeth all understanding *in* and, *all about you!* 21 trust 'the Way' and seek the Good! 22 And you will find Him! 23 Then, hold tight, and proclaim with zeal 24 the Kingdom of the 'Most High' has begun!

The Gospel

Page 9

1 Yet remember, 2 do not create new rules or laws beyond My instruction 3 as if you were Moses the Lawgiver, 4 lest they *bind* you, making you a slave to the Law. 5 After He had said these things, He left.

But after the Anointed left, 6 his disciples grieved 7 and wept; and said to each other, 8 'how can we go among the Gentiles and Unbelievers and preach that 'The Life to Come' has arrived!' And say 9 **Lo**, *the Gospel of the Son of Man and the Kingdom of Heaven* is here, and in you, and all around and among you even now, into the Age!' 10 *Afraid, the disciples remained anxious and said, 'why should seekers listen to us?' 'After all, their Ruler, "Error," and her Wicked Archons and Powers* slayed the **Son of Man.' 11** So, what would stop them from killing us or, anyone that listens to us?'

Mary Magdalene and Jesus

12 But then Mary stood up and greeted all the Brothers and Sisters. 13 She said to the disciples, and to everyone there, 14 'rejoice, and do not weep or grieve for Him, 15 nor, let your hearts be troubled. Choose forgiveness not division, peace not war and, Spirit over flesh. For it is by the grace of the 'Most High' we are saved! 16 Rejoice, for the Savior is with you, and will protect you from *'the False Spirit of Error.'* Rather, let us praise His greatness! 17 For the Savior prepared us for this 18 by making us into *"true Anthropos"* compassionate, knowledgeable, and giving human beings!'

19 When Mary finished saying these things, she turned their hearts and minds away from terror and toward the Good. 20 And they began (again) to debate the meaning of *'the Logos, the Word,'* and the *Savior*(that goes on to this very day).

Page 10

1 Peter then said to Mary, 2 'Sister, we know that the Savior loved you the most; 3 more than all the others (like yourself) following 'the Way.' For, we heard Him say, 'Mary, blissful art thou for I have perfected thee in mine mysteries, of the height, width, and breadth. Thou art a master, Mary, who rightly teaches the 'Gospel ' and, 'the Way.' For thou hath *already* entered the Kingdom!

4 Peter said, 'please, Mary, tell us the hidden words that the Savior spoke to you and that you alone heard. 5 Tell us *that* which we have not heard so we too can learn all the Savior's Words and Wisdom. 6 And, even *what* you heard *'in secret.'* 7 In response, Mary said, 8 *'If you wish, I will tell you what I heard Him say 9 that, otherwise would not be known.'* Here are the 'Saviors Words' that you have never before heard. 10 So Mary related her Vision of the Savior.

The Vision of the Christ

11 She said this, 12 'I saw the Lord today.' 13 I saw Him in a Vision,' and said to Him, *'Lord, I see you!'* 14 In response, He said, 15 'blissful art you my beloved, for you did not falter, nor tremble, nor were you overcome!' Then the Lord continued speaking, 'For many who see me *are* disturbed, shake and tremble and, faint away (…as "one who *hunts* us now" will do). Even more so, you did not fall on your face, nor run away!' 16 'For, where your heart and mind is, *'your nous,'* their lies your treasure!

17 Then I said to him, 18 'Lord, how does one who sees You, 19 in a Vision, perceive You?' 20 She further asked, 21 'is it by the Soul or, is it by the Spirit?' 22 In response, the Savior said, 23 'You do not see it by the Spirit nor by the Soul.' 24 'But in that place between them… *'the nous, your mind'*; which is… between the possible and real, between mind and matter, *and* between the soul and spirit!

25 There, is where you perceived it, Mary! That is how you saw and heard Me today.'

This new interpretation stops after extant page 10. Pages 11-14 are missing.

Overcoming the Powers and Understanding the Vision of Mary

(From the Extant pages 15-18)

Page 15

1 Later the 'False, Dark and Demonic Spirit,' the *Spirit of Craving* said to Mary, 2 'I did **not** see your 'soul' descend. 3 But, I saw '*it*' rising! 4 Liar! Deceiver!, **'Daughter,' you belong to me!'** Who do you think you are, Mary? For, before me, you were '*nothing!*' A hopeless, no account liar, and used up garment to throw out with the trash! 5 In response, and *in the Spirit,* Mary saith '*Dark, Spirit.*' 6 'Lo I saw you, O Evil One, 7 yet you do not know me, nor see the *real* me, and the Truth! 8 For He gave me, **Mary of Magdala,** *true, Sacred, Salvational Knowledge!*' 9 After her spirit communicated this, it flew upward, rejoicing.

10 *Error* called me, a soulless bit of flesh, a mortal body; *and* her molded puppet and slave! But she has failed! For '*the One*' brought me and taught me Wisdom and 'the Way.' With this precious Sacred Knowledge, I released all (I'd led astray)!' No longer ignorant, I 'possess Knowledge of the Sacred Spirit.' And the saving Sacred Knowledge within. With this I am rescued and set free! 11 When Mary finished saying these things, she left. 12 And her soul flew even higher, '*in the spirit*' rejoicing greatly!

The Archon of Ignorance

13 But ascending she faced (in the third aeon) 14 a mighty Power: 'Ignorance.' 15 Ignorance harshly interrogated her. 16 It said, 'Mary, where do you think *you* are going?' 17 '*You pathetic woman*'! **I bound you;** and you did iniquity, wrongdoing and sin!' 'So, you are chained here… *into the Age!*' 18 And Ignorance said to her, *who do you think you are?* **I will tell you… *you are one of us!*** Do not pretend otherwise! Then **Ignorance** said, 'you are already judged; foolish woman!'

19 Yet, her soul, mind and heart, '*in the spirit*' said this to that Archon… 'you are misguided, an unenlightened cretin! '*Little Horn… Unclean Spirit*' 20 Thinketh *thou* can judge me? The Truth is **I have been already judged! But not by you but by '*the One*' with true authority,** the '*Blissful One,*' the '*Lord of Spirits!* For, He judgeth me clean!' I was bound, but 'the Blissful One' loosened my

194

bonds. *And I had already freed my own prisoners!* 21 'Yet you (Archons, Dark Powers and the Demons of Wrath) presume to judge me and to *'do this through a false and counterfeit spirit.'* 22 But the Lords' 'Sacred Knowledge' bought my 'Salvation'. I am no longer bound to this time nor, to this aeon anymore. 23 For the Truth is clear. 24 All thou composeth will decompose back 25 into this earth, into this aeon, and to their root.

Page 16

1 When her spirit and soul had overcome that realm 2 it ascended even higher and faced the fourth Power. 3 This Power expresses itself by seven manifestations of (*ignorant and deadly*) sins or evil and wickedness (things she *had previously* expelled). For Mary, this brought back terrible fear, great anxiety and suffering. And *(as could happen to anyone)* she momentarily lapsed and let her defenses down… (and Error's counterfeit spirit, plans, methods, and schemes) re-entered her…

4 The first form was Darkness;

5 The second form, Desire; and Craving

6 The third form, Ignorance (*and*);

7 The fourth form, a Zeal for Death (…*even as before, a desire to harm herself*);

8 The fifth form said, 'only in the Kingdom of *Flesh and blood* 'can be found through carnal pleasures and the sensations you crave, true ecstasy!'

9 The sixth form, the Foolish 'Wisdom of Intoxication' said this to Mary, *'matter, flesh and wine is all there is!'*

10 The final, seventh form said, *recognize the 'Wisdom in Anger,' and, always be Angry. For in 'that' you will find fulfillment!* and,

11 'These are the seven Powers and Demons of Wrath.'

12 'Then the demons, and the Powers of Anger and Wrath, asked me, '*little one,* 'do you think you can just get up be off? How can you believe **that**? 13 For, will the *'One Who Is,* 'allow *you*, **a murderer of humanity,** to ascend?' 14 And pretend to be a heroine and strut about like 'a woman of courage,' and just *walk away* and be **exorcised**, *and be* **cured?** 'Vain and conceited girl! ' **…my deluded daughter.** 15 But Mary's spirit saith, 16 'the Savior slayed my previous selfish and amoral life and I am free!

17 In the Spirit she said, 'He released me from your oppression (*on this world*). 18 And my incarcerators have fallen away *in* this same, but *new* world… I am free! 19 Lo, no longer does uncontrollable desire and ignorance shackle me. Released, I have entered a higher, and Pneumatic *life!*

Page 17

1 **And it is a better, more loving and caring life!** 2 Yet this does not come from you, *'O false spirit below,'* 3 but, from 'Heaven Above'! I am no longer another's slave who must do evil; nor filled up by a *'false and counterfeit spirit'*. Finally I know right from wrong!' For I love now and am loved by He who calls me 'Blissful!' 4 Thus, from this time forward I wait… content in Repose *and* Silence… 5 into the Ages unto the Ages to Come. For he saith, 'Mary my Love, *the gates of Heaven Itself are already open for thee!'* 6 When Mary had said these things, she fell still. 7 Because, the Savior, 'in Silence' 8 had said this to her, and no more.

Conflict over Authority. Andrew Speaks

9 In response, Andrew said to all the other disciples, 'say what you will about what Mary just said, 10 but I for one, do not believe her.' 11 'The Savior did not say such things, nor 12 speak in this strange and mysterious way.' 13 'Mary's visions and report of the Savior's words are… strange.' 'And Her presentation of His Revelation seems different to the manner in which he spoke to us. *Is it (as she says) the 'New (and Full) Covenant'?* 14 In response, Peter spoke up…

Peter Speaks

15 Simon Peter said, did the Savior, 16 **'Did He,** *'the One,' of Infinite Knowledge and Love,* speak first with Her (and not with us)? Did He speak to this… **woman** and tell *her*, to instruct us? 17 How we should speak and how to preach? *'Amēn, amēn, I say…* Upright and devout Mary of Magdala is but, 18 must we change our customs and manners and mimic her? 19 Must we listen to her because (*she claims*), He taught *her* the deepest mystery, *and* the fullest knowledge? And taught her the most true Covenant: Salvational Knowledge, *and* the mystery of being *'One with Spirit?'* 20 Did He choose her over us?

Then Mary Wept

Page 18

1 Then Mary wept 2 and said to Peter, 3 'Brother… *Peter!* what are you implying? 4 Do you think I just made this all up? That I am an 'unstable' woman (*and, on top of that*) a fraud… *a liar?'* And that I contrived through **deceit** and artful imagination' and a **'Vision'** 5 'a fantasized resurrection?' 6 Then you must believe that I lie to heap up my own authority.

Brothers, you insinuate I, *Mary Magdalene* declare myself a **Disciple of the Lord…** And dare to teach with full authority, *and* in His name! But, I have always spoken and taught in His name and did so, with His approval *before* His death and to this day! For, *'Amēn, amēn, I say... the Truth is this,'* the Savior, like you, *picked me!*

7 In response Matthew ('Levi') *a highly educated Levite and former Roman tax collector* spoke up. And he said, 8 'Peter, you too quickly get angry'. 'Now you debate with Mary (one of) *the most,* **beloved** of the Saviors' disciples.' You know it and we all saw it! For He loved her deeply! She listened and heard and, taught the Word! 9Shame on you Peter for attacking her 10 as if she were evil and sent by the 'Adversary'! 11 Brothers, Sisters… the Savior guided her making her a worthy disciple! Remember what the Savior said? 'Mary will *do* the will of 'God'; *and as a Disciple excel all the rest!*

12 Mary has inherited the Light; 13 and is 'One' with the Lord. He (the Teacher) calls her His Disciple *in Spirit and in Union.* Therefore Peter, if our Lord said all this about her, who are we to reject her?' 14 'Without question, the Savior loved her more than us!'

15 'Rather, Matthew went on, we should be ashamed because we have strayed from His path 'of love and service'. Let us make atonement to Mary and, become compassionate human beings like her. 16 And strive to be those who love and help others in the image and likeness of the Lord, 'the Perfect (the Anthropos)' 17 instructing in His image and likeness by living out '*the Way*'. 18 Blissful are we, teaching Sacred Knowledge, Torah, and Salvation (as did the Son)! Let us deny ourselves and clothe ourselves in the **Perfect Man**. 19 So, that all of us will become compassionate '**sons and daughters, children of the Lord**' and of the 'Word.' 20 With His peace within us, we shall bear up under our burdens and spread the Gospel; 21 teaching nothing beyond what the Savior taught; teaching and preaching the Good!

Page 19

1 After Matthew finished saying these things, 2 they *all* got up and left. Blissfully, everyone (*Mary too*) walked forth to spread… *the News!* The Gospel According to Mary of Magdala.

-

James Brantingham PhD

Thousand Oaks, CA

5 19 2021

References for "The Gospel According to Mary of Magdala"

Akenson, Donald H. (2000.) Saint Saul a skeleton key to the historical Jesus. Oxford University Press. New York, NY

Akenson, Donald H. (2001.) Surpassing Wonder: The Invention of the Bible and the Talmuds. Chicago: University of Chicago Press

Bauckham, Richard. (2006) Jesus and the Eyewitnesses: The Gospels as Eyewitness Testimony. Eerdmans Publish- ing, Grand Rapids, MI 2006

Barbēlō (2019) in: https://en.wikipedia.org/wiki/Barbelo Accessed 4-19-2019

> I prefer Alastair Logan's (1996) explanation of this name, Barbēlō as from the Hebrew, *'barah ba 'lo,'* or "daughter of the Lord"

Barnstone, William. (1984) The Other Bible. HarperCollins. New York, NY.

Barnstone, William. (1984) *1 Enoch* (Book of Parables or Similitudes) *in:* The Other Bible. HarperCollins, New York, NY., 1984.

Barnstone, William., Meyer, Marvin. (2011) The Gnostic Bible: Revised and Expanded 1st ed. Boston, Massachusetts, New Seeds Books.

Barnstone, William. (2009.) The Restored New Testament: A New translation with Commentary Including the Gnostic Gospels of Thomas, Mary and Judas. Publisher W.W. Norton & Co. New York, NY

Bauckham, Richard. (2006) Jesus and the Eyewitnesses: The Gospels as Eyewitness Testimony. Eerdmans Publishing, Grand Rapids, MI 2006

Beischel Julie. (2013) Among Mediums: A Scientist's Quest for Answers. Publisher: Windbridge Institute. Tucson Arizona

Beischel Julie. (2014) From the Mouths of Mediums Vol. 1: Experiencing Communication (From the Mouths of Mediums: Conversations with Windbridge Certified Research Mediums). Publisher: Windbridge Institute. Tucson Arizona

Beischel J, Boccuzzi M, Biuso M, Rock AJ. (2015) Anomalous information reception by research mediums under blinded conditions II: replication and extension. Explore (NY). 2015 Mar-Apr;11(2):136-42. doi: 10.1016/j.explore.2015.01.001. Epub 2015 Jan 7. PubMed PMID: 25666383.

Beischel Julie. (2019) Investigating Mediums : A Windbridge Institute Collection. Publisher: Windbridge Institute. Tucson Arizona

Bem D, tressoldi P, Rabeyron T and Duggan M. (2016) Feeling the future: A meta-analysis of 90 experiments on the anomalous anticipation of random future events version 2; referees: 2 approved F1000Research 2016, 4:1188 (doi: 10.12688/f1000research.7177.2)

Bernhard, Andrew (10, 11, 2012). "How The Gospel of Jesus's Wife Might Have Been Forged" (in PDF). gospels.net. Archived from the original (PDF) on March 5, 2016. Accessed and Retrieved June 4 2018.

Betty, Stafford. (2011) The Afterlife Unveiled: What the Dead are Telling Us About Their World. O-Books John Hunt Pub. Ltd. Alresford, Hants UK.

Betty, Stafford. (2014) Heaven and Hell Unveiled. Updates from the World of Spirit. White Crow Books. Guildford, UK.

Betty, Stafford. (2016) When did you become less by Dying? After Life: the evidence. White Crow Books. Guildford, UK

Brantingham JW, Parkin-Smith G, Cassa TK, Globe GA, Globe D, Pollard H, deLuca K, Jensen M, Mayer S, Korporaal C. (2012) Full kinetic chain manual and manipulative therapy plus exercise compared with targeted manual and manipulative therapy plus exercise for symptomatic osteoarthritis of the hip: a randomized controlled trial. Arch Phys Med Rehabil. 2012 Feb;93(2):259-67. doi: 10.1016/j.apmr.2011.08.036. PMID: 22289235.

Brantingham, James. (2017) The Gospel of Philip. A New translation. CreateSpace Independent Pub. Amazon Digital Services LLC. Seattle, WA.

Brantingham, James. (2018) The Gospel of Thomas: Authors' own translation.

Brantingham, James. (2018) The Gospel of Mary: Authors' own translation and interpretation.

Brown, T. Patterson. (2014) The Gospels of Thomas, Philip and Truth. Available from http://www.freelyre- ceive.net/metalogos/files/intro.html Accessed 5 25 2014

Caruana, Laurence. (2015) The Gnostic Q Glossary of Gnostic Terms. Available at: http://www.gnosticq.com/az.text/glos.af.html Accessed 3 18 2015

Charlesworth, James H. (1973) The Odes of Solomon. Oxford University Press. . Oxford, UK (Charlesworth, James. Odes Sol 1973)

Close, ER and Neppe, V. (2015) Putting Consciousness into the Equations of Mathematics: the third substance Gimmel and trUE IQ Nexus J 7:4; 7.119, 2015 v4 160111 © ECAO

Close Edward R., Neppe, Vernon M. (2015) translating Fifteen Mysteries of the Universe by Applying a Nine Dimensional Spinning Model of Finite Reality: A Perspective, the Standard Model and triadic Dimensional-Distinction Vortical Paradigm, Part I. NeuroQuantology June 2015 Volume 13, Issue 2; 205-217

Close Edward R., Neppe, Vernon M. (2015) translating Fifteen Mysteries of the Universe by Applying a Nine Dimensional Spinning Model of Finite Reality: A Perspective, the Standard Model and triadic Dimensional-Distinction Vortical Paradigm, Part II. NeuroQuantology June 2015 Volume 13, Issue 3; 348-360

Close Edward R. Mathematical Unity of Space, Time, Mass, Energy & Consciousness in: Schwartz, Gary E., Woollacott Marjorie H. (2019) Is Consciousness Primary?: Perspectives from the Founding Members of the Academy for the Advancement of Postmaterialist Sciences (Advances in … the Advancement of Postmaterialist Sciences). Copyright 2019 © by the Academy for the Advancement of the Postmaterialist Sciences www.aapsglobal.com

Chronology of the universe. Wikipedia. Accessed (5 23 2021)

https://en.wikipedia.org/wiki/Chronology*of*the*universe*

Davies, Stevan. (2005) The Secret Book of John. The Gnostic Gospel Annotated & Explained. Skylight Paths Publishing. Woodstock, Vermont

Davidson, Gustav. (1967). A dictionary of angels: including the fallen angels. The Free Press Simon and Schuster. New York, NY

de Quillian, Jehanne. (2011.) The Gospel of the Beloved Companion: The Complete Gospel of Mary Magdalene. English Ed. Éditions Athara. ASIN: B0053HPQ2C

Delorme A, Beischel J, Michel L, Boccuzzi M, Radin D, Mills PJ. (2013) Electrocortical activity associated with subjective communication with the deceased. Front Psychol. 2013 Nov 20;4:834. doi: 10.3389/fpsyg. 2013.00834. eCollection 2013. PubMed PMID: 24312063; PubMed Central PMCID: PMC3834343.

DeConick, April D. (2001) Voices of the Mystics: Early Christian Discourse in the Gospel of John and Thomas and Other Ancient Christian Literature. Publisher T&T Clark, New York, NY

DeConick, April D. (2017.) The Gnostic New Age: How a countercultural spirituality revolutionized religion from antiquity to today. Columbia University Press. New York, NY

Ehrman, Bart. (2004) Truth and Fiction in The Da Vinci Code: A Historian reveals what we really know about Jesus, Mary Magdalene and Constantine. Oxford University Press. New York, NY.

Ehrman, Bart D. (2006.) Peter, Paul and Mary Magdalene: The Followers of Jesus in History and Legend. Oxford University Press. New York, NY.

Emmel, Stephan. (2021). The Dialogue of the Savior. The Gnostic Society Library. gnosis.org (Accessed 4 19 2021)

Funk, Wolf-Peter. (2007.) The First Revelation (Apocalypse) of James, in: Meyer, Marvin W.; Robinson, James M.. The Nag Hammadi Scriptures. HarperCollins. New York, NY.

Funk, Wolf-Peter. (2007.) The Second Revelation (Apocalypse) of James, in: Meyer, Marvin W.; Robinson, James M.. The Nag Hammadi Scriptures. HarperCollins. New York, NY.

Friedman, Richard E. (2017.) The Exodus. HarperCollins. New York, NY.

Gnostic Society Library, The. (2015) The Nag Hammadi Library. Available at http://gnosis.org/naghamm/nhl.html Accessed 2/7 2015

Grant, Robert McQueen. (1967.) Gnosticism. Columbia University Press. New York, NY

Grobel, Kendrick. (1960) The Gospel of Truth. The Valentinian Meditation on the Gospel. Publisher Abingdon Press. New York & Nashville TN

Grosso, Michael. (2015) The transmission Model of Mind and Body, a Brief History in: Kelly, Edward F., Crabtree, Adam., Marshall, Paul., Eds. Beyond Physicalism: Toward Reconciliation of Science and Spirituality. Publishers Rowman & Littlefield. Lanham, Maryland.

Heiser, Michael S. (2015) The unseen realm. Recovering the supernatural worldview of the bible. Hexham Press. Bellingham, Wa.

Hart, David B. (2017) The New Testament. A translation. Yale University Press. London, UK

Holy See Press Office (10 June 2016). "The liturgical memory of Mary Magdalene becomes a feast, like that of the other apostles, 10.06.2016". The Holy See. Retrieved 29 March 2018.

Hoeller, Stephan A. (1998 and 2010). Ecclesia Gnostica A Gnostic Catechism. Publisher: The Gnostic Society Press, Los Angeles, California. http://gnosis.org/ecclesia/catechism.htm Accessed 5-5-2015

Hooper Richard J. (2008) The Crucifixion of Mary Magdalene: The Historical tradition of the First Apostle and the Ancient Church's Campaign to Suppress It. Sanctuary Publications. Sedona, AZ

James, Montague Rhode. (1924) The Apocalypse of Thomas *in*,

The Apocryphal New Testament. Oxford, UK. Clarendon Press

"Lord of Spirits" (God the Father),

"Hear thou, O Thomas, for I am the Son of God the Father and I am the father of all spirits." Clearly "Lord of Spirits" could be drawn from The Apocalypse of Thomas (and other Revelations as it is taken from granted that the reader understand this term: the "Lord of Spirits" is meant to be "God," (or the Father, 'the One,' the 'Most High,' and similar.

Jenkins, Philip. (2001). Hidden Gospels: How the Search for Jesus Lost Its Way. Oxford University Press. New York, NY.

Jenkins, Philip. (2008) The lost history of Christianity. The thousand-year golden age of the church in the Middle East, Africa, and Asia--and how it died. Publisher HarperOne. New York, NY.

Jenkins, Philip. (2015). The many faces of Christ. The Thousand - Year story and influence of the Lost Gospels. Publisher Basic Books. New York, NY

Johannite Church, The Apostolic. (2018) Johannite Beliefs. https://www.johannite.org/

Keener, Craig S. Miracles. The credibility of the New Testament accounts volumes 1 & 2. Baker Publishing Group. Grand Rapids, MI 2011

Kilmon, Jack. (2019) Yeshua, the Enochian Jew. https://magdelene.wordpress.com/2008/11/07/yeshua-the-enochian-jew/Posted November 7, 2008 (Accessed 4-19- 2019)

King, Karin., MacRae, R. George W., Wilson, Robert McL., Parrot, Douglas M. The Gospel of Mary (BG 8502, 1) in: Robinson, James M. (1978) The Nag Hammadi library, ed. The definitive new translation of the Gnostic scriptures complete in one volume. Harper Collins, New York, NY

King, Karen L. (2003) The Gospel of Mary of Magdala: Jesus and the First Woman Apostle. Published by Polebridge Press, Santa Rosa, California

King, Karen. (2007) The Gospel of Mary With The Greek Gospel of Mary *in:* Meyer, Marvin W.; Robinson, James M. The Nag Hammadi Scriptures: The Revised and Updated translation of Sacred Gnostic Texts Complete in One Volume (p. 737). HarperCollins. Kindle Edition.

King, Karen L. (2003) What is Gnosticism? Harvard University Press. Cambridge, MA

Kloppenborg, John. (1987.) The Formation of Q. trinity Press International. Harrisburg, PA.

Kloppenborg, John S., Marvin W. Meyer, Stephen J. Patterson, Michael G. Steinhauser, eds. (1990.) Q Thomas Reader. Sonoma, Ca.: Polebridge Press.

Krippler, Stanley., Rock, Adam J., Beischel, Julie., (2013) Friedman, Harris L., Fracas, Cheryl L. (Eds). Advances in Parapsychological Research 9. McFarland & Company, Inc. Pubs. Jefferson, NC and London.

Leloup, Jean-Yves. (2002) The Gospel of Mary. Rochester, Vermont: Inner traditions.

Leloup, Jean-Yves. (2004) The Gospel of Phillip: Jesus, Mary Magdalene, and the Gnosis of Sacred Union.Rochester, Vermont: Inner traditions. *Leloup in Thomas per Logion 55 ...Whoever cannot free themselves from their brother and sister and does not bear their cross as I do is not worthy of me.*

Leloup, Jean-Yves. The Gospel of Thomas: The Gnostic Wisdom of Jesus (Kindle Locations 1999-2002). Inner traditions/Bear & Company. Kindle Edition.

Logan, Alastair, HB. (1996.) From Gnostic Truth and Christian Heresy. A Study in the History of Gnosticism. T&T Clark International. London, UK

MacRae, George W., Wilson., Robert. McL. (2000) The Gospel According to Mary. In Robinson, James M. Ed. The Coptic Gnostic Library. A Complete Edition of the Nag Hammadi Codices. Vol. 3. Koninklijke Brill NV, Leiden, The Netherlands

Marshall, Stevan. (2019.) A Homily for trinity Sunday in: Gnostic Society Library, The Nag Hammadi Library. Available at http://gnosis.org/naghamm/nhl.html Accessed 10 3 2019 http://gnosis.org/ecclesia/homily*trinity.htm*

Mattison, Mark M. (2017) The Gospel of Mary. gospels.net http://www.gospels.net/ and http://www.gospels.net/mary.html. (The following translation is public domain and may be freely copied and used, changed or unchanged, for any purpose. It is based on the Coptic text of BG 8502). Accessed Jan 2, 2017.

Mattison, Mark M. (2013) The Gospel of Mary. Coptic-English Interlinear. http://gospel-thomas.net/MaryInterlinear.pdf Accessed 2 2018

Max Planck; Brainy Quotes. https://www.brainyquote.com/authors/max-planck-quotes (Accessed 5 14 2021)

Mead, G.R.S. (1899; 2016). Pistis Sophia. London: Theosophical Publishing And The Gnostic Society Library. gnosis.org (Accessed 2016.)

Mead, G. R. S. (1921) Pistis Sophia. A Gnostic Gospel. A Gnostic Miscellany: Being for the most part extracts from the Books of the Savior, to which are added excerpts from a Cognate literature; (English). JM Watkins London. Kindle Edition.

Medved, Goran. KAIROS (2021). The Fatherhood of God in the Old Testament - Evangelical Journal of Theology / Vol. X No. 2 (2016), pp. 203-214 file:///Users/jamesbrantingham/Downloads/4Medved.pdf (Accessed 4 20 2021)

Meyer, Marvin W; Turner, John D. (2007.) The Book of Thomas in: Meyer, Marvin W.; Robinson, James M.. The Nag Hammadi Scriptures. HarperCollins.

Meyer, Marvin. (2005) The Gnostic Gospels of Jesus: The definitive collection of mystical gospels and secret books about Jesus of Nazareth. Publisher HarperOne, New York, NY

Meyer, Marvin with De Boer, Esther. (2004) The Gospels of Mary: the secret tradition of Mary Magdalene, the companion of Jesus. HarperCollins 10 East 53rd St., NY, New York

Meyer, Marvin W., Scopello, Madeleine. The Dialogue of the Savior in: Meyer, Marvin W.; Robinson, James M.. The Nag Hammadi Scriptures: The Revised and Updated translation of Sacred Gnostic Texts Complete in One Volume (p. 297). HarperCollins. Kindle Edition. (139, 11– 13).

Meyer, Marvin W., Scopello, Madeleine. (2007) Eugnostos the Blessed *in*, Meyer, Marvin W., Robinson, James M. The Nag Hammadi Scriptures: The Revised and Updated translation of Sacred Gnostic Texts Complete in One Volume. HarperCollins. 10 East 53rd St., New York, NY

Meyer, Marvin W.; Robinson, James M. (2007) The Nag Hammadi Scriptures: The Revised and Updated translation of Sacred Gnostic Texts Complete in One Volume. HarperCollins. New York, NY Kindle Edition.

Meyer, Marvin. Ed., Turner, John D. (2007). The Holy Book of the Great Invisible Spirit (The Gnostic Gospel of the Egyptians) in: The Nag Hammadi Scriptures. HarperCollins 10 East 53rd St., NY, New York 2007

Meyer, Marvin W.; Robinson, James M., Scopello, Madeleine (2007) The Dialogue of the Savior in: The Nag Hammadi Scriptures: The Revised and Updated translation of Sacred Gnostic Texts Complete in One Volume. HarperCollins. New York, NY

Monad-Wikipedia see: https://en.wikipedia.org/wiki/Monad*(Gnosticism)* (Accessed 2021)

Multiverse-Wikipedia (2021.) https://en.wikipedia.org/wiki/Multiverse# (accessed 2021)

Neppe, Vernon M., Close Edward R. (2012) Reality Begins with Consciousness: A Paradigm Shift that Works. Brainvoyage.com http://www.brainvoyage.com/RBC/perspective.php Accessed 4 27 2020

Neppe VM. (2020) Consciousness, science and spirituality: the broad conceptualization of consciousness through the prism of extending to the new physics Beyond EPIC applying the mnemonics PIERCED MOCKS. J Psychol Clin Psychiatry. 2020;11(1):18–38. DOI: 10.15406/jpcpy.2020.11.00666

Neppe VM. (2019) Meaningful Evolution ('ME'): triadic Dimensional Vortical Paradigm (TDVP) And Consciousness: A Refutation Of Darwinian Evolution ('DE') and a scientific addition or alternative to Intelligent Design ('ID'): Part 3 In Meaningful Evolution, abiogenesis and life solved through gimmel: translating from the infinite continuity to the discrete finite by applying the Neppe-Close triadic Dimensional Vortical Paradigm (TDVP). IQNexus Journal. 2019;11(2):20–25.

Olson, Roger E. (1999) The Story of Christian Theology: Twenty Centuries of tradition & Reform. Inter Varsity Press, Downers Grove, Il.

Pederson, Rena. (2006) The Lost Apostle: Searching for the Truth About Junia. Published Jossey Bass A Wiley Imprint. San Francisco. CA.

Pétrement, Simone. (1984). A Separate God. The Christian Origins and Teachings of Gnosticism. HarperCollins, Scranton, Pennsylvania

Pick, Bernhard. (1911) The Attack of Celsus on Christianity. The Monist 21(2): 223-266

Price, Robert M. A Complete translation of the Gospel of Mary. At: https://thegodabovegod.com/a-complete-translation-of-the-gospel-of-mary/. Accessed: May 2017

de Quillian, Jehanne. (2011.) The Gospel of the Beloved Companion: The Complete Gospel of Mary Magdalene. English Ed. Éditions Athara. ASIN: B0053HPQ2C

Radin, Dean. (1997) The Conscious Universe: The Scientific Truth of Psychic Phenomena. HarperCollins Pub. New York, NY.

Radin, Dean. (2013) Supernormal: Science, Yoga, and the Evidence for Extraordinary Psychic Abilities. Crown Publishing House a division of Random House. New York, NY

Radin D. (2014). Getting comfortable with near death experiences. Out of one's mind or beyond the brain? The challenge of interpreting near-death experiences. Missouri medicine, 111(1), 24–28.

Radin D. (2017) Electrocortical correlations between pairs of isolated people: A reanalysis. F1000Res. 2017 May 15;6:676. doi: 10.12688/f1000research.11537.1. eCollection 2017. PubMed PMID: 28713556; PubMed Central PMCID: PMC5490474.

Radin, Dean. (2018) Real Magic. Crown Publishing House a division of Random House. New York, NY.

Radin, Dean. (2019) Selected Psi Research Publications

http://deanradin.com/evidence/evidence.htm (Accessed 2 1 2019

Robinson, James M. (1990) The Nag Hammadi library, ed. James M. Robinson. Harper, San Francisco

^Robinson, James M., Hoffmann, Paul., Kloppenborg, John S., Moreland, Milton C. (2000) The Critical Edition of Q with Publisher Fortress and Peeters Press. Minneapolis.

Roche, Arthur. (2016) Mary Magdalene, apostle of the apostles (Congregation for Divine Worship and the Discipline of the Sacraments) 10.06.2016.

Romanoff, Katia. (2016) Sophia: Goddess of Wisdom & God's Wife. http://www.northernway.org/Sophia.html (*Accessed* 7-30-2016)

Saunders, Craig David. (2021) A Thesis submitted for the degree of Doctor of Philosophy. A Mediator in Matthew: An Analysis of the Son of Man's Function in the First Gospel. (Accessed 5 11 2021). Published 2017 for PhD. see, https://core.ac.uk/download/pdf/83948986.pdf

Schaberg, Jane. (1990.) The Illegitimacy of Jesus: A Feminist Theological Interpretation of the Infancy Narratives. Continuum Int. Press

Schaberg, Jane.(2002.) The Resurrection of Mary Magdalene. Legends, Apocrypha, and the Christian Testament. Publisher Continuum Int. New York, NY

Schaff, Philip., Ed. (2016) The Complete Ante-Nicene, Nicene and Post-Nicene Collection of Early Church Fathers: Cross-Linked to the Bible. Toronto, Canada.

Schaff, Philip. Origen. (2016). The Complete Works of Origen (8 Books): Cross-Linked to the Bible . Amazon.com. Kindle Edition.

Shoemaker, Stephan J. (2012.) The Life of the Virgin by Maximus the Confessor. Yale University Press, An MPG Books Ltd, Bodmin, Cornwall, UK

Schmidt, Carl., Schmidt, Violet MacDermot. Schmidt (VM MacDermot translator). Pistis Sophia. (1978) Volume 9. Leiden, Belgium. Brill

Smith, Andrew P. (2005) The Gospel of Phillip Annotated & Explained. Woodstock, Vermont: SkyLights Path Publishing.

Smith Andrew P. (2015) The Secret History of The Gnostics. Their Scriptures and Beliefs and traditions. Published by Watkins Media Limited. London, UK

Smith Andrew P. (2015) The Secret History of The Gnostics. Their Scriptures and Beliefs and traditions. Published by Watkins Media Limited. London, UK

Stevenson, I. (2006). Half a career with the paranormal. Journal of Scientific Exploration, 20, 13–21.

Strong's 'Shekinah' #4633: for 'skene' or 'skēnē' at: https://www.bibletools.org/index.cfm/fuseaction/Lexicon.show/ID/G4633/skene.htm

Stevenson, I. (2006). Half a career with the paranormal. Journal of Scientific Exploration, 20, 13–21.

Schwartz, Gary E. (2011). The Sacred Promise. Atria Books Division of Simon and Schuster. New York, NY.

Schwartz GE. (2010) Possible application of silicon photomultiplier technology to detect the presence of spirit and intention: three proof-of-concept experiments. Explore (NY). 2010;6(3):166-171. doi:10.1016/j.explore.2010.02.003

Schwartz GE. (2011). Photonic measurement of apparent presence of spirit using a computer automated system. Explore (NY). 2011;7(2):100-109. doi:10.1016/j.explore.2010.12.002

Schwartz GE. (2011) Photonic measurement of apparent presence of spirit using a computer automated system. Explore (NY). 2011;7(2):100-109. doi:10.1016/j.explore.2010.12.002

Schwartz GE. (2019). A computer-automated, multi-center, multi-blinded, randomized control trial evaluating hypothesized spirit presence and communication published online ahead of print, 2019 Nov 16. Explore (NY). 2019;S1550-8307(19)30552-X. doi:10.1016/j.explore.2019.11.007

Schwartz, Gary E., Woollacott Marjorie H., eds. (2019) Is Consciousness Primary? Perspectives from the Founding Members of the Academy for the Advancement of Postmaterialist Sciences (Advances in ... the Advancement of Postmaterialist Sciences).

Stapp, Henry P. (2015) A Quantum-Mechanical Theory of the Mind/Brain Connection in: Kelly, Edward F., Crabtree, Adam., Marshall, Paul., Eds. (2015.) Beyond Physicalism: Toward Reconciliation of Science and Spirituality. Publishers Rowman & Littlefield. Lanham, Maryland.

Throckmorton, Burton H. (1992.) Gospel Parallels. Fifth Edition. Publisher Thomas Nelson. Nashville, TN

Thomassen, Einar. (2007) The tripartite tractate in: Meyer, Marvin. The Nag Hammadi Scriptures. HarperCollins 10 East 53rd St., NY, New York 2007

Throckmorton, Burton H. (1992.) Gospel Parallels. Fifth Edition. Publisher Thomas Nelson. Nashville, TN

Turner, John D. (2001) Sethian Gnosticism and the Platonic tradition (The History of the Sethian Movement, Sethian Gnosticism and the Platonic tradition). Presses Université Laval, Paris.

Turner, John. (2019) Sethian Gnosticism: A literary History. https://archive.is/20121211123653/http://jdt.unl.edu/lithist.html (Accessed 5-8-2019)

University of New South Wales. (2020, April 27). New findings suggest laws of nature not as constant as previously thought. ScienceDaily. Retrieved 5-23-

2021 from www.sciencedaily.com/releases/2020/04/200427102544.htm

Werth, Nicolas; Panné, Jean-Louis; Paczkowski, Andrzej; (1999) Bartosek, Karel; Margolin, Jean-Louis, Courtois, Stéphane, ed. (1999) The Black Book of Communism: Crimes, Terror, Repression. Harvard University Press, Cambridge, MA

Wikipedia: Shekinah (in Wikipedia) the free encyclopedia https://en.wikipedia.org/wiki/Shekhinah#In_Judaism (accessed 23 21 2019)

James Brantingham PhD

4 28 2019

Thousand Oaks, California

The Gospel of Thomas

Introduction to the Gospel of Thomas

The *Gospel of Thomas* (*GThom*) is the most famous 'Gnostic scripture.' It may also be the most studied, argued, and fought over 'Christian document' in modern history. Many have argued about its "Canonical *or* Non-canonical status. Other than a few minimal comments by the Church Fathers, like Origen of Alexandria, Epiphanius of Salamis, and Eusebius, Constantine's first Historian of Christianity, other important "Church Fathers" such as Irenaeus seems not to know (or care) about it (Schaff, Philip., Ed. 2016).

But it was not until the Bedouins and Archeologists found the whole Nag Hammadi Coptic Gospel of Thomas that others recognized its import and previous consequential and even its far-reaching existence. Its first translators and scholars even believed it might be (part of) "Q" or the "Quell or Source" (see below). The date of composition is another fight. But some believe it stems from as early as 40 CE (at least in oral canonical memorizations - which are virtually variations of the same "Canonical" sayings by Jesus as found in Matthew or Luke.) But in this case, "sayings" are located in the *GThom*. And to others appearing as late as 140 CE, including unknown scriptures found in Thomas, including some so-called 'Gnostic' portions (Meyer, Marvin. 2005; King, Karen L. 2003)

It is worth noting that in the Septuagint Alexandrinus, LXX or 'the Jewish Greek OT *combined* with the 'Koine Greek Christian NT,' made up the totality of the Christian Bible in one book. The Codex Alexandrinus was a fifth-century (c. 400-440 CE) Christian Bible produced shortly after the first 50 Bibles Emperor Constantine I had ordered to be made and distributed by Eusebius of Caesarea (Schneemelcher, Wilhelm., Wilson, Robert McLachlan., Hennecke, Edgar. Eds. 1991; 2003; Schaff, Philip., Ed. 2016). The Alexandrinus includes (along with 1 Clement) also the "Letter of 2 Clement 12:2" which directly quotes from the Gospel of Thomas verse 22 - or another *very similar* text, obviously then also acceptable enough (at that time) to be included in one of the first Complete "Canonical" Christian Bibles. The quote is, *"For the Lord Himself, being asked by a certain person when his kingdom would come, said, 'When the two shall be one, and the outside as the inside, and the male with the female, neither male or female;'"* this "phrase" (uniquely when cited from this text) is still being recognized 'to this day' as "Canonical!" Codex Alexandrinus was created in the Fifth Century *after* the Council of Nicea. The Codex does not make all of "Thomas" Canonical. However, it suggests some still read it (or similar scripture) as non-heretical, with small fragments or 'similar sayings and scriptures' also showing up in the writings of Clement and Origen of Alexandria (and so it appears believed by them to be true oracular apothegms) or 'canonical sayings' of the Lord. So it (the *GThom*) had not yet been officially rejected by a council of the entire church (Meier, John P. 1991; 2016; Davies, Stevan. 1983; 1996; 2002; DeConick, April D. 2001; 2005; 2005; 2008; 2017; Pagels, Elaine. 2003; Patterson, Stephen J., Bethge, Hans-Gebhard., Robinson, James M. 1998; Brown, T. Patterson. 2014; Guillaumont A. et al., 1957; Grondin, Michael. et al., 1997; Brown, Patterson T. 2010; 2014; Kloppenborg, John S., Marvin W. Meyer, Stephen J. Patterson, Michael G. Steinhauser, eds. 1990; Mattison, Mark M. 2018; Lamambdin, Thomas O. 2000; Schneemelcher, Wilhelm., Wilson, Robert McLachlan., Hennecke, Edgar. Eds. (1991; 2003; and Schaff, Philip., Ed. 2016).

Scholars of great repute have gone to extraordinary efforts to elucidate it (in both positive and negative ways). Kloppenborg points out that the *GThom* has twenty-eight percent of 'Q,' or "Quell" sayings (the "Source" of the *apothegms* of Jesus found in Matthew and Luke but not in Mark or John.) They further state that the *GThom* has 37 (Canonical) out of 132 'Canonical Q sayings" brought out in the recent publication of the reconstituted "Critical Q" found in Matthew and Luke. It makes up to 28% of "Q" or the 'Gospel of Q' as Kloppenborg has called it (Köester Helmut. 1990; Meyer, Marvin W., Robinson, James M. 2007; Meyer, Marvin. 2005; Kloppenborg, John S., Marvin W. Meyer, Stephen J. Patterson. et al., 1990; Robinson, James M., Hoffmann, Paul., Kloppenborg, John S., Moreland, Milton C. 2000; Barnstone,

William. 1984; Barnstone, William., Meyer, Marvin. 2003; 2007)

The twentieth Century's most outstanding biblical scholars have argued over virtually everything in the GThom. They fight about its age, its provenance, its canonicity. And about it's the author (was it, famously, written by 'Doubting Thomas?') Did Judas Didymus Thomas ("Doubting write it? *Or… was it,* **Yehudah** just Judas? (Barnstone, William. 2009.) Both Eusebius and Saint Jerome reported that Elders had Pantaenus sent (one of the founders of the Catechetical Christian School in Alexandria) to see how the Indian or "Nasrani" (Christians) were getting along. They further reported that Pantaenus found the *Hebrew Gospel of Mathew* left in India by Saint Bartholomew. Some writers believe that the difficulty in understanding the language of Saint Thomas Christians mislead Pantaenus, who misinterpreted their reference to Mar Thoma (Bishop Thomas) as Bar Tolmai (the Hebrew name of Bartholomew).

Judas Thomas was thought in some circles, especially within Syriac Christianity, to have been a "twin" brother of Jesus (a rather shocking idea). But more likely, he was a cousin with some similar physical characteristics. But who could give Homilies (or preach) using the very words of "Jesus, his cousin," or his "brother" and was famous for making a powerful impression and deep, spiritual sermons, "causing people to feel as if an 'identical twin'" was talking. Otherwise, there would have been significant and extensive documentation of an *actual and true* "identical twin, which is not there" (Brantingham, James. 2019; Meyer, Marvin W., Robinson, James M. 2007).

And they argue over whether or not it is dependent upon the Four Canonical Gospels. How 'Gnostic' it is or isn't (a term most scholars of Gnosticism generally try not to use anymore). If they do use it, they do it with extreme hesitation, like Karen King (2003.) She argues the Gospel of Thomas is essentially not' Gnostic' (as does Thomas P. Brown 2014) and, so on and so on... But, it appears these arguments will continue... 'into the Age!' Yet, I do not doubt that (today) it is 'Holy Writ' for millions and millions of people ("modern Gnostics and otherwise). I suspect many who first read it would not (easily or immediately) identify it as Gnostic. Nor anything else accept Canonized Christian scripture (NSC Admin. 2021).

The twentieth centuries' greatest biblical scholars argue over its age, it provenance, it's canonicity, its author (putatively and famously, 'Doubting Thomas the Apostle' or, Judas Didymus Thomas) *or... was it,* **Yehudah** (Judas) 'as in, the Brother of Jesus?' (Barnstone, William. 2009). Many have fiercely argued over whether or not it is dependent upon the Four Canonical Gospels. How *'Gnostic'* it is or isn't (a term most scholars of Gnosticism generally try to steer clear of today - at least with other Scholars). If they do use it, they do it with extreme hesitation, like Karen King (2003.) She argues the *Gospel of Thomas* is essentially not' Gnostic' (as does Thomas P. Brown 2014) both believing it (acceptably canonical) and Christian. Though many agree many disagree with this assessment (Davies, Stevan. 1983; Meier, John P. 1991; 2016.) But it appears these arguments will continue for a long time maybe, 'into the Age!' Yet, I do not doubt that *today* it is 'Holy Writ' for millions of people ("modern Gnostics and otherwise"). Some Gnostics today do not consider that they are "Christian" in the modern sense (and this is the very reason they more comfortably approach Gnosticism while maintaining ties (even their main tie with other faiths - such as Buddhism, Judaism or some form of Hinduism; yet some Gnostics see themselves as "Christian" and think - this is the way the most "true Christianity" presented itself (Hoeller, Stephan A. 2002; Johannite Church, The Apostolic. 2018; Ecclesia Pistis Sophia. 2019.) I suspect many who first read it could not (easily or) immediately identify what is and is not Gnostic.

The 'New, New Testament or the, "Restored New Testament" or, "The Gnostic Bible"

Yet, it has recently been made 'canonical-*like*' by being included in 'The New, New Testament' by Hal Tussig (and His Associates). Dr. Tussig (now retired) was a Professor of New Testament at Union Theological Seminary in New York. And a Pastor at the United Methodist Church in Philadelphia, Pennsylvania *too*. So, he convened a 'council made up of nineteen important religious and spiritual leaders'; including, for example a non-Christian, but believing Jewish Scholar. Along with other 'newly' added texts Tussig, et al., and Barnstorm et al., have published, a '**New, New Testament** and Barnstone a "'**Restored' New Testament.**" William Barnstone and the late (great) Marvin Meyer also published "**The Gnostic Bible.**" Three of the Gospels and the SRevJohn (in this text, the second edition of *Holy Wisdom and The Logos of God*) are in both the "New New

Testament," or "The Restored, New Testament." And the *Gospel of Philip* is also included in "The Gnostic Bible." They are: *The GThom*, the *Gospel of Truth* (*Gtr*) and the *Gospel According to Mary* along with the *Secret Revelation of John or, SRev-John*).

William Barnstone has published a 'new' translation and 'restoration' of the 'New Testament' (2009). He is a Jewish scholar of the Bible (OT and NT). And of the whole of Biblical (OT and NT) literature or, as the title to his 1984 book states: 'The *Other* Bible' (1984). This includes Second Temple Jewish works like 1 Enoch and also the Dead Sea Scrolls, and all other Gnostic, Jewish and Christian Apocryphal literature (1984; 2009 2011). His 'Restored New Testament' includes the *GThom, GMary, GPhil, Gtr* and *Gospel of Judas*. He adds Hebrew names and much that was Jewish from the first century so that Jesus is called Yeshua, Andreas instead of Andrew and Yaakov for James. Pilatus is the infamous Pilate. And he brings much insight into the Jewish background of Yeshua and *of* the New Testament. He believes Christians have divested Yeshua and the New Testament from too much of its Jewish roots. And he draws from Hebrew or Aramaic whenever appropriate as was in the bible Yeshua read. A scholar of Greek he revisits the Septuagint and Koine Greek. This, Koine Greek was the Greek of the early Christian community. A Great Scholar, Barnstone's stunning and breathtaking work has informed me. And, I am in debt to his large and marvelous output. And really to so many more...

These 'new' (a 'New, New' or 'Restored') texts are "not yet" acceptable to Mainstream Christianity. But both chose for: pride of place (from the 'Gnostic literature') *The Gospel of Thomas*. There has been intense scrutiny applied to 'the *Gospel of Thomas*' and it is a near certainty that it was "Canonical or Canonical-like" for hundreds of years for the Syrian Thomasine Christians (which may have also written the, *Acts of Thomas (which certainly uses a verse from verse 13 in the "GThom,"),* the *Infancy Gospel of Thomas*, even (though probably not) the *Apocalypse of Thomas* . But at some point in time a 'man or woman' must at take a stand and share their work. I have felt this way in my publication of scientific research many times. But I feel it again regarding this book, *Holy Wisdom and The Logos of God*. I would only note that, as in the other works of this Book *Holy Wisdom and The Logos of God* (' *WisdLogos*') that the reader keep in mind these things. Within these texts in the first edition I was exegetically liberal and inventive. I have was liberal with interpolations from canonical, non-canonical and other gnostic texts. In this second edition I am more conservative (less exegetically liberal and use a smaller amount of interpolation.

My publication was only possible as a result of so many fine interlinear word-for-word Coptic to English translations. I used at least six now for the Gospel of Thomas alone. And there is a surfeit of wonderful translations (again with many fine interlinear word-for-word Coptic to English translations.) The world is changing (and, this is brought home in the *SRevJohn*). I hope readers enjoy all the texts here, including 'Thomas' *in*: Holy Wisdom and The Logos of God?

James Brantingham PhD
4 28 2021

Thousand Oaks

The Gospel of Thomas (the Gnostic Gospel)

Jesus Appears to Thomas

Now Thomas (also known as Didymus), one of the Twelve, was not with the disciples when Jesus came. So the other disciples told him, "We have seen the Lord!"

But he said to them, "Unless I see the nail marks in his hands and put my finger where the nails were, and put my hand into his side, I will not believe."

A week later his disciples were in the house again, and Thomas was with them. **Though the doors were locked,** *Jesus came and stood among them and said, "Peace be with you!" Then he said to Thomas, "Put your finger here; see my hands. Reach out your hand and put it into my side. Stop doubting and believe."*

Thomas said to him, "My Lord and my God!"... (John 20:28 After NIV)

Acts of Thomas, "Thomas says ...thou that didst call me apart from all my fellows and spakest unto me three words wherewith I am inflamed, and am not able to speak them unto others. Jesu, man that wast slain, dead buried!" "Jesu, God of God!" (James, MR. 1924)

Pro 3:19 19 By Sofia the Lord founded the earth; by the Logos he established the heavens (After: Kugel, JL. 2017)

John 8:51 'Verily, verily, I say to you, If a man keep my sayings, he shall never taste death.' (After the NIV)

The **Gospel of Thomas** (GThom) is the most famous, most studied, and most argued over Gnostic (Christian) Gospel in history. Scholars argue over its Age, its provenance, its canonicity, and whether it depends on the Four Canonical Gospels. And, much, much more. It has recently been named "canonical" by two new translations of the New Testament by Taussig's: "The New, New Testament" (Taussig, Hal., Ed. 2013) and by the Scholar William Barnstone and His "Restored New Testament" (Barnstone, William. 2009.)

THE GOSPEL OF THOMAS

1 Didymus Judas Thomas writes,

I, Thomas, inquired after the Living One, Jesus the Anointed. And he spoke to me and, I wrote down the words of our Rabbi; his hidden sayings and the Word. *Amēn, amēn, I say,* whoever finds His Wisdom within these words shall never taste death.

2 Jesus says,

One who seeks must keep seeking till they find. Yet many who find 'It' (*the Way*) art stunned, even troubled. For the 'Light' unnerves and astonishes everyone! But then their spirits lift. Free now, they reign over life!

3 Jesus says,

If your leaders say look, Heaven is in the sky or lo, it is in the sea, then birds and fish will arrive there before you. But Heaven is within you and all about you (though you see it not). Now many who do not know themselves, think they are close to Me. But, this is ignorance… in Truth, they are far from Me. First, know thyself then you will understand. For thout art made in the image of the Living One and art the sons and daughters of God Most High. But if thou do not know thyself, thou cannot know the Truth. Then thou liveth in ignorance and in poverty; know thee thy Truth for that will set you free.

4 Jesus says,

An elderly but wise man will not hesitate to query a little child; newly born and merely seven days old about, the 'meaning of Life'. After which he can reflect on the meaning and the purpose of his own life and on life itself. Then, through Sacred Scripture and Knowledge and in unity with God He will remember, and remembering He will live! The Lord's divine words and wisdom teach… that the first shall be last and the last shall be first!

5 Jesus says,

Hold fast; for 'the One' and, *'That Which Is,'* stands before thee! So remember, nothing hidden stays concealed **nor buried that is not unveiled.**

6 His disciples asked him,

Lord, what should we do to be holy, sanctified, and pure? And afterward, cleansed, how should we serve Thee? Which foods should we eat; how should we fast? How should we pray, and to whom should we give alms? Jesus says, So, do not lie. And in everything, do not do to others what you would not have others do to you! For every hidden thing will be revealed; every secret (under Heaven) made known.

7 Jesus says,

Blissful is the one who eats 'the lion' for this 'person controls his passions and himself." Blissful are they who control their zeal, conceit, and pride being caring and helpful souls. But when 'the lion' eats the person, this individual claws their way to the top. They rage out of control, covet power, and think those that do not take from others *anything* they want, vulnerable and weak!

8 Jesus says,

The Kingdom of Heaven is like a wise fisherman who cast his net into the sea. He drew up the catch, and a lot of small fish filled it. But looking closely, he found among them one large, beautiful, and magnificent fish, the best fish he had ever caught! Being wise, he threw the others back and kept that one only. Whoever has ears to hear, let him hear!

9 Jesus says,

Listen and understand, a farmer came forth sowing handfuls of seeds. He threw them out and scattered them. But some fell on a hard road and the birds flew down and ate them. Some fell on bedrock, and could not root into the soil nor, sprout sheaves. Some fell on thorns; and were stifled and caught and eaten up by worms. However, some seed fell on good soil. These seed rooted deep, and produced a bountiful, exceptional fruit. So these seeds produced sixty sheaves per measure and some, one hundred and twenty per measure!

The Little Apocalypse includes Verses 10, 11, 12, 13 and 16 & 111 (see below)

10 Jesus says,

Behold, when I come, I will cast a consuming fire on this World; and, on the Powers and Archons ruling this complex, savage place. And I will guard it until its blaze burns the unjustified and the unrighteous, away.

11 Jesus says,

When thou looketh to the Sky and the Heavens above, or the deepest Aeons below **Behold,** thout shalt see it all vanish with thine own eyes! *Lo,* the Heavens above and all the Realms below will pass away. For, the Cosmos itself drains away before thee! So, if thout art "dead," you will not live. Yet, they who sought and found the Light will live and shall never die! But when thou consumed lifeless food, your body gave it life (and Light). Now thout art unyoked and single. If thout art spiritual, step into the Light, and thy guardian Angel awaits and will joineth thee! What then, if thou doth not want this, will you do? Before thy existence, thou wert yoked as one. But, living in this world of matter, materialistic and fleshly things thee divided and now, ye no longer believeth in an 'Age to Come.' Nor doth thou wish to be forced into the Light. Or, join "some divided yoke" and be made one again. So, be it! But now, what will thou do?

12 The disciples said to Jesus,

You have said it, Lord, *we will lose you!* But after you leave us, teacher, who should our Rabbi be? Then Jesus said, No matter where you are, or what you have done, go to my brother James. James *is* Just; and 'he who lives by righteousness.' He will guide and sanctify you. **For He**(...*and* **the Anthropos**) **brought this whole world into being.** And the Blissful One shall teach you Word and Wisdom and lead you into Heaven *above* Heaven and, into the Life to Come.

13 Jesus says to his disciples,

Compare me and tell me whom do I resemble? Simon Peter says, Lord you are like a righteous angel. Jesus asks Matthew (Levi) whom do you compare me to? Lord you are like a wise philosopher of the soul, one who understands the heart and mind of the people. But Thomas hesitated... and then haltingly said, 'Rabbi, my mouth, and the words of my mouth; even my heart and my mind are worthless to answer thee, for I cannot comprehend who you are, nor am I fit to acknowledge Who or What You really are! Yeshua looked deeply into Thomas face and He said, 'Thomas, Brother Thomas, you are no longer my student for, you have drunk from my mouth the bubbling spring of the Word and Wisdom and become intoxicated with Knowledge and Faith.

And just then, he took Thomas away, withdrawing from the other disciples, and said to him in private 'three words'^ (*d, e, f, g, h, i, j*). Thomas, who had begun to entertain such thoughts, was *still* scandalized. Thomas understood He was claiming "equality with the One!" Shocked to his "Jewish" core, mind, and heart, he walked out. When he returned to the other disciples, they asked him breathlessly, 'what did Jesus say?' Yet Thomas said, 'if I spoke even one of the 'three words' He said, you... would pick up stones and stone me. But before you could do that, the rocks would explode. And their broken bits, shock, and flames would destroy you!

^*See below (^These Three Words Sources and Footnotes below)*

14 Jesus says,

If you fast, the sin of gluttony crouches at your door. And if you pray loudly that all might hear, men will scoff and judge you for they love the darkness, not the Light. Yet when you give to a charity *just* so that others might see, it violates and harms you spiritually. But remember, as you travel from place to place, if they listen to you and take you in, eat what they set before you. But no matter what they do, heal their sick and cure the ill. For it is not what goes into your mouth that defiles, but the words that come out that defile.

15 Jesus says,

If thou sees Spirit, which is not born of woman (or the flesh) prostrate thyself! Fall on thy face and bend thy head and worship, for He is 'the Lord of Spirits,' your Father.

16 Jesus says,

Many think, 'I Am' the Prince of Peace. Yet, society is not ready for peace. **Behold,** I come as an Avenging Lord; a Whirlwind of Fury, Judgment, and Fire! A 'Stumbling Block' to the people in this world. *Lo,* I stoke the fire and cut down all that rule by sword and by war. Look! Families tear each other apart in blood and conflict. Three against two; or, one against four; Father against son; daughter against brother; and (their) mother against them all! Like monks and nuns, each must stand alone on judgment day.

17 Jesus says,

I shall give to you what no human eye has seen, nor ear heard, nor human hand has touched nor, ' *that,*' which has even yet been conceived of,' in the human heart or mind!

18 The disciples asked,

Rabbi, tell us each what our missions will accomplish in the end? Annoyed by this, He said, 'you know **not** from where you came, nor who "*I Am,*" that is standing before you. Yet, you wish to know (before you've begun) the extent of your victory in the end! I say, 'blissful is one who, in the beginning, teaches 'the Way' for where thee doeth that is where thou goeth back! She who understands '*this*' will never die!

19 Jesus says,

Blissful is one who 'consciously remembers *being*' before 'being born, again.' For, if thou becometh my Disciples, these very stones beneath your feet will serve thee. Recall I taught that on a river in Paradise, thee seeth five trees growing next to each other. Seasons change but, their leaves do not. *Amēn, amēn, I say,* blessed art mine who understand this for thout shalt never die.

20 The disciples asked Jesus,

Tell us what the Kingdom of Heaven is like. And He sayeth, open thine eyes and see, thine ears and hear. Heaven above Heaven is like a small, tiny mustard seed. Yet, when this seed falls on the fertile ground, it grows into a mighty plant. And it becometh a home for the birds of the sky.

21 Then Mary asked the Rabbi,

What are your disciples like? Jesus says they are like children. But even more so, naïve children who lack wisdom and experience. Entrusted with a field to farm (which they do not own), they ask no-one for help or learn to farm it. Yet when the owners came back, there was no crop to take. Disappointed, they said, 'give us our field back.' So these little ones give it back, stripping away everything (even their garments).

Thus the Rabbi taught when an owner of a house knows thieves are on the way (and they will come!), he prepares. And, he makes his people ready before the bandits appear. For where the defense is weak, they will find it! And if the field is ripe, with a sickle in hand, they will steal the harvest. Be prepared! So that thieves cannot break in and plunder their house, field, or barn. Nor rob thee of thine true wealth. Those who have ears to hear, let them hear!

22 Jesus saw some infants nursing.

He said to his Disciples, 'Look and see these little ones being suckled. Their trust, and their full reliance allows them to enter the Kingdom of Heaven'. Then the disciples turned to Him and said, 'must we become like little children to enter Heaven?' Jesus said, *'when you make two into one and when you make the inside like the outside and above like below*; so that a male is not just a male and a female is not just a female but the two together, one; and together they are more than a man or woman. *And, when you see through God's eyes in the place of your eyes; and use God's hands in the place of your hands; and through love allow God's feet to guide your feet to aid and assist others*; then, Male or Female, Jew or Greek you become the image and likeness of 'the One' Above! Then — you will enter His Kingdom'!

23 Yeshua says,

I shall choose you, one from out of a thousand and two, from out of ten thousand. And through Sacred Knowledge you shall come to understand. Then thout shalt stand up righteous, chosen and saved… whole and complete!

24 His disciples said,

Rabbi, where do you come from? We must know, so we can seek it too. He told them: whoever has ears to hear should hear! Light exists within a person whose likeness is *(of) the Light.* If that person shines, it*is a* light for the entire world. But if he does not, the world is left in darkness

25 Jesus says,

If you hate the other but claim to be One with God, you lie! For it is written, 'the one who loves the other fulfills the law!' So I say, you must love one another and protect them as if they were the pupil of your eye!

26 Jesus says,

The 'speck' in your brother's eye (that blinds him from the Truth) you see. But the 'plank' in your own eye you deny. First, cast the beam from your own eye, then remove the sliver from your brother.

27 Jesus says,

Abstain thee, on the Sabbath from the world and, secular life. Or, thout shalt never know communion (or repose) with the Father, 'the One Who Is…'

28 Jesus says,

I incarnated into flesh and blood and stood up a man, the Messiah, for all! But I found everyone intoxicated and distracted by the flesh and the sensations, thrills and material things here below; in this world. None, no, not one thirsted for divine knowledge and salvation. My soul exceedingly grieved; I wept! For they (too) are sons and daughters, the children of God! But their eyes and minds, their souls were blind. 'For empty, they came into the world, and empty too they seek to leave the world.' But when they come too,' those who turn can see and hear and be saved.

29 Jesus says,

If a body comes into existence to serve 'spirit,' *that* is' astonishing. Yet if 'spirit' comes into being because of the body, that is an even greater wonder! The wonder of wonders! But I am amazed. For how did ' *noumena,*' '*spirit,*' become one with matter and flesh; making its home in such poverty?"

30 Jesus says,

Wherever they proclaim that there are 'three gods,' they are godless. But where they say God is One, I say, (*I and the Holy Father and Mother*) am with them. Split the wood and you will find me, lift the stone and, I am there.

31 Jesus says,

No prophet predicts God's will in his own home, nor heals there. For in derision, people cry out, *'Medice, cura te Ipsum!'* 'Doctor, first heal thyself!'

32 Jesus says,

A city on a hill is a light to the world. If attacked, it will not fall; but, neither can it hide (nor be left in peace).

33 Jesus says,

One who kindles a lamp does not set it under a basket nor hide it behind a hedge; but places it upon a stand where its' light allows everyone coming in or going out, to see. So then, what is whispered in your ears from the One Above shout it from the rooftops!

34 Jesus says,

If a leader guiding another is blind and will not see (nor hear) the Word or Wisdom, both may fall into the pit.

35 Jesus says,

Even an ordinary person can overcome a more muscular, ferocious thief and criminal. But, first, learn to bind the lawbreaker shrewdly. Then, plunder his home and take *his* ill-gotten possessions.

36 Jesus says,

Do not worry from morning until the night and from the evening until the next day; what to wear. Look! See how *God* clothes the lilies! They neither card nor adorn themselves. Yet, what more beautiful dress hast thou ever seen! '*That Which Is*' will supply you. Is not life more than just food, and the body more than just clothes? And who by constant worry improves their life?

37 His disciples say to him,

On what day shall we finally see you 'and know you for who you are?' Jesus said, "that day would come soon… for the Angel of Death will strip off your garments. Lo, if you can let 'your clothes and this life' slip away without fear or regret, you will see 'the Son of the Living One' and never be afraid again."

38 Jesus says,

Beloved, you have longed deeply, patiently yearning to hear My words and Holy Wisdom from Above. For I taught you stories that illuminated and brought thee Truth. Soon, the day will come when you will call me and seek me; but no longer find me!

39 Jesus says,

The Teachers and the Scholars of the Law dictate what you must do and how you should do it to live. Yet, they hide the keys to Salvational Knowledge (*Gnosis*). They do not do what they say *you* must do. Nor live the way they insist; *you* must live! Beware then to attain Gnosis; one must be as cunning as a serpent and innocent as a dove.

40 Jesus says,

A beautiful vineyard was planted but grew feeble and weak. For never set apart in gratitude to the Father, its roots were, without effort, pulled out and perished.

41 Jesus says,

To those who have much in hand, even more, will be given. But to those who have little, Lo, nothing, the world will also take that away!

42 Jesus says,

Thou shalt come into being as ye pass away! For, being *is* spirit. So, if thou art passing through uncouple *and* detach.

43 His disciples say to Jesus,

Who are You? You say (and do) unbelievable, incredible, even sinful things! Exasperated, He said, 'yet, *you still* don't know **Who I AM** from what I say? Nor **What I AM?**' from what I do? So be it, no amount of signs or words will persuade you.

44 Jesus says,

Blasphemy against the Father or the Son will be forgiven. There is no sin in tolerance, but one sins if they do not allow others their religious or spiritual beliefs. That person blasphemes against the Holy Spirit and commits the Unforgivable Sin.

45 Jesus says,

Grapes don't grow from prickly thistles nor figs from a thorny bush; neither plant gives edible fruit. So a good person does good things; and a bad person evil or wickedness from the goodness or iniquity within their hearts and minds.

46 Jesus says,

From the first soul born of a woman until today, no prophet was superior to John. He baptized us in living water and raised us to a new life, pouring death away. So the Baptist need not lower his eyes, nor head to anyone. Yet, thou who art least even humble as a child — will be greater than John, in the Life to Come!

47a Jesus says,

A man does not mount two horses nor pull back the strings on two bows, at the same time. So it is… a person cannot serve two masters. Otherwise they will love, serve and treat one with respect but hate, fear, and despise the other.

47b No-one drinks aged, excellent vintage and then call for new wine. Nor do they pour new and fermented grape juice into an old wineskin. It will burst the container. But an older wine poured into a new wineskin will destroy its' taste. So repairing a new garment using old cloth will cause it to tear.

48 Jesus says,

If two together, make peace with each other and say to a mountain 'move' it will move!

49 Jesus says,

Blissful are those 'the chosen' that carry on alone. Like monks and nuns, they live. Their experiential encounter with *God Above God* is such; they pass their life content to the end. On the last day, and through 'the Way,' they return to His Kingdom and Home.

50 Jesus says,

When you ascend, if the gatekeeping Archons or Angels ask you, 'from where have you come?' Say, 'we have come from the Father, the Father of Light'. For behold, the Uncreated said, 'let there be light, and the heavens opened and filled up with light; yet, not just any light… but, the quintessentially necessary, infinitely creative, illuminating luminescence; being from His Purity and Holiness, it is the Uncaused Cause of the All and All. The creator (in Truth) of everything: being from, God Above God: (the Father, Holy Mother and, the Logos) their

Spirit creating the very ground of being in which we, this cosmos and this world live and move and have its being.

'It is from there we have come from, the 'One Who Is'. 'And in His image and likeness God made us all'. But, if a Guardian Angel says, 'give us proof.' Say, 'We, the chosen sons and daughters of the Father, are the children of God Most High; come to carry out His will, bringing peace and repose'.

51 His disciples asked Him,

'Lord, when will the dead be resurrected, and find rest?' 'And when will Heaven above heaven, the New Jerusalem, that blessed New World arrive?' He answered, 'that which you look outward for already lies within and without and all around you! But, you do not yet understand or accept it, nor (can thee even) see it'.

52 His Disciples say to Him,

Twenty-four Prophets in the Torah and from the Word and full covenant speaketh about Thee, the Perfect Man, 'the One'. They saith, 'One like a Son of Man cometh on the clouds of Heaven'. Jesus saith to them, the One you await stands before thee, before thy face! Yet, thou wasteth time referring to the dead.

53

His Disciples say to him,

'Is circumcision required for salvation?' Jesus says, 'Abraham was chosen uncircumcised.' For the Father first picked Abraham then accepted and justified him. After that and upon the Lords' command, Abraham circumcised himself. So it is that, gaining wisdom and having a circumcised mind and heart comes first. 'Spirit cometh before the flesh or, we would have been born circumcised.'

54 Jesus says,

Blissful are those in poverty, even the poor in spirit, for theirs is the Kingdom of Heaven.

55 Jesus says,

'Whomever will not, 'stand on their own two feet,' but remain dependent on parents or siblings,' cannot be my disciple. **Lo, anyone that does not pick up their own cross and follow me, is not worthy.**

56 Jesus says,

A follower of 'the Way' sees this materialistic and fallen world for what it is, a corpse. Therefore, thou who understand… knoweth that the world is not worthy of thee. Nor can it judge; nor contain thy joy in knowing the Truth.

57 Jesus says the Kingdom of God is like this,

'A farmer and his workers sowed good seed and left the field. But another farmer, a lawless competitor came that night and sowed bad seed, weeds, among the first farmer's grain. But when the seed began to grow the farmer being wise, said to his workers, 'wait for both to sprout'. 'Do not pick them before the harvest. At that time, you will easily see the good seed from the bad. Then pull out the weeds and cast them into the fire.'

58 Jesus says,

Blissful are they who have suffered trials and tribulations for, they already entered and will soon enter fully, the joyous Life to Come!

59 Jesus says,

Do not liveth in ignorance. Thou who do not seeketh Him, 'Thine, the Living One,' will 'knoweth Him not' and be blind. For everyones days are numbered and death cometh for all. Then how can thee findeth Him? thout shalt not… and will searcheth in vain.

60 His Disciples said to Him,

Look at that Samaritan carrying an innocent lamb. Jesus asked, why is he carrying that lamb? They said to Him, so that during the festival he can kill it, cook it and eat it. Then He said to His disciples, *only if it is dead* will he cook it and eat it. So, as far as it is up to you, live in peace with everybody. But remain vigilant and aware lest, a vandal murder you and take that which is yours. *Lo,* even though you are as innocent as that lamb. Yet, many want to kill you; for in their eyes thout art vile, a renegade and a schismatic. They lie in wait to kill you; and after will desecrate your corpse. Then they will remove from your body anything of value; and leave it to the dogs. So find a site to defend; and stay out of harms way. For (*in this day*) only then, you (*who believe*) will know safety and peace.

61 Jesus says,

Two will lie upon a bed. One will die but the other shall live.

Salome said this to Jesus, and then asked,

Whom do you think you are you Sir? You talk and act like you are the 'One to Come,' the Anointed' *someone with great authority*! And you lay on my bed and eat from my table. So again, 'by what power or authority have you the right to do this!' Jesus then said to her, *Salome, 'I Am He'.* **'The One to come.'** For, I do the will of the Father, God Most High'. Salome thought about what He said and, stepping back saith, 'Lord, lord I was blind but now I see; deaf but now I hear. Lord, Accept me as thy Disciple'! Then Jesus said to her, 'when we unite in *His* Light we live… unto the Age! But if we do the will of the *Adversary,* lying, cheating and stealing, we *are* dark. And, we *live* in darkness!

Jesus says,

62 I reveal to the worthy, experiential knowing and awareness of all mysteries. These blissful ones are beyond doubt. They *have*, and they *know* **life and love.** But, they must give it away to keep it. So keep secret from your left hand the good the right hand does.

63 Jesus says,

There was a wealthy person. He possessed much money, many things and many treasures. He said to himself, I will skillfully use and save my money and, hide my assets (even from the family and those I love). Then no matter what happens I (at least) will remain rich my entire life! So he filled up his storehouse with every desire, and sat back in satisfaction. Those were his thoughts that day and as he went to sleep that night. **But,** *that very night the Angel of Death, the Reaper demanded his life and he died.* So I say, whoever has ears to hear, let them hear!

64 Jesus says,

A prominent man in the community wished to honor many important people in his town and so he invited them to a great banquet. When the food was ready he sent his servant out and said, 'summon these noble people to the feast tonight'. The servant went to the house of the first person and said, 'Sir my master asks you to remember to come to his lavish dinner tonight'. But he said to the servant, 'I am sorry but, I have a momentous banking matter to attend to tonight and, I cannot come'. Then the servant went to another man of distinction. But, he too could not come for he was purchasing a house and it would take up the whole day *and* night. He said, please tell your master I am sorry that I could not come! And so it went… All the important and influential people of the city (whom earlier had said they would come) withdrew and bowed out. So the servant went back to the master and said, 'everyone apologized but said they had other important matters they must deal with'. 'No one, *not even one…* could attend'. The master, angry and slighted said, 'go out into the streets and invite anybody you find, anyone willing to come! Even an outsider, a nobody, rich *or* poor! *Invite them all… educated, illiterate, the destitute, the blind and the lame!* For tonight *any* who come will share this great feast!

So it is in the Father's house. Any that seek Him, he invites in and they enter and feast with 'the One Above'! But those too busy buying and selling; working, and chasing after money, power, material things, *and* the flesh… these ones will always be to busy to come to the feast.

65 Jesus says,

A good and compassionate man owned land. On that land he planted a vineyard. He employed tenant farmers to cultivate the land for his family. His wish was to have a profitable vineyard (and out of this profit, to pay the tenants). Later he sent a servant to collect the fruit and the profits from their labor. But the farmers resented him and, and resented not owning the land. So they seized the servant, beat him severely and he was returned to the owner. He told the land owner what happened and that they gave him nothing. The owner thought, maybe they did not recognize he was my servant. So next he sent a different servant to collect the fruit and profits from his vine. They almost beat this man to death. The owner finally thought, I must send someone important; someone they will recognize represents me. So he sent his son. The tenant farmers *did* recognize him… the son! And they thought, this *is* our chance! And they beat him to death. 'Now the vineyard is ours, they crowed'! He who has ears to hear, hear!

66 Jesus says,

Show me the stone the builders rejected. For, it will be the 'cornerstone' that they needed the most.

67 Jesus says,

You may have great learning and education. And be accomplished in many skills; music, engineering and the building of bridges and castles and broadly taught Philosophy and the Word. You might *even be* a great author! The most educated person anyone has ever met… *But if you do not know yourself then, you know nothing!* Thus Solomon wrote… 'everything is mist, mere breath, …and a chasing after the wind'!

68 Jesus says,

Blissful are you when they hate you and persecute you. For, you will discover a place where they will no longer be able to find you nor persecute you ever again.

69 Jesus says,

Blissful are you who have been persecuted for your ideas and beliefs. Thou hath endured inconceivable abuse …even violent rejection. But rejoice! Thy hath seen the Father and know 'the Way' (and 'the Truth'). Blissful art thee who hunger, for thalt shalt be filled up and lack nothing.

70 Jesus says,

Blessed are you who bring forth *that* which is within you, for *that* which is in you, shall save you. But, if you have not strengthened that which is within, this lack… this debt, will kill you.

71 Jesus says,

Behold, destroy this temple and no human hands will rebuild it.

72 Said someone to Jesus,

'Sir, my brothers must be persuaded to divide our Fathers' estate so that each gets their fair share! Jesus says to him, 'who appointed me the judge and arbiter between you and your lands and your estates?' Then he turned to his disciples and asked, 'is that what they think, I came just to divide things; and to rend things apart?'

73 Jesus says,

The harvest is large but, but few work the fields. Petition the owner to bring more workers to the field.

74a A disciple says to Jesus,

Lord, many stand at the fountainhead. Yet, no one steps forth to drink.

75 Jesus says,

Many have prepared themselves and stand, waiting at the door. But only through the Bridal Chamber and in 'Sacred Matrimony,' can monks or nuns, husbands and wives (and thou) become 'One' again.

76 Jesus says,

The Kingdom or Heaven is like a merchant who acquired a consignment of goods. Yet within it he found a single, priceless and lustrous pearl. Wise and prudent, he sold off everything and bought the pearl for himself. So let it be with you. *It is written...* do not seek the treasures of this world, which moth and rust destroy and thieves break in to steal. But, lay up for thyself treasure in heaven!

77 Jesus says,

I AM the Light that shines over everything, good and evil left and right; right and wrong. I AM the sum of everything: *the All*. For everything cleaves off and, away from ME, and to Me, everything returns. Split the wood, and I am there. Lift up the stone, and you will find Me.

"It is I who am the light which is above ' them all. It is I who am the all. ic

78 Jesus says,

As the people and disciples left He called out, 'what did you come to the desert to see?' A fool dressed in camel hair? A Seer blown about by revolution, upheaval and change? Or, just expensive garments and clothes? 'Yes, the rich own costly clothes but, few of them own the Truth!'

79 A woman in the crowd yelled out to Him. 'Blessed *is* the woman who bore you and nursed you! But, Jesus said, 'even more so are those who hear the *Word*. And blissful are those who hear the *Word* of the Father and, through His Logos know the Truth.' 'For, in the days to come many will say, blessed are they who never gave birth; and whose breasts never nursed!'

80 Jesus says,

Many followers of 'the Way' discern in this season its corrupt and worldly, amoral inhabitants. Such people rely on *'lifeless:* icons and dishonest, materialistic and fleshly men *and* women' who perpetrate lawlessness and bring suffering and death. But the world is not worthy of them to whom this is revealed!

81 Jesus says,

One who, through hard work and effort, becomes rich when 'called' must put aside his life and (*for the greater good*) lead. But, those who amass monstrous and terrifying power (and use it only for what they covet and crave) must renounce this, for *the good of all*!

82 Jesus says,

Whoever comes close to Me is near to *the Fire*. But one who is far from Me moves away from *the 'Light,'* and away from Heaven Most High.

83 Jesus says,

The images of God's garment' were set in motion, *hidden in Light...* "But *the* Light' which created, maintains, and sustains reality and the world. For, the images of the Invisible Spirit and the Son of Man *are obscure;* and concealed by the panoply of unreality and the complexity of the All. Seek Him in the Logos, and the Hidden will be revealed.

84 Jesus says,

In life, we form a vision of our image and likeness; and when we perceive it, we are glad. But *only in the Spirit* or, *at the moment of death,* when we come face to face with 'the One' do we see our image in Truth. But **rejoice,** for your *Icon* will be yoked with our another; and the two, made into one! Measured thou shalt see what thy really were (good or bad) and that we never die!

85 Jesus says,

Adam came forth as a creation of great Wisdom and Power. But... his being was infected with Error. Alas, he was an unworthy 'son of God'. For he stood *not* in the congregation; ruled deficiently, and made egregious mistakes. For if he had been worthy, he would not have tasted death.

86 Jesus says,

The foxes have dens, and the birds their nests. But the Son of Man,' is a pauper here, with no place to lay his head or rest.

87 Jesus says,

Wretched is the flesh that depends on flesh. Even more so is the soul (or the mind) that depends on the flesh.

88 Jesus says,

Behold, angels, and prophets will come to you, and *from* heaven give you that which is yours. But, you must give back to Heaven that which *you gathered and caused to happen.* Remember then, and say to yourselves, 'someday they will come back and take, *that which is theirs'!*

89 Jesus says,

Why do you only wash the outside of the bowl? Do you not understand 'the One' who made the outside, made the inside too? So, clean up the contamination and filth on the inside as well.

90 Jesus says,

Come, all thee who seek. For, my lessons are a gentle yoke and guidance good; filleth thy heart with Wisdom and, know peace!

91 His disciples say to Him,

Tell us who you are so we may trust you and believe in you! Jesus says to them, 'you easily judge the state of the Heavens, of the earth and of its people'. **But when 'I Am,'** the 'One Who Is,' *the Lord and Logos;* (thy seek…) standeth before thee; thou doth not see Me nor recognize Me. *Nor understandeth thee the profundity of this moment.*

92 Jesus says,

Seek, and you will find Me. Yet, some who asked Me questions did not get the answers that they sought. But, I am willing still to speak, and you now understand, my answers are true! Yet even in your hour of need, you will not listen.

93 Jesus says,

Do not give what is consecrated to uneducated, unbelieving scoffers. Nor to those who mock it. For, to them, there is nothing above that should be hallowed below. They will and do treat both 'scripture and belief' in the same way as dung. So share *not* the pearls of scripture with fools or swine; lest scorning Wisdom they turn and tear you apart.

94 Jesus says,

Regardless of who, or what you are (or were), if you seek me you will find Me. For if you knock, and keep on knocking I will open the door.

95 Jesus says,

If you have money, don't lend it out at interest but give it to someone whom you know cannot pay it back.

96 Jesus says,

The Kingdom of Heaven is like a woman who had a tiny bit of leaven. She worked it into and throughout her dough and, transformed the dough into many large loaves of bread. So, whoever has ears to hear, let them hear!

97 Jesus says,

The Kingdom of the Father is like a woman carrying a full jar of grain. There was a long distance to go before getting home, and somewhere along the road (though she did not sense it), the jar broke. Ignorant to the loss, grain leaked out behind her. When home, she put the jar down and saw that it was empty.

98 Jesus says,

The Kingdom of the Father is like a human being who, when the time cometh - *to live or die*, slayeth even a mighty invader. But he had prepared for this invasion having everyone thrust swords into a wall. This strengthened their grip and made it powerful and steady. Then, the time will come (and it did!) and he stepped out of the shadows and, in self-defense slew a violent, invading looter.

99 Jesus says,

The disciples said to Him, 'your mother, brothers, and sisters are standing outside. They have been looking for you.' And He said to them, 'who is My true Father, (Brothers, Sisters) and Mother? Anyone who does the will of 'the Highest.' *They* are my true family! 'And the (perfect) children; the sons and daughters of God.' *They* will enter the Kingdom of Light above!

100 The disciples showed Jesus a silver coin and said, 'the Romans demand this coin be paid to Caesar as a tax. What should we do? He says, give to Caesar the things that are Caesars' and too God, the things that are God's. But *that* which was mine, give *that* back to me.'

101 Jesus says,

Whoever does not hate his Mother and Father as I do, cannot be my disciple. Yet even more so, whoever does not love the Holy Mother and Father as I do cannot follow me. **For, my earthly mother gave me death,** but my 'Holy Mother,' Life.

102 Jesus says,

Woe to the Doctors and the Purists who fanatically interpret the Law. The Word. They are like a sleeping dog who guards cattle. That dog neither eats nor allows the cattle to eat; and, both starve!

103 Jesus says,

Blissful is the person who knows where thieves and brigands will break through. That person prepares himself and his family to defend that place and, their home. For he teaches them, 'gird thy loins, collect thine money and (assets) and stow them; and, be ready!' For we must stop the thieves before they break in!

104 The disciples say to Jesus,

Rabbi, Lord, let us pray and fast! Jesus says to his disciples, 'why suggest this now?' 'What have we done; that our actions should be seen as wrong, or sinful?

If not sinful, why fast and pray even more? For, you do not see nor yet understand it, but later you will recognize this most hallowed day! For, I AM with you! The Bridegroom is here, the Son is here, so let us celebrate and feast! By all means pray and fast later, when the Bridegroom leaves the Bridal Chamber!

105 Jesus says,

He who knows His true Father and Mother, is He called rightly, the son of a whore?

106 Jesus says,

They joined together through love that, which was earlier apart. Yoked strongly in intention, makes the two into one. Then, the 'sons and daughters of the Son of Man' can say, 'mountain move and, the mountain will move!'

107 Jesus says,

The Kingdom of Heaven is like a shepherd who owned one hundred sheep. But his favorite one went missing. So anxiously, the good shepherd searched high and low, leaving the other ninety-nine alone. Haunted, he searched for it everywhere. Finally, he tracked the animal down. For he cared more for it than the other ninety-nine! *Amēn, amēn, I say,* 'that is how He, *God above God,* the Father loveth thee!

108 Jesus says,

Whoever drinks from my mouth, imbibing *Knowledge* will become me. I will become them, and they will divide my Word rightly, and the hidden will be revealed!

109 Jesus says,

The Kingdom of heaven is like a person who owned a field. Though he long plowed it, he never found its hidden treasure. So, he willed it to his son. The son, too, worked the field but decided to sell it and get on with life. So he sold it. The new owner worked it hard and plowed it deep. And to his profound joy, found in it, treasure; a treasure beyond words! Rich, he now lends money at interest to whomever he desires.

110 Jesus says,

Some can acquire much more than is needed to live; even more so, they prosper, becoming rich. But if 'God above God' and Duty call, they renounce their wealth and lead.

111 Jesus says,

Heaven and the earth shall roll up before you, an apocalypse before your very eyes. No longer trapped by illusions, deception, or a this-worldly, fleshly and materialistic world, '*the One*' revealed your authentic self! Living, and, 'one with the Living,' Ye no longer fear death and are free!

112 Jesus says,

Woe to the flesh that depends on the soul; even more difficult is it for the soul that depends on the flesh! *For it is written,* 'the soul is willing, but the flesh is weak.'

113 His Disciples said to Him,

When will the Kingdom of Heaven finally come? Today or much later; how much later? Yeshua says it is not coming in a way that you can say **Look,** 'here it is!' Or **Lo,**' there it is!' Instead, that Realm, *Heaven Above Heaven,* infinite, eternal, holy, and the transcendent Paradise of the Father is within; and spread out before you - everywhere! But humanity does not see it.

114 Simon Peter says to Jesus,

Rabbi, please tell Mary, "go back to Magdala and depart from here! She is a woman and knows nothing about Spirit. Then the Lord saith to Him (and all of them), 'do not cast Mary out, nor turn away anyone.' '*Amēn, amēn, I say to you,*' I will impart to *all,* Male or Female, Greek or Jew Sacred Salvational Knowledge; which, I already gave her. For Mary is Holy to, and a 'Living Spirit' like you!

Sources and Footnotes:

^**These three words:** I Am What I Am ('AHYH ASHR AHYH')

^ The "Three Words" from the "Gospel of Thomas" and the "I AM" or the "I Am What I Am" and the NT use of "I AM" and English.

^ 13 Jesus says to his disciples,

Compare me and tell me whom do I resemble? Simon Peter says, Lord you are like a righteous angel. Jesus asks Matthew (Levi) whom do you compare me to? Lord you are like a wise philosopher of the soul, one who understands the heart and mind of the people. But Thomas hesitated… and then haltingly said, 'Rabbi, my mouth, and the words of my mouth; even my heart and my mind are worthless to answer thee, for I cannot comprehend who you are, nor am I fit to acknowledge Who or What You really are! Yeshua looked deeply into Thomas face and He said, 'Thomas, Brother Thomas, you are no longer my student for, you have drunk from my mouth the bubbling spring of the Word and Wisdom and become intoxicated with Knowledge and Faith.

And just then, he took Thomas away, withdrawing from the other disciples, and said to him in private 'three words.'^ ('AHYH ASHR AHYH;' or I AM who I AM or God from God^) (*d, e, f, g, h, i and j*). ^ Thomas, fearfully heard these words, and though he had begun to consider this', yet it still scandalized his Jewish sensibility. Thus Thomas understood the teacher claimed "equality" with God, 'the Father'! Shocked deeply in his ("*Jewish*") mind and heart he walked out. When Thomas returned to the other disciples they asked him breathlessly, 'what did Jesus say?' Yet Thomas said, 'if I spoke even one of those 'three words' you… would pick up a stone and stone me. But before you did, the stones would explode. And the shock, the broken bits, and the fire and flames would destroy you and consume you'!

^**Gospel of Thomas Verse 13.** *More about the "three words:" (d, e, f, g h, i, and j notes:)*

More about *GThom* Verse 13 See: ^These three words below references.

^ d These three words 'Ahyh Ashr Ahyh' are strongly implied or indicated. But, admittedly are ***not*** actually written out in the Coptic. Thomas Patterson Brown (2014) makes an extended argument for this, 'the Holy Name'. I agree. See references Brown, TP (2014) and the URL address below for his Website. One can find Dr. Brown's supportive commentary and argument there. Jean-Yves Leloup (2005) makes a similar claim, but it is in his annotation alone.

^ The LXX or Septuagint and the Greek Tanakh (composed hundreds of years before the birth of Jesus) has: Ἐγώ εἰμι ὁ ὤν· . . . Ὁ ὢν ἀπέσταλκέν με πρὸς ὑμᾶς (Rahlfs-Hanhart). Or, from the Greek, "I am the one being. . . . the one being has sent me to you. I AM in Hebrew is אָנֹכִי. And one commentator apparently notes Paul (at times) uses "εἰμι ὅ εἰμι" ("I Am The I Am") or in Greek Εγω ειμαι it is a word order or construction that is considered by some forced or stressed (but it makes the point "mimicking" the "three words of the Hebrew." 'I Am The I Am" - in "Hebrew" אֶהְיֶה שְׁלָחַנ אֲלֵיכֶם). Or the transliteration of the Jewish words being three ('Ahyh Ashr Ahyh') or "I am who I am," that Jesus is thought by many to have said. There may be other solutions. (See: Stack Exchange Accessed Feb. 2021 below).

^"AM" is defined for Greek. A definition of "am" (εἰμι, transliterated 'eimai') is a verb often used with the word "I" as the first person singular version of the verb 'to be' (or Εγω or 'Ego.') So in Greek **Εγω ειμαι** or in transliterated English, "**Ego eimai**" means "**I Am**" and can be roughly construed (as used) by Paul's use of εἰμι ὅ εἰμι ("I" am the "I" am; Ego not being used in this formula). Yet this is translated non-theologically below.)

^e The *Acts of Thomas!* **Has an extraordinary alignment with the words implied in the** *Gospel of Thomas!*

In Greek "*The Acts of Thomas*" were not (and never) lost over the last two thousand years). When MR James translated this text he used a "three word phrase" - in English it is similar to the Apostle Paul's use of "εἰμι ὅ εἰμι" (I Am what I Am - see below). James wrote out "Jesu, *God of God*." Something of course supported by the Nicene Creed from the first Nicene Council in 325 CE (and further retained in last Nicene Council in 381 CE) which is the description of Jesus as: "God of God." The Acts of Thomas are believed conservatively to have come from around 250 CE or one hundred years before the Nicene Creed.

^εἰμι ὅ εἰμι (1 Corinthians 15:10) and ὅ or Greek for "The" = *literally*

"I am" or, "It is I" (but the "I AM" meant equally to the OT "I AM").

The High Priest Asks Jesus, "Are You the Christ, the Son of the Blessed One?" (And He says): "I Am…" (Ἐγώ εἰμι or 'Egō eimi') in Greek… " *εἰμι* =Am, 'Egō = I. "**I Am** *and you will see the Son of Man sitting at the right hand of Power and coming with the clouds of heaven*" (*After Berean*). ὅ is Greek for "The." So Paul was in effect saying (I)am the (I) am (vulgarly or colloquially, "I am what I am!" But constructing it to also mechanically mimic (in Greek) the three (Holy) Hebrew words, "Ahyh Ashr Ahyh" (εἰμι ὅ εἰμι).

^The *Acts of Thomas and 'God of God'*

^MR James (1924) translated from the Greek the *Acts of Thomas* (and many scholars accept that the *Acts of Thomas* are inextricably linked with the (*Gospel of Thomas* verse 13 and with other Apocryphal books featuring Thomas and Gnosticism too) **There were 'Thomasine communities'** in Syria (and possibly earlier from India and.) John, bishop of (Persia and) India was a Nasrani (or Christian) from the Coast of India specifically, "a Malabar Nasrani or Malankara Nasrani) is listed as attending the first Council of Nicea. So in this Apocryphal book of Acts, Thomas (the Apostle) states directly yet of near equal Theological Import and Meaning, "three words." And clearly they seem 'related to or to come right out of or from, Verse 13 of the Gospel of Thomas.'

^In the: "**Acts of Thomas**," Thomas says **"...thou that didst** *call me apart from all my fellows and spakest unto me* three words *wherewith I am inflamed,* **and am not able to speak them unto others. "Jesu, man that wast slain, dead buried!"** *"Jesu, 'God of God'"* (!) (James, Montague Rhode. 1924)

^ Coptic "I Am"

In *Gospel of Thomas* 77 Coptic, "I am": ⲁⲛⲟⲕ ⲡⲉ (or) ⲁⲛⲟⲕ ⲣⲉ (Brown, TP. 2014). Or "I am the Light:" ⲁⲛⲟⲕ ⲡⲉ p.ouoein - the light).

In*Gospel of Philip:* ⲁⲛⲟⲕ = "I am or actually I'm (or, I am myself...) functions as "I Am." So "I am a Roman" is actually literally: "I-myself... a Roman." Coptic for Roman is = Ϩⲣⲱⲙⲁⲓⲟⲥ. And the full phrase is: ⲁⲛⲟⲕ ou. Ϩⲣⲱⲙⲁⲓⲟⲥ (In Phillip "I am" usually uses the contraction, "I'm").

^**Words implied in the** *Gospel of Thomas* are similarly implied in the *Acts of Thomas* and by Paul in *Corinthians 15:10*

Like in God of God. So however it was meant by the Apostle Paul in 1 Corinthians 15:10 when he said the three greek words εἰμι ὅ εἰμι, (another way to say **I Am what I Am**) certainly could in some contexts mean, "God of God." It was a "way" to mimic the "three words" mechanically or the three Holy words: **Ahyh Ashr Ahyh.** from Hebrew. And so though some scholars say the phrase Jesu, *"God The God"* (in the Acts of Thomas) is uncommon or "strained" Greek. But would "technically" fit *GThom* verse 13 as "three" words.

^But eimí or "Am, exist" ("eimí" being the transliterated english pronunciation of the letters from the Greek word: εἰμι) is defined is in Thayer's dictionary as: "Am or "to be, too exist, to happen, to be present" and similar constructions). So "God of God" may also be "strained" from the Coptic (possibly ⲑⲉⲟⲥ ⲁ- ⲑⲉⲟⲥ or something similar). Here the coptic ⲁ- is the prefix of the imperative meant as "from" for literally, "God from God." Again roughly like the Hebrew **Ahyh Ashr Ahyh** or, "I Am What I Am," or as in the "Nicene Creed" **"Jesus, 'God of God"** actually in Greek (Θεὸν ἀληθινὸν ἐκ Θεοῦ ἀληθινοῦ) Or: **very God of very God,** "πολύ Θεός του πολύ Θεού" and another example (polý Theós tou polý Theoú). So later in the New Testament: κύριε κύριε (transliterated as Kyrie, and meaning, "LORD" which today is used of God Most High (in the OT) and Christianity today uses (in the NT) for Jesus, "Lord." 'Kyrie, eleison,' is "Lord, have mercy"). Kýrie Kýrie ("Lord, Lord' - repeated- meaning God). Or in Greek, Jesus applying it to himself in **Hebrews 1:10** And, Thou, Lord (Θεός του Ισραηλ... the

God of Israel). But, for example the NT "Hebrews" uses the word, "Lord" the Greek, Kýrie in the verse (and actually) kýrie kýrie. Hebrews 1:10: "In the beginning, O Lord, You laid the foundations of the earth, and the heavens are the work of Your hands."

f Healing My Religion (though a minor controversy - the "I Am" problem should be addressed).

Healing My Religion. Tag: Aramaic. A Blogging Website (2021) .

Healing My Religion. Tag: Aramaic. https://healingmyreligion.com/tag/aramaic/ This Website says *it is impossible* to say, "I AM" or, the *"I AM What I AM"* in Aramaic and suggests then that Jesus would not have used these three Hebrew words (Accessed Feb. 2021). I do not agree with this assessment *because* I believe Jesus would have readily used "Holy Hebrew" and that "Hebrew," 'Ahyh Ashr Ahyh,' I Am What I Am,' (was a phrase very probably "known by most humble or devout Jews") even by those who could, otherwise only speak and understand Aramaic. But if Jesus only used Aramaic the issue is a difficulty that logically flows from its assessment. I cannot refute this answer, but I think this writer's following suggestion (small "i" and big Ego "I") is anachronistically applying a modern (*modern* - Freud?) psychological explanation for the use in Aramaic of the so-called, "two I's." (see their argument below)" Or the small "I" or self, and the larger "I" or bigger self (similarly long used by Buddhism and Hinduism). Readers should know about the "Aramaic difficulty" with the "I am what I am," argument. The blogger comments and writes:

> "In Aramaic, the word that is later translated as 'I am' is really 'I-I.' Aramaic doesn't have a 'being' verb. You can't actually say 'I am' in ancient Aramaic, nor can you do it in ancient Hebrew, as far as that goes. So really what Jesus is saying is, 'I-I.' In other words: The connection of the small self, which in Aramaic is called 'nafsha', is the self that is growing, evolving, learning through life. And the connection between that and the greater self, or what would be called the 'only I', 'the only being', 'Alaha', or **'the One',** or 'God'." – Neil Douglas Klotz

I cannot tell you how many times some well-intentioned Christian person has reminded me that Jesus once said "I am the way, the Truth, and the light", as a way to justify their idea that belief in the person of Jesus is the only legitimate path to heaven.

It gives me no satisfaction whatsoever to spoil anyone's worldview in a painful way, but is of great significance to me that the word(s) "I am" would not have been linguistically available to Jesus in the language in which he was teaching at the time. Furthermore, if what he actually said was something closer to the Aramaic word for "I-I", this piece of Jesus' message – and it's theological implication – becomes totally transformed.

Curiously, in many other religious, psychological, and philosophical disciplines the idea of a relationship between a "small self" and a "greater Self" – as indicated by this Aramaic word "I-I" – is a common theme. This is more common in far Eastern spiritualities, where concepts of "Buddha nature", "Atman and Brahman", and "Tao" invite it's practitioners to seek spiritual enlightenment by liberating oneself from a "small-self only" orientation towards oneself and the world, and uncover a connection to… your favorite word for the divine, i.e. God, Source, the One, Only-I, etc. within.

…

…

So, here's what the phrase "I-I" means to me (the commentator continues at the "Healing My Religion website"):

"The way, the Truth, and the light" is accessible to everyone. There is no dogma that can dictate this path, and there is no governing body to decide how it must be done. There is just you-YOU. You, the vulnerable human being subject to all the vicissitudes of your daily experiences. And YOU, the you that's got a direct line to God.

Perhaps Jesus was saying, "Look, if you can get these two aspects of yourself – the human and the divine – communing with one another", well … that is the way, that is the Truth, and that is the light of human existence.

g Of course many Gnostic, Canonical, Orthodox and Other Christian translators will disagree. Yet, the Church of Jesus Christ of Latter-Day Saints has no trouble interpreting these ("Three words - as described above") to mean simply: the Will of the Father is the Will of the Son; the Father and Son are One (and Jesus is 'divine,' the *highest* prophet and Messiah; but not God.) *Some* Modern Gnostic Churches (but not all) hold similar views that Jesus is "the, or a Most High Prophet or Teacher," or one that metaphorically (and is reported as actually "ascended to" the Father. And so "Most High" spiritually yet not (in reality) God. They similarly define hims as "Godly" and "One with God" or with the "Most High." And interpret Jesus statements that I and the Father are "one," or if you have seen me you have seen the Father all through this lens. But ultimately as Origen states about John 14:28 "You heard Me say, 'I am going away, and I am coming back to you. If you loved Me, you would rejoice that I am going to the Father, because the Father is greater than I." *And so it was interpreted anciently in "Arian" churches for hundreds of years before the Nicene council. And for hundreds of years* after *the Council of Nicea and is today by various other Christians (See below: Brown, T. Patterson. 2014; Godhead. 2020; Ecclesia Pistis Sophia. 2019; James, Montague Rhode. 1924.)*

I hold that whatever definitions various "Christians" "Or Christian bodies, denominations, sects, churches and ecclesia use" they seem to have (at least) an acceptance about using the OT and NT to teach ethics, values and the commandments of God (or Jesus) such as the "10 commandments." However they all (whatever their name, denomination or non-denominational status) deviate from each definition or another.) Let us better tolerate different Christian theological positions (that at least hold a few things in common so being in this way a "singular body of Christians")! TP Brown made a strong argument that the *Gospel of Thomas, Gospel of Philip* and *Gospel of Truth* are "Christian" (see his reference and put the URL into the text field in a web browser to read T. Brown's full thesis). And I am sure he is speaking about Protestant, Catholic or even Orthodox beliefs alone. Nevertheless Brown strongly lists one by one the many "orthodox" Christian statements and values in each text (and indeed they appear to fit all Christian groups: Protestant, Catholic, Orthodox, Gnostic, Mormon and more)! It is true that *a few 'Gnostic' ideas are discussed in the introductions in each of these Gnostic Gospels (and especially the text of the SRevJohn) but they do not negate the whole of the Gnostic texts from being Christian - as Thomas P. Brown (2014) and Simone Pétrement's assert (1984).*

h. Historically, from the beginning and unto this very day, some "Christians" - (labeled heretical by others) interpreted the "I AM" statements of Jesus as professing - "Complete, Utter and Total Oneness in Will, Unity, and Purpose with God the Father." So it is interpreted in the "Church of Jesus Christ of Latter-Day Saints;" and in "Ecclesia Pistis Sophia" - both "Christian" churches, one Mormon, the other Gnostic. Neither claim "Jesus is God," but both claim to be Christian (and interpret these words of the New Testament "I Am" in a somewhat similar way).

Jesu, God of God (in: **The Acts of Thomas**)

iIn the *Acts of Thomas* the Apostle Thomas exclaims (in this text, a book never lost to history as were the books in the *NHL*)." Complete versions of the Acts of Thomas survived (all two thousand years) in Syriac and Greek. Epiphanius of Salamis - a heresy hunter - wrote about the Acts of Thomas. Though scholars agree it is a legitimate Apocryphal Christian book (considered by some as part of the original photo-canon). However it appears to have a few gnostic themes relating to death, Jesus death and resurrection (or "death seen from a more Gnostic perspective"). The "*Acts of Thomas*" (like the *NHL* texts) suggest "resurrection," be "done" in this life," so that one is (after baptism) brought into the "new life" now. And baptism (now) as a Christian assures survival of death and resurrection in the Life to Come. Death (the "Acts" say) is not a bad thing but one's position in the higher heavens above are improved as a result of inculcation and further practice of gnostic-Christian teaching, when that teaching is understood. An example of language in the "Acts of Thomas" which strongly echoes the Gospel of Thomas was presented above…

And how some believe the "Three Words" point to "a cognomen" for Sophia (or the middle word actually being Ashrh - being or pointing toward "Asherah" - as an expression of God with feminine attributes. It is asserted or suggested by some that the "Elephantine Jews used Ashrh." See: 'The Nazarene Way of Essenic Studies' 'I AM THAT I AM,' below and at website:

jI neither endorse or negate the following argument. Readers or Seekers can make up their own minds. And the argument is simply this: that instead of 'Ahyh Ashr Ahyh' what was said to Moses by 'the Gods'

(Elohim or Elohei) was: **'Ahyh Ashrh Ahyh'.** Or, 'I AM Mother God (Asherah) and Father God' (alone or God as depicted with feminine traits - which doesn't stress monotheism for "in His Image and Likeness He created them, male and female he created them"). Some suggest the Semitic Asherah was His wife or Consort (and which is believed it is said by some to have been confirmed by archeology - a Goddess they assert, equal to God (but a stress to modern monotheism). A short, concise argument about these hypotheses at 'The Nazarene Way of Essenic Studies' 'I AM THAT I AM'. http://www.thenazareneway.com/I%20AM%20THAT%20I%20AM.htm Or also see: http://en.wikipedia.org/wiki/

James Brantingham PhD

Thousand Oaks, CA 4 28 2021

References for "The Gospel of Thomas"

Armitage, Robinson (Ed). (1920) St. Irenaeus. The Demonstration of the Apostolic Preaching. McMillan Co. New York, NY

Bauman, Lynn. (2012) The Gospel of Thomas, Wisdom of the Twin 2nd Ed. Ashland, Oregon: White Cloud Press;

Barnstone, William., Meyer, Marvin. (2003, 2009, 2011) The Gnostic Bible: Revised and Expanded 1st ed. Boston, Massachusetts, New Seeds Books.

Barnstone, William. (2009.) The Restored New Testament: A New translation with Commentary Including the Gnostic Gospels of Thomas, Mary and Judas. Publisher W.W. Norton & Co. New York, NY

Barnstone, William and Meyer, Marvin. (2011) The Gnostic Bible: Revised and Expanded 1st ed. Boston, Massachusetts, New Seeds Books.

Borg, Marcus. (1999) The Lost Gospel Q: The Original Sayings of Jesus 2nd ed. Edition. Publisher: Ulysses Press. Berkeley, CA. 1999

Boyarin, Daniel. (2012) The Jewish Gospels: The story of the Jewish Christ. New York NY, New Press

Bourgeault, Cynthia. (2008). The Wisdom Jesus. transforming Heart and Mind- A new Perspective on Christ and His Message. Shambala Publications Inc. Boston, MA

Brantingham, James. (2017) The Gospel of Philip. Amazon Digital Services LLC. Seattle, WA. (Apple book) Paperback and Kindle. ASIN: B06XY2J951

Brantingham, James. (2019) Truth... What Is Truth. Holy Wisdom and the Logos of God. The Four Lost Apocryphal Christian Gospels: The Gospel of Truth. The Gospel of Philip. The Gospel of Thomas & The Gospel of Mary With the Secret Revelation of John. Pub. Amazon Digital Services LLC (Apple book). Kindle. ASIN: B08R7Z8KXD

Brown, T. Patterson. (2014) The Gospels of Thomas, Philip and Truth. Available from http://www.freelyreceive.net/metalogos/files/intro.html Accessed 5 25 2014

Brown, Patterson T. Hypertext interlinear of the Gospel according to Philip. http://www.freelyreceive.net/metalogos/files/ph*interlin.html* *(Accessed 5 25 2014)*

Chilton, Bruce. (2002) in Rabbi Jesus (Rabbi Jesus: An Intimate Biography). Publisher Double Day a Division of Random House, New York, NY

Davies, Stevan. (1983.) The Gospel of Thomas and Christian Wisdom 2nd Edition. Bardic Press. Oregon House, CA

Davies, Stevan. (1996.) Mark's Use of the Gospel of Thomas. *In:* The Journal of the New Testament Society of South Africa or Neotestamentica 30 (2) 1996 pp. 307-334

Davies, Stevan. (2002) The Gospel of Thomas. Annotated & Explained. SkyLight Paths Paths Publishing. Woodstock, Vermont

Davies, Stevan. (2005) The Secret Book of John. The Gnostic Gospel Annotated & Explained. Skylight Paths Publishing. Woodstock, Vermont

Davies, Stevan. (2002) The Gospel of Thomas. Skylight Paths Publishing. Woodstock, Vermont

Davies, Stevan. (1996.) Mark's Use of the Gospel of Thomas. In The Journal of the New Testament Society of South Africa or Neotestamentica 30 (2) 1996 pp. 307-334

Davies, Stevan. (1996.) Mark's Use of the Gospel of Thomas. In The Journal of the New Testament Society of South Africa or Neotestamentica 30 (2) 1996 pp. 307-334

DeConick, April D. (2001) Voices of the Mystics: Early Christian Discourse in the Gospel of John and Thomas and Other Ancient Christian Literature. Publisher T&T Clark, New York, NY

DeConick, April D. (2005.) Recovering the Original Gospel of Thomas: A History of the Gospel and Its Growth. Publisher: T & T Clark. London, UK

DeConick, April D., J. Asgeirsson, J., Uro. R. (2005) "On the Brink of the Apocalypse: A Preliminary Examination of the Earliest Speeches in the Gospel of Thomas." In Thomasine traditions in Antiquity: The Social and Cultural World of the Gospel of Thomas. Nag Hammadi and Manichaean Studies 59. Leiden: E.J. Brill.

DeConick, April D. (2008) Mysticism and the Gospel of Thomas. In: Das Thomasevangelium: Entstehung-Rezeption-Theologie. Edited by Jörg Frey, et al. BZNW 157. Berlin: DeGruyter. (Accessed 7 13 2019)

http://aprildeconick.com/gospel-of-thomas-articles-1

DeConick, April D. (2017.) The Gnostic New Age: How a countercultural spirituality revolutionized religion from antiquity to today. Columbia University Press. New York, NY

Ecclesia Pistis Sophia. (2019) https://www.sophian.org/index.html. (Accessed 6 -18-2019) The Fellowship.

Eusebius of of Caesarea (2018) Church History http://www.documentacatholicaomnia.eu/03d/0265-0339,*Eusebius*Caesariensis,*Church*History,*EN.pdf Accessed (6-25-2018)*

Godhead. (2020). Church of Jesus Christ of Latter-day Saints. https://www.churchofjesuschrist.org/study/manual/gospel-topics/godhead?lang=eng&r=1 (Accessed 9 26 2020)

Gott, Paula. (2016) I AM THAT I AM. Another look at how Elohim (the gods) answered Moses' question, "What is your name?". In The Nazarene Way of Essenic Studies. At The Nazarean Way http://www.thenazareneway.com/I%20AM%20THAT%20I%20AM.htm Accessed 11 1 2016

Grobel, Kendrick. (1960) The Gospel of Truth. The Valentinian Meditation on the Gospel. Publisher Abingdon Press. New York & Nashville TN

Grondin, MW. (2017) Coptic-English Interlinear translation.The Coptic Gospel of Thomas, saying-by-saying (Linked to: Andrew Bernhard's presentation of the Greek POxy fragments). http://gospel-thomas.net/sayings.htm (Accessed 1-2-2017)

Healing My Religion. Tag: Aramaic. https://healingmyreligion.com/tag/aramaic/ This Website says it is impossible to say, "I AM" or, the *"I AM What I AM"* in Aramaic and suggests then that Jesus would not have used the three Hebrew words (Accessed Feb. 2021). I (Brantingham) do not agree - see i *above*:

Stack Exchange Bible Hermeneutics at: (Takes up the "I am" question.)

https://hermeneutics.stackexchange.com/questions/13459/what-did-jesus-likely-say-in-john-858

The LXX or Septuagint and the Greek Tanakh (composed hundreds of years before the birth of Jesus) has: Ἐγώ εἰμι ὁ ὤν· . . . Ὁ ὢν ἀπέσταλκέν με πρὸς ὑμᾶς (Rahlfs-Hanhart). Or, from the Greek, "I am the one being. . . . the one being has sent me to you. I AM in Hebrew is אָנֹכִי. And one commentator apparently notes Paul (at times) uses "εἰμι ὅ εἰμι" a Greek word order or construction that is unusual or even forced (but it makes the point that it relates to and is the - I Am The I Am - as in the Hebrew word construction; and three words.) But to hearken back to the "Three Words" in "Hebrew" אֶהְיֶה שְׁלָחַן אֲלֵיכֶם ('Ahyh Ashr Ahyh') or "I am who I am" that Jesus said. There may be other solutions. (Stack Exchange Accessed Feb. 2021).

James, Montague Rhode. (1924) The ***Acts of Thomas*** in: The Apocryphal New Testament. Oxford, UK. Clarendon Press.

James translates from the Greek of the *Acts of Thomas* (whom many scholars now accept is linked with the *Gospel of Thomas* and Gnosticism too): "…thou that didst *call me apart* from all my fellows and spakest unto me three words wherewith I am inflamed, and am not able to speak them unto others. Jesu, man that wast slain, dead buried!" ***"Jesu, God of God"*** (God of God so three words).

Jenkins, Philip. (2017.) Crucible of Faith. Hachette Book Group. New York, NY

Kelly, Edward F., Williams Kelly, Emily., Crabtree, Adam., et al. (2007.) Irreducible Mind: Toward a Psychology for the 21st Century. Publishers; Rowman & Littlefield. Lanham, Maryland.

Kelly, Edward F., Crabtree, Adam., Marshall, Paul., Eds. (2015.) Beyond Physicalism: Toward Reconciliation of Science and Spirituality. Publishers Rowman & Littlefield. Lanham, Maryland.

King, Karen L. (2003) What is Gnosticism? Harvard University Press. Cambridge, MA

Kloppenborg, John S., Marvin W. Meyer, Stephen J. Patterson. et al., (1990) Q Thomas Reader. Sonoma, Ca.: Polebridge Press.

> The GThom has 28% of of the 'Gospel of Q' (or "the Quell" - italics mine) as Kloppenborg and Throckmorton see it (37 out of 132 Q sayings have a comparison in the Gospel of Thomas).

Köester Helmut.(1990) Ancient Christian Gospels: Their History and Development. Harrisburg, PA. trinity Press International. 1990

Kugel, James I. (2017) The Great Shift. Encountering God in Biblical Times. Houghton MifflinHarcourt Publishing. New York, NY.

Hart, David B. (2017) The New Testament. A translation. Yale University Press. London, UK.

Hoeller, Stephan A. (2002.) Gnosticism: New Light on the Ancient tradition of Inner Knowing. Publisher: Quest Books Wheaton, IL.

Hoeller, Stephan A. (1998 and 2010). Ecclesia Gnostica A Gnostic Catechism. Publisher: The Gnostic Society Press, Los Angeles, California. (http://gnosis.org/ecclesia/catechism.htm) (Accessed 5-5-2015)

Lambdin, Thomas O. (2000). The Gospel of Thomas. In Robinson, James M. Ed. The Coptic Gnostic Library. A Complete Edition of the Nag Hammadi Codices. Vol. 2. Koninklijke Brill NV, Leiden, The Netherlands

Leloup, Jean-Yves. (2005) The Gospel of Thomas: The Gnostic Wisdom of Jesus.Paris: Inner traditions

Lambdin, Thomas O. (2000). The Gospel of Thomas. In Robinson, James M. Ed. The Coptic Gnostic Library. A Complete Edition of the Nag Hammadi Codices. Vol. 2. Koninklijke Brill NV, Leiden, The Netherlands

Mattison, Mark M. (2018) The Gospel of Thomas. https://www.gospels.net/thomas/. The following translation has been committed to the public domain and may be freely copied and used, changed or unchanged, for any purpose. It is based on the Coptic text of NHC II, 2 (Accessed 5/25/2018)

Maier Paul L. (1999) Eusebius. The Church History. Publisher Kregal Publications. Grand Rapids, MI

Mead, George Robert Stow. (2021). Fragments of a Faith Forgotten: A Contribution to the Study of the Origins of Christianity in, The Gnostic Society Library. gnosis.org (Accessed 2021) Theosophical Publishing Society: London (1900; 1906).

Mead, G. R. S. (1921) Pistis Sophia. A Gnostic Gospel. A Gnostic Miscellany: Being for the most part extracts from the Books of the Savior, to which are added excerpts from a Cognate literature; (English). JM Watkins London. Kindle Edition.

Meier, John P. (1991) A marginal Jew: rethinking the historical Jesus: the roots of the problem and the person, vol. 1. Publisher Double Day. New York, NY

Meier, John P. (2016) A marginal Jew: rethinking the historical Jesus: Probing the Authenticity of the Parables, vol. 5. Publisher Yale University Press New York, NY

Meyer, Marvin. (2005) The Gnostic Gospels of Jesus: The definitive collection of mystical gospels and secret books about Jesus of Nazareth. Publisher HarperOne, New York, NY

Meyer, Marvin. Ed. (2007). The Nag Hammadi Scriptures. HarperCollins 10 East 53rd St., NY, New York

Mattison, Mark M. (2018) The Gospel of Thomas. https://www.gospels.net/thomas/. The following translation has been committed to the public domain and may be freely copied and used, changed or unchanged, for any purpose. It is based on the Coptic text of NHC II, 2 (Accessed 5/25/2018)

Meyer, Marvin W. (2007) The Gospel of Thomas with the Greek Gospel of Thomas in, Meyer, Marvin W., Robinson, James M.The Nag Hammadi Scriptures: The Revised and Updated translation of Sacred Gnostic Texts Complete in One Volume. HarperCollins. 10 East 53rd St., New York, NY

Meyer, Marvin. (2005) The Gnostic Gospels of Jesus: The definitive collection of mystical gospels and secret books about Jesus of Nazareth. Publisher HarperOne, New York, NY

Myer, Marvin. (2009) The Gospel of Thomas: The Hidden Sayings of Jesus. Publisher Harper Collins. New York, NY.

Pagels, Elaine. 1973; Johannine Gospel in Gnostic Exegesis: Heracleon's Commentary on John. Abingdon Press, 1973. Nashville, TN

Pagels Elaine. (1992) The Gnostic Paul: Gnostic Exegesis of the Pauline Letters. Published by Continuum International Publishing Group. New York, NY

Pagels, Elaine. (2003) Beyond Belief: The Secret Gospel of Thomas Random House, New York, NY

Pétrement, Simone. (1984). A Separate God. The Origins and Teachings of Gnosticism. HarperCollins, Scranton, Pennsylvania

Pick, Bernhard. (1902). The Apocryphal Acts of Paul, Peter, John, Andrew and Thomas. (Accessed 20/13/2020) https://en.m.wikisource.org/wiki/The The-*Apocryphal*Acts*of*Paul,*Peter,*John,*Andrew*and*Thomas*/Acts*of*Thomas*

Robinson, James M. (1990) The Nag Hammadi library, ed. James M. Robinson. Harper, San Francisco

Robinson, James M., Hoffmann, Paul., Kloppenborg, John S., Moreland, Milton C. (2000) The Critical Edition of Q with Publisher Fortress and Peeters Press. Minneapolis.

Schaff, Philip., Ed. (2016) The Complete Ante-Nicene, Nicene and Post-Nicene Collection of Early Church Fathers: Cross-Linked to the Bible. Toronto, Canada. Kindle

Schneemelcher, Wilhelm., Wilson, Robert McLachlan., Hennecke, Edgar. Eds. (1991) New Testament Apocrypha I: Writings relating to the Apostles; Apocalypses and Related Subjects. Westminster John Knox Press. Louisville, KY. 1991

Schneemelcher, Wilhelm., Wilson, Robert McLachlan., Hennecke, Edgar. Eds. (2003) New Testament Apocrypha II: Writings relating to the Apostles; Apocalypses and Related Subjects. Westminster John Knox Press. Louisville, KY. 2003

Smith, Andrew Philip. (2002). The Gospel of Thomas. Publisher Ulysses Books, Berkeley, CA

Smith, Geoffrey S. (2019) Valentinian Christianity. Texts and translations. University of California Press. Oakland, CA.

Throckmorton, Burton H. (1992.) Gospel Parallels. Fifth Edition. Publisher Thomas Nelson. Nashville, TN.

Taussig, Hal. Ed. (2013) A New New Testament. A bible for the twenty-first century. Houghton Mifflin Harcourt. New York, NY

Marshall, John W. (2017) The Five Gospels Parallels. Department for the Study of Religion, University of Toronto. http://sites.utoronto.ca/religion/synopsis/

(Accessed September 11-15- 2017)

The Gospel of Thomas

By James Brantingham, PhD

4 28 2021

Thousand Oaks, California

The Secret Revelation of John

Introduction to the Secret Revelation of John

The Demiurge or Yaldabaoth (and Sophia)

The Demiurge Yaltabaoth in the Secret Revelation of John

Without going extensively into Gnostic and Comparative theology, in the *Secret Revelation of John* also called *the Apocryphon of John,* (Waldstein M., Wisse, FW., *in,* Robinson, JM. 2000), we find that the 'god' of the Old Testament is presented (by John) as 'a Demiurge.' The Demiurge is *not the One, true God, but a lesser divinity or 'lesser god'* and this is a concept borrowed from Platonism. It is a noun meaning an artisan-like figure responsible for fashioning and maintaining the physical Cosmos. *"Lady Wisdom" ('Sophia') as found in Proverbs 8 in the Old Testament is such a Demiurge who helps* "God Most-High" *create in this positive way.* This "Genesis" needs to take into account that " the Aeons and Aeons, 'God,' and all the other divinities in this Vast Array of the Divine Fullness and the Universe Above," *pre-existed the creation of the Cosmos, the aeon of earth, and Wisdom's emanation of the its Demiurge.* It is so described in *On the Origin of the World (2007; 2011).* And it is inherent in *the Secret Revelation of John (2007; 2011).* These Sethian (or mostly Sethian) theological Gnostic books demonstrate that before *'chaos'* was… **the infinite.**

So the Scholars Barnstone and Meyer note it's similarity to the Biblical "Genesis" in their *"The Gnostic Bible"* and *the Nag Hammadi scriptures* (2007; 2011). Creation of the aeon of the earth, the world, its Demiurge and Realms and firmaments (above and below it) comes *after* this (Meyer, Marvin. Barnstone, William. 2007; 2007; Meyer, Marvin 2011).

The Demiurge and Yaldabaoth

The term "Demiurge" also means a "craftsman," "artisan," or "producer." But importantly, (in Platonism) it is a benign, virtuous, and noble "creator, divinity, or *'god.*" In the *SRevJohn* and Gnosticism more generally, he is the craftsman responsible for fabricating and molding this 'Cosmos,' and aeon of earth, this world and its realms and firmaments above and below. And as the Chief Ruler or Archon, the "*lesser god*" of earth. But he does not know this. He ('Yaldabaoth' as Sophia named him) ignorantly fabricates and molds the 'earth' unaware (that he is not) the "*One, true, God Most-High,*" nor, the creator of All, of everything, including indirectly himself! Thus the Demiurge expects ignorant human beings in his Cosmos to worship him. For, neither he nor human beings or fallen angels on earth know that they have (the true God's) 'spirit' within. When they come to know this (and know themselves), it can lead them to Salvation. The Demiurge (an Archon or Ruler created by "Sophia" - is a being between the Immortals and humans). She called it *Yaldabaoth* (who is a mixture of Good and Evil and, a Son of Chaos) is unaware that the Aeons and Aeons, the true One '*God*' and the Divine Fullness Above existed as 'the Proarchē' (before the beginning of the All; the Vast Array of the Divine Fullness and the Universe Above). And 'this Vast Array' existed before the beginning of the Cosmos" and before Yaldabaoth fabricated and molded this world. '*On the Origin of the World*' demonstrates that '*God*' emanated many Aeons, divinities, angels, and other divine beings before Yaldabaoth molded the local Cosmos and the aeon of the earth (Meyer, Marvin. 2007).

The Higher Pneumatic Sophia

There is a Higher Pneumatic Sophia (who in the Secret Revelation of John is also Barbēlō and is the Holy Spirit!). Sophia (Above) descends from the Highest heavenly Aeon, the Pleroma, "down and into" the void (or kenōma - the unspiritual lower world of phenomena and emptiness) below. Her descent below also meant the theft of light. And diffusion of the light into the darkness and emptiness of the kenōma. Sophia, bringing this light into the night (and dark) of the lower world, becomes Sophia (the "lower"). Because of these actions, She suffers. Out of this suffering and punishment, she appears to have created Yaldabaoth.

The Son of Sophia

So, Yaldabaoth (the son of Sophia - born but without a divine Father) is the Demiurge (*a lesser god*) but a powerful god-*like* entity or *demigod* ruling over the earth. He is a flawed and often demonic-like evil entity within the *SRevJohn* and most Gnostic texts. However because Sophia was emanated by the One (Good) God when she emanated Yaldabaoth part of "the Spirit of the true God" making up Sophia (or Wisdom) makes up a part of Yaldabaoth. So he can at times act neutrally or on occasion even be 'good.' However (though it appears he was assumed to exist by the authors of the following Gnostic Gospels) he the Demiurge, Yaldabaoth is **not** named in the *Gtr, GPhil, GMary* or *GThom*. But a Demiurge is strongly alluded to (especially as the 'Adversary and the cause of evil and suffering) in the *GPhil*. And 'Error' in the *Gtr* (though held by most Scholars to not be the Demiurge) often acts in a way very similar to how Yaldabaoth acts (Brons, David. 2019; Waldstein M., Wisse, FW., In Robinson, JM. 2000.).

In the *SRevJohn* he is the named the 'creator' of the Cosmos and Aeonic creator of Earth (and its firmaments) and creates the first earthly man (with a soul), or 'Adam'. Some (though not all scholars) suggest the Demiurge was the creator of Jesus "psychic or physical body" (though*not the Anointed* or *Christ* who has been eternally with '*God*'). But it was 'Sophia the lesser' who created and/or emanated Yaldabaoth. This is strange when one realizes that 'Canonical Sophia' is the Companion of God Most High. And a 'helpful demiurge and craftsman' in *Proverbs 8, Ecclesiasticus* and, other canonical scriptures. The earthly Demiurge (Yaltabaoth) is like the 'Apostle Paul's' description of the supreme Archon. He is 'the god of this world'. Yet, though often evil Yaldabaoth has within him a 'spark of the spirit of "God Most High' (though he does not know this). So, when the 'god' of this world emanates and creates human beings, angels and others they receive 'his breath or his spirit (which is actually from 'God' Most High, inherited as a result of being the son of Sophia'. This gives them 'life' and therefore all of his creation has 'the spark of the spirit' of the One, true and Good God!' But the allusions to the demiurge are only elusive in the *Gospels of Truth, Thomas,* and *Mary.*

Yaldabaoth is powerful

That said, Yaldabaoth is still a powerful god-*like* entity or *a demigod* who rules over the planet. He is a flawed and often a demonic-like evil entity within the *SRevJohn* and many other Gnostic texts. However, because Sophia was emanated by the One (Good) 'God' when *She* emanated Yaldabaoth, part of "the Spirit" of the true God making up Sophia 'makes up' a part of Yaldabaoth. So he does act at times neutrally and even on occasion benevolently or 'good.' However, it is not entirely clear what Yaldabaoth's status and powers are in *all* the books of the *NHL* (including associated texts like the *GMary*) found outside of the *SRevJohn*. But his status and powers are easier to understand in the books included within this collection, "Holy Wisdom and The Logos of God." Except for the *SRevJohn,* the "Demiurge" maybe only a near equivalent (expression of negative attitudes or harmful ways of thinking) such as the 'lawless enemy' found in the *GThom* verse 57 (and in other verses in these included Gnostic Gospels).

This parable in *GThom* verse 57 seems to suggest "the enemy" (who sowed weeds in the other farmer's land) is an adversary. *GThom* verses 68 and 69 bespeak other 'adversaries and enemies': That said, Yaldabaoth is still a powerful god-*like* entity or *a demigod* who rules over the planet. He is a flawed and often a demonic-like evil entity within the *SRevJohn* and many other Gnostic texts. But "the Spirit" of the true God making up Sophia makes up a part of Yaldabaoth. So he does act at times neutrally and even on occasion benevolently or 'good.' However, it is not entirely clear what Yaldabaoth's status and powers are in *all* the books of the *NHL* (including associated texts like the *GMary* found) outside of the *SRevJohn*. But his status and powers are easier to understand in the books included within this collection, "Holy Wisdom and The Logos of God (*WisdLogos*)." Except for the *SRevJohn,* there may be only near equivalent (negative attitudes or ways of thinking) in the 'lawless enemy' found in the *GThom* verse 57 (and in other verses). This parable seems to suggest "the enemy" (who sowed weeds in the other farmer's land) is an adversary. *GThom* verses 68 and 69 bespeak other 'adversaries and enemies':

68 Jesus says,

Blissful are you when they hate you and persecute you. For, you will discover a place where they will no longer be able to find you nor persecute you ever again (Brantingham, James. 2019)

69 Jesus says,
Blissful are you who have been persecuted for your ideas and beliefs. Thou hath endured inconceivable abuse ...even violent rejection. But rejoice! Thy hath seen the Father and know 'the Way' (and 'the Truth'). Blissful art thee who hunger, for thalt shalt be filled up and lack nothing (Brantingham, James. 2019)

But *Error* certainly acts similar to Yaldabaoth. And Sophia (as, *Lady Wisdom*) is there in the *GPhil, Gtr, GMary* and in the *GThom.*

In the *SRevJohn* he, Yaldabaoth is (finally) named. The 'creator' of the Cosmos, the Aeon of Earth, and its firmaments produces the first *earthly* man after the immortal Adamas (with a *soul or mind*), 'Adam.' But it was 'Sophia the fallen' or *lesser* who created or emanated Yaldabaoth. This is strange when one realizes 'Canonical Sophia' was the Companion of God Most High (but note, a Companion). And a 'helpful demiurge and craftsman' in *Proverbs 8, Ecclesiasticus, Ecclesiastes and the Letter of James* and in other canonical scriptures. The earthly Demiurge (Yaldabaoth) is akin to the 'Apostle Paul's 'description of the supreme earthly Archon. Like him, he is 'the *god* of this world.' But, when the '*god*' of this world, Yaldabaoth emanates and creates human beings, angels, and others, they receive 'his breath or spirit,' therefore Sophia's breath too (inherited from 'the One,' '*God Above God*'). So all receive *some* of the 'One true God's 'breath or spirit. Thus, it is '*God*' ultimately that gives Adam and humans' life!' Therefore, all of Yaldaboath's creation has 'some of the the '*Most High's* spirit within' (though they are ignorant that they have received this) from the '*One, true and Good God!*'

Barbēlō

The *SRevJohn* equates the 'Holy Spirit' with the mysterious deity or divinity Barbēlō. Barbēlō is, *at minimum,* equivalent to 'the Holy Spirit or the 'Holy Mother.' And it *is* an early expression of 'the trinity' (Logan, Alastair, HB. 1996) not yet agreed. At the same time, it was a part of several Tetrads found (only) in Gnosticism. Such Tetrads as; '*God,*' *the Father, Mother, and the Son.* Or, the 'Pneumatic (or Spiritual and Higher) Sophia, *Lady Wisdom* sometimes described as the Consort or Wife of the Father; and Jesus Christ yoked with the 'fallen,' (or lower) Sophia completing the Tetrad. Yet despite many suggestions about what the term Barbēlō means. 'God in four' or, a mysterious way of spelling 'YWHE,' I prefer Alastair Logan's suggestion that it is from the Hebrew,' *barah ba 'lo,*' meaning a "daughter of the Lord." (Logan, Alastair, HB. 1996.) Barbēlō is, in the *SRevJohn* associated with Gnosticism's famous designation of the "Godhead" as the '

Mother-Father.' Another way Gnostics expressed the 'One true God.' And is subsumed (at times) within descriptions of 'the Father' and the First Man. Barbēlō (relating to the above) is even given on occasions masculine characteristics. Barbēlō then is an extremely complex figure in the *SRevJohn* and other texts (Barbēlō. 2019, Barnstone, William., Meyer, Marvin. 2011; Meyer, Marvin W., Robinson, James M. 2007).

Holy Mother clarification

But though the 'Lower Sophia' that emanated the 'demiurge' is described as the 'Holy Mother'. But this 'Mother' is not to be confused (in Gnostic texts) with Jesus's earthly mother Mary, The Catholic 'Mary.' Mary being the earthly mother of Jesus will later (also) be called the 'Holy Mother.' And in Catholicism, and in the Orthodox churches today (but not in Protestantism) Jesus earthly mother is called the 'Holy Mother of God'. But in Gnosticism the 'Holy Mother' is 'usually meant as Wisdom or Sophia.' It is easy to see this in the *SRevJohn* and in most other Gnostic texts. Most Gnostics revere the earthly mother of Jesus so are quick to be very clear about just whom they are talking about (Hoeller, Stephan A. 2010; Brantingham, James. 2017; Brown, Thomas P. 2014; Meyer, Marvin. Ed., Turner, John D. 2007; Mead, G.R.S. 2016).

The Feminine and Barbēlō

Both Sophia and Christ are associated with this complex and mysterious being, 'Barbēlō'. 'Barbēlō' in the *SRevJohn* is part of the Highest and 'first' emanated Aeon of the first pre-Aeonic 'entities'. Yet, at the same time "She" in the *SRevJohn* is the 'first emanation.' And though Barbēlō is primarily seen as a feminine figure or 'Aeon with feminine attributes,' She, embodies many nuanced and complicated entities and beings (and from a 'trinitarian' point of view even '*God!*' But Barbēlō (the Mother-Father) is identified at times with a masculine 'virgin' identity and nature (and in other ways). I like most the definition proposed by Alastair HB Logan (1996) who notes that the Hebrew, *'barah ba 'lo,'* means the "daughter of the Lord." However, Barbēlō seems beyond any one singular 'persona' noted above. That said, a full rendering of 'Barbēlō' is beyond the scope of this book. But, this figure alone recognizes 'God's *irreducible complexity* (even) in late antiquity. As it is written... 'God is not just a man...' and (I say) ...is 'not just a Woman' too! (Meyer, Marvin. Ed., Turner, John D. 2007).

The Feminine

The canonical words of God Most High say: ...**God created mankind in his image, in the image of God he created them;** *male and female* he created them 'concretely affirms' the *"Mother-Father"* description of *'God'* in the *SRevJohn* (NIV). Or, as Psalm 82 says: 'I said, 'thou art gods, and all of thee, children of the Most High'. In this Psalm *'gods'* 'all of the children Most High.' And can be rephrased, 'I said, 'thou art gods and goddesses' and all of thee children of the

Most High'. This is not blasphemy as we understand *'God,'* theologically today. Since these 'gods' are those in the phrase (first from the OT) stated by Jesus when he says, 'Is it not written in your Law: 'I said you are gods'?

I have interpolated a few times into the *SRevJohn* from *1 Enoch* the term 'the *Lord of Spirits'* as another name for *'God'* the 'Father.' That (breaths into *SRevJohn* for me) a touch of Second Temple Judaism. For one Biblical Scholar whose work profoundly moves me is Donald H. Akenson (2000; 2001.) Akenson suggests that even the NT (and the early part of the Mishnah) can be considered an extension of Second Temple Judaism! I not only agree with him but would extend this into the 'Gnostic and related Scriptures (such as the Hermetic literature). Or as in all the uses above for the 'Holy Mother,' (the One) or *'God the Mother'* (from the Mother-Father) or just *'Mother'*. Thus these terms are non-blasphemous in Gnosticism (and intellectually in (non-Gnostic) Judaism and Christianity.

Modern Gnosticism, Hell, Universalism and Scientific Research

Modern Gnosticism takes from all past expressions of Gnosticism (from the Valentinians to the Sethians and the Cathars to the (still extant) Mandaeans. It feels free to utilize various expressions of Christianity from the Greek Orthodox to Catholics, from Protestantism and other forms of Asian "Orthodox Christianity." So, as in Greek Orthodox practice their clergy 'often do serious meditation' and have for hundreds and hundreds of years. Modern Gnosticism (even encourages interfaith meditation such as from Buddhist or other sources). 'There is (in the *SRevJohn*) a rejection of eternal suffering' in Hell' (and this is made quite clear in the *SRevJohn*). But though Jesus Himself states (in the *SRevJohn*) that most will be saved (a 'qualified Universalism,' in this text some may have to undergo some forms of *Purification or Correction* or - at least in the *SRevJohn* - even, some punishment. But then in the same text it is made clear that even the great majority of this small group of people (ninety-eight or ninety-nine percent) will eventually enter into 'the Life to Come' or (Heaven)! (See: Purification after SRevJohn References: Postlude A & B)

Yet a tiny few may face severe punishment and even destruction, but it appears to be their own choice (and *after* death not before). For Jesus goes down into Hell itself to bring Knowledge and to teach and bring out any that wish to leave Hell! Why would He not do this again? I believe this revived Christian (and Gnostic-Christian) teaching (as per Origen and Clement): that 'all will be saved' is, or was the true early Christian position (see the authors below on "that all will be saved" - all of their work is exemplary but John Wesley Hanson wrote his text in 1899 and it is filled with wonderful material about Origen and the early Church Fathers)! Yet the qualified Universalism found in the SRevJohn allows for a "Hell," for it does not rule out some form of correction, purification or even rarely punishment. But *it does rule out* "eternal horrific torture by a loving God." Is a Billion years of horrific torture enough, or a trillion years? Or maybe Twenty trillion years will finally hit the mark (and Mao, Stalin and Hitler will join us above)! It is an incomprehensible, untenable position for the Christian (or Gnostic-Christian) **God of Love** in the *Gospel of John* (Beauchemin, Gerry. 2018; Beauchemin, Gerry., Reichard, D. Scott. 2007, 2010, 2016; Hanson, John Wesley. 1899; Hart, David B. 2019).

Many of these ideas are shocking. And on top of that Gnosticism seems generally to believe in 'Reincarnation' (but it is a varied and nuanced 'belief' in Gnosticism which I cannot do justice for in this introduction). To many who first approach Gnostic texts or their congregations, reincarnation is a practice that they have been led to believe *is Pagan, even demonic that other* religions believe. But there is a growing body of 'scientific evidence' about the "after-life," "transcendence as in Near Death Experiences and Out of the Body Experiences," even communication with those who are deceased, and with Telepathy (reading minds) and Precognition (prophecy) and much more… and it has been going on very strongly now for about fifty years! It is being carried out by rigorous scientists (using… rigorous scientific methodology in their research and studies)! One area of rigorous collection of evidence by Psychiatrists is in reincarnation. I have a PhD in Clinical Research from the University of Surrey in Guildford, UK and have read the books and papers I list and they are compelling! (Hoeller, Stephan A. 2010; Stevenson, I., Keil, H J. 2000; Stevenson, I. 2006; Tucker JB. 2016; Matlock, James G. 2019; Rohr, Richard. 2019; Schwartz, Gary E. 2011; Radin, Dean 2013; 2018; 2019; Kelly, Edward F., Crabtree, Adam., Marshall, Paul., Eds. 2015; Williams Kelly, Emily., Greyson, Bruce., Kelly, Edward F. 2007; Greyson, Bruce 2021; Schwartz, Gary E., Woollacott Marjorie H., eds. 2019).

For references see 'References' for the Introduction to Holy Wisdom and The Logos of God.

The Secret Revelation of John (the Gnostic Book)

by James Brantingham PhD

The Teaching of the Savior & The Hidden Revelations and Mysteries Concealed Now (For Aeons in Silence) That He Revealed to John, His Disciple

With Contemporary Inspiration From, the 'Greater Gnostic Johannine Community' Illuminating The Prophetic Knowledge Of The Past Forward, and Into the Third Millennium

Prologue

One day John, the brother of James, a son of Zebedee, was going to the Temple.

A Pharisee and learned Rabbi named Arimanios challenged him, saying, "Where is your teacher now, that Rabbi, that - minim that you followed?"

John replied, 'He has gone back to His Father, to the Most High in Heaven above. Back up from where, he came down.'

The Pharisee then said, 'That Nazarene misled you, He lied to you and closed your hearts to your own people.' Arimanios went on, 'He has turned you away from Abraham, Moses and the traditions of your Fathers; even from right understanding of Torah.'

When I heard this, I turned away in uncertainty and, worried. I fled from the temple and went high up a trail until, I found a solitary place on a mountain.

There I grieved. Unhappy and confused I thought, 'why did the Lord choose Jesus? And why did *'God Above God'* allow His Anointed Savior to be tortured; even to die? 'And, even more so, why would *'God Above God'* send his only Son to be so shamefully killed? What type of a Father would do this and allow this to happen to his only begotten son'? (See below)

> Hereafter singular notations of 'God' with a capital 'G' and in Italics are meant to express this title: *'God Above God'*. *God* in late antiquity was, the Monad or the, Unknown God Most High. *'God'* (in italics) means the *God Above God* or (the) *God* above, every human conception of any 'God' (or 'gods'.)

John thought, 'after all, where is this Heavenly Aeon, this Pleroma, this place of Fullness, where dwelleth the Most High *God* in the Highest Heaven in the Fullness above? And when will He, the Father (and His Son) bring it down to us, the Kingdom of *God* in power; fully here, and fully below? For only through Heaven comes the enduring and trustworthy world; our true Home and, the Home of the Father, of Holy Wisdom and of the Savior. For, He, the Savior said it... 'this world here John, is modeled on the Imperishable, Incorruptible World of the Father Above.' The Aeon that is Above all Aeons. For Christ said it, pray this way... 'Your Kingdom come, Your will be done, on earth as it is in heaven...'

'Even so, He did not teach me as much as I desired about it, nor instruct me in its many details... I wanted him to stay longer; and, to have taught me more about His, 'the Saviors Holy, transcendent way' and, about His deep understanding of life and of 'the Life to Come'. And, even more so, to have instructed us further, and much more deeply, spiritually, metaphorically and mystically in His Beautiful, Powerful and transcendent Way, His truly Spiritual Way of interpreting Torah! Then, I would be more able (trusting in His judgment) to effectively proclaim His Christhood and make known the Kingdom of *God*, in Power… But now, the Anointed has ascended.

I meditated on these things (in the Spirit) and suddenly,

Behold!

The heavens opened.

The whole of creation shone with a bright light from above. Then the world began to shake and I fell on my face. In fear I looked up and,

Behold!

Out of the light a child appeared before me. I continued looking into the light and, the child transformed into an old man, then, changed again into a young man, like a servant.

Yet what was I was seeing? I could not understand it. Was I dead? I shook with fear. Then, the likeness began to merge and coalesce but still changed. Changing over and over, through and into the three-forms. Each appeared, one after the other, as in a vision.

Then He spoke,

'*John… John…*' why do you wonder? Why are you so afraid? For it is I, your Lord.

Do you not recognize my form? You have seen me before, have you not, look!

Do not be faint-hearted and be not afraid. As I told you before. I am with you,

Always!

I am the Father, the Mother, and the Son.

Undefiled, uncontaminated, and pure; I am the enduring One unto the Age into the Ages to Come' and the living One.

Now I have come to teach you what is,

What was and, what is to come!

Listen and you will learn.

Learn about that which has remained hidden and not revealed, and the hidden, invisible word will be known.

And you will know it, and teach it, 'that which really is' and 'the Way' to those who follow Me, the Perfect Man.

Raise up your head. Lift up your face and eyes and look upon Me. Understand. Then with understanding share what you have learned. Share it with others in, or those who are, followers of, 'the Way'. Lift up their spirits, and strengthen them making them steadfast, faithful disciples.

John, the son of Zebedee then asked Jesus the Anointed the Truth about *God* Most High, 'the One,' the Inexpressible.

Jesus teaches on the One

The One

God is One (but many)

Creator of the cosmos born from Light;

Profoundly complex yet absolutely simple

Perfect yet without us, incomplete

Uncreated yet By Its Own Nature, Self-Generated

And first Begetter and Womb of the All

The Primal Ineffable Father and Mother;

though not just a 'Father' nor just a 'Mother' (nor just a man nor just a woman)

Greater than the greatest and Less than the least

He is the Imageless Image.

The Monad emanates Diversity in Unity

Nothing has authority over it, nor does anything rule it

For nothing is superior to it

The One exists, but not as we exist; nor not exist as we do not exist.

We see Him and see His Works; He, the Great Invisible Spirit.

The One is uncontaminated, and undefiled

Pure light; yet, which no human eye can look within…

For it is written… 'Thou cannot… see my face and live'.

Yet we look for Him and see Him everywhere; in everything, everyday and every way, the Virgin Invisible Spirit.

Inside and Outside every and all borders; though everything and anything that is, is inside of His borders

He must not be conceived as simply 'a god' or simply 'the god'; nor in any similar, mundane way

For He is *'God'* (above every human conception of any god or 'gods')

He is beyond human understanding and expression

But expresses himself by our words, through revelation and mighty acts of power.

He dwelleth in life, but can dwell with the dead

For He is life and, He is death!

The first Uncaused Cause,

The Cause of Something rather than Nothing

Though all that exists, exists through Him, or within Him or below or beside Him; but He is superior to all… through, within, without, below or apart from Him

Everything that exists, exists because He decrees it so.

When He is far from us, we are close to Him

When we are far from Him, He is next to us.

He is not this nor that, nor a-thing, nor that-thing, nor any one or a multiple or a myriad of-things; He is nothing!

He is unmeasurable for, nothing was outside or apart from Him that could measure Him

The One is noncontingent and eternal, knowing neither light nor darkness as we do

He needs nothing provided to Him, though He provides all that the cosmos needs

For, if He needed anything, He would not be complete; and lacking, He would be in need of completion.

But rather, He is Perfect; for the One, 'He Who Is' is always Complete; and Perfect in light or darkness

Without limit, He is the illimitible for, no one nor anything existed prior to Him to set His limits.

He is unnamable and unknowable, for nothing existed prior to Him to know Him to name Him; nor to describe Him or define Him

He, the eternal, exists through the Ages upon Ages into the Ages to come. Before the creation of time, space and the Universe He was. Thus 'the One Who Is' does not partake of any one Aeon, or Age or Realm, because He existed before, through and after time and, before through and after Space; and before, through and after all matter, movement and repose.

He is 'not perfect, not blessed, not divine'; because He is superior to all such inadequate concepts; superior to them all

God is not corporeal nor incorporeal; not 'large' or 'small' but, ('on the far side of; on the other side of; further away than; behind, past, after) beyond… all such quantifiable things. He is not a creature (like us) but the 'Creator Who Is'. Nor can anyone know Him; For He is not at all 'just a human being' who may be known; but is superior to all that is, that is known and unknown

His Image and Likeness

Yet, *'the One Who Is'* contemplates His Image and likeness (being of inestimable majesty, being, and spirit); for it is in 'the Image of God's Likeness,' that *'the One'* created them… *male and female God* created them!

He is the light and, the One who created light!

Light!

He is the blissful One and gives blessedness

The Knowledgeable One who gives knowledge.

The Merciful One, who gives Mercy

The Chief of all Aeons and Pleromas, Heavenly Beings and Dimensions in every and all the Realms of Fullness

And the Begetter of all Aeons, of Everything; and the All in All

For, the Sage said it… with a single word He said, 'be' and it was!

And the Sage said it… with a single word He said, 'light,' and there was 'light!

Light!

But not just any light; it is the quintessentially necessary, infinitely creative, illuminating luminescence; being from His Purity and Holiness the Uncaused Cause; becoming the very cause of the All and All and all that is, and the creator (in Truth) of everything: that being, the entire cosmos! For He *God*: (the Father, Holy Mother and, the Logos) by the Spirit are the very ground of being in which we, this cosmos and this world lives and moves and has its being. For, They existed before all things, and it is Through Them that, all things were made, and without Them, nothing was made that has been made.

And, They are before all things, and by Them all things hold together! The Universe and the All in All, existing into the Ages and Ages, unto the Ages to Come; World Without End!

Indestructible

Silent in Repose

Peaceful

And the 'One Who Is' Sustains and Maintains it all through Goodness

The Origin, Truth and Reality Before and After Creation. And, the Hidden Future, this Beguiling Moment and, the Past

Yet we would know nothing of these hidden things about *God*, except He, the Anointed came forth from the Father to instruct us. He alone gives us the Truth, the Word, informing us fully.

Surrounded by this Pure light; the Father appreciates Himself reflected in the 'Water of Life'. Which is *'That'* which creates and sustains space, time, being and the *All and All* into the Age. For, conscious that His Being and **Spirit** surrounds everything; He causes it, the 'Water of Life' to pour fourth from hidden fountains forming everything; the *All in All* and *All Creation!*

'Even now from the *'Contemporary, Gnostic Johannine Community…'* comes Inspiration…'

The **Seer** by intuition, and by foreknowledge glimpses an image of the true reality. And he (John) is enlightened… and he sees coming into this world 'of classical reality' (*a reality that, cannot be 'known' by human sense*) the Father's 'Ennoia' or Wisdom. She, From His first thoughts is the Glorious Barbēlō who comes 'in His Image and Power,' the Holy Mother who, stands before Him and before Them all. For this is the will of *God*. Brought forth by the Father She will help Him lay out all of the foundations of the world and of the entire universe! And together with (His pronoia) or, forethought they will bring to all that need it (and seek it) 'His Providential plan for Salvation'.

The **Seer** understands then that this world and 'reality' is not the 'true reality' but merely a semblance, and a invention of our minds; an illusion. For Matter, Materiality, and Flesh are merely the emergence of forms from what is behind the 'true reality'. For, **Behold!** concealed, underneath and deeply below this phenomenal, 'fathomless' world, is that which supports this reality above (and *there…* there is no differentiating 'before from after'.) Nor do they see that *from there* (comes the 'fundamental, primary, primordial' creations and emanations, out of Fathers' being and substantiality). This, 'space' is really a three dimensional ersatz, apocryphal expanse made up of, 'quasi, virtual lines'! Behold, one stroke 'attaching to another; and that line attaching to a third…' this creates the dimensions or the worldly 'emergence of space'. **Lo, 'matter** ' 'can build and make things' and when used as objects, clothes, tools or weapons even kill, maim and crush. But 'Matter (from which flesh comes too)' is an illusion.

For all of this is but the 'emergence' out of the properties underlying this indispensable yet truest actuality that makes up the real but hidden reality. That Truth is (in fact) that all of 'beingness' is made up of an ever moving (non-stationary, wave-*like*, quivering) knowledge or 'particle-*like*' forms. These tools and instruments of information and knowledge are mere 'minims and motes' so small they are (veridically but) largely, (and) substantially *nothing…* all matter being in fact mostly 'space' so empty it is rightly compared to 'a particle of sand' measured against 'the space of the earth!' Yet misleadingly understood as 'things' utilized by humanity, by animals and the world as… 'something… rather than nothing'. Yet this 'something is very near-*too* nothing!' Such things came 'to the *Seer*' through, the spirit'.

Behold, First Thoughts

Yet even before the foundation, His Protennoia (or earliest thoughts) and Pronoia (His Providence) had become real. One of the first thoughts appeared before Him, Perfect in Purity and Power. Look! She, Barbēlō is His luminescence and manifests as the Holy Spirit and 'Mother,'. For He, the Holy Father; with Her (together) are Perfect in Power. Thus arising in and from His '*nous*' (His mind and heart) and, in His likeness, image and power is the Mother who 'is one' with the Father in will. She, with the *Logos* and as *Wisdom* completes the Word. Therefore they are the Providence of the plan of salvation for those who will have need of it.

Wisdom and the first Man

'Wisdom,' (or Sofia from Barbēlō) helped bring about *God's* plan for Creation, Salvation and the Chosen people of Israel. Because, see: Wisdom is spoken of by the prophets from Moses …who says of Her in Genesis (out of the Oral Torah) 'Wisdom *is* the Holy Spirit…' and this Spirit hovered over the formless, chaotic void… over the murmuring deep. And even more so, said the prophet who walked with *God* and was no more, 'Wisdom took her seat… next to *God* …superior to the angels… and even the Chosen (while in the garden of Eden.) **Elohim (the Good)** noted She, Wisdom breathed (His) *pneuma,* life and consciousness into mortal Adam. Yet He had inspired into Eve such a 'depth of mind and heart' and of *Soul* that through this Her deep 'Sacred, Salvific Knowledge' would set Adam free. With this, Adam was brought 'into being' and arose, the first mortal man with a soul. And Adam would find this saving knowledge… or, so it is said by Baruch in scripture *and,* by Baruch (in Justin) (Barnstone, William., Meyer, Marvin. 2011).

Consider this, David and Solomon prophesied extensively about 'Wisdom' (or 'Sofia') in *Proverbs* and, in the *Wisdom of Solomon* and in *Baruch* (in the 'Greek' Septuagint LXX). And, repeatedly by *Sirah* in the LXX. …And by Paul in *Corinthians* and in the full covenantal word which also saith, **'Christ 'the Logos'** *is* (the…) **Wisdom of God'**. And in *John*… who wrote, **'He, Christ ('the Wisdom of God')** which with the *being* of the Logos is, 'the One'. This *God* is *God* Most High; the One Good, *God* of Love and Truth! Therefore, as the 'Spirit' of *God*

'She, Barbēlō, *is* the Spirit (and the feminine Wisdom, Holy Spirit or Shekinah) of the Most High Above (Karen King. 2003; Barnstone, William., Meyer, Marvin. 2011; Schaberg, Jane. 2002.)

Barbēlō is:

Wisdom, (but as Sofia the Greater *and* Lesser) the universal creator For He, *God* saith… 'Wisdom …(was) with Me before all time …before My works of old; …before I prepareth thy heavens, **Lo,** She sayeth to the Father 'I was there; before Thou established the clouds above; and the fountains of the deep; I was there. And by Me kings, princes (and) nobles reign, and intercessors decreeth righteousness…' For, Thou writeth in Sira (She *is*) '…the Holy Spirit'. And the Father poureth Me out over and upon… those that love Him. Behold, 'intelligence, Wisdom,' cometh before everything! For, 'Barbēlō,' as 'Wisdom,' is the twin; the created (and creator) who, as our 'faithful Sofia the Lesser,' is yoked with the Wisdom of Jesus Christ!

And She is the inscrutable Womb and Begettress of everything in, *the All and All*!

Barbēlō is:

The Holy Mother and Holy Father;

Barbēlō is:

The First Man (Adamas): 'a trace' of the likeness of the Invisible Spirit or 'the Father,' as seen in the watery image reflected in the firmament. And so (portending) an image of the Last Adam, the Anointed (She too is… verily the 'image of the unknown God').

Barbēlō (Higher Sophia) is:

Holy Spirit

And,

Thrice male,

Thrice Powerful,

Thrice named (*the* Father, Mother and Son)!

For Barbēlō is the Androgynous Principle and Power; with Power over all the Aeons and Realms of the Age, into the Ages to come. First to arise outside of it all; She… outside of space, time and being is and was; before the beginning.

She, Barbēlō, the Holy Mother (and Spirit) is an ever-enduring ageless (androgynously acting) 'Ruler' over Matter, Power, Time and Space. She has Authority over all Pleromas, Aeons, Aeonic or Heavenly beings in the Heavens; and those that pre-existed the creation of the material and fleshly lower cosmos below. But, acting in her capacity as our Sofia the Greater, She is a 'creator, a fabricating craftsman and molder' of the earthly cosmos and aeon, and its' matter, and flesh (beneath) and its firmament above; and in the Abyss beneath. For, as Holy Mother, Barbēlō was the first to arise (and emanating with the Logos, She separated from and stood apart from, God).

Barbēlō, the Holy Spirit praised the Father and asked She be granted His divine integrity, and His wisdom through His revelations as she went forth to create. For, She then created 'That Which Would Be'; the Aeons and Heavens even the Aeonic Abyss'; but for and by The Father's Will alone. And She praised the Father, the Great Invisible Spirit, for He granted it to Her, Barbēlō to execute! Thus her wish was fulfilled even before the generation of the earthly aeon below.

Thus the Mother placed all her thoughts, revelations and plans before Him. He approved and, she commenced to complete them. And humanity, formed in the image and likeness of the Invisible Spirit was given 'free will'. Thus note, it is for this reason that there must be good and evil, right and wrong and **Lo,** suffering of all types and degrees! For only with these things and with such a 'world' (of 'the right, the good and a place to heal,' set against that which is 'wrong, and evil, and a place of suffering') will there be choice. Because, for a human being to 'learn' to act godly and to 'learn' to be like-*too* a 'god,' undergoing theosis… it requires choice (*'for, is it not written in the law, the Anointed said, Ye are gods?*). Therefore, She established the Fathers' plan of providential salvation for those beings (many who will suffer…) but, who can come forth now or later. She brought this before Him and, before the Logos (who would descend too); for He, the Word was of the greatest import to the providential plan of the Father. Together, they stood before this Plan; all of Them, praising it to the Holy Mother and Father!

The Fathers' Will

She, Barbēlō, to carry out The Fathers' will made a few requests before making all that would be (and, the ground upon which all would become… *that*) which are **all substances, materials and phenomenalities needed to make** the earthly cosmos, earthly aeon and its 'creation,' realms and firmament (above *and* below). To accomplish this She, Wisdom, The Holy Mother was emanated from *God* as one of His 'first thoughts' but, separate and apart from the Father… So She, Barbēlō asked to be able to prophesy, to see ahead and plan for the future through prescience and foreknowledge; and, She asked for Incorruptibility, and for Life into the Age; so to be able to discern the Great Invisible Spirit's Truth and, Desire. And to be able to righteously wield His Power. For He, the *'Lord of Spirits,'* and the Son (with Adamas the First Man) agreed and praised Her, and the Father gave Her all that She asked for.

Thus Barbēlō told Them She would always use these great powers in a trustworthy way, too express *God's* Will. And... She, and They: and *all* the Hosts of Heaven stood before the Father and glorified and praised Him, the Great Invisible Spirit.

After this, She began to bring under Her control (for it was His will) all further Spirits, Aeons, Aeonic beings, Archangels, Angels and Archontic Heavenly and Human beings. This was according to His Plan of Providence. After this, all the Hosts of all the Aeons and Heavens Above praised Her and the Father, the *'Lord of Spirits'*. When this was completed, He - *the Logos* came down from Heaven descending to earth; for He too is a vital part of the Father's plan of salvation.

And to be clear the powers working with and under Her, Barbēlō's control, included 'Reason,' 'Prophecy,' 'Sapiential and Apocalyptic vision by precognition,' and the steadfast and immovable congregation and community of 'the Unbreakable Ones' (the 'Seed of Seth'). And the 'Hosts' (the Sabaoth) of the Highest Heavens Above (that) exist to protect Her, Barbēlō, (and *'God'* the *Father, Mother and Son*) into the Age unto the Ages to come (everlastingly). These ones Make up 'the Ten' a 'Pentad' (a Powerful, Five Fold Realm of Heavenly or Aeonic Beings, each yoked into a 'singularly' powerful being). These *yoked pairs* make up an 'androgynously and disparately linked' opposite gendered, 'heavenly, human' and/or, 'other entities' who are (all) singularly powerful beings'; exceptionally mighty, consecrated *and,* the Guardian-Angels of Heaven Itself.

The First Man

And the First Man, Immortal Adamas was:

In the image of the One,

In the plan of salvation

By the plans of the Holy Mother (Barbēlō) from the 'first thoughts' of the Father and Holy Mother because She, Wisdom (or Barbēlō) is:

The future, righteousness and Truth unto the Age;

Who brings forth salvation through knowledge and 'yokes' human and angel together as 'one' ('Syzygies') into the Age!

The Unbegotten Father and Barbēlō, bring forth the 'Light of Life'

The Unbegotten Father brought forth Wisdom; revealing the sacred name of 'Barbēlō,' 'the Mother,' who comes from out of His pure light. **Behold** the Father (the Virgin Invisible Spirit) looking back and into Her, caused Her to conceive the **light** (*of* **life**); for She had received the 'the Spark' of the Fathers's Light.

The Son Empties Himself

This brought forth the *only-begotten,* **the Logos**... the Son who would descend into and become the Anointed. Yet He, the Logos (the only begotten Son) had existed from before the beginning and from the Age upon the Ages and into the Ages, having always been 'in the mind and spirit' of 'the Father, the One,' the *'Lord of Spirits'.*

Yet, *Behold, as it is written...* the Son did not regard equality with 'God, the Father,' a thing to be grasped. But... emptied Himself, taking the form of a lowly slave, becoming (*as* the Anointed) 'one like a son of Man'; and in the likeness of Adamas (and Adam) and-*like* all men (and women) on earth. For in Heaven, the Father, Mother and Son are in spirit, *and are ecstatically, and in actuality... and in sacred verisimilitude, equal,* **'and One,'** as it should be on Earth!

So, *'for his time lived upon the earth'* He, the Son has a blessedness similar too but not equal with, Barbēlō or, 'the One'. For, *He said it... 'Amēn, amēn, I tell you, the Son can do nothing by himself... for whatever the Father does, the Son does too'.* In this sense then He, the Anointed and Redeemer, was *it is written... '... made a little lower than* Thee'. *For, He saith it... 'I go to the Father, for the Father is greater than I'.*

Book of the Living

Sorrowfully, and grieving for the children of the Most High, the Logos, the Anointed with saving knowledge and Wisdom was despised and rejected by all men! Obediently yet, knowing human fear He was nailed by human Archons to 'a tree,' and enduring this torture unto death, this became His testament and His 'dispensation.' For (**Lo, *it is the reason why*)** the Word **was fastened to that cross...** because it was the only way... that He could - in this, His *final act,* as the Son of God *give up* His garment... *freeing those who had loved him to write 'the Book of the Living'.*

Wisdom ('Mother' Sofia) Came Forth

Yet, the 'Spirit' celebrated the light; for, 'the Son' had come forth from the Father because of and due to Barbēlō; **both:** from the first thoughts of the Father. 'Wisdom' came forth too as 'Mother Sofia, Sofia the Greater' 'Companion of *God'* who had emanated (from Barbēlō too) and His Pure Light, Above.

The Great Invisible Spirit, the Father anointed the Son with 'Christhood'; and with unlimited 'kindheartedness, humanity and benevolence,' so He would go down as 'the Logos and Savior'. And, blessed by the Great Invisible Spirit, *'God' poured spirit over, poured it out, and upon Him mightily* (the **Son**). *And the Father Rained Hard (on Him) His Righteousness and Love; and Upon Him His Own Spirit, and from His Mind, Fullness; Giving him every, and all... full measure of Goodness.*

The Divine Self-generated One, the Father, Mother and Wisdom: allow, direct and create the Cosmos and Universe

Then He (yoked with the Holy Spirit, Barbēlō) brought forward His and the Holy Mother's Divine Self-Generated One the Logos, the Anointed One (*Christ*) to completion. And the Son glorified the Great Invisible Spirit the Father, with a mighty voice... *and,* with a crash of thunder; and by the sound of rushing waters even by a 'a whispering' from the Father. Angels sang antiphonally Gregorian Chant (from a specious future, retro-causally: see below). For the Father would Incarnate and embody Himself as a man. And because of His Providence, and by His great mercy and love for humanity, He would descend down through all the Aeons *to arrive as the Anointed with full Authority and Power.*

Authority over it all!

And the Great Invisible Spirit would put the 'Son,' the Divine Self-Generated One (the Logos) in authority over everything; with authority over every divinity, humanity, angels and rulers; and in fact over the *All and All*; over matter, time, and space itself! For no authority (of any kind) would be superior to him *and,* all would be subservient (*even the Adversary*). And, the Logos would instruct in 'the Way' and in 'the Truth' and teach those (who seek it) everything...

The Son (yoked with Sofia, the Lesser or Wisdom below) descended to carry out the Fathers' Will, and the volition of the Father's Desires. He asked to be given His Father's Divine Mind (the '*nous*') and the '*Lord of Spirits*' agreed. In Silence, the Father's will would become the actions of the Son; the Son's thoughts the Father's thoughts. And His mission would align with the Providential plan of 'the One'. After this they stood (the Son, and the Holy Mother Barbēlō or Wisdom) Glorifying 'the Father'.

And the Word incarnated and became Christ the Man, the Divine Self-Generated One (on earth). For, through Him (and in concert with the Father and Barbēlō) Christ (the Divine Autogenes) created *the entire* Universe **and in fact, the All in All;** and, *'They'* allowed the aeon of earth and of this world and everything in it, contrived by Sofia the Lesser (and in fact by 'Her' son, the '*lesser god, Yaldabaoth*') to be 'shaped' and formed. So Yaldabaoth believed this 'his cosmos, his world, and this earth and, its aeon, and realms (above and below) and the firmament of this singular cosmos, was his (and solely his creation)!'. **After that, the Son and Sofia the Lesser stood together and glorified** *God* **and** *Barbēlō.*

His will being One with the Father, *God* honored Christ's Plan of Salvation. For the Anointed would teach Sacred Knowledge through 'the Way,' and bring disciples unto 'Truth, and *Gnosis*' and this would bring them to 'Salvation'. For, trusting in the teaching and instruction by the Anointed, the suffering denizens of earth could (if they sought it) find it... 'Sacred Knowledge and Redemption'. And, all of this would come by the *Grace of God,* a **'Lifeline'** to experiential Union with *'the One'* and to *'Life Into the Age'* in the Highest Heaven Above...!

The Great Invisible Spirit and the Gift of the Four Fundamental Principalities and Powers

First, the Great Invisible Spirit (the *Lord of Spirits*; *God*) gave a gift to the Self-generated Son; three aids or 'lights,'. And these protective angels or 'lights' presented themselves before Him and were:

Will (the angel of sacred volition)

Thought (Angels who inform the *Lord of Spirits* about everything); *and,*

Life Into the Age ('the angel with the gift of everlasting life, enduring unto the Ages and Ages into the Age'),

The Four Fundamental Powers, their Principalities (the Luminous Lights or Archangels)

Then the Father gave the Son Four fundamental and Great Lights or Luminous Powers (Archangels) who arose directly out of and, from *God*; to be of *any* help to the 'Son,' as He deemed necessary. And they pledged themselves before Him, the Divine Self-Generated One (the Logos) and stood before Him… Immortal, Imperishable and the Upright Logoi of Light.

These Luminous Angels were sent to the Son and named for Grace, Understanding, Perception and Judgement.

Harmozel (from Grace) is also called 'Charis' and stood before Him. *Harmozel is 'the first light or Luminous Archangel'* who stands with Him by God's Grace and is, a mighty power and a companion. Harmozel, stands over the First Aeon or Heaven. There, the Great Depth of the Father and the Profundity of the Most High is revealed by His 'compassionate judgement, and empathetic understanding'. Harmozel, himself is protected and accompanied by another angel called Gamaliel. Gamaliel dwells with three other helping angels or lesser lights,

Grace (or Charis) with

Truth and,

Form, (the Guide) and with

Oriel (Oroiael; who is the Archangel Uriel who enhances Perception) *and he is the second Luminous angel* with a Sobriquet of, 'the Fire of God and the Seer of Truth'. And he stands with Seth over the Second Aeon, Heaven or Realm. And with Oriel are three other helping angels or lesser lights,

Providence ('the Way' to Knowledge and Salvation)

Perception (for Insight and Reflection) and,

Memory (for Remembrance) and then:

Daveithai, the third Light or Luminous Angel stands over the Third Aeon or Heaven, and he comes with the Understanding, and the Enlightenment of the 'children or, seed of (the Righteous) Seth.' *Daveithai is an Archangel with the 'moniker' as 'the Rock'* and with him are all the souls of the Saints known and unknown, divine, incorruptible, unshakeable, and those of earlier blissful 'communities' (earlier enlightened, mystical, divine and righteous people who obtained sacred knowledge attained from their redeemer Seth). Seth and the Sethians were righteous exegete's of the spirit and philosophy of the Good. *For… before Abraham was, they were the sons and daughters of, and the children of God*. And with these Sethians are three other helping but lesser lights, and angels:

Understanding,

Love, and,

Idealists (contemplative mystics or the *'gnostike,'*) and finally,

Eleleth **is the forth Great Light or Luminous Archangel,** with a name derived directly from 'El' and, by Wisdom's (Barbēlō's) Judgement, Eleleth stands in the Presence of the Holy Spirit, *and looks astonishingly into the* **actual face** of *God*!

Here in this Fourth Aeon, dwell the 'complicated souls that (even though) they had acquired divine salvational knowledge, *even, experiential union with 'the One'*; and Wisdom, and Unity with 'the Creator' *yet, let it all go…* And **purposely returned to Ignorance, Hard-Heartedness and Sin.**

Even knowing what they had known, and having experienced heaven (some still chose to and return to ignorance and sin). But for most immediately but for others only after prolonged, and terrible suffering… do they gain knowledge and repent (though some refuse to repent; persisting and choosing darkness into the Age). Most of these Apostates *or, almost all* by Wisdom and right Judgment, repent and return. Then casting away their ignorance (and sin) and, after being purified are welcomed back amidst great rejoicing (*as the prodigal sons and daughters of God*). And welcomed into the *Heaven of Eleleth* where they can remain into the Age, into the Ages to come. Yet, their rebellion remains a mystery… but no matter, they have returned (and many joyfully 'yoke themselves' with their guardian angels and heaven) becoming servants. And with them come these helping angels:

Perfection

Peace and,

Wisdom (Sofia)

And these make up the (the four lights) and twelve Luminous Aeons of Archangels and Angels.

They all stand ready to guard the Logos, the Autogenes and Lord Christ! For no mattereth whom thou art (now) or what thalt shalt have done (before) it is by the Fathers' volition and desire that, through His Word and Wisdom *that the Plan of Salvation be offered to all!* And offered again and again until seventy times seven… And, they who return are greeted by the Holy Mother (Barbēlō) and by the Son, the Logos; **but *God* says choose, and reminds them all,** thou art beloved; and, *'He'* saith, 'beloved come back…'

For these things are established too, through Foreknowledge, Revelation and by the Perfect Man and by the Mind and Heart of the Anointed. *For the Father saith again; 'thou art loved' and; 'beloved, come home…'*

The Perfect Man Adamas and the Aeon or Realm of Harmozel the first Light

Through the goodness of the Great Invisible Spirit and the Self-Generated Son, the Perfect, true Man came forth: the first man, Immortal Adamas. *God* placed Adamas over the Aeon of Harmozel and with the divine Self-Generated Christ. The first, immortal man possesseth great abilities for the Invisible Spirit gaveth him an invincible, indomitable spiritual consciousness and power.

Adamas stood and he praised the *'Lord of Spirits'*, saying to Him, 'Lord, it is by Your Grace, Truth and Design that the quintessentially necessary, infinitely creative, illuminating luminescent 'Light' brought forth this earthly aeon and cosmos (and the entire Universe) and the '*All in All*'. 'Thou, art that Light (and Perfect Power) that shineth over everything, good and evil, right and wrong, left and right (and now and forever)! For Thou art the sum of everything *Lo*, of all that is!'!

'Seth and Sethians' an elect community

Sethians, (from Seth the son of Adam) were an earlier elect community of 'the One'; and those that followed him are the seed of Seth, Seth's descendants; sons and daughters of *'God'* and souls of the known and unknown Saints that cometh before Abraham was… Saved by Noah, 'a Sethian' gave birth to Shem, Shem to Arpachshad, Arpachshad to Abraham, Abraham to Isaac, and Isaac to Jacob; Jacob (or Israel) to King David and 'he' to Joseph (His Father with, His mother Mary) *to* the Anointed. For the Christ, the Logos 'was in the beginning before the Ages into the Ages to Come (and hath been so, everlastingly) the Son of *'God'*, timelessly. Therefore Seth who came (before the 'earthly incarnation') was incarnated by 'the Logos, the Christ, in Spirit' which, therefore 'makes Seth and all Sethians, Ancestors of Israel; and Israelites' too (by the mechanism of a retro-causal past; this *specious* moment but a part of the inclusive temporality including everywhere and every-when)! *For the Prophet saith it…* 'from them (the Israelites; the Jews) cometh the glory, the covenant and instruction, worship and thine promises and so, 'by the flesh or by Adoption,' a chosen people of the 'Most High *God*'. *Yet it is written…* Seth and Sethian's descendents prophetically recognized the trinity: 'the Father, Mother and the Son' (Marshall, Paul. 2015)

The Baptist, Seth, Jesus and the Children of the Most High God and Israel

For it is written… Adam *knew* his wife again; and, she bareth him a son, and called him Seth (ancestor of all the generations of the righteous): For *God*, saith Eve, hath appointed me another seed… one, like a 'son of Man' and, in his likeness and image…!

Behold, a prophet came in the 'Spirit and Rebirth' of Elijah

Behold, It is written… in the beginning was the Logos… Christ, the Wisdom of *God*

Behold, It is written… in the beginning… *God* created Wisdom …his spirit (or breath) with power (and strength) before (the beginning) and so… before his work, his emanation of the Universe began…

Israelites, 'the Children of Seth and of Abraham; of the One God'

For this reason too and *like,* John the Baptist… who …*saith the Logos* comes 'in the Spirit' and as a 'rebirth' of Elijah So, Seth came antecedently (by the mechanism of a retro-causal past; into this *specious* moment… part of the inclusive temporality including everywhere and every-when)! So 'in the Spirit' and as a 'rebirth' Seth came as, 'the Word'. For Jesus the Christ, the Logos 'was,' as John said, 'in the beginning, the Word.' And the Word was '*God,*' and therefore had existed from, Ages upon the Ages Past into the Ages unto the Ages to Come (*with* the Father forever, and from before, and in and beyond the Age, endlessly); and is now '*the One*', forever and ever; World Without End.'

Therefore Seth came (before the 'incarnation') as 'the Logos, and in the Spirit' and, in 'the image and likeness' of Christ. Then, Christ Jesus (the incarnated) came *'later'* 'in the spirit and in the flesh' and with 'the image and likeness… and the righteousness of, and *within the 'rebirth' of* Seth! All these ones were, 'temporally, spatially and diversely spread as *'God'* wills'; and, all were the 'children of Abraham, Israelites by flesh or by adoption!' (Marshall, Paul. 2015; Stapp, Henry P. 2015)

And as it is with 'the One' the Father, who is inside and outside, in any, or on the other side of, or in any state of time now, or in the past, or in this specious moment or the future; and after this… He, the Father is even from before and from beyond; from throughout *and from the whole of all time…*) So all stood before Him and praised the Great Invisible Spirit!

Sethians ('Sons and Daughters of God, were Israelites for an Age *and* Messianics' for an Age; and were…) **and are once more again**, ancestors of, if they choose to be it: righteous Israelites or Gnostics again!).

Look!

Creation of the World, and the Crisis of Wisdom

In 'the beginning' was the Logos (*and it is written… it*, the *Logos* is…) …the **'Wisdom of *God*'**. So the *Logos,* 'with Wisdom' was **with** *God,* and, the *Logos* 'with Wisdom' *is* **'One with'** *God*. And *God* (Father, Mother - *or Sofia the Greater* and, the Son… are like-*too* the yoking in fulness of Barbēlō) and unified… Because, they are of the same mind, substance and essence. **For, it is written…** 'the One' said, *'let there be 'Light' and their was Light!* …but not just any light; the 'quintessentially necessary, infinitely creative Light'. *That* which emanates *all* things, all realms; and all dimensions including (and inclusively) *all* energy, time, space, matter And (unknowingly *to Yaldabaoth - even himself,* the 'lesser god,'). Yaldabaoth in his molding and concocting of the aeon of earth and, in his invention of its realms above and below and of its firmament (is *ignorant* and a deceived divinity). He deludes himself that fabricating this 'singular cosmos and aeon of the earth' is actually the creation and emanation of… the all (the Universe). Even of all of the sublime, bewitchingly mesmeric, incredibly commensurate, highly refined and proportional 'laws of nature'… Behold the 'natural laws' that let this cosmos emerge (and, which is unknown to Yaldabaoth) produced this inflating 'Anthropic, and now infinitely, expanding Universe.' A universe generated 'for human being'; for, Anthropos. Yet, it was not through the '*god*' of this world (but 'the One,') who is… the Father, Mother, and the Son… (together, who are) the Great Begettress and Womb of the Universe, who is Barbēlō, who created it All! (Meyer, Stephen C. 2009; 2014; Marshall, Paul. 2015; Stapp, Henry P. 2015; Meyer, Marvin. 2005; Kelly, Edward F. 2015; 2015)

The Perplexed 'Maker;' and 'troubled Creator' of the World'

But it happened then (at that same time) and by her own volition (but through jealousy) Sofia 'the Lesser,' created her 'own son and divinity,' Yaldabaoth. And *he, the 'god' of this world* was *not* '(as 'he believed') **the** 'creator'. But he was merely a 'sculptor, a formatter; and (*only*) the 'maker' of this world's outward, superficial appearance; and designer of many functions of the living things and beings upon it.' He wrongly convinced himself *'he'* had created this aeon and cosmos (which he mistook for the entire universe and all the realms above and below)…

The World, the Firmament and its Cosmos

Nevertheless *'he, Yaldabaoth'* put *'this, his'* cosmos an 'immense distance away' from His Mother Sofia and Her Aeon (and therefore all other Aeons above). Despite that, and because of what he had inherited through Sofia's great power and spirit; and, because of *that* which he had *stolen* from her... Yaldabaoth 'ordered and assembled' superficially, this discrete, and localized aeon and world. He, *who is also called Saklas the fool,* and *Samael the blind; a stumbling block, is ignorant and he believes,* **'he and only he' created this entire world and Universe!** But, the Truth is: he merely (and without knowing it) outwardly contrived and molded this earthly aeon and its' Heavenly Realm and firmament above: *the* moon, stars and sky' and, its realms below... Because, all this happened through his Mother's Error. For, Sofia had desired to *'improve'* creation and to *'demonstrate Her worthiness'* but had failed. She alone (and without the Father's guidance or consent) had blundered disastrously attempting to bring forth a 'sacred divinity'... but, *'it'* was neither in His (nor in Her) image and likeness.

But, in Her Realm Sofia *is* a mighty power. And Her 'reproductive' thought there was effective. Unfortunately the 'divine being She gave birth' to, was *imperfect; different,* '*...odd, off...*' **And, a misshapen, unfamiliar half animal, half man (and not even with a 'human-like' image)**. This aeon, and this 'lesser god' provoked fear in anyone and everyone that looked upon it. But even more so, he was *not* in 'the image and likeness' of the Father. Realizing Her failure, Sofia the Lesser became afraid.

When Sofia examined Her creation and focused on it she was shocked. Looking closer she saw a Serpent-like being with a Lion-like face. Its eyes full of anger... its soul full of fire, blood, violence and desire; ...part dragon with a lion-*like* head! Horrified, She surrounded it with a luminous mist and a high perch and palace, and then *cast 'it' all outside; and even more... outside the Outer...* so that no one, especially the Immortals could see him. Yet Wisdom (Barbēlō) above, the companion of the Father saw it all...

Yaldabaoth the 'Son of Chaos'

As a result of creating 'it' without the Father (or His consent) She gave rise to an *Error* and to *Evil*. Seeing what She had *'created'* She cried out, 'yaldā bahuth,' which means (I have made a) **'Son of Chaos'**. For he is not from the Light but from the Dark. And immediately it was clear that he was supremely arrogant, ignorant and sadly, hostile... yet a powerful immortal. A daemonic divinity that received his name from her cry of horror: 'Yaldabaoth'. (**See:** *Addendum 1* below: 'Yaldabaoth and yaldā bahuth' after *SRev John* references)

An evil, lower deity; he is *'a lesser god'*. Yet, in spite of that **he** *'is (as it is written...) the god' of this world,* of earth. And Sofia, who had created him, did not immediately inform the Most High, nor anyone else in the Heavens Above.

Yaldabaoth, thinking all above and around him was created by his Mother (or himself), stole from Her (without Her knowing) more of Sofia's Spirit and Power. And, using this he further molded the 'lesser aeon of earth,' and 'fallen humans, angels, demonic Archons, people, leaders and rulers' of this world. He then added a little bit to the firmament and it's realms' of the unseen above and the domains below.

Sofia tried to stop Yaldabaoth but, She could not control him. So in distress She cried for help. But, it was too late… Yaldabaoth had taken steps to protect himself and his 'Kingdom'… Yet the Holy Spirit, *the Mother of all Life* heard Her cry, because 'Wisdom' sees everything…

Despite this Yaldabaoth became the Chief Ruler (or Chief Archon) and, 'the *god*' of this aeon, and of earth. As the Chief Archon and Ruler of this aeon and its realms, its firmament and its Abyss, he seized it. Thus even to this day, this cosmos and its firmament burns luminous in the background with an after-glow that still persists! This petty, powerful ruler begot divine and human archons, many powers, principalities and authorities. These are to carry out his dictates, and to make effective his every wicked, base and unholy wish and desire.

The Fashioning of 'the aeon of earth' and Mortal Humanity

Here he dwells; with great power because, when Sofia created him She breathed into him a *'spark of the spirit of the true God'* (unknowingly) passing to him great power! Yet within Yaldabaoth the spirit of the One was transformed into (*'a False and Counterfeit Spirit'*). For, though She was separated from the true God; 'the One Most High, Sofia is nonetheless a hypostasis (of the Father) as Yaldabaoth is not. And Sofia being of the same substance as the Holy Father (and the Holy Mother *and* Son) She too desires to do the will of *God*'!

A Jealous God

After this first creation, and in a *'demented and crazed-like'* 'mania' he cried out, *'it is written that…,* **I am a jealous God, and there is no God but me!**'

But those he created (or that joined him) from above or from below; dark, evil and, fallen angels, daemons, humans and others, said to each other, *'if there is no other 'god,'* 'why does he waste his time saying this? Who is he jealous of'?

Spirit Moving Over the Murmuring Deep

Because of all this, 'Barbēlō' (the Spirit) became greatly agitated, and began moving to and fro, over the waters and the murmuring deep. And, the brightness of the earth dimmed and, the world became a darker place.'

John then said to Jesus, 'Rabbi, what does it mean, 'Her Spirit moved to and fro over the waters of the deep?' And, 'the brightness of the earth dimmed and, the world became a darker place?'

The Savior smiled and said to John, 'Moses misspoke or, was misunderstood for, not only did water cover it but, much greater confusion and ignorance spread over the entire earth *and,* it became a more ***wicked, unholy*** and ***spiritually*** darker area in which to live!'

Earthly Creation, Construction and Fabrication Continues

After the earthly aeon and world was created, Yaldabaoth the Evil Chief Ruler copulated with one of his female demons called, 'Madness'. Though she was deranged, nevertheless Yaldabaoth found her 'attractive'. And… though a thoughtless, selfish, even *'crazed and demented female'* he did not care because, she filled him with carnal lust. So, he 'took her and entered her'. From this fornication were begotten many 'Powers'; the 'Power' of Wickedness, of Jealousy, of Discord and of Desire. And she, 'Madness' (and many others like her) gave birth to myriads of dark, fallen and nefarious 'Archons, rulers, angels, demons and humans.' And these corrupt, foul and depraved humans became his evil Ruling Archons and, *'his host'*. **And they worshipped Yaldabaoth;** *'their god'*.

Eloim and Yave and 'Elohim' and the Inscrutable Existence of the Aeon of Earth

Yet **Behold** *in 'Baruch,' Justine writes…* the demiurge *Edem* (is a feminine personification and representation of the first feminine soul of earth.) Formerly the wife of **Elohim,** Elohim breathed soul into the first man too, and allowed Yaldabaoth's 'wicked' invention… 'his creation of' this lower aeon and earth; and also his concoctions and its distortion of and torture of human beings, dark and lesser divinities; of which the first demonic pair he named *'Eloim and Yave'*. But, (inscrutably) this was *allowed* to exist by *God.* Why? Because the true Father (*Elohim*) and, by the *Wisdom* of Barbēlō, (*'God,* the Good Father, Mother and Son') had already 'seen it' and had 'planned for it'. **For Behold** it is the will of **God Most High** that the 'lesser *god'* of 'this aeon and earth,' exist… (Barnstone., William. 1984; Barnstone., William and Meyer, Marvin. 2011)

Further, Yaldabaoth (in the manner above) gave to these divine beings twelve ruling angels, and (to each of them) seven 'lights' (or seven lesser angels); and… (*though the 'god' of this world did not understand it*) they were modeled on the good angels, authorities, powers and other immortals, humans and other beings above. Like the 'Immortal Adamas,' he created 'mortal Adam' as, 'the First Man' from his and his mother's 'archetypal memories'. These became his 'host and army, his spies and warriors' (his *Sabaoth'*). They are dark imitations of the Good Father's Pleromas, and, His Good Aeons and Aeonic beings and, His Righteous Host in Heaven, Above.

And to each Archangel of the earth he gave three powers. Ultimately the '*god'* of the earth created 365 fallen 'angelic' beings (and other humans or daemons) under his rule.

The Seven Heavens and 'Spheres or Dimensions' (over the aeon of earth)

The names of these first Archontic creators and rulers of the seven heavens or spheres above earth (who helped in the creation of mortal, and a flawed humanity and earth) follow:

So, over the First aeon, of the seventh heavens or spheres 'was' **Athoth** (who is also called 'Wisdom'). The second was **'Hermes** (trismegistus') whose knowledge and wisdom leads to the *'Nous,'* or the mind, heart and intellect; toward the Good and toward Sacred Knowledge. Then comes **Galila** (who guides other Archons in making for Yaldabaoth, earthly human beings such as) **Yabel**; **Adonai**; **Sabaoth**; **Cainan** and **Abel**!

The Abyss (the Vale of Hinnom or in English: Hell)

But Malevolent Archons, Authorities and Powers rule over the Abyss of Darkness, the Vale of Hinnom. This sphere includes: **Abrisene**, and **Armoupiael**; **Melcheir-Adonein** until one comes at last, and finally too, **Belial**, *a daemon, the devil*, and the *'Accuser himself'* who… arose from the Holy Spirit (*or Breath*) of **Pistis-Sofia** blown on his face, the 'face of Chaos' in the lowest principality. This is (*in spirit*) Yaldabaoth's 'true father'. He, **Belial** rules the lowest Aeon, Gehenna… Hell Itself!

Exorcism

And all these Archons, Authorities and Powers have two sets of names. One name reflects the desires and wrath of 'the *god*' of this world. But the second set of names were given (*secretly*) by the Father, and the Holy Mother. One name resembles names found in the Heavens above and are deceitful. While the other name… (given by Yaldabaoth's alter persona's '*Saklas the blind* and *Samael the fool*) exposes their *true*, *base*, *corrupt*, and *fallen lower* 'selves' and true natures. So by identifying these 'base and corrupt natures' a 'healer or ancient doctor' can weaken it and cast 'it' out, the demon that besets a diseased part of the body, through exorcism.

'And so Yaldabaoth ordered seven to be created as his wicked Rulers or Archons. He made them 'Kings,' over their Spheres, the 'Seven Heavens' and this earthly aeon Above. And five others, led by King 'Sabaoth' and, King 'Adonaios' were especially delegated to rule over the underworld… Lords over the Pit and the Abyss used to purify the wicked and strengthen the fallen *below* the aeon of earth.

Power from his Psyche or Soul and his 'False and Counterfeit Spirit'

And he, Yaldabaoth shared his 'psyche' or 'soul, and his *'false and counterfeit spirit'* and power with his followers; **but not all of it.** *For it is not his… 'full power, light and spirit' inherited from his Mother.* Because he (rightly) understands that, it is only *this power* that keeps the evil soulless ones from taking *his (Yaldabaoth's)* life and *his* leadership.

Yaldabaoth, the accuser with many faces

The Adversary, Yaldabaoth dons many faces and so disguised, 'act outs, even violently'. As an Archontic Ruler he takes any action he desires (disguised as human) on earth. Or he can present himself as the *'god'* of this world. And direct others to carry out tasks.

He and His Archontic rulers have shocking visages: Athoth dons a sheep's face; Eloaios a donkey's face; Astaphaios a hyena's face; Yao a seven headed snake; Sabaoth the face of a dragon, Adonaios the face of a monkey; and Sabbataios a face of flame and fire!

Authorities and Rulers over the aeon of earth

These divergent authorities and deficient rulers are emanations by Yaldabaoth to command and rule on earth. For he has his own protective Seraphim, Cherubs and Angelic beings…

Yet even on Yaldabaoth's world there are beings that are good, filled with spirit and light from his Mother. Though a mystery… they are from the Father too (the One, Unknown *Good God*). With 'Spirit' from the Holy Father *sent through* the 'Holy Mother, Barbelo'… or 'Sofia,'. They eagerly await Sacred Knowledge.

These beings do not worship Yaldabaoth. So he blocks and blots out their memories. Especially the good memories or sparks of *God's* light or spirit. And blocks the 'light or spirit' from *the Good* or from *from Heaven Above*.

He, the *'god'* of this aeon created (around earth) seven heavens with 'wondrous but, deceitful names'. He made 'heavens' to be ruled over by His Archons, Powers and Authorities (modeled on his 'archetypal memories and dreams' of the 'true' Higher Aeons or Realms Above) such as:

Goodness the first power (is associated with 'Thoth' or Athoth) another name for Hermes (or, 'Hermes trismegistus') who was considered an 'Egyptian' divinity of wisdom, knowledge, philosophy, intellect, and rationality. And a writer of the most ancient core Truths and scriptures; including the Word of *God and* about that which holds all things together; (even on the resurrection and the life to come). like Enoch, these Hermetic writings reflect sacred knowledge and salvation. (Freke, Tim., Gandy, Peter. 1997; Smith Andrew P. 2015; Barnstone, William. 1984;)

Forethought the second power, is also called 'Eloaios' (derived from the Hebrew root for 'God,' 'El') and an indication of great power). This Aeon can anticipate problems, is prudent and farsighted and is capable of visions (including prophetic vision).

Divinity the third (is the power of Yaldabaoth's 'daughter') and she is also called 'Astaphaios'.

Lordship, the fourth power, is called Yao, a son of

Ya-ldaboth (derived from the ineffable name of *God* Most High): the true Father whose existence the demiurge denies.

Sabaoth, the fifth power, 'a Kingdom' is derived from 'Adonai Sabaoth,' or the 'lord of hosts'; and 'the leader of armies'. He, is a son of Yaldabaoth with the ability to control chaos and, subdue others.

Adonin is the sixth power and it represents Jealousy and Zeal.

Sabbataios is the seventh power, and is derived from knowledge and understanding stemming from the Hebrew term 'Sabbath' or Shabbat and thus, is a term denoting 'the seventh or the number seven' (a holy number); as in the last day. And it is a term of power used by the 'heavenly host'.

The Aeon of Earth

This aeon he modeled from his ideas that come from, 'that which is above' (or 'archetypal memories and dreams' inherited from his mother). But in fact 'Samael,' is blind and does not believe there are other 'Holy Aeons, Heavens, and Pleroma's Above'. For (despite) his own unimaginable creation and existence, he otherwise does not believe in a Loving, Holy Father, or that any *God* exists; at all. For he knows nothing about the true reality of the Holy Father or Mother (Barbēlō).

And he certainly does ***not*** believe he and his mother (nor any other God) has existed from the Ages and into the Ages to Come (*or everlastingly*). So, blind and ignorant he, believes himself sole 'creator' of the 'cosmos' (and of the universe). And as sole creator he demands ***all*** worship him (in obeisance to their '*god*'). *And this makes him feel full, needed, meaningful, important* and *powerful* and, (like smoking the opium poppy) He can never get enough. Therefore all must continuously praise, worship, and exalt him!

Sofia In Sorrow Repents and Seeks Help

The Breath and the Wisdom of *God* entered Sofia's mind. She realized Her creation 'Yaldabaoth' lacked illumination. That his 'spirit' was dull and ignorant. Then She learned that the Holy Father did not approve of 'this, *his* creation' nor of 'this destructive *minor* divinity's shallow assertions. Yaldabaoth proclaimed that as 'creator' of the earth; and of *this world and aeon and firmament,*' and of all its realms and (mistakenly) all its beings that the people must worship him (and him alone). Then Sofia the Lesser finally understood, She by herself could not correct this deficiency. And She grew depressed…

Then I, John asked Him, Lord Christ, 'What should Sofia do?'

The Lord said, the Holy Mother saw the evil in the Adversary's theft of light, power and life by this 'god' and *his dark host*. This *'lesser god'* led an ignorant rebellion and *Sofia* now repented her benighted contribution to it; and to all the darkness and misinformed actions this rogue, ignorant 'contender' and his hosts, had inflicted on the earth. **For,** *if Sofia had forgotten* **Her need** *of the Father and of Heaven Above*; how could she expect her 'son' to accept this too? She knew that he would never accept rule by the true God Above. Remembering this, She was ashamed… and repenting, wept.

But oblivious to all this, the Adversary, the Son of Chaos raised himself above his creation. And with his host of daemons and fallen angels watching he 'preened and polished himself'. Then, standing erect he felt sublimely filled with mighty power! But 'Holy Wisdom,' the Holy Spirit and 'Mother' realized the damage wrought by Sofia's actions… Finally, and with the help of the Father and the *Holy Mother*, Sofia understood what to do. Repenting she lifted Her face, eyes and arms *up* to Heaven and cried out for help; praising Heaven and asking for their help.

Heaven responds

Considering that the whole Pleroma (including the Aeons) *had not previously heard Sofia's repentant prayer*; when they did hear it, they were deeply moved. All wished to help Her; and to help the 'children of *God*' below. Those *lonely human beings and souls,* caught up in the Adversary's earthly abyss; and living in the misfortune and mayhem below.

And they praised Sofia for her repentance and asking for help from the Great Invisible Virginal Spirit. They beseeched Him, 'Father 'bless Her, help Her' and help the 'children' suffering below'.

And the Father, and His consort the Holy Barbēlō approved. Then the Holy Spirit poured forth mightily the love and understanding and divine knowledge of the Father's Plan of Salvation. Sofia, comprehending his plan and with great love for the children of 'the One' below, was shown 'the right path,' and 'the Way,'.

The Father Comes Down, as the Incarnated Logos

For He, the Father - *in an unprecedented act,* came down as the Word (the Logos) through all the Aeons to her level. Exceedingly painful to do, he entered as the 'Logos…' into matter and flesh; and into Jesus, of Infinite Sweetness. *This the Father did, to help Sofia, and all those human beings and souls suffering under this deficiency.* Beings, that at that time were filled with a craving for material, fleshly, sensual and dark pleasures and desire. Without help from 'the One' above it would have remained a shadowland of death and sorrow.

Behold the Father came down as 'the Logos, the incarnated Word and Son'. And by the Logos, and with the help of Wisdom they brought His Providential Plan of Sacred Knowledge, leading to 'Gnosis' and Salvation.

All given a choice

Nevertheless, Sofia would not be allowed (for an Age) to return to the Aeon of the Father or to the Highest Heaven Above. She must remain in the Ninth realm until the 'deficiency she caused is filled' and, until the amnesia imposed on humanity… by the *'son of Chaos'* is removed.

A Voice From Above Proclaims Humanity (Men and Women) Exist; and, the Son of Man Exists!

Then a voice came from above; from *God* Most High and out of the Highest Heavens Above; from the most exalted Aeon. It said, 'men, and women exist, and in Our Image and Likeness *humanity* exists'. And even more so He said, *'in* my *image and likeness,* the Son of Man *exists!'*

Even so when the Adversary, the Chief Archon Yaldabaoth and his 'host' heard this… they thought it was his Mother, Sofia calling to him. Or maybe, it had just been a bad dream from which he had now awakened. He was not sure though… of its' source.

Nevertheless the Father's Plan of Salvation, His Providence and Wisdom unrolled below (as foreseen). So the **'Son of Man'** (the Logos) came forth in the 'Image and Likeness' of the Perfect Man, His Father!

And the earth and its aeon, Yaldabaoth and his Archons and, all of the fallen host were shaken! The very foundations of the Abyss opened wide and shook beneath them.

The First Man (Earthly Adam) and His Creation

The First Man Above (**Adamas**) one like a son of Man appeared in the Sky above; and could be seen in the waters of the firmament (in the world of physicality). In the image of the 'true God' Adamas appeared.

And though Yaldabaoth's disciples listened to him, that dark authority, these fallen angels, daemons and others gazing at Adamas said to themselves, 'let us mold a *mortal man* in the likeness of Immortal Adamas and the '*god* of *this earth* and aeon below'. For, Yaldabaoth and his host knew Adamas had Great Spirit,

Power and Illumination; and, they thought they could create a mortal Adam and obtain these things for themselves.

The First Man (and Humanity) with a 'Soul'

On that basis and, by the Authority of their Chief Archon they set about creating '**Adam**,' *the first earthly, fleshly, and 'Psychic', 'man (**a man with** a soul')*. So creating him they placed in him, self-consciousness, mind, and heart. And because 'Providence' had participated (*indirectly through Sofia*) he received (unknown to them) a spark of the Father's 'Spirit and Light' *and… through that,* hidden help from the Good and Good Powers Above. Still, Evil had also entered Adam through Sofia's insistence on creating him by herself alone; an unavoidable mix of good and bad. And also from Yaldabaoth's immoral and malevolent slaves helping in the design, fabrication, and molding of every part of **Adam**… from his flesh and bone, tissue and sinew to his body, being and mind.

Names of the Demons (and Fallen Host) Associated with Adam

Nevertheless, by divine forethought (and as part of the Providential plan) the name of each lesser, wicked and malignant divinity, angel or demon that had worked on each and every part of Adam was recorded. Later this could be used 'by those that had molded him' to provide understanding and help (**See below: Appendix 1.**)

Adam Is Constructed in the Image and Likeness of Adamas

But first and foremost, **Adam** (*and Eve who had been hidden within him by Ennoia, or God's forethought*) was given a mind and heart, or a soul. So Adam became the first man (in this world) with a 'psyche' or soul. Some of the Powers that worked on him were:

Divinity (in concert with other Powers) formed the bones of this first man with a soul.

Goodness (in concert with the other Powers) formed his sinews, tying bones together; in this first man with a soul.

Providence (like the others) formed the structure of his bones; for this man with a soul.

Lordship; being his Christhood and Goodness (from the hidden *Ennoia*) formed the very marrow of the bones of, this first man with a soul.

Fire; the fire of baptism for this fleshly being filled his 'soul' and his entire constitution and, the form of his body.

Understanding and even Envy, created his skin, teeth, nails and hair; in this first man with a soul.

Wisdom Eventually (and in concert with all the authorities, powers, demons and angels) brought together each and every thing of matter, flesh, materials, substance, elements, or 'technical skill' needed to complete Adam. From his bones to his hair too, his body and his soul they brought Adam to life.

Adam is Formed and is Given Knowledge and Experiential Truth (See **Appendix 1 & 2)** after references for the SRevJohn

Eventually the demons and powers (even some that were good) and associates of the *'god'* of this world, finished his creation. Here are a few that worked on Adam:

The first fallen, and dark angel working on him was Eteraphaope-Abron who fashioned, designed, and created Adam's head; then Meniggesstroeth the brain; Asterechmen the right eye; Thaspomocham the left eye… Akioreim the nose; Banen-Ephroum created lips; Amen the teeth… (and) Adaban the neck; *and a myriad of other demons and beings worked to make Adam live…*

(Here see: 'Appendix 1' below for where all the rest are named and who worked to create and complete Adam.) And for the full chapter on creation)…

And others were sent to govern the creation of Adam's perceptions… and (his) senses… imagination and… for the integration of it all… including all his impulses and, impulsive manner)… **(Again see** *Appendix 1 below SRevJohn references)*

Extensive details about these myriads of beings may be found in the Book of Zoroaster. And today in other *extant and searchable books and texts…* **(See Appendix 2 below SRevJohn references)**.

The Salvation of Adam and Eve

Eve (or 'Zoe' with Barbēlō) is called the: '*mother of life* and *a giver of souls*'. She came to assist and toil with Adam. For the Father had secretly, and out of a deep compassion for the two, filled her with divine knowledge and taught her everything filling her up with 'His mind and heart'. Eve, was a woman of the Light; gentle and full of wisdom. For Eve had been given '*Experiential Gnosis*' and thus '*Salvational Knowledge*' and sent to share this with Adam. Even more so, she was taught 'the Way'. **Consider this,** she led Adam into the 'Holy of Holies' in his mind and heart …and to the true temple which is within'. Thus she taught him, how to ascend back to the Father and Paradise above…

Sensing something was wrong, and being alarmed by this, the '*god*' of this cosmos took counsel with his hosts and powers. Before Adam was even fully created they took action to stop Eve. Unfortunately Adam and Eve did not know that they had been made from 'the dust' of this world so that their minds and bodies would react, **automatically against the will of the Father, the Mother**

and the Logos Above. Out of these elements the *'god'* of this world and his host produced Adam (and Eve) in a manner so as to control them. And Yaldabaoth and his demons shackled and fettered them within human bodies made of matter, flesh and bone. Outside of the Garden they were compelled... nearly every second to find food and a place to dwell to survive!

Yaldabaoth and his Host celebrated the fabrication and finishing touches (putting crippling emotions, fears and desires into the mind and body of Adam). This made him less an Image of the Immortal Adamas above'. **Behold** Adam (and Eve) are mortal and outside of the 'Garden' live in the shadow of death every day. And Adam was filled with ungovernable desire and lust; a *'gift'* from the Abyss, from Belial himself!

Yaldabaoth loses spirit

However, Adam would not move until his Mother told the Archangels of light that Yaldabaoth, 'should breath into the face of Adam'. And this breath gave Adam life. Suddenly Adam could move and live. And was strong. But in doing so the Chief Ruler felt a loss of his (own) enlivening 'spirit'. This frightened Him, so, he made up his mind to take back the spirit and power from Adam.

In fact Yaldabaoth and the entire Host watched and interacted with Adam. And, as they did they all became jealous and afraid. For they quickly recognized he was greater, smarter and 'more creative' than they. Adam learned more quickly, rapidly and gained knowledge and made use of it; availing himself of it skillfully! This alarmed and terrified them more.

If there were many more of his kind, how would they survive? So they decided his creation (by Yaldabaoth) had been botched; and that *they* had carelessly given him too much of themselves and and their powers.

So the *'god,'* Yaldabaoth (and his demons) threw Adam 'out' of Eden; out of Paradise! And Adam (and Eve) fell into the lowest part of their worldly aeon and into matter and flesh. *Lo* deeper; into the 'tomb,' and the prison of bodies below!

Paradise, Adam and Eve and, the 'tree of the Knowledge of Good and Evil' and Salvation

But before all of this happened the *'god'* of this world, Yaldabaoth and his fallen powers, angels, daemons and others placed Adam (and, unknowingly Eve) in 'their' earthly paradise. They said to Adam, 'let this Paradise be a setting of bliss, where thou may eat freely and do no work; let it be a delight to thee and a place of repose unto the age'. So they urged him, 'eat, relax, do no work; be idle!' Yet, in this Paradise, was the 'tree of Life' and, the 'tree of the Knowledge of Good and Evil'. And, the fruit on these trees looked delightful and delicious. Yet the '*god*' of this world had created this garden, and he did not tell them the Truth about the 'tree of the Knowledge of Good and Evil'. Yaldabaoth and his Host knew that if they ate from this 'tree of Knowledge' they (Adam and Eve) would know too much; and they would leave him. *For he said it…* 'Of every tree in this garden thou may freely eat **but, of the tree of the knowledge of good and evil, thou shalt not eat of it. For in the day thou eat of it, thalt shalt surely die…**

And in a clairvoyant moment Adam heard this…

> 'For this fruit is bitter and it's beauty a hoax; which is not from above (but *below*) and thus not from the Good *but from the Enemy*; (therefore it is '**Godless**'). Except for the tree of 'the knowledge of Good and Evil'.

Salvation

Then the Logos spoke to Adam, 'the Chief Ruler and his fallen hosts have made a plan for you'. They do not want you to eat from the Knowledge of Good and Evil. And because they gave you a '*false and counterfeit spirit*'; it keeps you afraid and in ignorance.

But Eve watched a very large snake, 'a serpent' eat the fruit… and without harm; and pondered on this. Eve then said to Adam 'because we each have a spark of the spirit of the Father, the Logos showed me we can eat the fruit of that tree'. Then Eve urged Adam, and both ate the fruit. 'For then thou will attain divine knowledge, wisdom, and unity' that leadeth to salvation.

Banished from Eden

So when the '*god*' of this world and his demons found out that they *had* eaten from this tree they banished them from Paradise; ejecting them out. And the '*god*' of this world caused Adam to forget and, he became Amnesic. He forgot his spark of 'the true spirit from the Father within,' and Yaldabaoth fill him up (again) with his '*counterfeit, false spirit*'. But **Behold** …Adam had received Wisdom from the Father's 'spirit'. The Spark of Light from the One, true, Loving God Most High! And this spirit (this light; and His knowledge and power) could not be destroyed nor taken from him. And Adam was reminded of this by his 'Epinoia,' Eve.

Eve told him, 'remember that you are a man with a soul and you have the 'true Father's' spirit within'. For you were modeled after your immortal self, Adamas! *Lo*, Adam, Adamas is modeled after the Father. So remember that you come from Heaven too, and from the Highest Aeon (or Adamas) Above. For only when thou remember this, shall thee find 'the Way'. And turning seek, and seeking find… Heaven and the Great Invisible Spirit, again.

But the Chief Archon caused him to forget all of this. And Adam turned away from wisdom and knowledge and descended onto the earth, to its material, matter, and fleshly desires. So at first, Adam gave himself to it fully for an Age…

The Prophet speaks

For indeed the prophet said it… 'I will make the heart of this man dull, his ears closed, and shut his eyes; lest he see with his eyes, hear with his ears… and understand with his heart and turn, and be healed…'

"But Rabbi,' John said, 'didn't *the Serpent* lead Eve to eat the fruit of that tree?'

The tree of knowledge of Good and Evil

And he said, 'in point of fact John, it was I that *allowed* the Serpent to persuade Eve to eat and then, to offer the fruit to Adam.' For, after eating it they stood under the tree, looked up into the sky and when they looked up… began to understand. For they had begun to think rationally, to seek out 'knowledge,' and especially to know right from wrong.

After gaining knowledge they became unified with the Father. And they understood his purpose for them. For at their deaths they would ascend to Heaven, and to Paradise. However, with this understanding they recognized their nakedness and indecency.

But in Truth, Eve (at first hidden within Adam) hung onto the spark of Sofia's 'spirit, knowledge and wisdom'. So, that after she was removed ('or cut') out of Adam's body, she still brought Him sacred knowledge.

And the *'god'* of this world and his fallen hosts saw that Adam was smarter and more clever than they. And Yaldabaoth hungered to get back from Adam his 'Spirit and Power.' So he tricked Adam. And he put Him into a deep, deep sleep; *a coma of insensibility.*

Then I, John, asked, 'Lord,' 'What is this deep coma of insensible sleep'?

'This,' John, *'is* the cost of eating that fruit and, the price to be paid'. But this insensibility was a blessing (in one way) for, Adam passed out and felt nothing when Yaldabaoth and his hosts cut Eve out of, his flesh. The Chief Ruler also hoped to recover his power and spirit at that time.

Eve, (Zoë) the Woman Without Whom Adam Would Not Have Been Able to Survive

Yaldabaoth sensed Eve was a threatening power so he 'surgically' 'removed Eve' from his side. Yet he took just a little flesh (Adam's rib). And Eve was within it. Then using that flesh, he raised up the woman, Eve or Zoë. And, she stood before them all.

The light-filled Epinoia (or Eve) smiled when Adam awakened and by that smile alone, he was blessed with Wisdom. The scales fell from his eyes, and the veil that had dimmed his mind was pulled off. **Behold,** Adam in a *spiritual ecstasy* could see Heaven above Heaven! …for he was no longer lost, nor in darkness. And with this, Adam 'came to' and the dullness of his mind cleared.

In great joy Adam looked at her and recognized his counterpart and, his beloved companion (his divine twin) and his helpmate, Eve! Joyfully he exulted saying, 'Blissful am I, for I have been set aside to share this life with Eve, a companion who gives me immeasurable joy.' 'For, today I am happy and rejoice'! So he looked up at her and said, '…this… *this is indeed*, 'bone of my bones' and 'flesh of my flesh'. As it is written… 'therefore, shall I leave my Father and Mother, and cleave to my wife. And we shall be one flesh'.

So important was this, that Sofia (innocently) came down 'as Wisdom' to help rectify her mistake. And to fill the deficiency; and regain what she had lost and given wrongly to Yaldabaoth. Therefore, both Sofia (and Eve) are called 'the mother of life'; and Sofia, the 'mother of the living'. And Eve, a 'daughter' of *God.*

For Sofia is a daughter of 'the One' (of Wisdom, and of the Holy Spirit) and comes down to bring (for any who seek it) Divine Salvation; from the Providence and Authority of Heaven and, from *God* Above.

The Eagle Observes

Standing on a branch of the tree of Knowledge of Good and Evil but hidden from sight, perched an Eagle. I am the Providence of His Plan. I, the Anointed have brought down to Humanity, Salvational Knowledge and Truth. For I come from the Pure Light and, from Heaven Above. And as the Epinoia I woke them up and, by the Spirit and Wisdom of the Father, I raised them up. They are no longer ignorant but are 'enlightened'.

But the '*god*' of this world Yaldabaoth, noticed too that something had changed. Adam and Eve withdrew from 'worshipping' him. And their thoughts had turned away from him. Yaldabaoth was infuriated and wished to attack them. So, *he cursed them, cursed the earth, and cursed the woman. He made her weaker than Adam; increasing her dependence upon him, and her need and desire for Him as her husband.* Yaldabaoth made Adam Eve's 'master,' and Adam ruled over her. For Yaldabaoth did not yet know the Father's plan of salvation for the couple.

In spite of this, Adam and Eve were afraid. And they were terrified to renounce and curse Yaldabaoth, the Adversary of the Good. For he was against 'the Way' and anyone leaving him or his aeon. In this moment of fury Yaldabaoth had cast them out of Paradise. Into the night and darkness; and into a world of bitter work and fear and, the daily struggle to survive.

The Rape of Eve

Then the 'blind and foolish *god* and his host' ('the others' who had been watching) saw Eve (the attractive 'Zoë') a young and beautiful woman. But when '*the god*' of this aeon heard her speak, he realized she had a profound knowledge and was like Adam. For, she spoke of a divine salvation and that she had been sent to attain this for them by 'Providence'.

So when Wisdom and the true *'God'*, God Most High saw what was about to happen, Barbēlō sent divine assistants to remove from Eve (her) divine Knowledge, and her true divinity within.

Yaldabaoth and his host, filled with hate and violent lust for Zoë, attacked her. Yaldabaoth raped and defiled Eve (desecrating her flesh). And later, many of the fallen hosts would rape her too. Eve bore them many children… half-angel and demon, half-men and angel' with most evil, but a few that were good.

Eve bore Yaldabaoth two demonic sons:

And so Eve (the flesh of Zoë) bore Yaldabaoth two demonic sons'

Eloim, who was like a bear (whom he maliciously named Cain) was evil, and

Yavai, who was like a lion (whom he dishonestly called Able) and who was 'righteous'

Yavai commands fire and wind, desire and spirits; and

Eloim commands water and earth and the darkness under the earth. And so he called them Cain and Able.

And the '*god*' of this world has deceived humanity (about these 'demons') to this very day. For it was then that the '*god* of this world,' made (*nearly*) everyone crave the flesh. He put lust into everyone by his '*false and counterfeit spirit*'. Even after this incredible violation, Eve still wanted to be a wife to Adam, but also (and equally) had a desire for family, for a husband and its protection through family and a tribe.

So, more and more people were born and the 'demon *god*' Yaldabaoth blew his breath into each. But he did not actually comprehend what he was (really) doing. For his breath contains a spark of the Father's 'spirit'. So, **understand John** all human beings have a spark of the Breath or 'Spirit' of the true God, the Father Above! For with this Knowledge they can re-learn that within them is the 'Great Invisible Spirit, *God*' and that if they seek Him, they can find Him, and become: *sons and daughters of the Perfect Man.*

Further, the '*god*' of this world gave his (and his hosts) and Adam and Eve's progeny, various and different abilities. And with different abilities they utilized their hands and minds and slowly began to gain control over nature and the elements; to plant and to harvest and, to farm animals.

Eloim and Yavai

Yaldabaoth therefore appointed his 'two progeny to be the Mighty Archons and rulers over humanity'. These two mighty Archons (***fallen Archangels*** and '*lesser gods*') were to rule over his earthly aeon; its' principalities and powers and, all of it's nature. And they ruled over humanity who remained ignorant and imprisoned in their tombs of flesh. In this manner, more and more people came to 'worship Yaldabaoth' to satisfy his (the '*god*' of this world's) every need and desire.

Seth and the sons (and daughters) of God, the Holy Mother, Adamas and the Perfect Man

Adam knew Eve again; his helpmate (who was also made in the image of *God*). For Eve is the 'mother of life'. And so with Prophetic knowledge, guidance from the divine and with deep experiential unity with God the Father, Zoë begot her third son, Seth. **Seth was begotten in the image of the Perfect Man** *and so too, was a* '**Son of Man**'. Seth's later descendents included Shem, Abraham and, Jesus the Anointed. For *Lo*, he, Seth is a righteous man and those who follow his teachings are a righteous 'race' (or 'community'); the '*seed* of Seth'. Later, the seed of Seth would become Israelite *and* Christian, for an Age.

Seth, was in fact the image of the first man, Adamas (the Perfect and true Man in Heaven). And he came through the Holy Mother and descended with the Holy Logos, to prepare the aeon of this world for the Anointed…

Seth 'put on' the garment of the divine Autogenes (the self-generated) Christ. And they combined their great power and goodness. Then as the (friend of the) immortal Son of Man, through the divine Shekinah (or Holy Mother)… he descended below the firmament to the aeon of earth. For before the Incarnation of Christ, Seth, and his people had long worked to prepare a place for the descent of *'the Very Word of God,' the Logos and, the Anointed'* (and to bring the full covenant and to all, the '**Book of Life**').

But the Adversary began to see much of humanity was 'losing' interest in him; and, for reasons that were unclear. So, he forced every human being on earth (including the 'seed of Seth') to drink from 'his intoxicating waters of forgetfulness'. And, by use of this great intoxicant they forgot where they came from, and from whom, and who they were (or to where they should return). They forgot that they were, the 'children of Adam and of Seth' and (later) 'Abraham'. Nor could they recall that they were *'the children of the Logos and God'* and that (as they were previously taught through Wisdom, Sofia) that they had the Fathers' Spirit within them. ***His Aeon is their true home!*** And even more so, they are **all** descendents of the One, the true God and the Father of the All. For, their true family and residence is in His Aeon Above Aeons; *not, this World of Darkness and, Death below.*

> Indeed, many of the sons and daughters of Seth had long ago forgotten their beginnings. For it was only when, through the Fathers' Providence that the Anointed Jesus descended from above… that, their 'archetypal' memories (*as the seed of Seth*) returned. Then the Holy Mother raised them up and as the children of Seth and of Christ they rejoiced. For Christ's teachings are also (part of) the eternal '**Book of the Living**,' that led Seth and will lead them too, to '*Divine Salvational Knowledge, Gnosis* and Salvation!

Six Questions that John asks the Savior About life (and the Savior Prophetically answers):

"Jesus answers John the Seer regarding six questions (found here in the SRevJohn). Also, there is a "Discursus" or discussion of this material below the references especially related to questions 1 and 2 (a scribal addition not part of the SRevJohn). All Six Questions are answered here (See:Appendix 2a and b for the SRevJohn.)

Question One

I, John, asked the Savior, 'Please tell me, Lord, will every soul be saved and enter the Light? Do we, when death comes, enter into the Life to Come? Into Paradise? For, Thou, LORD, Thee saith, 'He loves us all (Good and Bad, Right and Wrong) unreservedly! So is this true, or is it not! Do some go to the 'Abyss and others to the Light?'

He answered John and said, "These are common sense questions that arise in everyone's mind. Yet, it is hard to explain, except to the righteous unshakeable, untroubled children of 'the One' (the Righteous One)! They did indeed pass down 'the Way,' for ages and ages into the age; and with these simple Truths: be loving, caring, and give! 'Lo,' and they have done so since the first man was endowed with a soul! These have followed the Unshakeable One, the Truth from Ages upon Ages into the Age (and now follow Me)! Because upon them the Great Invisible Spirit descended, and when that happened they 'turned, and turning found 'Divine Salvational Knowledge' ('Experiential Knowing, or blissful 'Gnosis')!' Becoming perfect and with Knowledge these ancient ones waxed toward kindness, toward loving, giving and caring for all, 'Behold,' even thine enemies!' John (who stared past His Vision and out onto the ocean) said to the Lord, Your angel Lord, Your angel 'Metanoia' frees them all; frees them of evil, anger, jealousy, envy, desire, and greed! For now I and Thy Children look without fear even on the ever-approaching Angel of Death (and Death itself)!

For we have endured all and born everything thrown at us by the World and, the by the World's 'false and counterfeit spirit,' the 'lesser god.' Because of our Sacred (and Secrete) Knowledge, we have lost all of our (previous) rage, envy, jealousy, desire, and craving. No longer filled with anxieties or unfulfilled desires to 'get' or too 'have everything' before we die, we have finished the race! We know! Death is not the end (but) a rebirth into the Life of the Age! (Turner, John., Meyer, Marvin W.; Madeleine Scopello., Robinson, James M. 2007; Davies, Stevan. 2005). (Also see: *Discursus* after SRevJohn references)

Question Two

Then I said to Him, 'Lord, what about the souls that didn't do anything to help people, or to pass on divine salvational knowledge to others; or to improve others' lives (even their own families?); though the Wisdom of the Spirit (the Spirit of Life's power) descended upon them?

He answered and said, "John, sometimes the Virgin Invisible Spirit (and the Holy Mother) descend upon people formerly extremely wicked, very evil, and lacking in all morality. Just their transformation into someone who no longer hurts themselves or others is a big, big change (and for the better)!' This power from outside and above (must generate a soul and mind). And it must descend upon all for, without it, no one can "even be or live." If the good, Spirit of Life increases in them while alive, power (and even Spirit) fills and strengthens their souls and minds. Nothing then can lead them astray or into wickedness. But in those who turn to and let into their minds (and hearts) 'the lesser god of the air,' the evil artificial and counterfeit Spirit, of this World it can lead them into iniquity and Error!" (Turner, John., Meyer, Marvin W.; Madeleine Scopello., Robinson, James M. 2007; Davies, Stevan. 2005). (Also see: *Discursus* after SRevJohn references)

Question Three

Then I asked Him, Lord when the souls leave their dead flesh behind where do they go?

He said, 'if the soul is Holy and the good Spirit has grown, it will be stronger than that which comes at them from the false or counterfeit spirit, and they will flee all ignorance, wickedness, and evil' and enter heaven above.

Question four

'Savior,' I said. 'What of the souls of the people who did not know of (nor ever hear about, nor read about nor were told about) the Father, the Logos, or Wisdom and Divine Salvational Knowledge? Do they have a chance to meet and learn from the people of 'the Way?' Or are they lost?'

And He said, 'everyone in this life, by choice or by rebirth, are given a chance. To seek Salvation, and if they seek it, they can find it!' 'For Look, the righteous in the sight of God follow 'the Way' (by whatever it is called)!' And... they live by trust. And by trusting will find the 'Logos, Wisdom or 'Gnosis' and Salvation!

Question five

Then I asked the Anointed One, 'Lord, can a person re- enter the insides of their mother or become again the seed of their father?'

So, Jesus, understanding this to be the same question Nicodemus had asked said, 'you mean, ...can a grown man be born again?' 'Or can he enter his mother's womb, and know 're-birth'? So the Savior explained... 'Amēn, amēn, I say... except a person be born again or, undergo 're-birth' in spirit (or in the flesh) that person will never know the 'Kingdom of God'. But, he said, 'Blissful art thou John, for asking this!'

But, here is the answer to attaining '*Gnosis*!'

A soul (who seeks to be reborn) must trust in 'the Savior, the 'That Which Is.' Because the Sacred Word, Wisdom (and the Logos) saith the Congregation will find thee another who hath already 'walked that path'... To Gnosis' and too 'Salvation!' Then, follow this mentor who will lead thee there and, 'if thou hath ears to hear and eyes to see, thalt shalt find Salvation!'

Question six

Lord, what happens to the souls of people who achieved transcendence by trusting in You and living 'the Way'. But, (and John said this is horror) even after this, turn back and resume their old, ignorant, and sinful ways and live as they lived before!

And He said to John, 'these lost ones usually do not simply walk away. Yet, if they choose to separate from the Sacred Spirit and this Community, it is their 'free will' and... and by their choice! It is not the 'choice of Heaven. Some (like the fallen angels before them) throw off salvation and choose carnality and evil instead!'

But even more so, some of these turn back and attack those who live by 'divine knowledge and faith'. And attack *'all who believe in any'* expression of sacred knowledge, spirituality, or religion (or any practice of transcendent activities). For, the demons know scripture well and are keen on 'quoting it'… They quote Solomon (to those) pondering a return to a materialistic and fleshly existence. "Solomon saith," 'it is written... there is nothing better for a person under the sun than to eat, drink and be merry...'

for...

'the dead know nothing, neither have they any more a reward; for memory of them is forgotten...'

Personal Doubt

The Lord sayeth, *up to this very day...* 'some are filled up by *Error* and *Malice*, and beareth not a word about (a, or any) *God*... nor will they hear about *any* 'spiritual, religious or transcendent beliefs or practice. It is not personal doubt, they *know* no God or Spirituality or Spiritual practices are real; and, that they are a lie!"

But, personal doubt or an inability to believe is not (in and of itself) ignorance, or a mortal sin. *For it is written... all unrighteousness is sin: and doubt through ignorance is not a sin* and does not *lead to death...* **But, there are ignorant, dark sins that are mortal and deadly... leading to 'death' spiritually, and, ...even worse.** *For, it is written...* the Apostles and, Messengers of 'the One, of the Logos and That Which Is' spoke or wrote about this in scripture. And, outlined *that* which does (and *that* which does not) lead - to the loss of salvation... It is for those who continuously and ignorantly (**and purposely**) commit the unforgiveable sin. *Most just go round and round and are eventually thrown back into the fetter of flesh, to grow...*

Horrific and Murderous Apostates, Gehenna and Hell

But, (because the Lord is merciful) even those who completely disbelieve and push others not to believe,' *even they* **do not** *commit the unforgivable sin!* This preventeth *not* entrance into the the Life to Come (Heaven), for 'such ideas and emotions' are quite common within a life-time... Hell is reserved (and this for an Age; or for a tiny minority... Ages and Ages) to those who commit repetitive horrific torture and murder of innocents... including bad, evil, 'wrong,' imperfect, unethical, immoral, unholy, even cruel people! For they too are made in the image and likeness of *God*! The ultimate denial (the **"true** unforgiveable sin") and the **"true,"** Cursing Of the Holy Spirit is such unjustified vast and monstrous murder and torture! They will *not* be pardoned (for an Age or even Ages upon Ages into the Age); and rarely, a singular individual (who given a chance to change their mind, but will not) - by their choice - goeth - unto destruction! (Thomassen, Einar. 2007).

So I asked Him, 'Lord, where did the *'False Counterfeit Spirit'* come from and with such strength?' And he told me: from the Adversary and Idolatry for, "I am become as a demon apart, who dwelleth in matter and light is not in him, and I am become as a counterfeiting spirit, which is in a material body and light-power is not in it (Mead, George Robert Stow. 2021).

The Chief Archon and Ruler, Yaldabaoth (the Adversary of the Aeon of Earth and Fate.)

The Holy Mother and Father working together as Barbēlō, as: *God, 'the Holy Mother, Wisdom and the Son,'* together (or alone) who are the 'The One Who Is' Their insight, forethought and deep mercy allowed humankind to come into being. **And it is in their plan and it is their will,** *that all be saved!* For He who lifted up the sons and daughters of Seth, of Abraham and Moses, and of Jacob and Jesus, (even *all true* messengers of *'God Above God'*) will, that all be saved!. These, the Father said, are the *true* children of light (and are the assembly, and congregation, of) *'God.'* These are 'the children of the Light,' and the 'Perfect and Unshakeable Race of Seth'!

Adam and Eve's Exaltation

But the *'god'* of this World, the Chief Ruler and Archon, *ha-satan* of this realm realized, Adam and Eve (and *their* children) were superior, smarter, more exalted and clever than he. Or... his host. Shocked, it was a blow so hard that Yaldabaoth could not take it! Jealous and angry and, filled with bloodlust he set out to kill them all! So, he and his followers set a trap. Then when ready, they struck!

The trap and Rape of Sofia

Mindlessly, Yaldabaoth and his fallen hosts and demons *trapped* and *violently raped* Sofia; repeatedly… For they hoped that from these 'unions,' their own half-human children would be compliant and worshipful.

For they want all human beings to believe: 'fate, and their destiny is set'. It is pre-determined and unchangeable. By theirs, or any other being or power. They must accept their lot, for their future is fixed and they are Yaldabaoth's slaves.

So he fettered them in flesh and bound them there, and told them, 'be free; do anything thou wish! So in a 'drugged-*like* and a drunken-*like*' stupor, and in a *'loss of control'* they did! And they were filled up by an insensate hatred, horrible anger and with violent lust; remaining this way in ignorance *and in* 'Yaldabaoth's image and likeness!' (Simon, Bernard. 2017)

Noah and the Arc

Some of humanity were so 'out of control,' so 'destructive, so violent and unpredictable' that, from moment to moment not even the Chief Archon could keep them under his power! So eventually even he, 'the *god'* of *this* aeon came to regret *'his creation'*; 'both of earth and of it's humanity'. Thus he sent a great flood to destroy them all and do away with this failure. Then, he would start it all over again.

But the Spirit of the Most High, the true God warned Noah.

And Noah preached to the children of Seth and, to the sons and daughters of men warning them about, the coming end. But they knew him not nor listened to him; nor even if they did, did not believe him; and, many did not care…

The true 'Arc'

> Answering a question from John, the Savior said to him, 'It was not as Moses said John, 'that, they hid in an ark.' But they hid in a special place, provided by Noah. And not just Noah but by his family and many other people who believed in Noah's prophecy… (earlier followers of 'the Way,' and of *God Most High,*'the One'). For they recognized 'that in Truth the spirit, the law, and the required instructions for living and life *'were written upon their hearts'* and 'listening to their hearts,' these ones followeth Noah. But instead of a sea-going Arc they hid in a sheltered place, a 'luminescent cloud' that preserved and veiled them. This 'sanctuary' obscured them in a protective mist, **concealing them in an 'Arc' of safety…** and in clouds of light (above the waters and the death and destruction below*)!*

But Noah, a prophet of 'the One,' recognized his delegation, his divine Lordship and Leadership. And **Behold,** the Angel of the Lord and 'of the Light' illuminated them. So he countered the Chief Archon, the Adversary and, the *'god'* of this world; who poured out darkness and water over everything and everyone. Death was everywhere…

For the High Archon conspired with the fallen powers, authorities and, unchaste and immoral angels and demons to control or kill them all. And he sent down, the 'Benim Eloim' the 'Watchers,' (the fallen 'hosts' and Grigori) who, watching the women of earth lusted to go in to them. And he sent them down and they raped these women as they raped Eve. And gave birth to a 'new' race of half men and, fallen angel or daemon. Yet (even) a few of these were good, but most were bad… and the good were known as the heroes of old, men of renown. Thus these 'good Nephilim' helped destroy the fallen. For it is written… that, 'god (the *'god'* of this earthly aeon and world) stood in the divine assembly of the Nephilim; and said, 'Ye are '*gods*' even sons of the most high! But *Lo,* they were lesser *gods or archangels;* 'and all 'sons and daughters of Yaldabaoth,' the *'lesser and fallen god'* of this world.

Even so, thou must listen to me, or thalt shalt die like all men, and fall like prince Astaphaios did…

Thus these half men/half daemons failed to repopulate the earth. And when it became clear they could not succeed, Yaldabaoth and his host made a new plan, plotting and scheming.

And *these* fallen angels molded themselves 'despicably, and inhumanly,' into the 'likeness' of the these women's husbands and went 'in to them.' Fooled by this, and believing they were with their mates 'these evil ones' went into these 'wives or women' again and again. And they were filled up (in ignorance) with 'their seed'. So they created many for Yaldabaoth; many more fallen 'humans' who lived and re-populated the world. Yet (unknown to him) most still had a spark of (Sofia's) spirit (procured by each) from the breath of Yaldabaoth…

And to win these women over, the fallen ones, who disguised themselves as their mates, they brought them Gold, Silver, Iron, Presents, and Money. They also brought them Copper, Iron, and other Metals and all kinds of materialistic things including, cosmetics, jewelry and other gifts. They maneuvered these women (and people) astray… by deception and by lies… tricking them into fornication again and again.

So these *sons and daughters of Perdition* took women, (and the women took men) and went into them begetting children of darkness. And such has continued, up to this very Day!

The Providential Hymn of the Anointed

For we know 'the Truth,' the ontological, 'real,' and freely chosen reasons, that determine clearly our perceptions of right and wrong. For **John See,** I became human, and I ('the *Logos*') walked the earth…

So, I, the *Logos* entered into this aeon of darkness, of matter, materialism and of fleshly desires and death. And, 'this I did to *'experientially live as a human being'*. **Behold,** I experienced everything (all that a) human being could do or will ever do or experience (throughout all of the Ages upon the Ages)! And, I know *that* which 'maketh thee up'! I knoweth thy minds and thy souls and, the fetters of, and suffering of the flesh'; *and,* 'knoweth that which would have been otherwise unfathomable'.

Yet for descending into humanity, and giving sacred knowledge and becoming 'One' with thee in unveiling salvation… I was hung on a tree. But after resurrection I went down into *Gehenna* (the Valley of Hinnom; into *Hell*). When I appeared there to Belial and the 'dead,' this caused the cosmos (and the world) to shake; like an earthquake it shook. But as I looked… my face lit up with joy; for, I saw all of the 'Saints and Sinners,' and, all that were locked up. Their flesh and bones debased or decaying, and some were 'worn-out' with the flesh falling (or fallen) off their skeletons. Thine wert in a 'deep, deep sleep'. Upon my arrival most 'awoke'. And those who had never heard it before could choose, sacred knowledge (and even there) and if they wished, receive (at that moment) utter and total '*Gnosis*' gaining knowledge and salvation and exiting that Abyss and straight-away going to Heaven and Repose. And their souls and spirits were released from the Pit, and they entered into Paradise… into the Age upon the Ages to Come. Yet **Look, Behold!** some *even then* chose to stay!

They remain with Belial in the shadowland, some until purified - and even some, into the Ages upon Ages everlastingly and forever! Yet a small number are thrown back into the tomb of flesh.

And I cried out, 'Anyone who heareth Me, Ariseth and get up from thine deep sleep!' And many wept and shed bitter tears. And one saith, 'who is it that calleth out my name and from where, and from whence hath this hope cometh, for all of us, to be released from this, our prison? 'Who giveth hope to us who laith chained here, whose bones have withereth into the dust (to we who were in deep distress and without hope); seemingly unto the Age?'

But, 'I said to them, '**I am** the **Providence**' (**I am the Fathers plan of salvation**). And, I have been sent from Above and by 'He Who Is'; and from the Pure Light. For the Son, the Logos hath been sent through the compassion of the Great Invisible Virgin Spirit (*God*). **For *I am He*, who raiseth you up** (saints and, sinners, good and the bad, prophets and seekers and many, many more); those who seek it now, enter thy true and honored place into the Aeons and the Repose thou deserve!

Raise Thee Up!

Arise, stand thee up! And remember it is to you that I hearkened; and this time, 'follow your Root; *follow the right path to your true Root and, the Source*: 'the One,'. Cometh thou now to the Aeon of Paradise and to the Holy Father, Mother and to the Son! **For I, the Logos am merciful.**

But guard yourself against the Adversary, his fallen angels, and his demons of poverty (*who speak Ignorance and Lies*). Guard against the 'Liar himself, Belial,' '*that being of Chaos*'; and against his deceits and fabrications; and *listen not* to his fallen hosts who would ensnare and, bind you again. Beware of their subterfuge, and neither eat nor drink their food or wine. *Nor listen thee to their dark, and ignorant philosophy!* For accepting such falsities, hypocrisy and darkness can put thee back here; into the Abyss; back into the paddock and Pit, the 'lock down,' his camp in Hades, and into the flesh once again!

So I raised them up   giving them a precious rebirth (in resurrection!) *and I sealed them up in the light and water of the five seals, giving them their 'robes and garments of light,'* and, 'baptised them' through living water and by fire (*Chrism*) and 'enthroned them in Glory,' anointing them and granting them their *Kingship* (or *Queenship*) in Heaven Above Heaven, into the Age…!

The Bridal Chamber

Look, I led them *in the Spirit* to a Vision, So that they could see the Holiest of sacraments; the deepest mystery. It is that which is carried out in the Bridal Chamber (the Holy of Holies). There, the Holy Sacrament of Marriage or Union with 'the One' (monks or nuns singularly with, the Christ; or 'the One' or, with 'God') is accomplished. And it is where human Lovers and Beloveds, in the Bridal Chamber vow in holy matrimony, to be faithful to each other and with *God*, forever enduring into the Age. For I will raise thee up! And I will 'seal thee with the light and Water of the Holy Seals'. So from this moment, thou may step into rebirth and into the abundant life now and, into the Life to Come, even into Paradise unto the Age! *Halleluia!*

For, death will no longer rule thee, nor cause thee terror again; for those who have followed 'the Way,' *or,* 'the One' from this time on will, into the Age and so into the Life to Come, *know* peace. For **See** I, His Son (the *Logos*) ascend for them (and show them 'the Way'). Here, 'is the path to the Perfect Aeon and, to the Holy Father, Holy Mother and to *'Paradise,'*!

For '*in the Spirit*' thalt shall enter Heaven Above heaven, into the Age. For… *Thou hast seen it and I have completed everything; and, 'it is finished'!* And it is accomplished in your sight and within your hearing and, is now lodged in your minds and hearts forever!

The Conclusion of, and the Commission to John to Teach This Secret Revelation to Fellow Spirits and Disciples

trust in Me John, for I have revealed to you the Hidden Mysteries. Write these Revelations down and share these words of Holy Wisdom and Sacred Knowledge that saves. Share it with fellow spirits. But beware! *It is written… 'do not give what is holy to scoffers… for the 'fool' is reckless and, in their heart does not believe.* They say, 'there is no *God*'; and by this justify all types of abomination, murder and wickedness. Calling that which is good bad and, that which is bad, good. Yet even after doing that which is evil in the eyes of *God,* they sleep well… Because, 'the *god*' of this world (and his ignorant *human* Archons) have dulled their minds.

The Savior finished speaking and said to John, 'Guard these scriptures carefully and keep them secure'. 'For John…, cursed is anyone who exchanges this book as a simple gift or, for clothes *or for anything else besides,* the Wisdom and the Salvation to be found in reading it'. *'That person will be cursed'!*

These hidden words came to John while he was *in the spirit* and, in a mystery. But, as the Savior had instructed him John *immediately* wrote them down.

Then he, John went to his fellow disciples and revealed to them these hidden Oracles and this Revelation from the Savior. And they all rejoiced mightily!

Secret Revelation of John (The Apocryphon of John)

Jesus the Christ

Amen!

James Brantingham PhD

4 18 2021

Thousand Oaks, California

References for The Secret Revelation of John 4 28 2021

Armitage, Robinson, Ed. (1920) Irenaeus Bishop of Lyon. The Demonstration of the Apostolic Preaching. The Macmillan Co. New York, NY

Bancell, PA., Nelson, RD. (2008) The GCP Event Experiment: Design, Analytical Methods, Results. Rigorous exploration of GCP data: Correlations, structure, implications. *Journal of Scientific Exploration,* 22(3)309–333

Barbelo or Barbēlō (2019) in: https://en.wikipedia.org/wiki/Barbelo (Accessed 4-19-2019)

Barnstone, William. (1984) The Other Bible. HarperCollins. New York, NY

Barnstone, William. (1984) *1 Enoch* in: The Other Bible. HarperCollins. New York, NY

Barnstone, William., Meyer, Marvin. (2011) The Gnostic Bible: Revised and Expanded 1st ed. Boston, Massachusetts, New Seeds Books.

Barnstone, William., Meyer, Marvin. On the Origin of the World in: (2011) The Gnostic Bible: Revised and Expanded 1st ed. Boston, Massachusetts, New Seeds Books.

Barnstone, William., Meyer, Marvin. (2003) The Hypostasis of the Archons in: The Gnostic Bible: Revised and Expanded 1st ed. Boston, Massachusetts, New Seeds Books.

Barnstone, William. (2003) Three Forms of First Thought in: Barnstone, William., Meyer, Marvin. The Gnostic Bible: Revised and Expanded 1st ed. Boston, Massachusetts, New Seeds Books.

Barnstone, William., Meyer, Marvin. *Baruch* by Justin in: (2011) The Gnostic Bible: Revised and Expanded 1st ed. Boston, Massachusetts, New Seeds Books.

Beauchemin, Gerry. (2018) Hope For All: Ten Reasons God's Love Prevails. Malista Press. Brownsville, Tx.

Beauchemin, Gerry., Reichard, D. Scott. (2007, 2010, 2016) Hope Beyond Hell The Righteous Purpose of God's Judgment (p. 27). Malista Press. Kindle Edition.

Bedard, Moe. (2019.) The Gnostic Warrior. http://gnosticwarrior.com/yaldabaoth.html (Accessed 3 18 2019)

Beischel J, (Ed.) Amenti, Ankhasha., Bray, traci., (2014) Campbell, Dave., Cox, Carrie D., Gerber, Joanne., Justyn, Daria., Marlowe, Nancy., McLean, Sarah., Nash, tracy Lee., Parkinson, troy., Quinlan, Ginger., Rey, Eliza., and Russo, Kim. (2014) From the Mouths of Mediums. Volume 1: Experiencing Communication. The Windbridge Institute, Tucson, Arizona

Beischel J, Boccuzzi M, Biuso M, Rock AJ. (2015) Anomalous information reception by research mediums under blinded conditions II: replication and extension. Explore (NY). 2015 Mar-Apr;11(2):136-42. doi: 10.1016/j.explore.2015.01.001. Epub 2015 Jan 7. PubMed PMID: 25666383.

Beischel, J. (2019) Contemporary methods used in Laboratory-based mediumship research https://www.google.com/search?q=Beischel%2C+J.+Contemporary+methods+used+in+Laboratory-based+mediumship+research&oq=Beischel%2C+J.+Contemporary+methods+used+in+Laboratory-based+mediumship+research&aqs=chrome..69i57.1762j0j8&sourceid=chrome&ie=UTF-8 (Accessed 2 1 2019)

Beischel Julie (2019) Investigating Mediums. Windbridge Institute. Tucson AZ

Bem DJ., Honorton C. (1994) Does Psi exist? Psychol Bull. 1994; (1)115:4-18

Bem D, tressoldi P, Rabeyron T and Duggan M. (2016) Feeling the future: A meta-analysis of 90 experiments on the anomalous anticipation of random future events version 2; referees: 2 approved F1000Research 2016, 4:1188 (doi: 10.12688/f1000research.7177.2)

Betty, Stafford. (2011) The Afterlife Unveiled: What the Dead are Telling Us About Their World. O-Books John Hunt Pub. Ltd. Alresford, Hants UK.

Betty, Stafford. (2014) Heaven and Hell Unveiled. Updates from the World of Spirit. White Crow Books. Guildford, UK.

Betty, Stafford. (2016) When Did You Ever Become Less by Dying? Afterlife : The Evidence. Whitecrow books. Hove, UK.

Bosch, H., Steinkamp, F., Boller, E. (2005) Examining psychokinesis: The interaction of human intention with random number generators—a meta-analysis. Psychological Bulletin, 132, 497–523.

Bösch H, Steinkamp F, Boller E. Examining psychokinesis: the interaction of human intention with random number generators--a meta-analysis. Psychol Bull. 2006 Jul;132(4):497-523. PubMed PMID: 16822162.

Brantingham, James. (2017) The Gospel of Philip. A New translation. Amazon Digital Services LLC. Seattle, WA. Paperback and Kindle. ASIN: B06XY2J951

Brantingham, James. (2019) Truth... What Is Truth. Holy Wisdom and the Logos of God. The Four Lost Apocryphal Christian Gospels: The Gospel of Truth. The Gospel of Philip. The Gospel of Thomas & The Gospel of Mary With the Secret Revelation of John. Pub. Amazon Digital Services LLC. Kindle. ASIN: B08R7Z8KXD

Bauckham, Richard. (2006) Jesus and the Eyewitnesses: The Gospels as Eyewitness Testimony. Eerdmans Publishing, Grand Rapids, MI 2006

Burgess, Stanley M. (1989). The Holy Spirit: Eastern Christian traditions. Peabody, Mass.: Hendrickson Publishers.

Caruana, Laurence. (2015) The Gnostic Q Glossary of Gnostic Terms. Available at: http://www.gnosticq.com/az.text/glos.af.html (Accessed 3 18 2015)

Chilton, Bruce. (2002) in Rabbi Jesus (Rabbi Jesus: An Intimate Biography). Publisher Double Day a Division of Random House, New York, NY

Christ... the Wisdom of *God* (1 Corinthians 1:24); Christ Jesus... who became... the Wisdom from God, ... (1 Corinthians 1:30)

Davidson, Gustav. (1967). A dictionary of angels: including the fallen angels. The Free Press Simon and Schuster. New York, NY

Davies, Stevan. (2005) The Secret Book of John. The Gnostic Gospel Annotated & Explained. Skylight Paths Publishing. Woodstock, Vermont

Davidson, Sean. (2019) Aleteia. https://aleteia.org/2017/07/22/why-mary-magdalene-can-help-us-receive-communion-with-greater-love/) Accessed 7 29 2019.

> Note: in Luke 7:36-50 the woman who 'lived a sinful life' anointed Jesus feet... anointing him before his crucifixion. So, it should be remembered that, along with this woman being a sinner (in this verse) so it is the same for us all! Paul says in Romans 3:23 'for all have sinned and fall short of the glory of *God*'! All, everyone... and this verse in Luke no longer need be associated with prostitution; as Mary Magdalene is an Apostle and there is no evidence she was a prostitute... (Holy See Press Office 10 June 2016)

> Luke 7:36-50: 36 When one of the Pharisees invited Jesus to have dinner with him, he went to the Pharisee's house and reclined at the table. 37 A woman in that town who lived a sinful life learned that Jesus was eating at the Pharisee's house, so she came there with an alabaster jar of perfume. 38 As she stood behind him at his feet weeping, she began to wet his feet with her tears. Then she wiped them with her hair, kissed them and poured perfume on them. (NIV)

DeConick, April D. (2017) The Gnostic New Age: How a countercultural spirituality revolutionized religion from antiquity to today. Columbia University Press. New York, NY

Delorme A, Beischel J, Michel L., et al. (2013) Boccuzzi M, Radin D, Mills PJ. Electrocortical activity associated with subjective communication with the deceased. Front Psychol. 2013 Nov 20;4:834. doi: 10.3389/fpsyg.2013.00834. eCollection 2013.

PubMed PMID: 24312063; PubMed Central PMCID: PMC3834343.

Thomassen, Einar. (2007) The tripartite tractate in: Meyer, Marvin. The Nag Hammadi Scriptures. HarperCollins 10 East 53rd St., NY, New York 2007

Ecclesiasticus 1:1; 9-10 Sofia (Our daughter) is (a hypostasis of) Wisdom, is from the true *God*, and hath been always with him, and is before all time. ...*God* created her in the Holy Spirit, and saw her, and numbered her and measured her. And he poured her out upon all his works, and upon all flesh according to his gift: and hath given her to them that love him.

Dawkins, R. (1986). The Blind Watchmaker. New York: W. W. Norton & Company.

Dawkins, R. (2006). The God Delusion. Bantam Books. New York, NY

Encyclopædia Britannica, Inc. (2021). Valentinus Gnostic Philosopher. Britannica Online". britannica.com. https://www.britannica.com/biography/Valentinus Corporate Site. (Accessed 27 January 2021)

Encyclopædia Britannica, Inc. (2021). Basalides Syrian Philosopher.. Britannica Online". britannica.com. https://www.britannica.com/biography/Basilides

Freke, Tim., Gandy, Peter. (2008) The Hermetica: The Lost Wisdom of the Pharaohs. Tim Freke Publications. Kindle Edition.

Gieseler, Johann Karl Ludwig. (1818) Historical = critical experiment about the Genesis and the earliest fates the written gospels, Leipzig 1818. Entire text is found at: http://www.traditionshypothese.de/texte/gieseler.html (Accessed 18 10 2018) See: *Addendum 1: 'Yaldabaoth and yaldā bahuth'*

Genesis 1:2 (2018) And the earth was without shape or form (italics - mine) and void, and darkness was upon the face of the deep, and the Spirit of God moved upon the face of the waters. The Blue Letter Bible (from: the Septuagint). (Accessed 9 18 2018) https://www.blueletterbible.org/lxx/gen/1/1/t_corr_1002

Gnostic Society Library, The. (2015). The Nag Hammadi Library and the extensive resources for The Secret Book of John. Available at http://gnosis.org/naghamm/nhl.html and/or http://gnosis.org/naghamm/nhlsbj.htm Accessed 2/7 2015...

Gnostic Society Library, The. (2019). Brons, David. Valentinian Theology in: The Nag Hammadi Library. Available at http://gnosis.org/naghamm/nhl.html (Accessed 1/23/2019)

Hanson, John Wesley. (1899) Universalism the Prevailing Doctrine of the Christian Church During Its First Five Hundred Years . Universalist Publishing House. Kindle Edition.

Harris, Sam. (2004) The End of Faith: Religion, Terror, and the Future of Reason. Norton. New York, NY

Hart, David B. (2017) The New Testament. A translation. Yale University Press. London, UK.

Hart, David B. (2019). That All Shall Be Saved: Heaven, Hell, and Universal Salvation. University Press. New Haven and London

Hoeller, Stephan A. (1998 and 2010). Ecclesia Gnostica A Gnostic Catechism. Publisher: The Gnostic Society Press, Los Angeles, California. http://gnosis.org/ecclesia/catechism.htm (Accessed 5-5-2015)

Hoeller, Stephan A. (2002.) Gnosticism: New Light on the Ancient tradition of Inner Knowing. Publisher: Quest Books Wheaton, IL.

Honorton C., Ferrari DC. (1989) Future telling : a meta-analysis of forced-choice precognition experiments 1935-1987. Journal of Parapsychology. Vol 53; 1989: 281-308

'In …the beginning…' (as found in Genesis 1:1 ('God'); John 1:1 ('the Logos') Proverbs 8:22 ('Wisdom'). The Apostle Paul says in 2 Cor. 4:18 'While we look *not* at the things which are seen, but at the things which are not seen: *for the things* which are *seen are temporal*; but *the things* which are *not seen* are eternal. In this regard 'we, humanity' did *not* see (*eternal*) 'Sofia' or 'Wisdom' when She 'helped: (*from before the earth existed… in laying or bringing forth… the depths of the ocean and separating dry land from the seas; in making the clouds that bring rain from the sky; in building up hills and mountains; in creating the fields; in preparing the Heavens (or Aeons) and in setting up habitable lands and Kings and governments and so on…* (Italics mine taken from Proverbs 8:1-31)

> In fact the 'Logos' throughout Johannine literature connects the Christian understanding of Jesus to the philosophical idea of the Logos and the Hebrew Wisdom literature. They also set the stage for the later development of trinitarian theology early in the post-biblical era.

'In the Origin was the Logos…' (also: Genesis 1:1; see Hart David. 2007 The New Testament above)

Joe, Jimmy. Dark Mirrors of Heaven. https://www.darkmirrors.org/ (Accessed 10 10 2018)

Jenkins, Philip. (2008) The lost history of Christianity. The thousand-year golden age of the church in the Middle East, Africa, and Asia--and how it died. Publisher HarperOne. New York, NY.

Jenkins, Philip. (2015). The many faces of Christ. The Thousand - Year story and influence of the Lost Gospels. Publisher Basic Books. New York, NY

Kasser, Rodolphe., Meyer, Marvin., Wurst, Gregor. Eds., (2008) Francois Gaudard. The Gospel of Judas. 2nd Ed. Published by National Geographic, Washington, DC

Keble, John (1872). The Five Books of St. Irenaeus Bishop of Lyon. Against Heresies. On the Detection and Overthrow of the So-Called Gnosis. With the fragments that remain of his other works. James Parker and Co. Oxford, London

Kelly, Edward F., Williams Kelly, Emily., Crabtree, Adam., et al. (2007.) Irreducible Mind: Toward a Psychology for the 21st Century. Publishers; Rowman & Littlefield. Lanham, Maryland.

Kelly, Edward F., Crabtree, Adam., Marshall, Paul., Eds. (2015.) Beyond Physicalism: Toward Reconciliation of Science and Spirituality. Publishers Rowman & Littlefield. Lanham, Maryland.

Kelly, Edward F. (2015) Toward A Worldview Grounded In Science And Spirituality in: Kelly, Edward F., Crabtree, Adam., Marshall, Paul., Eds. Beyond Physicalism: Toward Reconciliation of Science and Spirituality. Publishers Rowman & Littlefield. Lanham, Maryland.

Keener, Craig S. Miracles. (2011) The credibility of the New Testament accounts Volumes 1 & 2. Baker Publishing Group. Grand Rapids, MI 2011

King, Karen. (2006) The Secret Revelation of John. Harvard University Press. Cambridge, Massachusetts

Krippler, Stanley., Rock, Adam J., Beischel, Julie., Friedman, Harris L., Fracas, Cheryl L. (Eds). (2013) Advances in Parapsychological Research 9. McFarland & Company, Inc. Pubs. Jefferson, NC and London.

Layton, Bentley, (1987) The Gnostic Scriptures. A New translation with Annotations and Introductions. Publisher Doubleday & Company. Inc. Garden City, New York.

> In the Sethian school, for example, the Demiurge is a hostile demonic force who creates the material world in order to trap the spiritual elements.

Leloup, Jean-Yves. (2002) The Gospel of Mary. Rochester, Vermont: Inner traditions.

Levinson, John R. (2002) The Spirit in First Century Judaism. Brill Academic Publishers Inc. Boston.

Lossky,Vladimir. (1991) The Mystical Theology of the Eastern Church, by Vladimir Lossky, Cambridge UK James Clarke & Co Ltd.

Lumpkin, Joseph. (2011) The Books of Enoch: The Angels, Watchers and the Nephilim. Fifth estate Publishers Blountsville, Al.

Mashour GA, Frank L, Batthyany A, Kolanowski AM, (2019) Nahm M, Schulman-Green D, Greyson B, Pakhomov S, Karlawish J, Shah RC. Paradoxical lucidity: A potential paradigm shift for the neurobiology and treatment of severe dementias. Alzheimers Dement. 2019 Jun 19.

Matlock, James G. (2019) Bibliography of Reincarnation Resources Online. http://deanradin.com/evidence/Matlock%202012.pdf Accessed 4 22 2019

Maier MA, Dechamps MC, Pflitsch M. (2018) Intentional Observer Effects on Quantum Randomness: A Bayesian Analysis Reveals Evidence Against Micro-Psychokinesis. Front Psychol. 2018 Mar 21;9:379. doi: 10.3389/fpsyg.2018.00379. (see commentary

Marshall, Paul. (2015) Mystical Experiences as Windows on Reality in: Kelly, Edward F., Crabtree, Adam., Marshall, Paul., Eds. Beyond Physicalism: Toward Reconciliation of Science and Spirituality. Publishers Rowman & Littlefield. Lanham, Maryland.

Mead, G. R. S. (1921) Pistis Sophia. A Gnostic Gospel. A Gnostic Miscellany: Being for the most part extracts from the Books of the Savior, to which are added excerpts from a Cognate literature; (English). JM Watkins London. Kindle Edition.

Mead, George Robert Stow. (2021). Fragments of a Faith Forgotten: A Contribution to the Study of the Origins of Christianity in, The Gnostic Society Library. gnosis.org (Accessed 2021) Theosophical Publishing Society: London (1900; 1906).

Meyer, Marvin (2003) The Secret Book of John in: Barnstone, William., Meyer, Marvin. The Gnostic Bible: Revised and Expanded 1st ed. Boston, Massachusetts, New Seeds Books.

Meyer, Marvin W. The Holy Book of the Great Invisible Spirit or The Egyptian *in:* Meyer, Marvin W. The Gnostic Gospels of Jesus: The Definitive Collection of Mystical Gospels and Secret Books about Jesus of Nazareth HarperOne. Kindle Edition.

Meyer, Marvin. (2005) The Gnostic Gospels of Jesus: The definitive collection of mystical gospels and secret books about Jesus of Nazareth. Publisher HarperOne, New York, NY

Meyer, Marvin. (2007). On the Origin of the World *in:* The Nag Hammadi Scriptures. HarperCollins 10 East 53rd St., NY, New York 2007

Meyer, Marvin W. (2007) Dialogue of the Savior *in:* The Gnostic Gospels of Jesus: The Definitive Collection of Mystical Gospels and Secret Books about Jesus of Nazareth. Publisher HarperOne, New York, NY

Meyer, Marvin. Ed., Turner, John D. (2007). The Gnostic Gospel of the Egyptians also called: The Holy Book of the Great Invisible Spirit *in:* The Nag Hammadi Scriptures. HarperCollins 10 East 53rd St., NY, New York 2007

Meyer, Marvin., Scopello, Madeleine. (2007). Eugnostos the Blessed in: The Nag Hammadi Scriptures. HarperCollins 10 East 53rd St., NY, New York 2007

Meyer, Marvin W.; Madeleine Scopello., Robinson, James M. (2007) Dialogue of the Savior *in:* The Nag Hammadi Scriptures: The Revised and Updated translation of Sacred Gnostic Texts Complete in One Volume (p. 303). HarperCollins. Kindle Edition.

Meyer, Marvin W., Poirier, Paul-Hubert. (2007) Thunder, Perfect Mind in: The Nag Hammadi Scriptures. HarperCollins 10 East 53rd St., NY, New York 2007

Meyer, Marvin W.; Robinson, James M. (2007) The Nag Hammadi Scriptures: The Revised and Updated translation of Sacred Gnostic Texts Complete in One Volume. HarperCollins. 10 East 53rd St., NY, New York 2007

Meyer, Marvin. (2007). The Nature of the Rulers in: The Nag Hammadi Scriptures. HarperCollins 10 East 53rd St., NY, New York 2007

Meyer, Marvin., Madeleine, Scopello. Eugnostos the Blessed in: The Nag Hammadi Scriptures. HarperCollins 10 East 53rd St., NY, New York 2007

Meyer, Marvin W.; Robinson, James M. (2007). The Nag Hammadi Scriptures: The Revised and Updated translation of Sacred Gnostic Texts Complete in One Volume (p. 473). HarperCollins. Kindle Edition.

Meyer, Marvin; Robinson, James M. (2007). The Second Discourse of Great Seth *in:* The Nag Hammadi Scriptures. HarperCollins 10 East 53rd St., NY, New York 2007

Meyer, Marvin; Robinson, James M. The Gospel of Judas *in:* The Nag Hammadi Scriptures. HarperCollins 10 East 53rd St., NY, New York 2007

Meyer, Marvin W.; Robinson, James M.. The Nag Hammadi Scriptures: The Revised and Updated translation of Sacred Gnostic Texts Complete in One Volume (p. 523). HarperCollins. Kindle Edition.

Meyer, Stephen C. (2009) Signature in the Cell: DNA and the Evidence for Intelligent Design. HarperCollins Braun, Seattle WA.

Meyer, Stephen C. (2014) Darwin's Doubt. The Explosive Origin of Animal Life and the Case for Intelligent Design. HarperCollins Braun, Seattle WA. 2014

Moore, Edward. (2018) Gnosticism. Internet Encyclopedia of Philosophy. St. Elias School of Orthodox Theology. (Accessed 11 13 2018) https://www.iep.utm.edu/gnostic/

Mossbridge J, tressoldi P, Utts J. (2012) Predictive physiological anticipation preceding seemingly unpredictable stimuli: a meta-analysis. Front Psychol. 2012 Oct 17;3:390. doi: 10.3389/fpsyg.2012.00390. eCollection 2012. PubMed PMID:23109927; PubMed Central PMCID: PMC3478568.

Mossbridge JA, tressoldi P, Utts J., (2014) Ives JA, Radin D, Jonas WB. (2014) Predicting the unpredictable: critical analysis and practical implications of predictive anticipatory activity. Front Hum Neurosci. 2014 Mar 25;8:146. doi:10.3389/fnhum.2014.00146. eCollection 2014. Review. PubMed PMID: 24723870; PubMed Central PMCID: PMC3971164.

Nelson R, Bancel P. (2011) Effects of mass consciousness: changes in random data during global events. *Explore* (NY). 2011 Nov-Dec;7(6):373-83. doi: 10.1016/j.explore.2011.08.003. PubMed PMID: 22051562.

Ninan, MM. (2018) Adam and Eve Outside of Eden. Lulu.com Normal, Ill.

Pagels Elaine. (1992) The Gnostic Paul: Gnostic Exegesis of the Pauline Letters. Published by Continuum International Publishing Group. New York, NY

Pagels, Elaine. (1973) Johannine Gospel in Gnostic Exegesis: Heracleon's Commentary on John. Abingdon Press, 1973. Nashville, TN

Pagels, Elaine. (1979) The Gnostic Gospels. Random House, New York, NY

Panné, Jean-Louis., Paczkowski, Andrzej., Bartosek, Karel., Margolin, Jean-Louis., Werth, Nicolas., Courtois, Stéphane., Kramer, Mark. (Editor, translator), Murphy, Jonathan (translator). (1999) The Black Book of Communism: Crimes, Terror, Repression. Harvard University Press. Cambridge, Mass.

Pearson, Birger A. Melchizedek in: The Nag Hammadi Scriptures. HarperCollins 10 East 53rd St., NY, New York 2007

Peel, Malcolm L., Zandee, Jan. (2019) The Teachings of Silvanus. *in:* The Gnostic Society Library. http://gnosis.org/naghamm/trimorph.html (Accessed 1/22/2019)

Pétrement, Simone. (1984). A Separate God. The Christian Origins and Teachings of Gnosticism. HarperCollins, Scranton, Pennsylvania

Plank, Max. (2019) Brainy Quotes: https://www.brainyquote.com/quotes/max*planck*211839 (Accessed 7 25 2019.)

Plantinga, Alvin. (2018) 'Evolution, Shibboleths, and Philosophers'. The Chronicle of Higher Education. April 11, 2010. Accessed 9-25-2018

Proverbs 8:1-36 see especially 22; 23 and note 8:12;14; KJV; also: Proverbs 8:22-23 Jewish Publication Society; the Tanakh 1917

Quispel, Gilles (2008). Van Oort, Johannes, ed. Gnostica, Judaica, Catholica: Collected Essays of Gilles Quispel. Leiden: Koninklijke Brill NV.

Radin, Dean. (1997) The Conscious Universe: The Scientific Truth of Psychic Phenomena. HarperCollins Pub. New York, NY.

Radin, Dean I. (2004) Electrodermal Presentiments of Future Emotions. Journal of Scientific Exploration. 18 (2) pp. 253–273,

Radin D, Nelson R, Dobyns Y, Houtkooper J. Reexamining psychokinesis: (2006) comment on Bösch, Steinkamp, and Boller. Psychol Bull. 2006 Jul;132(4):529-32; discussion 533-7. PubMed PMID: 16822164.

Radin, Dean I. (2006) Psychophysiological Evidence of Possible

Retrocausal Effects in Humans In: D. Sheehan (ed)., Frontiers of Time: Retrocausation Experiment and Theory. American Institutes of Physics.

Radin, D. I., Borges, A. (2009) Intuition through time: What does the seer see? *Explore*. 5(4) 200–211.

Radin, Dean. (2013) Supernormal: Science, Yoga, and the Evidence for Extraordinary Psychic Abilities. Crown Publishing House a division of Random House. New York, NY

Radin, Dean. (2018) Real Magic. Crown Publishing House a division of Random House. New York, NY.

> ††† In Radin's above 1997; and 2018 book he cites Utts and the evidence for psi (and see Radin 2019)… to send or receive thoughts from another person (or 'Telepathy,') and perceiving people, objects, locations, or physical events via super-natural 'second sight' now called 'Remote Viewing' or 'Clairvoyance'; and an intuitive feeling about the future, especially one of foreboding (a 'Presentiment' which is also a form of 'precognition'), Implicit precognition (or the ability to perceive future events, also a type of precognition but all called anciently 'Prophecy'); and moving things by the mind such as Influencing changes in random number generators (RNGs) or a form of Psychokinesis (or Telekinesis). And this will be a difficult time for 'scientists' who (by nature and not by observation and testing) will never accept 'a God of the Gaps' or 'a super-natural (or as Radin calls it a 'supernormal') explanation of the Gaps'. For these scientists believe in nothing, deny everything (especially God Most High; or the 'the One'); or that 'life' has any meaning or purpose (they practice 'Scientism run amok')!
>
> ††Professor Jessica Utts is chair of the statistics department at the University of California at Irvine. In 2016, she was also president of the American Statistical Association (ASA), the world's largest community of professional statisticians.

Patricia Utts said... about Radin's, Bem's and others Paranormal or Parapsychological research:

'For many years I have worked with researchers doing very careful work in parapsychology, including a year that I spent full-time working on a classified project for the United States government, to see if we could use these abilities for intelligence gathering during the Cold War... At the end of that project I wrote a report for Congress, stating what I still think is true. The data in support of precognition and possibly other related phenomena are quite strong statistically, and would be widely accepted if it pertained to something more mundane. Yet, most scientists reject the possible reality of these abilities without ever looking at data! And on the other extreme, there are true believers who base their beliefs solely on anecdotes and personal experience. I have asked the debunkers if there is any amount of data that would convince them, and they generally have responded by saying, "probably not." I ask them what original research they have read, and they mostly admit that they haven't read any. Now there is a definition of pseudo-science—basing conclusions on belief, rather than data!

†† (continued) Dean Radin states: ...the overall evidence for **psi** is provided by classes of experiments that have exceeded the six-sigma threshold. This refers to studies where the overall odds against chance, after careful consideration of all known experiments investigating the same topic, are assessed to be over a billion to one...

†† (Continued) these powers or paranormal abilities studied are:

Each of these experiments used protocols that avoided all known design flaws... Telepathy, Remote Viewing (or clairvoyance), Presentiment (a form of precognition), Implicit precognition, (Influencing) Random number generators (RNGs) a form of Psychokinesis, and a 'Global Consciousness Project,'(assessing (see Radin, Dean 2018)

††(Continued). In sum, when considering the Statistician Utts's statements to the world's statisticians, the six classes of experimental protocols that exceed combined odds against chance of 1 billion to 1, and two other protocols headed in that direction, there is no need for further proof-oriented scientific evidence. Debates will persist over ways to best explain and interpret these data, but the existential question—that some forms of psi exist—is for all practical purposes settled (Radin, Dean. (1997, 2013; 2019)††

Radin, Dean. (2019) Selected Psi Research Publications

http://deanradin.com/evidence/evidence.htm Accessed 2 1 2019

(Seth) Genesis 4:25; 5:4–5

Schneemelcher, Wilhelm., Wilson, Robert McLachlan., Hennecke, Edgar. Eds. (1991) New Testament Apocrypha I: Writings relating to the Apostles; Apocalypses and Related Subjects. Westminster John Knox Press. Louisville, KY. 1991

Schneemelcher, Wilhelm., Wilson, Robert McLachlan., Hennecke, Edgar. Eds. (2003) New Testament Apocrypha II: Writings relating to the Apostles; Apocalypses and Related Subjects. Westminster John Knox Press. Louisville, KY. 2003

Schaberg, Jane. (1990.) The Illegitimacy of Jesus: A Feminist Theological Interpretation of the Infancy Narratives. Continuum Int. Press

Schaberg, Jane. (2002.) The Resurrection of Mary Magdalene. Legends, Apocrypha, and the Christian Testament. Publisher Continuum Int. New York, NY

Schaff, Philip., Ed. (2016) The Complete Ante-Nicene, Nicene and Post-Nicene Collection of Early Church Fathers: Cross-Linked to the Bible. Toronto, Canada. Kindle

Schwartz, Gary E. (2011). The Sacred Promise. Atria Books Division of Simon and Schuster. New York, NY.

Schwartz GE. (2010) Possible application of silicon photomultiplier technology to detect the presence of spirit and intention: three proof-of-concept experiments. Explore (NY). 2010;6(3):166-171. doi:10.1016/j.explore.2010.02.003

Simon, Bernard. (2004) The Essence of the Gnostics. Arcturus Publishing Limited 26/27 Bickels Yard, 151–153 Bermondsey Street, London SE1 3HA Copyright © 2017 Kindle Edition.

Smith, Andrew Philip. (2009) A dictionary of Gnosticism. Quest books. Wheaton, IL.

Summit Publications (2019) Mysteries of the Divine Names: YHVH Tzevaot ("Lord of hosts") (Part 4.) https://www.summitlighthouse.org/names-of-god-series-kabbalah/ Accessed 3 19 2019.

Stapp, Henry P. (2015) A Quantum-Mechanical Theory of the Mind/Brain Connection in: Kelly, Edward F., Crabtree, Adam., Marshall, Paul., Eds. (2015.) Beyond Physicalism: Toward Reconciliation of Science and Spirituality. Publishers Rowman & Littlefield. Lanham, Maryland.

Steinkamp F., Milton J., Morris RI. A Meta-analysis of forced-choice experiments comparing Clairvoyance and Precognition. The *Journal of Parapsychology* Vol. 62, September 1998 (pp 198-218)

Samuel. 2 Sam. 22:2: The LORD is my rock, my fortress and my deliverer; my God is my rock, in whom I take refuge, my shield and the horn of my salvation

(NIV). David praised God as his Rock in the scriptures as a 'royal thanksgiving song' and as his last song as cited above.

Stevenson, I. (2006). Half a career with the paranormal. Journal of Scientific Exploration, 20, 13–21.

Stevenson, I., & Haraldsson, E. (2003). The similarity of features of reincarnation type cases over many years: A third study. Journal of Scientific Exploration, 17, 283–289.

Stevenson, I., & Keil, H. H. J. (2005). Children of Myanmar who behave like Japanese soldiers: A possible third element in personality. Journal of Scientific Exploration, 19, 172-183.

Stevenson, I., & Samaratne, G. (1988). Three new cases of the reincarnation type in Sri Lanka with written records made before verification. Journal of Scientific Exploration, 2, 217-238.

Storm L, tressoldi PE, Utts J. Testing the Storm et al. (2010) meta-analysis using Bayesian and frequentist approaches: reply to Rouder et al. (2013). Psychol Bull. 2013 Jan;139(1):248-254. doi: 10.1037/a0029506. PubMed PMID: 23294093.

Storm L, tressoldi PE, Di Risio L. (2010) Meta-analysis of free-response studies, 1992-2008: assessing the noise reduction model in parapsychology. Psychol Bull. 2010 Jul;136(4):471-85. doi: 10.1037/a0019457. Erratum in: Psychol Bull. 2010 Sep;136(5):893. Psychol Bull. 2015 Mar;141(2):403. PubMed PMID: 20565164.

Storm L, tressoldi PE, Utts J. (2013) Testing the Storm et al. (2010) meta-analysis using Bayesian and frequentist approaches: reply to Rouder et al. (2013). Psychol Bull. 2013 Jan;139(1):248-254. doi: 10.1037/a0029506. PubMed PMID: 23294093.

Thomassen, Einar. (2007) The tripartite tractate in: Meyer, Marvin. The Nag Hammadi Scriptures. HarperCollins 10 East 53rd St., NY, New York 2007

Theophilus of Antioch. Theophilus to Autolycus Book 1. Early Christian Writings. (Accessed 1 11 2019) http://www.earlychristianwritings.com/text/theophilus-book1.html

tressoldi PE., Massaccesi S., Maartinelli M., Cappato S. Mental Connection at Distance: Useful for Solving Difficult Tasks? Psychology. 2011. Vol. 2. No. 8. 853-858. SciRess

Tucker JB. The Case of James Leininger: (2016) An American Case of the Reincarnation Type. Explore (NY). 2016 May-Jun;12(3):200-7. doi:10.1016/j.explore.2016.02.003. Epub 2016 Mar 2. PubMed PMID: 27079216.

Turner, John D. Three Steles of Seth *in:* The Nag Hammadi Scriptures. HarperCollins 10 East 53rd St., NY, New York 2007

Turner, John D. Zostrianos *in:* The Nag Hammadi Scriptures. HarperCollins 10 East 53rd St., NY, New York 2007

Turner, John D. (2001), Sethian Gnosticism and the Platonic tradition (The History of the Sethian Movement, Sethian Gnosticism and the Platonic tradition.) Presses Université Laval, Paris.

Turner, John D. (2016) trimorphic Protennoia; the Book of Thomas in: The Gnostic Society Library. http://gnosis.org/naghamm/trimorph.html (Accessed 2/17/2016)

Turner, John D. (2016) trimorphic Protennoia *in:* The Gnostic Society Library. http://gnosis.org/naghamm/trimorph.html (Accessed 2/17/2016)

Turner, John D. (2016) Zostrianos in:he Gnostic Society Library. http://gnosis.org/naghamm/trimorph.html (Accessed 2/17/2016)

Turner, John D. (2016) Marsanes in:he Gnostic Society Library. http://gnosis.org/naghamm/trimorph.html (Accessed 2/17/2016)

Turner, John D. (2016) Interpretation of Knowledge in:he Gnostic Society Library. http://gnosis.org/naghamm/trimorph.html (Accessed 2/17/2016)

Turner, John D. (2016) Allogenes in:he Gnostic Society Library. http://gnosis.org/naghamm/trimorph.html (Accessed 2/17/2016)

Van der Toorn, K. (1992). Anat-Yahu, Some Other Deities, and the Jews of Elephantine. Numen, 39(1), 80-101. doi:10.2307/3270076

Waldstein M., Wisse FW. The Apocryphon of John. (1995). In Robinson, JM., Klimkeit HJ. Eds. The Nag Hammadi and Manichaen Studies. EJ Brill. Leiden, The Netherlands.

Waldstein M., Wisse FW., Robinson, JM., Klimkeit HJ. Eds. (1995.) The Apocryphon of John Nag Hammadi Codices 11,1; 111,1; and IV,1 with BG 8502,2 in: The Nag Hammadi and Manichaen Studies. EJ Brill. Leiden, The Netherlands.

Waldstein M., Wisse, FW., In Robinson, JM. (2000). The Apocryphon of John. In Robinson, James M. Ed. The Coptic Gnostic Library. A Complete Edition of the Nag Hammadi Codices. Vol. 2. Koninklijke Brill NV, Leiden, The Netherlands

Waldstein, Michael., Wisse, Frederik. Ed. Owens, Lance. Gnostic Society Library, The. (2018). The Secret Book of John - The Secret Revelation of John (The Short Version) from the: Berlin Codex (BG 8502, 2) & Nag Hammadi Codex III, 1 in: The Nag Hammadi Library. Available at http://gnosis.org/naghamm/nhl.html Accessed 7 18 2018 The Nag Hammadi Library

Waldstein, Michael., Wisse, Frederik. Ed. Owens, Lance. Gnostic Society Library, The. (2018). The Secret Book of John - The Secret Revelation of John (The Long Version: Nag Hammadi Codex II, 1 & Nag Hammadi Codex IV, 1) from the: Berlin Codex (8502,2) & Nag Hammadi Codex III, 1 in: The Nag Hammadi Library. Available at http://gnosis.org/naghamm/nhl.html Accessed 7 18 2018 The Nag Hammadi Library

Wisdom of Solomon 7:25-27 For she is the breath of the power of God... and a pure influence flowing from the glory of the Almighty: therefore can no defiled thing fall into her. 26 For she is the brightness of the everlasting light, the unspotted mirror of the power of God, and the image of his goodness. 27 And being but one, she can do all things: and remaining in herself, she maketh all things new: and in all ages entering into holy souls, she maketh them friends of God, and prophets. (KJV)

Wisdom *is* 'Sofía' (Σοφία) in Greek. Often spelled 'Sofia' in English scripture.

The 'Holy Spirit' as studied through the Christian theology of 'Pneumatology' can refer to the *inspiration* of prophets, and the *indwelling* of the Holy trinity (which in itself covers many different aspects... *including Wisdom*- italic mine). See: Burgess, Stanley M. (1989) above.

Wisse, Frederik. Gnostic Society Library, The. (2018).The Secret Book of John - The Secret Revelation of John in: The Nag Hammadi Library. Available at http://gnosis.org/naghamm/nhl.html (Accessed 7 18 2018)

Appendix 1

Here: '*Adam is Formed* and is Given Knowledge and Experiential Truth'.

Eventually the demons and powers (even some that were good) and all the fallen and associates of the '*god*' of this world worked to finish the creation of his limbs and body:

Adam is Formed

The first ones Eteraphaope-Abron fashioned, designed, and created Adam's head; Meniggesstroeth the brain; Asterechmen the right eye; Thaspomocham the left eye; Yeronumos created the right ear; Bissoum the left ear; Akioreim the nose; Banen-Ephroum created the lips; Amen the teeth; Ibikan the molars; Basiliademe the tonsils; Achcha the uvula; Adaban created the neck; Chaaman created the vertebrae; Dearcho the throat; Tebar (produced) the right shoulder and Ararim the left; Mniarchon produced the elbow; Abitrion the right underarm; Evanthen the left; Krys the right hand; Beluai (made) the left hand; treneu the fingers of the right hand; Balbel fashioned the fingers; Kriman the nails; Astrops made the right breast; Barroph the left; Baoura created the right shoulder joint; Ararim the left shoulder joint; Areche made the belly; Phthave the navel; Senaphim produced the abdomen; Arachethopi the right ribs; Zabedo created ribs; Barias the right hip; Phnouth the left hip; Abenlenarchei produced the marrow; Chnoumeninorin the bones; Gesole created the stomach; Agromauma made the heart; Bano the lungs; Sostrapal the liver; Anesimalar formed the spleen; Thopithro the intestines; Biblo created the kidneys; Roeror designed and created the sinews; Taphreo created the spine; Ipouspoboba the veins; Bineborin formed the arteries; Aatoimebpsephei made muscles to move the limbs; Entholleia created all the flesh; Bedouk formed the buttock; Arabeei the penis; Eilo the testicles; Sorma fashioned the genitals; Gorma-Kaiochlabar made the right thigh; Nebrith the left; Pserem designed and made the kidneys on the right; Asaklas the left kidney; Ormaoth (created) the right leg; Emenun left; Knyx produced the right shin-bone; Tupelon the left; Achiel fashioned the right knee; Phneme the left; Phiouthrom formed the right foot; Boabel its toes; trachoun created the left foot; Phikna its toes; Miamai designed and fashioned the nails of the feet; Labernioum of the hands (*After*: Waldstein M., Wisse FW., Robinson, JM., Klimkeit HJ. Eds. 1995.)

And seven appointed to supervise all of these beings:

Thoth,

Hermes,

Galila,

Yabel,

Sabaoth,

Cain

Able

And those appointed to enliven and drive the limbs and many other muscles were these:

For the head was Diolimodraza, the muscles that were enlivened and moved the neck were created by Yammeax; the right shoulder Yakoubib; the left Verton; moving the right hand was Oudidi; the left one Arbao, and the fingers of the right hand were moved by Lampno; the fingers of the left hand Leekaphar; of the right breast Barbar; the left breast Imae and of the chest Pisandraptes. Moving the muscles of the right shoulder joint was Koade, and of the left Odeor. Of the right ribs was Asphixix, and the left ribs Synogchouta; but of the belly Aroup. For the womb Sabalo, and for the right thigh Charcharb; but the left thigh Chthaon, and including all the genitals was Bathinoth; while those of the right leg Choux, and of the left leg Charcha. And for the shin muscles of the right leg Aroer, and of the left shin-bone Toechtha. But for the right knee Aol; the left Charaner. And for the right foot Bastan and its toes Archentechtha; the left foot Marephnounth and its toes Abrana.

Seven reign over all of those above:

Michael, Uriel (Oroiael, or Oriel) Asmenedas, Saphasatoel, Aarmouriam, Richram, Amiorps Three hundred and sixty-five demons and angels worked together to create the 'first psychic man' (Adam); the first with a soul.

And they kept at it until his entire frame, body, and psyche (his 'nascent soul was attached') and finished.

And those who are rule over the senses, Archendekta. And another rules over perceptions, Deitharbathas. And in control and, the creator of the imagination, Oummaa. And the one that allows assent, Aachiaram. And the one over letting free impulse, Riaramnacho.

And the source of these daemons established throughout the entire body is fixed at four: heat, cold, wetness and dryness. And the mother of them all is matter: (materialism and the flesh). The one who regulates heat is, Phloxpha. And the one who regulates cold is, Oroorrothos. The one who regulates what is dry is, Erimacho. And the one who regulates wetness is, Athuro. The mother of them all is, Onorthochrasaei who is boundless for, she stands in their midst and mixes with them all. And truly, she is matter, material and substance… Lo, and the informational, self-organizing content by which she nourishes them (these four daemons below):

Ephememphi causes the quest for pleasure. Yoko invokes desire. Nenentophni increases grief. Blaomen increases fear. The mother of them all is Esthensis-Ouch-Epiptoe. These passions fill the body and mind and come out of these four daemons. For from grief (comes) envy; jealousy, suffering; from trouble, pain and, from a lack of consideration, heartlessness, anxiety, mourning, and more. For many, too much pleasure comes from doing wickedness, and being 'puffed-up' with empty boasting and similar things. From desire (comes) anger, wrath, bitterness, bitter yearning, insatiable greed and similar things. From dread (comes) horror, panic, undeserved flattery, anguish and shame. These resemble virtues and vice. But genuine insight into another's true character comes from Anaro, who is the head of the material soul which dwells with the seven senses or Esthensis-Ouch-Epiptoe. And this is the number of all the angels: altogether they are 365. They labored on Adam it until, part by part, the psychic and material body was completed. Now others whom I have not mentioned to you rule over the rest.

Then God noted Yaldabaoth's finished creation of Adam's psychic body. And that a soul was attached to a man (and to him, 'Eve,'). And to the first man with a soul, Barbelo (the 'Mother and Father') secretly sent Eve as Adams' Epinoia to guide him; and to help Adam to develop 'insight, reflection, and intuition'. So in the end, both had not only a rational mind but also a heart: and therefore with a 'mind and heart' both had souls. And Adam and Eve came to understand that within each of them, was a spark of The Father's 'spirit'; and therefore behold, they were children of One Most High! (After: Waldstein M., Wisse FW., Robinson,

JM., Klimkeit HJ. Eds. 1995.)

If you want to know more about them, it is written in the Book of Zoroaster; yet many details about these daemons (or demons) and entities are found in literature to hand (and is extant now) and accessible in, a 'Dictionary of Gnosticism' or in 'Gnostic Q' (see below.)

Appendix 2

Here: Extant books with extensive details about myriads of beings

Extensive details about these myriads of beings may be found outlined in the Book of Zoroaster. But accessible and extant texts today that can be obtained (in paper and online) and that are searchable; and that cover information about all of these powers, angels, beings and the hundreds and hundreds of fallen daemons, angels and related others mentioned, and cited above. And for many their specific roles and definitions in the design, fashioning and creation of Adam's body in the 'Sethian and Gnostic theology or revelations' described in this and a number of sources see these books or texts; 'living texts,' sources such as (Waldstein M., Wisse FW., Robinson, JM., Klimkeit HJ. Eds. 1995) *And especially see*: **AP Smith's 2009 Dictionary of Gnosticism** and Laurence Caruana's '2015' 'the Gnostic Q') .

Addendum 1: 'Yaldabaoth and yaldā bahuth'

It is a possibility that Gieseler (1818) chose (by 'intuition' or in some limited way, even by 'precognition' the term *'yaldā bahuth'* (see: Dean Radian, 2019 above) for, the name of the demiurge especially the, 'Son of Chaos'. Because (not known in 1818, this later 'term' is confirmed by the associations of Yaldabaoth (the 'craftsman; the demigod, or demiurge) found in the nearly 52 early Christian and Gnostic texts from the Upper Egyptian town of Nag Hammadi in 1945. And in fact a few finds... even a hundred years before the 'Nag Hammadi Library' included the *Secret Revelation* (or *Apocryphon*) *of John*. But this *SRevJohn* also gave a similar reading to Yaldabaoth as... 'a son, or 'the, or, an angel or a Aeon' including the term and the word (for the son of) 'Chaos' or, the son, 'in Chaos'. He is so named and similarly inscribed in the:*The Holy Book of the Great Invisible Spirit,* where as Nebrouel (See Marvin Meyer's 'The Gnostic Gospels of Jesus' 2005) and in*The Gospel of Judas* also described as 'Nebro' (a recognized variant of 'Nebrouel') both terms meaning one (or a 'son') of 'Chaos'. Meyers' notes, that DeConick and Turner even suggest that *Judas* (in this, the recently restored Gospel of Judas) *may* (and I paraphrase the statement) 'exceed all of those... who sacrifice to, and do evil ...the *greatest evil).* For the 'god' of this world in the Gospel of Judas is (a) diety ...a *'lower or lesser god'* for the other eleven apostles; **and is named a 'son of Chaos'.**

And Yaldabaoth is 'the Chief Creator of Chaos' *in: On the Origin of the World (Barnstone and Meyer 2003).* Yaldabaoth 'pursues Chaos' *in:* the *Hypostasis of the Archons* (Barnstone and Meyer 2003). And Yaldabaoth in the text *'Pistis Sofia' (or Faith and Wisdom)' is* ***'Chaos,'*** and the very place where they dwell is 'created by

Yaldabaoth' and is 'part and parcel' of this world; Chaos being the 'very Cosmology, and their Ground of Being' for Sofia and all the rest in this realm. He is the cause of '…the Great Chaos' which is the 'intermediate world' or 'outside the outer' a hazy and confusing environment of the 'lost' (not entering heaven upon death) throughout this entire text and world. **Yaldabaoth is the head Demon who controls all '49 demons' in Hell and, those who act on earth**; certainly a 'demon of Chaos' (Mead 1899). Hoeller (2010) also notes 'Yaldabaoth' is commonly called the 'child of chaos,' and in later times (by the 'Gnostics' in France, the Cathars) he was transfigured as simply 'the demiurge, the demigod, the 'craftsman' but in their literature identified with **(and is)** *Lucifer or Satan, the prince of the powers of the air (the 'demiurge or the 'god,' of the Old Testament.)*

Moe Bedard (2019) *makes an extended argument that the name 'Yaldabaoth' is derived from:* 'yal'db,' 'meaning a boy or man who has is surrounded by a bright yellow or glaring color *(as in 'a golden glow' or by 'luminescence' around the boy or man)* and states essentially, that this is one direction from where the name for Yaldabaoth may be derived… *Further Bedard seems to posit that …hence, Yaldabaoth…* was… the first-born Gnostic who rebelled against *God* (or would appear or come to be 'the fallen angel'; (a nod toward the 'devil or satan'.) But Bedard also brings up that the name Yaldabaoth attached to the 'Sabbaoth of hosts' a well known form of as the 'Lord of Hosts' or "Lord YHWH of Hosts" ('hosts' here being defined as 'Armies').

Yet a Kabbalistic-*like* site appears to posit that the name 'Yaldabaoth' (see: Summit Publications 2019) comes from some form or modification of **YHVH Tzevaot** ('**Lord of hosts**') as a name for '*God*'. And in English *'Tzevaot'* is written 'Sabaoth'. These biblical sources slightly altered can give: *YH TZevaot* (or names close to: Yaltabaoth) and easily 'tease out from that name Yaldabaoth (or similar). Possibly using a term such as '*YH Tzevaot* or *Yahtzevaot* - or any - both by early non-Christian Gnostics or Gnostic-Jews as a way to 'pronounce the name of Yaldabaoth' without saying the full Holy name of 'YHVH' (or YHWE). And instead they used 'YH or Yah' (acceptably spoken for 'Yahweh' (just as they used the euphemisms 'Adonai or HaShem'… for *God*). Sometimes following it ('YH or Yah') with the spoken word 'Tzevaot of Sabaoth'. In late antiquity Layton (1987) writes that in the 'Sethian school,' the Demiurge (Yaldabaoth) *was* the hostile demon or 'demonic force' who had created the material world *to trap* the 'spiritual elements.' And Barnstone writes… 'the Great Angel Eleleth called out, '…where did this 'chaos' come from… the underworld?' '…Suddenly there appeared the **great demon** who rules over the lowest part of the underworld *and chaos…***he is called Sakla, Samael, and Yaldabaoth'** '…who stole power away from 'innocent Sofia or Wisdom' (Barnstone 2003). But ultimately the name Yaldabaoth remains a mystery. However these are a few of the many reasons I decoded to Keep Gieseler's (1818) term (in spite of other scholars discounting it) 'yaldā bahuth' too mean, the 'Son of Chaos'.

Postlude A & B - Purification or Correction

David Hart (2017) notes that of the two dominant rabbinical schools of Christ's time, Shammai and Hillel, both spoke about a place (after death) of purification correction (or very rarely punishment) for the few unrepentant in the face of Hell **yet, each to be of a limited period And this was reserved for the intractably heinous, vile and evil (or who do evil).** For, some of them (a very small number) they believed, would suffer an eternal or final shame, remorse, suffering, and ruin. Shammai grimly suggested a third of humanity would suffer this fate. But Hillel (whom many compare to Jesus) is quoted as saying…, 'That which is hateful to you, do not do to your fellow. That is the whole Torah; the rest is the explanation; go and learn' Hillel believed the power of God's mercy greater. For Shammai, Gehenna was a place with a refiner's fire for the soul (like refining gold) and for neither just the incorrigibly wicked nor blamelessly good, but those subjected to this 'refining fire' would ultimately ascend up to paradise.

Hillel saw Gehenna as a place of final punishment and even annihilation (body and soul) for the utterly depraved, but thought their number extremely small. Hillel it appears, believed no one suffered in the Gehenna for more than about or around twelve months (though, what would modern Jewish theologians think today about Hitler and Stalin)? Yet this was an idea espoused by the famous Rabbi Akiva, a generation after Christ. However we really don't know what Jesus believed regarding these well-known views of Jews in late antiquity about Gehenna (or Hell). But, he certainly spoke metaphorically or allegorically about it and many other things using such language as ovens (to burn up weeds or waste). He said, *as it is written…* 'Wherefore, if God so clothe the grass of the field, which today is, and tomorrow is cast into the oven, shall he not much more clothe you, O ye of little faith? Or harvests, *as it is written…* 'Therefore saith he unto them, The harvest truly is great, but the laborers are few: pray ye therefore the Lord of the harvest, that he would send forth laborers into his harvest… or threshing floors and so on. Jesus seemed to believe that his listeners would understood what was meant by this particular allegory or metaphor. Clearly, then it seems unlikely he would have always meant that His discussion of 'Hell' (*After*) be taken in a literal sense (David Hart 2017).

Discursus: Modern Gnosticism, Christianity and World Religions Today

Granted, "the many religions, religious and spiritual practices" are unquestionably better understood (and defined) today (in this ecumenical age). But with all due respect, at this earliest period in Christianity, we are not speaking about (and with no disrespect meant) "Christian-Hindusim." More than ever before, today the "commonalities" between the world's "Religions" are demonstrated by research (Greyson, Bruce. 2021). Highly trained Scientific Researchers using the scientific method have been carrying out and doing superlative experiments on "paranormal, parapsychological, near-death and related 'Psi or 'ESP' powers and abilities" (Beischel, Julie. 2019; Radin, Dean 1997; 2013; 2014; 2017; 2018; 2019; Schwartz, Gary E. 2007 ; 2011; 2011; 2019).

And, there is now a substantial body of evidence from this

research; research that has been repeated and corroborated, gives robust support to the "reality of some religious or spiritual commonalities." Such research appears to outweigh the Dissimilarities. But, at this time though there are some variations between the world's religious ideas and practices that seem irreconcilable… Yet, less than that which is irreconcilable between such sciences as Relativistic (Newtonian-Einsteinian 'or big') and Quantum (or Subatomic, Quantum mechanical, 'or Small') physics! Am I making a claim that "science has proved the existence of God?" No, it has not. Am I making a claim that "science has proven beyond one hundred percent doubt that the existence of some Paranormal, Para- psychological, ESP or Psi realities are real? No. But research into these areas using the methodology of science has demonstrated great statistical significance for many of these experiments - and stronger statistically significant (and numerical) evidence than science has, for many areas which it takes for granted are supported by evidence (Utts J. 1996; Mossbridge JA, tressoldi P, Utts J., et al 2014)! One such area is 'metaverses.' Many physicists and other scientists appear to believe' metaverses' (millions and millions or billions and billions of universes have been demonstrated to exist). In fact there is no direct evidence, not even that a one systematic re- view of a falsifiable hypothesis or (any) hypothesis has been falsified (or confirmed)!' Belief in Metaverses is not justified nor should they be used to explain anything related to physics or a kind of "evolution" of our own Universe (See Appendix 1 after the references for Truth. What Is Truth?)

Psi and Paranormal Research

No statistically significant hypothesized evidence supports more than one Universe at this time. There is no demonstration of controlled or non-controlled hypotheses falsified or confirmed for the existence of more than one Universe. Data completed and published in peer-review journals have failed to "prove" "a quantum field existed before the Big Bang. The Beginning or Big Bang created Physics (Relativity or 'big' physics and Quantum Mechanical or 'small' Physics). A Quantum field did not exist before the Big Bang created Physics! So it is simply a "wish-fulfillment" by some scientists that another "Universe" existed before this Universe existed! Of which there is no "evidence." They hypothesize that a Quantum field, Quantum fluctuation, and Quantum inflation caused the beginning of the Big Bang and created the Universe. Wanting this to be true does not make it true! Positing a Supreme Being or Entity (or Consciousness) causing this Universe fits Occam's razor better than asserting it is the 'Goldilocks Universe' simply a product of chance found with- in "billions and billions and billions of Universes!

The "Universe" hereafter (in this book) will mean: "Creation, the Entirety, the All in All, and the World, this earthly Cosmos, and aeon,' and space, above and below the Heavens, the firmaments, all realms, and all existence and infinity) will be expressed using the words, "the Vast Array of the Divine Fullness and the Universe."

On the other hand, the research of Drs. Dean Radin, Gary Schwartz, or Bruce Greyson (and many other scientists) working in Paranormal or Psi fields has gathered a large body of significant evidence about such phenomena. Much evidence and data on Near-Death Experiences (NDE's, Out of Body Experiences (OBE's), Telepathy (Reading or Communicating with another's Mind), Precognition (Prophecy), Communication with hypothesized "Deceased" (after their death or with them in, the Life to Come) and so on is supported. These researchers have amassed many repetitive, statistically significant, numerically large, and meaningful amounts of actual evidence. They have collected data on commonly report- ed "supernatural, paranormal or parapsychological abilities." "Abilities" found in Spiritual texts or Spiritual Practices. It is acceptable that some happen, or have happened" (and do) exist! Dr. Schwartz's scientific papers (impinge directly upon Gnostics beliefs) and are freely available at Pubmed (down- loaded in 2019). His book will surprise anyone interested in Gnosticism! See, The Sacred Promise publicly available through Atria books. And get and read Professor Schwarz's three papers in Pubmed. (Schwartz, Gary E. 2011; 2011; 2019; Radin, Dean 2013; 2018; 2019; Kelly, Edward F., Williams Kelly, Emily., Crabtree, Adam., et al. 2015; Greyson, Bruce., Edward F. 2007; Greyson, Bruce 2021; Schwartz, Gary E., Woollacott Marjorie H., eds. 2019).

Discursus, psi and sources

SRevJohn. References for "The Discursus " (a modern scribal addition - added here at the end to the SRevJohn for clarity). See below for comprehensive references used by the "Discursus": (Stapp, Henry P. 2015; Radin, Dean 1997; 2013; 2014; 2017; 2018; 2019; Brown, Thomas P. 2014, Bem, D., et al. 1994; 2016; Mossbridge JA, tressoldi P, Utts J., et al. 2014; Mossbridge JA, Radin D. 2018; Beischel J, Julie., et al. 2007; 2013; 2014; 2015; 2015; 2019, 2020; Betty, Stafford. 2011; 2014; 2016; Storm, Lance., et al. 2010; 2010 and 2013; tressoldi P. et al. 2011; Honorton, Charles. et al., 1989; Kelly, Edward F. et al. 2007; 2015; Stapp, Henry P. 2015; Delorme A, Beischel J, Michel L., et al. 2013; Stevenson, Ian., et al. 1998; 1989; 1990; 1993; 2000; 2000; 2003; 2005; 2006; Tucker JB. 2005; 2016 Tuck- er, James. 2006; 2014; Matlock, James G.2019; Schwartz, Gary E. 2002; 2006; 2011; 2011; 2017; 2019; Sarraf M, Woodley Of Menie MA, tressoldi P. 2020; Krippler, Stanley., Rock, Adam J., Beischel, Julie., et al. 2013; Keener, Craig S. Miracles. 2011; Hart, David. 2017; 2019; Mashour GA, Frank L, Batthyany A, Kolanowski AM., et al., 2019; Meyer, Stephen C. 2009; 2014; Waldstein M., Wisse FW., Robinson, JM., Klimkeit HJ. Eds. 1995; 2018; Waldstein, Michael., Wisse, Frederik. Ed. Owens, Lance. In, Gnostic Society Library, The. 2018; 2018; Davies, Stevan. 2005; King, Karen. 2006;

Barnstone, William., Meyer, Marvin. 2003; 2009; 2011; Gnostic Society Library, The. 2015; Thomassen, Einar. 2007; Assante, Julia. 2012.)

The true Reality

Jesus answered, 'those to whom the Great Invisible Spirit, mysteriously descends and who accept His help, but do not help others will, in any case be transformed and (at least) leave most of their ignorant and evil ways behind and cause less suffering to others.

But the Father Above allowed the 'god' of this world to create earth and many of the people in its aeon. The Father permitted it, and so... by the 'to and fro, the up and down, the sweep and swing and a very unlikely, likelihood 'the world,' which is actually made up of wavering oscillations, slackened and settled. These rippling infinitesimal specks and motes collapsed and resolved (when we looked at 'them') into the recognizable, everyday non-living and liv- ing objects of this world. The entities we perceive, such as people, animals, structures and objects we can't see, even a tiny insect (and the air we breath). They are, 'that which is' or, existence itself!

Consider! This 'generation' (like others before it) is ultimately responsible for what is or, why there is something rather than nothing which includes this earthly aeon and everything else within (and without) it! This process of quavering and undulating bits and motes folding and crumpling into intelligible structures... 'or that which is,' allows the existence of life, essentiality and 'being' itself. And, without these 'invisible processes of nature' neither this aeon nor, this world would exist!

The Universe in Its Totality (including many who suffer on the aeon of earth) is Good...

Clearly 'outward existence, being, and reality' seem to appear solid and substantial, actual and tangible but in fact: 'more real,' then what is the actual true reality underneath that normal human senses (usually) cannot detect. So, the Apostle

Thomas comments: Jesus says,

I incarnated into flesh and blood, and stood up a man and, the Messiah, for all! But I found every- one, everywhere intoxicated, and distracted by material things and flesh and, by the sensations and thrills found here below; in this world. None, no, not one thirsted for divine knowledge and salvation. My soul exceedingly grieved for them all; and I wept... For they are the sons and daughters, the children of God! But I could see in their eyes that, their minds and souls were blind. For... they do not understand that they come empty here; with most unable to see 'the Way'. But when they 'come too' and 'sober up,' those who turn can, turning see (or listening, hear) and, be saved.(Brantingham, James. 2019 GThom)

Jesus says,

If a body comes into existence to serve 'spirit,' that is' astonishing. Yet if 'spirit' comes into being be- cause of the body, that is an even greater wonder! The wonder of wonders! But I am amazed. For how did ' noumena,' 'spirit,' become one with matter and flesh; making its home in such poverty?" (Brantingham, James. 2019 GThom)

John 14:2-7 My Father's house has many rooms. If that were not true, would I have told you that I'm going to prepare a place for you? If I go to prepare a place for you, I will come again. Then I will bring you into my presence so that you will be where I am. You know the way to the place where I am going. Thomas said to him, Lord, we don't know where you're going. So how can we know the way? Jesus answered him, I am the way, the Truth, and the life. No one goes to the Father except through me. If you have known me, you will also know my Father. From now on you know him through me and have seen him in me. (GW)

The outward world is what we choose to see, evaluate and judge!

The outward world of the tree, rock, person or table beside you is the 'articulation, the token or epiphenomenon' of that which is the 'true reality' hidden beneath... but, though 'this world' seems the bona fide and genuine one, yet 'it...' is an illusion. For Behold, it is the unseen, improbable, seemingly crazy, unbelievable and even impossible... (which 'Scientists' now know) makes up the 'real, and true reality behind all existence'. And it is 'that' which makes up matter and flesh, the solid, tangible and seemingly 'concrete substance,' of all that we see, touch, feel, hear and interact with. Thus... the veridical basis of reality seems 'incomprehensible, baffling, and irrational'.

Many of these Natural Philosophers cannot believe 'God' (or 'any god') or even a 'godless cosmos' could create such an ersatz universe. A world that is a phantasm... made up of illusory phenomena and phenomenal appearance that simulates 'another world' but, not the 'world as it really is (in itself'.) And that the real world or noumena (the perceivable and perceptible world is simply that, which is taken ac- count of)... How could a 'world' be brought into being this way... Such an... outrageous, bizarre, crazy, demented, and an insane-like place... How could this phenomenal world not be 'the source behind' the hidden cosmos, universe and the All and All'?

But this sacred knowledge has 'always' been known' (anciently by mystics) but providently unknown and unexplainable until now, (by science) to the masses. Yet this will be commonly known (in that specious age to come)... So, that which was known by a tiny few (through the spirit) from the beginning (will be known to many later, through science). And then too only by a tiny number of mystics and scientists for generations. It is the recognition of 'that which has been known since the beginning of history' by many undergoing theosis and, becoming one with God' or, with 'the One'. And much, much later by some Natural Philosophers, by, perceiving the underlying 'veridical matrix' of reality. These few saw the Truth and 'the true reality' from the beginning. As it is written... 'All matter originates and exists only by virtue of a force... We must assume behind this force the existence of a conscious and intelligent Mind. This 'Mind is the matrix of all matter' (... Quotes 2019).'

Whatever the case is, it suggests that the Logos, the One, or the source and sustainer of all life, God approves of this hidden 'reality '. And this includes the small, singular cosmos of Yaldabaoth, where that ignorant 'god,' and Chief Archon oversees great human suffering (but, also despite everything he does to stop it... great human joy and happiness. For, as it is written... As Above So Below (or... 'on earth as it is in heaven'). Thus even this 'cosmos' below is like-too the Greater Universe of 'God'. Since the 'One true God,' the Father is Good (the Universe is good too) there- fore (overall) the Universe is, in its totality (including the fallen aeon of earth) 'part of that' which is Good... !

For it is not just 'if we lacked a 'mind or consciousness,' we would not nor could not, live, move or even be able to stand'; but even more so that (without a mind or consciousness) this world and cosmos (itself) would not exist. Lo, not even the aeon of earth, nor its people and things; not even Yaldabaoth would exist!

Yet, if in those who have souls, seek and find Spirit; and if through the Holy Spirit (and not the 'Counterfeit Spirit') they have been strengthened through Sacred Knowledge and 'Gnosis' then upon death they will ascend to Heaven.

For it is written...'Let one who knows seek and find and rejoice'... For those who choose it can find their way back to the divine, and Sacred Salvational Knowledge (even union) with, the Father. Thus, nothing will ever lead them back to that place of ignorance, wickedness, terrible and... deadly blindness again. Therefore they will ascend! And are done with this aeon! Attaining 'Gnosis,' they will enter Heaven and, the Life to Come. Freed from the perpetual turn of the wheel their soul and spirit will forever be free! For, they have entered salvation and rest unto the Age.

This Section deals with "Science and God or Spirit and/or Spiritual Observance or Practice" *and has been placed below* the references and can be skipped over if one is not interested or so desires (**See Appendix A**)

'Grand Unified Theory' (of Quantum and Relativistic Physics) or Also see: Edward Close's "Mathematical Unity of Space, Time, Mass, Energy & Consciousness," and related Science (After Appendix A see below Appendix A on Barbēlō and Consorts)

A brilliant writer, Philo's ideas (from two thousand years ago) echo recent scientific, peer-reviewed and published mathematical studies in physics by Vernon Neppe and Edward Close. Their research gives evidence that 'Reality' isn't just Space, Time and Energy *but* may be better or best described as: 'Space, Time and Consciousness' (2012; 2015; 2015.) Theses studies by Vernon Neppe, MD, PhD and Edward Close PhD have ultimately resulted in (the Physicist and Mathematician) Edward Close publishing his "Grand Unified Theory" or *'Mathematical Unity of Space, Time, Mass, Energy & Consciousness' (2020).* Edward Close and Vernon Neppe a Mathematician and Physicist with a Psychiatrist and Neuroscientist specializing in Consciousness make a strong argument that the reason the Standard Model of Physics cannot explain certain fundamental findings nor produce or generate falsifiable hypotheses is because, it does not accept Consciousness exists independent (or outside) of the brain. Thus most scientists 'model' rules out such things as 'Super-conciousness'. And yet Bruce Greyson MD, PhD, after fifty years of research, notes that there is no better explanation for why Reality is, at bottom, Consciousness. "Consciousness does exist independently of the brain, Dr. Greyson notes. For nothing else makes sense of the data he has seen in the great body of research he has undertaken in paranormal science (2021).

Mathematician and Physicist Edward Close's "Mathematical Unity of Space, Time, Mass, Energy & Consciousness," or a 'Grand Unified Theory' (of Quantum and Relativistic Physics)' explains the 'Source' of gravitation, electromagnetism, the weak interaction, strong interaction and all known physical forces (such as 'Space, Time, Energy and Mass') because, it includes as his development of a unique outcome measure, the 'calculus of distinctions.' The 'calculus of distinctions' as an outcome measure can be (and has been) mathematically assessed. Dr. Close has utilized the 'calculus of distinctions' (and other measurements such as 'trUE Units' and more - see below) to find the missing 'key' (or 'key force,') that allowed him to succeed in unifying Relativity and Quantum Physics. This 'key' is *'consciousness'*.

Max Planck (a co-discoverer of Quantum Physics) said over one hundred years ago… "All matter originates and exists only by virtue of a force... We must assume behind this force the existence of a conscious and intelligent Mind. This Mind is the matrix of all matter."

Planck also said, "We have no right to assume that any physical laws exist, or if they have existed up until now, that they will continue to exist in a similar manner in the future" (Max Planck 2021)

Neppe and Close state that in this infinite reality, there is a way to measure 'information meaningfully utilized.' Close calls this a 'Quantum (or *Qualit*) of consciousness.' A 'Qualit of information,' of our 'finite reality' (is a 'Quantum-like,' or, smallest part of the information meaningfully utilized that makes up and sustains reality.) But it is not of Space, Time and Energy but of Space, Time and *Consciousness!* Only this succeeds in offering a 'Grand Unified Theory.' A core understanding about this is that: 'infinite reality' is unending and contains all information and is therefore, the very definition of, 'a higher or supreme and thus aware consciousness.'

If the *'existence of information'* in the Universe *and* outside of the Brain is questioned then think about this (and try to answer it)! Did humanity 'create' mathematics or create the 'fine-tuning' of the Cosmological and Physical constants: or the 'Laws of Nature,' *that holds the Universe together?* Or do they exist apart from the "mind of humanity?"

My own *peccadillo* in this argument (since I received a Bachelors of Music and remained a musician as well as a scientist) is, 'did humanity create music,' or did it discover it? Again: Did humanity "create these the laws of nature" *and* the "vibrations of various materials that cause the sounds we label 'music,' that we associate with composers, or did they discover them?" This question applies to whatever you listen to... Bach, Mozart, or Stevie Wonder!' The information needed (the 'tools or musical instruments to make these sounds) *had to exist 'potentially and realizably'* long before humanity existed. Construction of (the first) musical instruments (such as various 'flutes,' and eventually other 'instruments') allowed people to 'play' different sounds. Yet the materials (and the fabricating of different musical instruments) allowed humans to cause (inherent to the materials of the various musical instruments) various sounds, "playing" what would later come to be called music!

The Laws of Nature (Physical and Cosmological Constants)

These the "laws of nature" or "Physical and Cosmological Constants" are the Universe's fine-tuning of Physical Constants - and in fact, many other aspects of reality (such as 'life,' weather, or the distance between the Sun to the Earth). The "laws of nature, or 'nature'" existed billions of years before life *and* humanity came to live. And it isn't just "the fine-tuning of the 'laws of the Universe'" but it is the overwhelming fact that many associated events (secondary or 'emergent' due to nature) caused actions or effects at the right time and in the right place.

Without these random but fortuitous events, humanity would not have 'evolved'! When you look at what most (or nearly all) physicists and scientists write "about the created Universe," most (not all) say the 'cause' of the Universe is or was a Multiverse. Some physicists and scientists hypothesized (that beyond our one Universe), there are groups of multiple universes. Together, these scientists assert that the multiverses (also called "parallel universes," "other universes," "alternate universes," or "many worlds") create and form all of this Universe's laws of nature and existence. They are the cause of the entirety of space, time, matter, energy, information, and the physical laws and constants that describe them (in this, Our Universe)! In effect, multiverses carry out "creation" of this Universe instead of 'God!'

But, I am a scientist that has conducted research (at the highest levels) and published it in peer-reviewed scientific journals (Brantingham JW, Parkin-Smith G, Cassa TK, et al., 2012). I have a PhD from the University of Surrey in Guildford, England, and, *I read these scientists' papers.* One of the 'hottest items' currently proposed as the cause of the big bang, or the creation of the Universe and ultimately us, is a hypothesized multiverse such as described above. Positing a 'multiverse' solves all the problems found with just a singular Universe. With the possibility of millions and millions (or billions or trillions) of 'universes,' one can predict a 'Just Right Goldilocks' universe (statistically impossible) but with eternity… a *probable* 'Anthropic Universe' so finely tuned that we humans exist within it.

A Multiverse' creates 'an eternity of *the creation of infinite Universes.*' Yet, we cannot even predict that *this Universe* is eternal. But with an infinity of Universes, anything can (and will) happen! Including (*and note*) the 'Big Bang' *and* 'miracles in an 'Anthropic Universe!' The "multiverse is a way of getting around," 'a Beginning - or from 'Nothing, getting Something' (without the need of a "Creator"). Many that support "string theories in physics" support the multiverse. But to support something untestable is a metaphysical belief not science (Stapp, Henry P. 2015; Multiverse-Wikipedia 2021; Chronology of the universe. Wikipedia 2021).

Cosmologist Paul Davies notes,

> "Extreme multiverse explanations are… reminiscent of theological discussions. Indeed, invoking an infinity of unseen universes to explain the unusual features of the one we do see is just as ad hoc as invoking an unseen Creator. The multiverse theory may be dressed up in scientific language, but in essence, it requires the same leap of faith."

This 'Multiverse' is a way of allowing near infinite time, and an infinite number of Universes (through a kind of evolution) to get, a 'Goldilocks,' or 'just right Universe' (and eventually, evolutionarily - with no help from God, and with a Universe without meaning, purpose or intention to produce - 'us'). Thus many of these scientists confidently tell us that we "need no God" to explain our Universe. Now, some say this is *nearly* true because it is justified (by the way the Universe formed). This magical 'Goldilocks Anthropic Universe' was a "predestined event" due to *how* the big bang unfolded and the important "event" of "Inflation."

Some hypothesize **Inflation** happened just after the *it,* the Big Bang, "banged" or "exploded" at (*less than*) or at about <10^{-32} seconds after *it* the 'bang' began. Then the Universe expanded "**faster than the speed of light**" *by a factor in the order of* 10^{-26}! And, this all happened over a period between 10^{-35} to 10^{-32} seconds! Though this "period" is calculable (but impossible) for a human being to isolate and "experience," it exists. So, because of "*inflation*," many scientists state the "multiverse hypothesis explains it all." They say this because "they believe," *Inflation* is an inherently quantum phenomenon! *It is a circular metaphysical argument.* In other words, these scientists claim to know where "something rather than nothing came from." When there was '*nothing*' including "physics, quantum physics or the 'laws of nature" and *before* the Big Bang, this is what happened (they describe). With multiverses, "a quantum fluctuation - possibly by a "Higgs-Boson" particle, occurred." Somehow this "particle" caused the big bang and the creation of space, time, matter, and energy." *It also (by the way)* **created** Physics, and simultaneously Quantum Physics. For *they are the same thing* but appear in two different states somewhat like "water and ice!" **But this is an illusion** (*Stapp, Henry P. 2015; Multiverse-Wikipedia 2021; Chronology of the Universe. Wikipedia 2021).* To posit that a 'quantum field' existed before it existed is metaphysics! It (the quantum field, they say) existed "eternally" ("because there was a 'multiverse' before the big bang with 'physics - or quantum physics' causing a quantum field fluctuation, some virtual particle, then the Big Bang and etc., etc.)! Since all of these remain unproven hypotheses, why is this better than something else causing the Universe?

But, *first,* this hypothesis that there is an eternally existing "quantum field" is saying you can get Something from Nothing (and this does not exist in our Universe and Physics). Those who believe this hypothesis (a pre-existing Universe and Quantum field before the Big Bang) have yet to produce a testable "falsifiable theory." In layman's terms: there is *no evidence* that such an eternal quantum field from an eternal 'multiverse' exists!" No more than there is evidence that a "unicorn exists." *Second,* even if trillions of Universes have existed there still had to be one that existed first (you don't get something from nothing) and an infinite regression is impossible (without a beginning). So then, from *a statistical point of view* regarding 'all of these necessary things and coincidences to have happened at the right time and in the right place and in the right way,' by "Occam's razor" we can conclude there is an equal chance that a God... or, "G.O.D." (Schwartz, Gary. 2006), a Guiding, Organizing and Directing (benign) Entity could have created the Universe. '*God*' then as "Eternal Infinite Information or Consciousness" could have created the smallest unit of information needed as the 'basic fundamental unit' (the Qualit, or Quantum of information meaningfully utilized') that supplies the information needed to stabilize 'reality' and make up the "ground of being." And so G.O.D. created and sustains the existence of our Universe (Close Edward R. 2019; Schwartz, Gary. 2006). Whether it be defined as a Super-Consciousness or as Super-Information, *or All Information* potentially *and* that actually exists; "It, 'God,' 'That Which Is,' "brought itself and the Universe and "us" into existence. Super-Information or Super-Consciousness *or, All Information* that *'potentially* and or *that actually exists'* is by definition aware or conscious (Schwartz, Gary. 2006.) This upholds the "Primacy of Consciousness in Close's Grand Unified Theory." (Close Edward R. 2019; Neppe, Vernon M., Close Edward R. (2012) and (Schwartz, Gary. 2002; 2006, 2010; 2011; 2011; 2019; 2019.)

A 'Quantum (or *Qualit*) of consciousness' is a measurable unit never before defined (but which Close names and uses in his Unified Theory. And, Close's, **'Theory Unifying Relativity and Quantum Physics'** requires "consciousness." Consciousness is the ground of all being and reality. So, the transcendence and Mysticism in Reviewing "Science and Quantum Physics" (which so many scientists hate and seem to want to explain away), cannot be 'explained away'!"

Fine-tuning'

Take Omega (Ω) or the density parameter of the Universe. The density parameter is the ratio of the average density of matter and energy in the Universe to the *critical density*. The 'critical density' is the watershed point at which an expanding Universe stops, and begins to contract. This ratio of the mass to density of the universe is the critical density of > five atoms (of monatomic hydrogen) per cubic meter in the Universe. But if the expansion of the Universe should stop and begin to contract back to an infinitely small point it would be < than five atoms. But in fact the average density of ordinary matter in the Universe is believed to be only about 0.2–0.25 atoms per cubic meter. So, what gives it a density greater than five atoms per cubic meter? It appears that it is: **Dark Matter** and *especially* **Dark Energy** that are the sources of this "extra density" (= > 5 atoms per cubic meter) creating the 'Cosmological Constant or (Lambda) $\Lambda = 2.036 \times 10^{-35}$. That is, 10^{-35} is -35 followed by 34 zeroes or: 100, 000, 000, 000, 000, 000, 000, 000, 000, 000, 000, 000. At this time, and from this one physical constant, the Universe, Time and Space should (this scientist says) expand infinitely - and that is what we appear to see (Rees, Martin. 2000).

Yet if there was a slightly larger quantity of dark energy, or in effect a slightly larger value to the cosmological constant, space would have expanded so fast that galaxies would have been unable to form thus life (as we know it) would not have come about. Take Epsilon (ε). Epsilon is the nuclear efficiency of the fusion of hydrogen into helium, measured at 0.007. This causes four nucleons to fuse into helium, with and efficiency of 0.007 (or 0.7%) of their mass, which is otherwise converted into energy. If this value of "ε" had been 0.006 or 0.008 neither hydrogen nor the complex chemistry (and human life; or all of life) would have been possible. Or look at 'Q,'. It is the ratio of the gravitational energy required to pull a large galaxy apart which is around 10–5. This is what it is, but if it was smaller than this no stars could have formed, and if much larger, again, no stars could have formed because the universe would have been to violent (Rees, Martin. 2000).

Many scientists hate such 'fine-tuning' issues and consider it merely the same as 'intelligent design' or "gobbledygook or quantum voo" (which to them is the same as *fundamentalist Christians holding up snakes and dancing down the aisles' and,* is a 'barbaric belief and superstition(s) that brings into the argument '*the God of the Gaps.*' This is they say is, "Superstition." But to *believe in* "a huge number (or even two other) Universes existing before our Universe came into existence (without a "shred of evidence") is the height of science (when actually "it is the *religion* of scientism")!

These scientists do not see that they (too) hold a metaphysical ('scientistic') position or in fact a 'religious stance.' But since their 'hypothesis' is (actually) also like a religion, and *cannot* be falsified they often believe in it with the ferocity of the most fundamentalist zealot. That another Universe created our Universe and 'life' (and us) is based on: *no, none, nil, zero, nada* evidence! These scientists practice what is called 'Scientism' or 'a Scientistic Religion' because to them, all legitimate knowledge can only come forth from 'science' (and 'scientists!') But, this too is non-falsifiable…

When 'information is meaningfully utilized,' it is a '*Quantum or Qualit of consciousness*'

When Information is divided or, makes up a part of our reality as the 'calculus of dimensional distinctions' defines it, it is a '*Qualit of information meaningfully utilized*' or, a way of using complex mathematics to measure and compare '*consciousness*' to other quantal measurements (of other things). Using this distinction of one thing from another Edward Close modified as a measurement tool an outcome measure called the 'calculus of distinctions.' In physics (Edward Close with Vernon Neppe) developed a 'calculus of dimensional distinctions' or (CODD) for examining consciousness. This is a measurement of phenomena as finite, non-zero distinctions relating to integers of quantum reality. With that can come an exploration (in depth) of the deep relationship between mathematics, reality and, *consciousness*. Ultimately Close and Neppe assert, 'Space-Time-and Mass (S-T-M) is derived from, *Space-Time and Consciousness* or 'S-T-C'. But these three factors cannot be separated. These 'three forces' have been fundamentally and inseparably tethered from the beginning… (2020). This tethering manifests they state, and as Close writes in (2019) **elucidates the basis of reality** across, between and within, 9 multiple fluctuating dimensions. I would note that these are "dimensions," like up, down and to the side (not parallel universes).

Developed by Close and Neppe (2015; 2015; 2020) and Close (2020) they have named this *'measurement of consciousness,'* a 'Qualit of Information meaningfully utilized'. And these particular units (of information) they call, 'triadic Rotational Units of Equivalence' (or 'TRUE Units'.) These measurements allow equations with falsifiable hypotheses to be developed and tested. This research is going forward as this is written. Close and Neppe have asserted (especially Close) that they have found the solution to the 'Grand Unified Theory'.

Close has shown that it is mathematically dependent (for the first time in history) on *consciousness'* (2019.) And, there is other supportive evidence but is beyond the scope of this small article. See their joint text: 'Reality Begins with Consciousness' (2012) and Closes' 'Mathematical Unity of Space, Time, Mass, Energy & Consciousness' (2019.)

Using TRUE Units is a new basic way of describing elementary particles. TRUE units cannot be derived from our usual 3S-1t perspective (or 3 Spacial dimensions in 1 moment of 'present' Time (or '3S-1t'). Thus 1 TRUE Unit (has been named and) is equal to 1 *'gimmel'*. It was necessary to define it in this manner (for computation) because Close and Neppe say there is *not* a 'half a quantum unit, or half an atom' nor is there a half *'gimmel.'*

This quantum, or 'qualit of consciousness' is found in a *'rotational or vortical entanglement with mass and energy'*. Such an additional unit of entanglement (as Close's equations demonstrate) must exist. It was determined that it must exist to create the stability needed for subatomic particles, atoms, elements and molecules to spin near the speed of light, *and* to keep them from flying apart. Without this quantum of *'gimmel'* subatomic particles in a finite 'spacial association' and, not (as denoted previously in physics) an 'association of virtual points' such as 'quark points,' would not securely combine. If that occurred, then the 'proton' (the most 'permanent or stable' subatomic particle) would lose its stability and the Universe would 'fly apart' and be destroyed. To define and work out *gimmel*, the third form, or substance of reality, Close used the *Pythagorean Theorem* to define the rotation and orthogonal projection from one dimensional domain into another, and ultimately arrived at its' stability through *9 dimensions* . Next Close used the addition of integers cubed by *Fermat's Last Theorem*. This theorem demonstrates that any combination of elementary quanta of any cubic volumetric combination (that is), any *two* atomic or subatomic particles or components, cannot achieve stability without *Gimmel*. Thus two nuclei comprised of neutrons and protons with orbiting electrons (but no quantum or' qualit of information') cannot produce stable atoms. But they can with the addition of *Gimmel*.

Gimmel is the 'massless, energy-less, substance made up of a spinning vortex of instructional information, or 'information meaningfully utilized' which is (or must be from) a 'higher consciousness'. It is the answer to what Steven Hawking queried, 'what… *puts* the fire *into* the equations' causing Space, Time, and Consciousness and in fact reality!' *Gimmel* necessarily links together the 'whole'. Nothing would exist without this third component (*Gimmel*). And there would be no 'periodic table' including the crucial elements for life. For all is 'tethered together' and entangled!

Such quantum entities must combine with quantum equivalence units (TRUE Units) or*gimmel* to be integral and symmetric and so as to function and (not be torn apart) and survive (Close ER. 2019; Neppe VV. 2019; 2020 Close Edward R., Neppe Vernon V. 2015; 2019; 2020). Close's paper (on a Unified Theory) went through peer-review and is published. Other scientists (even you) can read it and come to their own conclusions.

'Consciousness and Reality'

Both the living biological brain and the apparent infinite Universe and the reality or 'consciousness and knowledge' (outside of the brain) require this profoundly important third component for stability of all particles, waves or information. Thus for the stable existence of our quantum cosmological reality: '*Gimmel*,' is required. The *'Gimmel'* is the third letter of the Semitic alphabet (or ג) and a revolutionary solution to the conundrum of the so-called Grand Unified Theory. For it is in fact the solution for a 'Theory Unifying Relativistic Physics and Quantum Physics.' And, Close has developed testable and falsifiable Hypotheses; some components of which have already been falsified and helped him to construct this Grand Unified Theory and show how it is mathematically intact (Close ER. 2019; Neppe VV. 2015; Close ER. 2020). A *Gimmel,* or a 'quantized qubit of consciousness, or reality' is as much a part of our cosmology as the (quantum) existence of the universe. Thus infinite Information or 'Consciousness' pervades 'the entirety of Existence and Being'. Or to put it another (*spiritual*) way I (and Philo posited two thousand years ago) is to say, *the 'Logos'* pervades the entirety 'of Existence and Being' from the micro to the macro. And yet Philo discussed such similar ideas two thousand years ago (Grosso, Michael. 2015); Close Edward R., Neppe Vernon V. 2015)!

-===

Appendix 3

Some Gnostic Theological Ideas (not in the *GMary* but possibly underpinning some of its ideas, stories and exegesis). **And notes about "Wisdom" or Lady Wisdom/Sophia & Barbēlō and Consorts**

This is additional information is found in the full Nag Hammadi Library (and other Gnostic texts, with information about "Barbēlō" who is in these three other texts: (like the SRevJohn). She is inThe Holy Book of the Great Invisible Spirit, the trimorphic Protennoia, Pistis Sophia and many other texts that reveal and outline the many associations between "Barbēlō," "Sophia" and 'Wisdom,' as well as their associations with the "Holy Spirit" (or "Holy Mother" or "Mother").

It seems that 'Gnostics' were very concerned about presenting '*God*' as 'One'. But with Barbēlō (as the Holy 'Mother-Father'; the 'Perfect Aeon') we have a complex entity beyond simply the 'Holy Spirit'. The *SRevJohn* uses one of the many derivations from 'Wisdom as Sophia' (and in some way a or, the 'Higher Sophia') and/or *as* Barbēlō' to describe (through Gnostic exegesis) the 'true virginal conception of the Christ'. It occurs when the Virginal Holy Father 'looks back and into the 'face'' of the Virginal Holy Mother (here meaning the 'Holy Spirit'). At this moment in 'temporal time,' Jesus is baptized by John and the Holy Spirit enters Jesus and he becomes Jesus Christ. Barbēlō is roughly analogous to Judaism's use of the feminine noun for the 'Holy Spirit' or the 'Shekinah'. But 'Barbēlō or Wisdom and Sophia' is complex: Barbēlō represents the male and female attributes of God the Father, God the 'Holy Mother or, Spirit' (and in the *PS* and *SRevJohn*) 'She,' is the Companion *of* the Holy Father. Together 'They' immediately bring about 'the *Logos* or the 'Son'.

Sophia, Wisdom and Barbēlō

In English "Sophia" is the word 'Wisdom' which represents both (Jewish Chokmâh, pronounced, 'Hokmah') and the Greek' ('Wisdom' or Sofia) in the Canonical Scriptures. And the Hebrew 'Sapiential or Wisdom literature' was translated by the Jews into Greek and found in the **Septuagint LXX.** This **'LXX'** was adopted by those who first followed Yeshua the Anointed and (some of) His later disciples who later called it the **Old Testament** (or 'OT'). This literature became the "Wisdom literature" and was personified as, 'Sophia'. 'Lady Wisdom or Sophia' is *God Above God's* forethought, and was "with Him" (as John's Prologue) states at the beginning and as in the Proverbs. Or, as the Father said, **'Wisdom …(was) with Me before time …and before My works of old; …before I prepared the heavens,** *Lo*, **before I, the Most High, established the clouds above; the fountains of the deep below… For She… 'Wisdom,' was**

334

there from the Ages past unto the Ages into the Ages, and upon the Ages, and Ages to Come!

And Wisdom or Sophia came early into Gnostic-Christianity from the OT, the
Deuterocanonical and Apocryphal scriptures *(but also from the: SRevJohn)* as Sophia and Barbēlō. So John said in the *Secret Revelation.* and in, "The Holy Book of the Great Invisible Spirit, *the* trimorphic Protennoia, *the Gospel of Judas,* and the *Three Steles of Seth.* And in: *Zostrianos,* Marsanes, Melchizedek, *and* Allogenes!

Arising (self-generated with the Father, the Son and the Logos) She (Barbēlō) arose within the Father's '*nous*' or in and from His mind and in His heart. Barbēlō was with *God Above God* and the *Logos, before creation and before it all…* For, like the incarnation of the Son, She was already in *His* Mind, in *His* Image and, in *His* likeness and had (and has) the Power of God Most High! For it is written, Moses even in *Genesis…* (coming from the Talmud said, "She" (Chokhmah) *is* the 'Word yoked to righteousness' of the LORD' *Prov. 8:8) And Moses said it:* 'Wisdom *is* the Holy Spirit…' and further, She *was **that*** which hovered over the formless, chaotic void… the murmuring deep! So to the prophet Enoch noted… 'Wisdom took her seat… next to God… She, Wisdom or '*Sophia*' was and is the feminine emanation of *God Above God*, the *Shekinah*! For the spirit of the Lord shall rest upon the Anointed and upon Wisdom, and, upon the spirit of knowledge! For 'Wisdom' (in the *Secret Revelation of John*) as *Sophia* was the first thought of the One (true) and, Most High God or, *Her* alter Persona as 'Barbēlō;' *the* Holy Spirit (*and* 'Holy Mother') who *is* the 'Wisdom' of God Most High! And, as the Holy Spirit sits at the left hand of *Power…*

Barbēlō is often depicted as a supreme female principle, with the name "Holy Mother" (or feminine Holy Spirit or "ruaḥ ha-kodesh"), the 'Mother', and even the androgynous Mother-Father (among other names). She is the Father's (or 'God's') first-thought and co-creator of all other emanations (and reality and being) including Yeshua!

Barbelo

She (Barbēlō) is the first thought of the true God. She is his image. But importantly she becomes the womb of every-thing (of all creation). The *Very* Womb of Creation! For she is prior to creation and prior to them all. Barbēlō is explicitly described as giving birth to or secondarily emanating Sophia (thus Wisdom). Of course this associates her with canonical Wisdom. And 'Wisdom' is 'Sophia' and (though it is not obvious) is canonically a co-creator with God. So this is Barbēlō's direct association with Sophia. And of course Messiah Yeshua is associated with (and "yoked with") the exact same "Wisdom!"

It must be remembered that first and foremost Gnostics and Gnostic Christians considered themselves "Christians." As Christians they *also used* the proto-canonical "catholic" scriptures (though they interpreted them through Gnostic texts and analogy and metaphors). Since "Wisdom or Sophia" was strongly associated with Yeshua, this (Gnostically) associated Yeshua with Barbēlō. All of these complex associations lead to descriptions of Barbēlō as an androgynous or even at times, a male. For example she is… "the Mother-Father," "the first man, the Holy Spirit, Thrice-male, Thrice-powerful, Thrice-named, the androgynous eternal 'Aeon' outside of all, and outside of all the realms of time, space and matter! And is among the Invisible Ones that first to came forth! (*After* Davies, Stephan. 2005)

Where does the name Barbēlō come from? As His first "thought" or emanation I like most Alastair, HB Logan's suggestion. It is from the Hebrew or, *'barah ba 'lo,'* which means, "daughter of the Lord" (1996). There are many other explanations and suggestions.

However Isenberg, one of the first translators gives a hypothesis that the gnostic gospels may derive from a single comprehensive Gnostic Christian text. And that most of 'their excerpts' derive from a single book. A "harmony" (possibly like the Diatessaron). If it exists It certainly is (or was) "a Gospel" that transmitted many words of the Lord (Yeshua) and *'God Most High,'* those who bring Salvation. Clearly Gnosticism's metaphors, dynamic spirit, boldness of spirit and images, and its' palpable greatness is both mysterious and enigmatic. This being one (very) probable reason for its' growing popularity and push (and draw) to be read. Like quantum physics, more and more readers turn and read Gnostic texts every day (Schneemelcher, Wilhelm., Wilson, Robert McLachlan., Hennecke, Edgar. Eds. 2003)!

Temporally, on the aeon of the earth (as noted) the 'virgin birth' (initially defined by Gnosticism and other Christian groups) occurred when John, *'in the spirit'* baptized Jesus, and he and the humanity around them witnessed 'Reality, or *the Heavens*' split open and the Spirit of Holiness enter Jesus (as a dove). The lesser *'god,'* the Ignorant Yaldabaoth or the 'demiurge' is not openly seen, hinted at nor ever clearly described in the *GMary*. But *'attributes and personifications'* of a 'Chief Ruler or Evil demiurge' as Paul describes him - the *'god'* of this world' *are* easily identified and intelligibly described.

'Mary, being human *is attacked by these* 'attributes and personifications' such as 'forbidden desires'. And, by the personification of 'Evil, Darkness and especially Ignorance. She is filled with a Zeal for Death. And conversely, a desire for 'Pleasure and, the Pleasure of the Flesh'; whom, call Mary back. Darkness and the 'Chief Ruler' are ignorant. They (and humanity) lack knowledge about this local little 'backwater' cosmos. This *we* (today) now know (though it had to have been and, was always known by the Most High *God*.) And so the *'lesser god'* Yaldabaoth shaped and molded this 'small' cosmos and its' Seven aeons in the firmament above and similar aeons or 'Hell' the 'Shadowlands' below.

And, it (creation of the Cosmos and Aeon of earth and emanation of 'the Error' Yaldabaoth (or Yaltabaoth) the *lesser god* of the OT (happened *after* the creation of Universe) or as it is written after the: *'all, the vast array of Aeons and Aeonic beings'* and all the other countless Aeons, Realms, Dimensions and Heavens (of the uninterrupted) Universe were previously created. Or as it says in Genesis 1:1-2, In the beginning, God created the *'heavens, all the heavens…'* and the earth…. in *all* of their *vast* array. Or in modern vernacular, the 'self-generated' caused 'the Beginning'. 'Wisdom' (in the *SRevJohn*) is further labeled 'the Holy Spirit' and/or the 'Holy Mother'. And the 'Holy Mother' is often just labeled, 'Mother' (pointedly this is not Jesus earthly mother Mary). 'She' (the 'Holy Mother' is found in the *SRevJohn* but also in the *GPhil* too. And found there and in other Gnostic texts as Barbēlō (who though usually depicted in a feminine guise) in fact is a very complex entity (as in the *SRevJohn*.) In the *SRevJohn* Barbēlō is the 'Mother-Father', 'God in a *feminine* persona', and 'God the Father, the Holy Mother, the Logos, and the Son'. She (Barbēlō) has been labeled 'Sophia the Greater', a Consort of God the Father and, described with both masculine and feminine attributes. truly a complex entity. It appears that all this is taken for granted as the background for Barbēlō in the *Pistis Sophia*. And as 'the Holy Mother' makes sense of the *Gospel of Thomas* verse 101:

101 Jesus says,

Whoever does not *hate* his Mother and Father as I do, cannot be my disciple. Yet even more so, whoever does not *love* his Mother and Father as I do cannot follow me. For, my **earthly mother** gave me death, but my '**Holy Mother**,' Life (*GThom* Brantingham, James 2019)

Hear us, Father, just as you heard your only-begotten Son, and received Him to yourself, and gave him rest from His Labors. You are 'the One ' whose power is invincible. Your armor is indestructible because it is from 'the Light.' Your Word is life, and Your touch heals. The Truth, the Word, brings Repentance and Life. For this has come from you. You give us the thoughts that complete our serenity (of the Solitary.) Again: Hear us just as you heard your elect. Through your Son's sacrifice, these will enter; through their good works, these have saved their souls from their blind (and dumb) limbs so they might exist eternally. Amen! (*After*: Emmel, Stephan. The Dialogue of the Savior

In the *GMary* and the *Pistis Sophia* (and was recognized by the Catholic Holy See in 2016 that in the New Testament today) Mary Magdalene is a full Apostle (for in the *Pistis Sophia* the only criteria for Discipleship is the ability to understand and speak through the Spirit). Jesus himself states (in *PS*) that, 'Mary, thou blessed one, I perfected you in all mysteries; those of the height, of discourse and in openness of the All in All, for thy eyes and heart are raised to the kingdom of heaven more than all thy brethren' and He further notes '…Mary Magdalene and John the Virgin will be superior to all my disciples'! Yet what is actually and fully meant by this is their (and her) ability to hear, perceive and instruct in the mysteries Jesus is teaching them now (*Pistis Sophia*.) All of this appears to be the background from and in which we receive the *GMary*. Many believe some or part (or nearly all of this) will be found in the missing 10 pages supporting this characterization and importance of Mary; but specific evidence for this is maddeningly not found in the *GMary*.

James Brantingham PhD 6 15 2021

Thousand Oaks, CA